ADMINISTRATION

Carol Carysforth

NVQ level 2

Student Handbook

Heinemann Educational Publishers
Halley Court, Jordan Hill, Oxford OX2 8EJ
a division of Reed Educational & Professional Publishing Ltd
MELBOURNE   AUCKLAND
FLORENCE   PRAGUE   MADRID   ATHENS
SINGAPORE   TOKYO   SAO PAULO
CHICAGO   PORTSMOUTH (NH)   MEXICO
IBADAN   GABORONE   JOHANNESBURG
KAMPALA   NAIROBI

First published 1994

98 97 96
10 9 8 7 6

A catalogue record for this book is available from the
British Library on request

ISBN 0 435 451308

Typeset by 🅰 Tek Art, Croydon, Surrey
Printed in Great Britain by Clays Ltd, St Ives plc

Dedication

This book is dedicated to the memory of my mother – whose support and encouragement I have missed for longer than I care to remember – and to my father, whose aim in life appears to have been to foster in his children a critical evaluation of everything they see, hear and read!

Ackowledgements

I would like to acknowledge personally the co-operation, assistance and support of all those who have helped me in the writing of this book – from friends and colleagues to the inumerable employees of commercial and public sector organisations who, yet again, have been helpful and informative in keeping me up-to-date with developments.

My thanks are due to Sue Bramwell for her advice and guidance on security, to the British Security Industry Association for their permission to reproduce the chart shown on page 68 and to the Heinemann staff who inspired me so much in March! Especially thanks are due to Margaret Berriman of Heinemann, who is now more friend than editor, and Sheri Hill, her assistant, for her attention to detail in seeing this book through.

Personally, my thanks are due to Antony, Paul, Matthew and Roger – who suffered by being virtually ignored for several weeks – and to Mike – for everything.

Carol Carysforth
May 1994

Contents

Information on option units

This book contains the eight compulsory units you will need to complete your NVQ 2 Administration award but you will also need to choose *one* option unit from a choice of seven. You are advised to think very carefully about this. If possible, select the unit which links the most with your job or career prospects. If you are on a full-time course, discuss the options with your tutor and, if possible, select one in which you will be able to have some practical experience. This will make it much easier for you to prove your competency.

Content of option units

Unit 9 Maintain and issue stock items

Choose this option if you are – or want to be – involved in ordering, monitoring or maintaining stock and issuing stock items on request. Because this is an administration award, the emphasis is on office stationery and equipment as stock items, not on general retail stock.

You will learn about different types of office consumables and equipment, how stock is controlled and monitored and how to handle and store stock properly.

Unit 10 Process documents relating to goods and services

This option is involved with ordering goods and services and processing claims for payment – which may be invoices or expense claims. If you work in a purchasing office or an accounts office then this may be your most suitable choice.

You will learn about the policies and procedures involved in ordering different items and will need to understand the documents used and how claims should be checked before payment.

Unit 11 Organise travel and accommodation arrangements

This unit is concerned with the different types of business travel, how arrangements are made and the factors to consider when booking accommodation. If you work in a company where executives or other personnel regularly travel on business then you may want to gain experience in this area.

You will learn how travel arrangements are made and how different methods of travel compare, as well as how to understand some of the documents involved. Booking accommodation both within the UK and abroad is also covered.

Unit 12 Contribute to the arrangement of events

You may work – or want to work – in a department or organisation which is often involved in arranging external events, from a small sales meeting to a large conference. This unit is concerned with the various types of arrangements required to ensure that the facilities match requirements, the correct resources and materials are provided and those attending are looked after properly.

You will learn about the different facilities available, the types of resources required and the procedures involved in looking after visitors and delegates, such as transport, registration, security and catering requirements.

Unit 13 Produce and present business documents from provided material

This unit is concerned with using a keyboard to produce a variety of documents from notes, manuscript and amended typescript in a variety of formats.

Choose this option if you are learning keyboarding and especially if you are taking typewriting or word processing examinations in conjunction with your NVQ course. You will learn how to deal with different types of material and produce finished documents which are accurate and well-displayed.

Unit 14 Produce and present business documents from recorded material

This unit relates to audio typing and related skills in this area, i.e. keyboarding, interpretation of recorded instructions, choice of paper, layout of documents and basic English skills such as spelling and punctuation.

This option may be your choice if you are studying audio typing or regularly use an audio machine at work. You will learn how to produce a wide variety of documents from recorded instructions and how to produce these in a variety of styles and formats.

Unit 15 Produce and present business documents from dictated material

This is the unit to choose if you want to link shorthand skills with your NVQ award. To achieve this unit you must be able to take notes at a minimum of 70 wpm.

Choose this option if you are learning shorthand and especially if you regularly use this skill at work. 'Office-style' dictation, rather than 'examination' dictation is quite acceptable for proving competency and, indeed, is more realistic. You will have to provide letters, memoranda and short reports as evidence – and these will have to be accurate!

The options covered in this book

If you choose any of the units from 9–12 then you can obtain the information you need from the relevant chapter in this book. However, you will find that the structure of the option chapter is rather different than those for the compulsory units, and the chapter is also shorter. The reason for this is two-fold. Firstly, we are sure that you don't want to buy a book which has dozens of pages in it which you don't need – and this would be the case if the option units were very long. Secondly, it is likely that you will be studying your option towards the end of your course. It may even be the last unit you do. Now, therefore, is the time to prove that your personal skills have improved (*see Unit 1*) and you really can take more responsibility for your own learning. You should be able to do a little more on your own.

For that reason, although all the main points you need to know are covered, there are more ways in which you are actively involved in your own learning. You can use this requirement as part of your action plan and – in many cases – to prove that you can find the information you need and deal with this according to instructions (*see Unit 5*).

If you choose any of the last three units then you will not find information on these in this book. This is because all these units are *skill specific* and, although you obviously do need to acquire a certain amount of knowledge to prove your competency, this will be taught to you as part of your skill lessons. If it is not, then there are specific books on the market which deal with keyboarding, audio and shorthand skills. The material contained in these books comprehensively covers all the knowledge requirements of each unit.

However, you may like to note that if you are using the Activity book which accompanies this book to help you to prove your competency in a working situation, then activities *are* included which cover *all* the option units, including the skill units.

1 Develop self to improve performance

This unit of your NVQ course relates to your personal development. In particular, it emphasises **self**-development. What is self-development and why is it important?

Everyone needs to achieve something as they go through life. Achievement helps people to feel good about themselves – to have self-respect and self-confidence. Regardless of what they may say to other people, most people are disheartened and demoralised when they make a mess of something or fail dismally – or receive a report with 'could try harder' or 'could do better' written all over it! Equally, they feel good inwardly when they do something well and this is commented on by other people.

CHECK IT YOURSELF

Imagine that a friend of yours goes abroad and you don't see each other for five years. When you meet again your friend asks what you have been doing since you last saw one another. How would you like to be able to respond? Which answer, from those below, would you want to give?

a 'Nothing much.'
b 'I'm still in the same job I had when you left.'
c 'I've had a few jobs and tried several courses, but nothing seems to have got me anywhere.'
d 'I've done quite well really, I've improved my qualifications and ended up in the job I always wanted.'

Personal and professional development

Most of us would prefer to answer **d** because being successful usually also implies

- better pay
- greater job satisfaction
- greater personal satisfaction.

Development can, therefore, be related to work. Most people starting out on their career don't expect – or want – to be doing the same job in five or ten years' time as they are doing at the moment. Most people want to progress in one way or another. However, development also applies to other areas of your life – your personal and social skills should develop so that you learn to take in your stride situations which may worry you now. You learn to be more independent and self-assured. You learn to cope with life's problems more easily – and don't expect or need someone else to be on hand to solve them for you.

The self-development journey

The best way towards personal and professional development is to

- set clear, realistic but challenging goals
- take the responsibility for setting and achieving these **yourself**
- review your goals at regular intervals to see
  - how far you have progressed
  - what has gone wrong and why
  and then adjust your goals accordingly.

In other words, you have to **plan** your development by

A identifying where you are **now**
B identifying your **goals** (where you want to be)
C working out what you have to **do** to get from **A** to **B**.

Setting out on your journey from A to B without planning is like going on a journey into the unknown without a map! This unit is therefore designed to help you to

- collect the information to work out your own development needs
- create your personal action plan (your own personal route map)
- review your progress along the way – and learn how to alter your plans if necessary
- keep a record of your progress so you have proof for yourself, your employers and your tutors (both now and in the future).

Why this emphasis on self?

You must bear in mind that *you* have to be actively involved with this process all the time. No-one else *really* knows what you like doing and what you don't, what your real ambitions are, where you feel confident and where you don't. No-one else, therefore, can set your goals for you. This is what is meant by the word *self-development*. You take the responsibility for managing your *own* progress and identifying areas where you are doing well and those where you are not. Equally, you are the only one who truly knows whether a failure to meet a goal is because of genuine problems or because you really couldn't be bothered!

CHECK IT YOURSELF

You have a project to finish for work or college. Your only option, if you want to hand it in on time, is to work until about 3 am to complete it. You are more likely to do this if you really are interested, involved and committed to finishing it. In other words, the only person who can *make* you finish it on time is *you*!

Regular reviews

The main problem with self-development is that you may be enthusiastic at the beginning and then lose interest later on. Try to guard against this. You really do need to review how you are doing on a regular basis. If you are doing well, this will motivate you to keep going. If you are having problems, then a review is absolutely essential before you and your objectives part company altogether!

What are the benefits?

If you are persistent and determined to persevere then the benefits are considerable.

- You will become more motivated to do well because you will know *why* you want to succeed.
- You will be able to concentrate your time and your energy on those areas which will give you the greatest benefits.
- Your self-awareness will increase so that you will start to know more instinctively what is right for you – and what is not.
- Your self-esteem will increase as you continue and realise that you can be successful in your own right and in your own way.
- You will know, and be able to explain to others, what you are doing and why – and how long it will take you to do it.
- Your expectations of yourself and other people will start to change. You will have less patience for those who want to waste your time. You will probably start to reassess your own goals as you begin to realise that you are capable of far more than you ever believed possible!
- You will collect evidence which will prove your achievements to your current employer and any future employer. This evidence will not be restricted just to academic or professional qualifications but will give a much fuller picture. From it you will be able to compile an excellent CV and, at an interview, will be able to talk more confidently and knowledgeably about yourself.

 SPECIAL NOTE

The units in this book normally have a review of the main points covered at the end of each element, together with a test of your knowledge and understanding. However, because of the nature of this unit only **one** unit review and knowledge/understanding test is included at the end of the whole unit.

Element 1.1

Identify and agree own development needs

What is development?

When you were born you could do nothing for yourself. Someone had to feed, wash and dress you. Very soon you learned to do all of these things for yourself. As you grew up you learned many other things

- how to play games
- how to write
- how to get on with people.

This is known as learning or development and can be broken down into three main areas.

Knowledge	how many pence in a pound, where to buy the best pizza, when the bank is open
Skills	how to use a calculator, how to drive a car, how to make cheese on toast
Personal development	how to look after a pet, how to be patient with old people, how to ask your parents for a loan, how to explain to your tutor that your homework will be late.

DID YOU KNOW?

If you join the Duke of Edinburgh's award scheme or an organisation such as the Scouts or Guides, you will find you are developing all three areas as you progress within that scheme.

Where are you now?

Everyone has different personal development needs, depending on what they have achieved already. In any group of people there may be some common factors but there will also be considerable differences depending upon people's backgrounds and their individual strengths and weaknesses, likes and dislikes. For this reason, identifying your own needs is something that only *you* can do and the process will be personal to you. It won't apply to anyone else. You can ask other people for help and advice, but no-one else can do it for you!

Where do you start?

The first stage is to work out, as accurately as you can, where you are *now*. To do this you need to think about

- qualifications you have already gained
- other important achievements in your life
- yourself as an individual person.

To do this you need to collect as much information as you can to obtain a clear picture of yourself.

Self-assessment methods

Everyone finds it difficult to assess themselves objectively. To help, try this exercise. Imagine that you have been involved in a car crash and have lost your memory. You desperately need to find out as much information about yourself as you can. If you were a private detective, investigating your own case, what would you do? Here are two methods you could try.

1 Collect as much documentation as you could which proves what you have done (from GCSE certificates to swimming awards, from details of a holiday in France to information on a Saturday or holiday job). This might include

- school reports
- references from past employers
- certificates from school or past courses
- work experience reports
- information on your hobbies or interests.

2 Interview as many people as you can who know you well. They could fill in the gaps on your achievements and give you information on what you are like as a person – fiery tempered or patient, introvert or extrovert, organised and always punctual or disorganised and frequently late!

However, you would need to be careful *who* you interviewed as some people give you a more accurate picture than others. Your parents, employer or tutors may be more prepared to tell you the truth in some areas than your best friend would!

TEST YOURSELF

1 Collect as much documentary evidence as you can on your own achievements. Make a summary list under the two headings

   a qualifications
   b other achievements and experiences

and then check carefully that you haven't left anything out. You may find it useful to check your list with your parents and/or close friends from your school days.

2 List all the people you could interview to find out more about yourself. List *only* those people who you think would tell you the truth!

3 Try to identify the problems with finding out about yourself from others. Think in terms of

    a how well do they *really* know me?
    b how does it feel to listen to people talk about me like this?

SPECIAL NOTE

If you have already prepared a National Record of Achievement at school or college then you will already have a good basis on which to start. However, in relation to your personal goals and aspirations it is important that you distinguish between those which were relevant *previously* and those which *still apply.* You also need to discount anything you may have included because it sounded good or you thought your tutor wanted to hear you say, rather than something you know to be a true reflection of yourself!

Who am I?

For various reasons, no-one really sees a person in the same way that they see themselves. You may go to a party with friends and not want them to know how you dread walking into a room full of people, you may pretend to your supervisor or your tutor that you find a job easy when you don't, you may hide problems from your parents or friends rather than worry them.

Knowing yourself well is very important if you are trying to set realistic goals for yourself. The more accurately you assess yourself, the more appropriate your goals will be and the fewer problems you will meet trying to reach them. It is useless to pretend, as the only person you are fooling is yourself!

There have been dozens of quizzes written to help people assess themselves. If you buy any magazine you may see something very similar. Below are two different self-assessment questionnaires. Try them and see what you find out.

Self-assessment 1 – Assess your personal skills

Use the quiz on page 7 to give yourself some idea of your own personality. Don't pause too long on a question – often your 'gut reaction' is the most accurate. If you are in doubt in any area, think about occasions when this has been tested. Can you offer any evidence to back up your answers?

Finally, go through the quiz with a good friend. See if he or she can 'second-guess' the answers you gave. (This is a better and more reliable method than just asking a friend for his/her opinion of you!) Bear in mind that your friend will give you an idea of how *other people* see you – rather than how you really are. If there are any differences between your answers and your friend's, then discuss possible reasons for this.

Quiz – Assess your personal skills

Achievement profile

- Are you competitive or laid back?
- Are the targets and goals you set yourself realistic and well thought out?
- How do you react to failure – do you decide to do better next time or give up?
- Do you ever put the blame on someone else when you have made a mistake?
- Would you cheat to get what you want?
- Do you achieve what you set out to do – or are you full of good intentions?

Emotional profile

- Do you get upset easily?
- Are you easily bored – if so, do you show it?
- Are you easily depressed?
- Are you ever aggressive?
- Do you jump onto the defensive if someone comments on something you have done?
- Do you think you are tactful?
- Can you compromise with other people when necessary?
- Do you sulk or bear grudges?
- Have you got a strong temper – if so, can you control it?
- Do you think before you speak?

Work profile

- Do you like work which calls for accuracy and detail?
- Do you think and plan out a job carefully?
- Are you well organised and tidy – do you find what you put away?
- Do you like a known routine or do you like new things to happen on a regular basis?
- Are you observant?
- Do you have a good memory?
- Are you sometimes difficult to work with – and in what way?
- Do you write neatly?
- Do you take great care when you do a job or are you rather slapdash?

Social profile

- Do you make friends easily?
- Do you like a busy social life?
- Do you like being in with the crowd?
- Do you like being on your own?
- Are you always friendly?
- Can you keep a secret easily?

- How do you react if you find someone doesn't like you?
- Are you easily impressed?

Life profile

- Are you always in a rush?
- Do you burn the candle at both ends?
- Do you like to keep fit?
- Do you work quickly?
- Are you a worrier – or does nothing bother you?
- Do you quickly grasp what to do or need it spelled out for you?
- Do you find it difficult to relax – or even harder to get going?
- Do you often put things off – especially if you don't want to do them?

Self-assessment 2 – Assess your strengths and weaknesses

The quiz on page 9 is rather different. This time you are asked to identify those areas which you find easy to cope with (your **strengths**) and those with which you have difficulty (your **weaknesses**). Below the list of statements are three blank lines. This is to indicate that the list is not necessarily complete! If you feel that you are particularly strong or weak in an area which is not mentioned, then you should add this to the list. However, do **not** write in this book if it has only been lent to you, but copy out the list for yourself.

Quiz 2 – Strengths and weaknesses

Identify your strengths and weaknesses by ticking the most appropriate box alongside each category. If you have any particular strengths or weaknesses which aren't included then add these at the end.

Identify your support group

At this point you need some help to make sense of what you have found. Your support group could include any or all of the following people.

- your teacher or tutor
- your employer or line manager
- your careers counsellor or adviser
- your managing agent or work supervisor
- your parents or friends
- your social or youth worker

Different people on your list will be able to help you in different ways. At this stage you need to talk through what you have found out about yourself with someone who has the time to listen and who has an interest in your self-development programme. This is likely to be those people who are most involved with helping you to achieve your NVQ award – either at work or at college.

	Can do easily	Can do with assistance	Can do with difficulty
Personal/social skills			
Work on my own			
Work with other people			
Join in discussions			
Thank people			
Apologise to people			
Accept criticism			
Give an opinion clearly, fluently and unemotionally			
Listen to and respect other people's opinions			
Work skills			
Arrive on time			
Discuss my work with my boss or tutor			
Write about myself			
Research information			
Use a telephone			
Accept responsibility			
Keep to a schedule			
React to a challenge			
File documents neatly and quickly			
Persevere when things get difficult			

TEST YOURSELF

1 Identify *at least two* people with whom you can discuss your findings and make appointments to see each of them.

2 Discuss what you have already achieved and found about yourself with each of them. Take with you your answers to the quizzes you did earlier and identify any areas of personal development you particularly need to work on. Make brief notes on your discussions to add to your 'evidence' file.

3 Make a summary list which records

a what you like doing and what you don't like doing

b your strengths and weaknesses – and the areas on which you should concentrate at the moment.

 DID YOU KNOW?

The term 'line manager' is used to describe the person at work to whom you are directly accountable and who is also responsible for you. This may – or may not – be your actual supervisor.

The word 'line' comes from the way an organisation chart is drawn. Below is shown a chart for a small office. Sarah's line manager is Paul and Tom's line manager is Bob. You can see this from the clear vertical line which links them. You can also tell that Sarah and Tom are at the same level in the organisation – and so are the two managers, Bob and Paul.

Bob Sharman ———————————— Paul Richards

Tom Dray   Hasra Bota   Sam Ford   Sarah Hunt

 TEST YOURSELF

1 Can you say who is Hasra's line manager, and who is Sam's?
2 See if you can obtain an organisation chart of your workplace and use this to check who is your particular line manager. Alternatively, obtain one from another source (such as your school, college or work experience placement) to see how it works in practice.

Organisational needs

All organisations have several common needs. They need to

- make a profit
- keep their customers or clients informed and satisfied
- operate within the law (e.g. obey Health and Safety regulations and complete tax returns)
- have a harmonious atmosphere for their staff
- keep documents safely
- process work promptly
- give a good impression to their customers, shareholders, suppliers and the community in general.

These are general needs. Other needs will be more specific and will depend on what type of business is carried out. A food manufacturer needs to make certain that hygiene standards are met, goods are advertised and promoted and are distributed on time. A computer consultancy would have different needs. There may be greater emphasis on rapid response to customer enquiries and staff may need to work more flexible hours.

Therefore, although all organisations will need you to have certain knowledge, skills and abilities, these may be slightly different depending upon where you work. In addition, organisational needs can change. The type of jobs available and their content can vary if, for instance, new technology is introduced. Today, most organisations want their employees to be computer literate and to be able to use basic software packages.

If your personal needs are totally at odds with those of the organisation for which you are employed, then you need to rethink *either* the type of organisation in which you should work *or* your career choice in general. If your main need is for freedom and the great outdoors you would hardly be suited to working in a bank! If you enjoy your work, then matching your needs with those of your organisation will help to make you a better employee and far more likely to be seen as someone suitable for promotion.

The needs of the job

The actual job you do within an organisation will affect the attributes and qualities which are expected of you. A receptionist will be expected to have a pleasant manner, to be outgoing and friendly, speak well and communicate easily with a wide range of people. Such skills would not be as essential for a word processor operator. Accuracy, proofreading skills and rapid keying in would be more appropriate. It is important that you consider both your natural attributes and those qualities you think you can develop in relation to a particular job.

 DID YOU KNOW?

Some people prefer to operate 'on the front desk' and others 'in the backroom'. If you are shy, nervous with strangers and find social conversations almost impossible then you would be better off as one of the 'support team' than aiming to be the mainstay of the customer service group! Try to choose a job where you feel comfortable in the role. If you grow out of the job, as you gain in confidence then you can always change direction later.

 TEST YOURSELF

Four jobs and four sets of qualities are given on the following page. Can you match each with the correct job?

Jobs

1	wages clerk	**3**	sales office assistant
2	switchboard operator	**4**	secretary

Qualities required

A   tactful, patient, unflappable, clear speaking voice, good memory

B   neat, accurate, an eye for detail, good basic maths skills, good communicator

C   good organisational skills, smart appearance, discreet, diplomatic, good writing skills

D   creative, imaginative, good communicator, flexible, persistent, works well under pressure

Personal and core skills

You may have noticed that communication – in one form or another – is required for virtually every job in business. This is a **core skill** – one that is essential. Other core skills in business include the ability to

- work with figures
- be computer literate and use a range of IT packages
- manage yourself (e.g. time-keeping, appearance, taking responsibility)
- work with others as a member of a team (e.g. cope with opinions opposite to your own, help weaker members of a group)
- solve your own problems – and to be able to recognise those which are unsolvable and refer them to the correct person.

On many courses and programmes, core skills development is included and regularly assessed and reviewed. If this is not the case on *your* course there is nothing to stop you assessing these skills yourself – and keeping notes on your progress.

CHECK IT YOURSELF

1   Read the three mini-case studies below and decide

   a   which employees are suited to the job – and which are not

   b   whether their planned actions are appropriate and, if not, what they should do.

Case study 1

Mark started work at a firm of accountants last September and successfully completed his NVQ 2 award in Administration this summer. Although he works mainly in the general office, he wants to move on in the company. He likes working with figures and has recently started using computers at work, which he enjoys. He has decided to find out which courses he could move on to which are more closely linked to accountancy, and to talk to his boss about what he should do next.

Case study 2

Victoria loves animals and originally wanted to work for a vet. She enjoys dealing with people and was good at this when she had a Saturday job in a local store. When she left school, Victoria decided to take a part-time NVQ/secretarial skills course in the hope that this would enable her to apply for any jobs as a receptionist for a vet. For four days a week she works in the production office of a local paper mill as an YT trainee. The work keeps her busy but she doesn't enjoy it very much. She has decided to see her supervisor on Monday to say she doesn't like the job.

Case study 3

Jimmy didn't know what he wanted to do when he left school. His family own a Chinese restaurant and he has helped out there for quite some time. He enjoys the work but has decided he doesn't want to work in catering himself. However, he felt some business skills would be useful so he started an NVQ Administration course full-time. He spent his last period of work experience in the personnel office of a large company. He got on well with his colleagues and other visitors, as he finds it easy to get on with people after all his experience in the restaurant! He has decided to find out more about personnel work and what he should do if he wants to become a personnel officer in the future.

2 Make a list of the needs which you consider are relevant to your own organisation. Discuss this with your supervisor or line manager and fill in any gaps. (If you are studying on a full-time course, you can start by making a more general list of organisational needs and complete this when you are on work experience.)

3 Match this with the list of your own needs you compiled on page 10 and your own individual preferences. Discuss with *at least one person* from your support group whether you are suited for the type of job you are doing (or thinking of doing) or not.
If you are suited to the job, your next step is to find out how you can advance your career further – what additional qualifications, skills, abilities and experience you will need. If you are not suited to the job then read the next section very carefully indeed!

DID YOU KNOW?

Many people drift into jobs rather than make a positive career choice because

● they don't know what there is available

- they are not qualified for the type of job they want
- they don't know where to get information and/or help.

Equally, many people make a positive choice, only to discover later that it was wrong or that their personal needs and preferences have changed. They then change direction later in life.

This can often be the case with people who decide to take a business qualification. There is a vast range of business courses and careers in business and many people only know about the obvious ones. If you feel that your information is sadly lacking in this department then it is time to put things right!

Sources of advice and information

Before you can prepare a formal statement of your development needs, you need to check that you have obtained sufficient information on

- what you *have* achieved up to now
- what you *want* to achieve in the future
- what you *need* to achieve in the future, bearing in mind your current job and your career goals.

If you need to obtain more information about a possible career or specific qualifications then you can visit your local Careers Office, the Job Centre or your local college.

If you know the career in which you are interested then it is worth finding out if there is a professional body which issues information and literature, e.g. the Chartered Institute of Marketing or the Institute of Personnel Management. Find out the address by visiting your local or college library.

Alternatively, talk to your line manager, supervisor or tutor about career development – or visit your personnel department.

Finally, it is worth talking through your proposed plan with any of your support group to see if they have any suggestions which you may have overlooked.

CHECK IT YOURSELF

If you have any doubts or queries about the type of job you want to do, you are recommended to do each of the following.

1 Visit your local Careers Office, Job Centre and the student advisory centre at your local college. Find out as much as you can about the type of jobs to be found in

- different departments, e.g. production, sales and marketing, distribution, purchasing, personnel, administration and finance

- different types of organisation, from a local solicitors' office to the National Health Service, from your local town hall to a large organisation such as British Telecom.

2 Target those areas which interest you and obtain more detailed information on qualifications, training, appropriate courses, salary levels and so on. You may need the assistance of several members of your support group to help you to obtain and analyse the information you need, but it is worth it to put yourself on the right route.

Preparing a statement of your development needs

By now, you should have obtained a considerable amount of evidence about yourself, i.e.

- documentary evidence on your own achievements
- records of interviews and discussions with others
- your self-assessment answers from the two quizzes you completed
- notes from any work reviews you have had
- details of your own needs and your organisation's needs
- information on your chosen career route.

The time has come to assemble all this information into something useful which you can use as the basis for your future development.

You may find it easier if you think in terms of

1 professional skills
2 personal skills
3 knowledge.

Under each heading you need to note down

a what you *have already* achieved
b what you *want* to develop
c what you *need* to develop
   - immediately
   - in the next few years.

 DID YOU KNOW?

Your supervisor or tutor may have a pre-printed form which already contains these headings if he or she has the tutor pack which accompanies this book.

CHECK IT YOURSELF

Prepare your statement in draft form and discuss this with *at least two* people from your support group. See if they can offer useful suggestions to improve it in any way. In particular, if you are working then you should involve your line manager or supervisor and if you are on a full-time course then your personal tutor should be involved. When you have agreed your statement with the most appropriate people then prepare a final printed version.

Be prepared to amend your statement regularly over the next few months, as you start to fulfil some of the needs you have identified. Bear in mind that your amendments should be agreed with *at least one* other person. If you consider that you have suddenly become the most punctual person in the world it is wise to check that your supervisor or tutor holds the same opinion!

Element 1.2

Prepare and agree a plan of action to develop self

There is a very old saying which says 'never look a gift horse in the mouth'. Basically, this means never turn down a golden opportunity – or miss one altogether because you didn't realise at the time how much you could benefit. Opportunities for self-development occur both inside and outside work and usually when you least expect them to! You may be offered the chance to

- attend a company training course
- stand in for somebody else at work
- help out in another department when they are very busy
- go on an 'away day' training programme
- go on a residential course to develop your personal skills
- work on a special project
- read an interesting book or article
- watch a television programme on a work–related topic
- go on holiday to a different country.

All these, and many others, are golden opportunities for self-development – though you may not recognise them as such at the time.

 TEST YOURSELF

Think back over the past twelve months and list any opportunities for self-development you may have had (at work, at college or in your personal life). Try to think as broadly as you can. It will be easy for you to think of things you actually did – and less easy to think of opportunities you ignored or turned down!

Taking advantage of opportunities

If you want actively to pursue a programme of self-development then you can't afford to ignore any such opportunities in the future. The first step you should take, therefore, is to talk through your statement with someone who can help you to

- identify opportunities for meeting your needs
- agree specific objectives which will help you to meet your needs.

The best person – or people – to choose will depend on your situation and who is responsible for your own training and development.

CHECK IT YOURSELF

Look back at your statement of self-development needs and identify *at least ten* ways of meeting your needs. Ask your tutor or supervisor for help if you need to. Then underline all the ways which are possible and score through all the ways which are not feasible. As an example, if you need to learn more about making travel arrangements, it is sensible to do the NVQ option on that topic but rather less feasible to book a worldwide tour to find out at first hand what to do!

Don't forget to include methods which involve you finding out, researching or studying information **on your own**! (*See also Element 5.2*.)

Organisational training and development

In most organisations, staff training and development is undertaken by the personnel department. There may even be a special training officer to organise these events. Training programmes may be

- organised on the company premises. These are called in-house or on-the-job training programmes.
- offered by external agencies. These can be private training providers, your local college or even your local fire brigade (e.g. for a course in fire fighting).

Some topics are ideally taught on-the-job. If you work for a company which wants you to learn to use their switchboard, you will be taught how to do this – probably – by the existing switchboard operator.

Other topics are best taught outside work. Fire fighting is an obvious example, so is first aid. You can hardly practise bandaging half the office staff during the lunch break! Most courses which lead to professional qualifications are run by outside training providers. Therefore, when you have completed your NVQ course and decided on a specific career path, you may be advised to attend college on a day-release or evening only basis to obtain higher qualifications.

Employees who really want to get on may attend college on one or two different nights a week (as well as working full-time) to obtain their qualifications. Courses in Personnel Management, Marketing and Management Studies are often run on this basis.

Organisational policy and procedures

Different companies have different policies and procedures in relation to staff training. For example, some companies have a specific induction programme for all new staff to tell them about the company, how it is organised and structured and the products or services it supplies. Other companies do not. Some companies have their own in-house NVQ training programmes, while others use their local college. Some pay for all additional training, others expect their employees to pay some or all of the cost.

If you want to attend a course or training programme – whether in-house or external – you may be able to do so if your line manager agrees, or you may have to have your application approved by the personnel department.

It is therefore wise not to assume any specific policy but to ask your line manager or colleagues yourself – and find out exactly what to do if you want to know what is on offer or attend a course yourself.

CHECK IT YOURSELF

1 Your sources of advice on training and development will vary depending upon your circumstances. Make a list of *at least five* useful sources of advice you could access and check these are suitable with the most appropriate person of your support group.
2 Obtain information on *at least one* course in which you think you may be interested in the future.

The role of colleagues

The people with whom you work or train can often be a mine of information. Regardless of the people you have listed as your support group, it can be a friend or colleague who tells you

- how to complete a form and when to hand it in
- whether a training course was good or a waste of time
- the areas in which your particular manager or tutor is especially interested
- which areas your colleagues think are important
- which areas your colleagues think *you* should consider important

- of the latest bit of news which will help you to achieve your objectives.

Whereas friends may tell you what they think you want to know, colleagues are often more honest! They have to work alongside you every day – and put up with you – whether they like it or not. For that reason, you are likely to receive fairly practical and objective advice from them if you enter into any discussions relating to your own self-development.

 ## DID YOU KNOW?

A **mentor** is someone who gives somebody else useful advice and information which will help their self-development. A mentor can have a formal role or be an older colleague who knows the system, has a personal interest in you and wants to help you by giving you useful information and guidance.

Some organisations and training establishments appoint official mentors for junior staff who are on training programmes. This sometimes works well but is never as good as the unofficial mentor. If you find your best mentor is an older colleague who is super to work with and gives you invaluable advice, then you are very lucky. Never take their help for granted and always carefully consider their opinion before you make a decision.

Learning and self-study

You may get rather a shock if some of your colleagues observe that a major problem is that you don't take much action *yourself* to learn anything independently. Part of everyone's self-development, especially as they get older, is learning to be self-reliant and not expecting other people to provide information they need. Learning to work alone, to organise yourself and master things one step at a time is an important part of your self-development and will pay dividends in the future as you won't have to depend on other people to do things for you.

You can improve your own knowledge in numerous ways. Some of this will be more relevant to your professional development than others. Reading an interesting article in the newspaper about your rights as a consumer is likely to be more beneficial than reading a road test on a sports car or scanning the fashion page!

 ## TEST YOURSELF

1 When did you last visit a library?
2 When did you last read an article in a newspaper which hadn't a sensational headline?
3 When did you last watch the news on television *to the end*?
4 When did you last discuss a serious topic (e.g. the budget) with your friends?
5 When did you last study something on your own?

Learning styles

Everyone learns in different ways. Some people remember everything they see on a video but forget what they heard in a classroom. Other people get the most out of group work or discussions. Honey and Mumford[1] identified four learning styles. Which one do you consider you use the most – and which one the least?

1 The activist

You like to get on with things immediately. You are impulsive and will try anything once and worry about the consequences later. Change doesn't worry you. You fill your spare time with numerous activities but are easily bored, hate routine work and dislike detailed preparation before you can get on with a job. You often have good ideas but don't often put them into practice. You are sociable and optimistic with lots of friends and like to be the centre of attention.

2 The reflector

You think a lot. Before making a decision you will try to think about a problem from every angle. You will listen to other people and then carefully think about what was said before you act. You are careful, thoughtful and methodical. You may be considered to be a slow and/or quiet worker who prefers to work alone rather than join in with the group.

3 The theorist

You are objective and unemotional and like to know where you stand. It irritates you if someone is offhand or flippant. You like to think things through step by step to see how they fit. You are good at asking relevant questions and are self-disciplined. You don't like to commit yourself.

4 The pragmatist

You prefer action to discussion. Before too long you become impatient with ideas and theories and want to see if they will work in practice. You prefer practical rather than theoretical work and like a challenge. You are a very down-to-earth person but may occasionally rush in too quickly with the first obvious solution to a problem.

Honey and Mumford believed that you need to be able to adopt all four styles to learn, as some styles suit some situations more than others.

CHECK IT YOURSELF

1 The activist style can be related to the next practical and urgent task with which you are involved – either at work or at college. Concentrate

---

1 Peter Honey and Alan Mumford, management consultants and training and development experts

on getting involved *quickly* and learning by experience. Talk about your experience with a member of your support group later. Activists will enjoy doing work to move forward but may struggle at keeping records of their personal development.

2   The reflector style is best used in relation to planning. Looking back and thinking about what happened comes naturally to a reflector. Apply this style when you have to think over your experiences and relate them to your action plan.

3   The theorist style can relate to discussions you have with your colleagues, your tutor, your line manager or in class. Develop the technique of *listening* to other people *before* you leap in, *considering* their opinions carefully and *thinking* carefully before you make a reply. As a theorist you will be more able to learn from your experiences and revise your plans successfully.

4   The pragmatist style can be developed when you attempt a task after learning about it for the first time. Often you need to adapt your theory to fit the real world! For instance, you may have some fanciful ideas and objectives but would have to make them fit reality. You will be more able to plan successfully if you adapt a pragmatic approach.

DID YOU KNOW?

There is nothing more frustrating than being surrounded by information and not having a clue how to organise it all, let alone remember it. Self-study is a skill which, like all other skills, can be learned.

Learning techniques

If you know how to learn effectively, then you will find learning far more enjoyable as the reward for your efforts will be so much greater.

The main areas on which you should concentrate are given below. Answer each question carefully – and work out the areas where you need to change your habits to learn effectively.

1 Do you use your time to maximum advantage?

Time management is an important aspect of learning. Learning or study time must be **planned** – to a realistic timetable which allows for your leisure activities and has some built-in flexibility (to allow for the unexpected).

Main points to remember

- Set yourself a realistic target to achieve.
- Don't work for hours on end – an hour at a time is usually enough.
- Everyone learns better when they are attentive and fresh – not exhausted. Burning the midnight oil is not usually a good idea.

- You can only remember things which you understand.
- End every session testing yourself to find out if you've achieved your target.

2 Can you write notes quickly and accurately which cover the main points and understand them later?

You need to apply this skill on many different occasions – e.g. when you take a telephone message. Use abbreviations, making up your own if it helps. Keep your layout clear and simple with headings, sub-divisions, underscoring – even diagrams if you want.

3 Can you find your notes within minutes, even months later?

Being organised is essential. File notes immediately under a relevant subject heading or in a labelled folder.

4 Do you expect to be able to learn information just by reading?

All learning should be **active**. You learn very little by just sitting and reading. If you have an article or several pages to read and consider then go through these steps.

- Look through the material first.
- Make sure you understand what you are reading. Ask if you are not sure.
- Read it again and highlight the main points.
- Make **brief** notes of the main points.
- Check if you can recall the main points from memory.

5 Do you recognise that you can often learn from other people?

You don't always learn from formal sessions. Informal conversations, discussions, exchanges of views and even arguments with a friend or colleague can help you to understand material, clarify information and even give you a different point of view. To benefit you must learn *when to talk* and *when to listen* so that you don't just sit waiting until it's your turn to speak again!

6 Do you know *how* you learn?

We all learn in different ways. Some people prefer to break information up into small chunks, others learn in wholes. Some people remember text, others prefer pictures.

You can improve your memory by

- creating an association (like being able to remember a telephone number because it contains four figures of your birthdate)
- creating a **mnemonic**, which is a short word containing the initial letters of the facts you are trying to learn
- linking your facts together.

7 Can you clearly identify the different ways in which you would read a telephone directory, a recipe and a novel? Or do you think they are all the same?

There are **five** ways in which you should read. Each is designed for a different purpose.

- You **scan** material if you are looking for something specific, e.g. a telephone number or book index. When you put yourself in 'scan mode' you shouldn't get distracted by other things you see!
- You **skim** material if you are looking through something but not for something specific, e.g. when you look through a magazine to see what's in it.
- You are involved in **light reading** when you read a novel or magazine article. Your recall is poor, especially after some time.
- You read **word by word** if you are following new or important instructions, e.g. how to set a new video player for timed record, how to mix a solution to dye your hair!
- You **read for study** if you are trying to learn something. This means slow and repetitive reading and taking notes where appropriate.

DID YOU KNOW?

You can increase your reading speed by

- increasing the number of words you 'see' at one time
- adjusting your speed to the difficulty of the material
- always reading forwards – not looking back or re-reading words
- improving your vocabulary.

TEST YOURSELF

With a friend, try improving your memory by playing a different version of 'Kim's game'. Imagine you have entered a competition and are going to be shown 20 objects in quick succession. You can keep all those you can remember!

Your friend should write down 20 'prizes' – from a sports car to a tennis racquet to a barbecue, then read out the list to you saying one item every three seconds. See how many you can remember and repeat back afterwards.

The trick is to link each object by incorporating it into a 'story'. For instance, for the three items mentioned above, picture yourself driving a sports car, whilst you hold a tennis racquet, on your way to a barbecue. It doesn't matter how ridiculous or improbable your story is – in fact the more silly it is the more likely you are to remember it!

You will find if you practise that you can quite easily remember 20 items and repeat them. Then try 30 – and so on!

Action plans

An action plan is a document which clearly states what you want to achieve in the future. Ideally, each goal you set yourself should have a target date. This might be in a few weeks' time, a few months' time or in years to come. The idea is that you can then work out how to reach each target by the date you have given.

Planning a course of action may mean you have to change your existing work habits. You may need help from your line manager, your supervisor, your colleagues or your tutors to achieve your targets. Whatever you do *don't* set yourself unachievable targets – you'll only get fed up and decide the whole thing is a waste of time. Your targets need to be clear and realistic. They should also stretch you a little. Setting a target you can achieve already is cheating!

Once you have set a target then you need to map out the steps you need to achieve it. Stick to these whenever you can. If you have a real crisis in your life then it is quite understandable – and essential – that you review your target. If you were going on a journey and the train broke down halfway you would *have* to review your arrival time!

TEST YOURSELF

Discuss the contents of your NVQ course with your line manager or tutor. Think about

- what is involved in each unit
- the number of elements in each unit – and whether these are different from each other or linked
- which jobs you do at work and which units or elements you should find easy to complete
- which units or elements you will need to study carefully because they contain new information
- which units and elements are 'ongoing' (i.e. will be continued throughout the course; **note** – this is one of them!)
- which units or elements you will need to do as simulation because you can't do them at work.

Now try to work out a realistic schedule for completing each unit. As a start, use the following format.

Unit/ element	Target date for achievement	Actual date of achievement
1 Develop self	on-going (so state review dates)	

Check your schedule with your line manager/tutor to make certain it is realistic and achievable.

Action planning for other areas

Your complete action plan may include more than one qualification. It should also cover areas such as

- personal skills
- core skills
- current weaknesses and concerns
- current strengths and successes
- additional job-related qualifications (e.g. in IT or foreign languages)
- other achievements (e.g. in relation to your hobbies and interests)
- your career aspirations – both now and in the future.

Aims and objectives

The difference between an aim and an objective is that an **aim** is a general statement which says what you intend to do, and an **objective** is measurable. This means you can prove that you have achieved it! A person may have the aim of losing weight before going on holiday and might set themselves the objective of losing between three and five pounds a week which would be both sensible and realistic. (One pound a week is too little and ten pounds a week is too much. In both cases someone on a diet would give up almost before they had started!) This is a typical case of turning an aim into a realistic objective to retain motivation.

 DID YOU KNOW?

Slimming and keep-fit clubs have made a fortune out of setting objectives for people and keeping them motivated! By recording people's progress, giving them feedback and praising them when they do well, they have produced a 'formula' to help people succeed and reach their goal. You can apply the same formula if you bear in mind the key points.

Setting your own objectives

Imagine that one of your aims in life is to be a more punctual person. Your objective should be stated in terms which you can measure, e.g. 'I will not be late for work or for class on more than two occasions in the next month.' You can now measure your objective against your performance and test if you have achieved it.

A more difficult case is when you have an objective which is less easy to **quantify** (or put into numbers). Imagine that one of your aims is to become a more sociable person. How are you going to measure this? You may decide to set yourself an objective of going out more often, or having more friends. Both these would be measurable. As a second example, if you set yourself the aim of being a more tidy person you would have to work out how to quantify this. You could set an objective of always having a tidy desk when you leave each night, or filing papers every day. You can use self-observation to see if you have achieved this – and also count statements from other people. If your supervisor remarks on week 3 that your desk is an example for others to follow then you are really achieving your objective!

TEST YOURSELF

Below are given *six* general aims. Can you work out suitable objectives in each case?

1 I'll learn some useful French phrases before I go on holiday next year.
2 I'll get better at answering the telephone at work.
3 I'll do something to keep fit.
4 I'll find out which courses I can do after this one which will help me to move on in my chosen career.
5 I won't put things off as much.
6 (*The hardest!*) I'll be much nicer to my friends.

Objectives and action planning

Your action plan should include your objectives, rather than a series of general aims. Only then will it be possible for you to measure if you have achieved them.

TEST YOURSELF

1 Draft out an action plan which includes the development needs you identified during Element 1.1 and any other areas you want to develop which you have since identified.
2 Set yourself clear objectives for each of your key areas.
3 Discuss your plan, and the timescale you have set yourself with your line manager, any mentors you have at work, your tutor and any other members of your support group who you feel will be able to help you.
4 Discuss the action you need to take to achieve each of your objectives. Be prepared to change or modify this if your tutor or line manager feels any are unrealistic or unachievable.
5 Agree a method of setting out your action plan so that it is clear and easy to follow. If there is a standard way of setting out action plans in the organisation you work for, or if you are following a college system, then you may have to follow an official format. Otherwise you can design your own.
6 Now prepare and **date** your own action plan and keep it safely. Note that because this document has to be regularly revised, it is useful to prepare it on a word processor and to store it on disk.

Element 1.3

Implement and review a personal development plan

Before you get muddled up between 'action plans' and 'personal development plans', one thing must be made clear – they are virtually the same thing. If you call it a personal action plan then you probably can't go far wrong!

Your action plan is a *temporary* personal development plan – because it declares what you wish to achieve at this moment in time. Technically, your personal development plan would be all your action plans put together over a period of time. If you are sensible then you will keep all your documentation together – as it will undoubtedly be very useful in the future – for you, your employer, your tutor and the verifier who will check your evidence for this course.

Portfolio of achievement

All NVQ courses require a considerable amount of evidence to be produced which proves that you are competent in all the stated areas. You must also prove that you have covered the performance criteria for each unit, the range statements and that you understand the knowledge requirements. A scheme verifier will check all this carefully to make sure that you deserve your award.

All your evidence must therefore be stored carefully and **dated**. This proves that, in units such as this, you have *regularly* updated your evidence. At the end of your course you can create a final personal development plan which states what you want to achieve after completing your NVQ award. In addition there will be clear records of what you set out to achieve during the award, where you were successful and where you weren't (and why!).

Your supervisor or tutor may have his or her own ideas of how your portfolio should be structured. It is usual to have a lever arch file to contain all your evidence and numbered dividers for each unit.

CHECK IT YOURSELF

Check if this is the case for your course and obtain the folders and dividers required. Label these clearly and neatly and, behind the first divider, carefully file all the evidence you have obtained so far. *Don't* file actual certificates and diplomas. Simply list these and ask your supervisor or tutor to verify your list by signing it at the foot of the page. If you have followed the instructions in this book carefully, you should already have collected quite a number of pages to file!

Implementing your action plan

Now is the time to start **implementing** your plan. This means putting your plans into action. Don't try to move forward on everything at once – it'll overwhelm you. Choose one or two straightforward objectives to start with and tackle these first. Then you can move on to other areas. Try to learn your action plan, so that if unexpected opportunities for self-development suddenly arise, you know to take advantage of them.

The trick is not to forget to record your progress. You can do this

- by keeping a diary or weekly record of your achievements, progress or new experiences
- by talking to other people and noting down their comments
- by keeping records of any training courses you attend or other discussions you have which relate to your progress.

Your progress record should be the basis of your first review session as this document is proof of what you have achieved against each of your objectives.

 ## SPECIAL NOTE

If you regularly forget to write down what you have done, then this skill should perhaps be added to your list of objectives at your first review!

Reviewing your progress

It is absolutely essential that you review your progress at regular intervals with someone whose opinions you respect and who you can talk to freely and honestly. A review implies *two* things –

- looking back at what has happened over the past few weeks and analysing where your plan has worked (and where it hasn't)
- looking forward and changing your plan in the light of experience.

There is a saying that anyone can get something wrong *once* but only a fool repeats the same mistake. When you were a child, you quickly learned not to touch anything hot – or you would get burned. You didn't need to keep repeating the experience to get the message.

It is therefore quite acceptable to find that you went wrong when you first made out your plan. It is far less acceptable to keep getting it wrong!

Preparing for your review

Prepare for your reviews by

- comparing your progress record against your action plan
- making a note of your successes and progress
- identifying any areas of weakness or problems
- updating information where necessary (e.g. if your ambitions or job has changed, or if you have taken up a new hobby or interest)
- thinking through the three areas of skills, knowledge and understanding in relation to both your professional and personal development.

SPECIAL NOTE

It is a good idea to schedule regular review sessions right at the beginning and have fixed times for these. The longer you go between reviews the longer you have to work on your own. However, don't be frightened of reviewing your progress yourself and *initiating* a review. If you feel that a sudden problem means you would benefit from a review then pencil in the updates to your action plan, and make an arrangement to discuss these with your line manager or tutor as soon as possible.

Appraisals and work reviews

All organisations have some procedures in place for monitoring the work of employees, students or trainees. If you are employed then your organisation probably has a system of reviewing your work. These are often called **appraisal interviews**. At an appraisal interview you discuss various aspects of your work with your supervisor or line manager. This gives you the opportunity to discuss problem areas and areas in which you are interested and want to develop further. It gives your supervisor the chance to answer queries, to find out more about you and to help you in your self-development programme.

Schools and colleges may have a similar system during tutorials. You will probably have a personal tutor with whom you will discuss such matters – and you may be expected to keep your National Record of Achievement up to date.

If you are on a training programme such as YT, your managing agent or trainer will discuss your progress with you at regular intervals and complete a monitoring form.

All these systems can be classified as **work reviews** and information and evidence from these reviews is vital in helping you with your assessment of your own development needs. They will usually result in specific organisational documentation which you can include in your portfolio.

Attending an action plan review

It may be that, whilst you are taking this award, your action plan reviews are included in any of the types of work reviews stated above. Whether this is the case or not, before the review date make sure your documentation is complete and you have prepared properly. Hopefully, your tutor or line manager will also have listed comments to discuss e.g. areas where you have been particularly strong (or weak).

Talk to your line manager, supervisor, colleagues or tutor about any difficulties you are having achieving your objectives. Don't be frightened about admitting that you are having problems – everyone has problems with certain things at some time or other. Consider whether

- you have been too ambitious
- you simply lost heart
- you were lazy
- there were too many distractions and/or other events for you to cope
- circumstances genuinely worked against you
- it just seemed like a good idea at the time – but wasn't.

Review each objective in the light of these considerations. You can

- leave it as it is, and try again
- make it easier to achieve
- discuss alternative methods of achieving your objective
- remove it altogether.

Concentrate on your achievements and successes, rather than your failures. Congratulate and reward yourself for any area in which you did well and update your action plan. If you did really well, perhaps you should add some more targets to your list?

Updating your action plan

At the end of your review you need to create an up-to-date version of your action plan. This is then your basis for action until your next review session. If you have saved it on disk it is a simple matter to recall it, update it and take a new print-out. Give a copy to your line manager or tutor and any other member of your support group who has been helpful. Keep all your documentation filed neatly, in a separate folder from your main portfolio if you wish.

At the end of your course you should derive a great deal of pleasure from looking back at where you first started and reviewing your achievements. You can then look forward to moving on in life – and developing an action plan to take you even further into the future and towards your goals.

UNIT REVIEW

By the end of this unit you should have worked with appropriate people from your support group and have

- identified and collected relevant information on your own achievements to date
- identified opportunities for developing yourself and linked these to the needs of the organisation for which you work and to your own job and career plans
- agreed a formal statement of your development needs
- agreed specific objectives for your own development and the appropriate action to take to achieve these
- prepared an action plan and put this into effect
- kept a record of progress against your action plan
- attended regular reviews and adjusted objectives where necessary
- started to keep a personal portfolio of your achievements.

REVIEW YOUR KNOWLEDGE AND UNDERSTANDING

True or false?

1 Review sessions can only be scheduled by a line manager or tutor.
2 Many organisations organise their own training courses for employees.
3 We should scan a document if we want to find a particular item quickly.
4 Many people have different careers during their working life.
5 Reviewing your progress means looking backwards and looking forwards.

Fill in the blanks

6 The _____ department is responsible for training and development of employees in a large organisation.
7 A scheduled review interview for employees at work is called an _____ interview.
8 Trying to find out more about yourself and your own wants and needs is called _____

Work it out

9 Becky attends her NVQ course one day a week. She works as a clerical assistant/typist in the environmental office at the local town hall on a YT scheme and dreams of working abroad one day. Her mother thinks her ideas are unrealistic and tells her to think more sensibly.

    a Find out if there are any departments in a local authority which would be more suitable for Becky.
    b Identify *four* things Becky could plan to do which would make her dream more likely to come true.

10 During a progress review with your line manager you find out that

    a she is keen for you to develop your numeracy skills – but you don't like working with figures

    b she thinks some of your plans are unrealistic

    c she is doubtful about your story that you couldn't complete the last unit you were studying on time because you weren't feeling well.

Consider how you would react in each of these cases and the best way to handle the situation – which would involve both communication and negotiation skills.

Discuss your ideas with other members of your group, your colleagues, supervisor and/or tutor.

2 Monitor and maintain a healthy, safe and secure workplace

This unit is concerned with your role, as an employee, in understanding the importance of health, safety and security procedures and taking an active part in helping to monitor and maintain a safe and secure working environment for yourself and your colleagues.

Legislation on health and safety is continually being updated and it is important that you are aware of both your own and your employer's responsibilities in law. Security procedures are becoming more important as crime increases. Employees and their belongings, as well as the organisations themselves, may be targets. Cars are stolen from company car parks more frequently than valuable computer data is tampered with or destroyed.

This unit is divided into two elements. The first of these is concerned with health and safety and the second with security in the workplace.

Element 2.1

Monitor and maintain health and safety within the workplace

Health and safety is an important issue for all organisations. Absenteeism through poor working conditions or accidents is costly to any company and people do not work as productively if they are ill, tired or in an unsatisfactory environment. Even more importantly, an organisation which does not comply with current legislation on health and safety is committing a criminal offence and can be prosecuted.

Since 1974 employees have also been required to comply with health and safety legislation – and their role has been increased with the new EU (European Union) regulations which came into force in January 1993.

Health and Safety legislation

The most important Act relating to Health and Safety is the **Health and Safety at Work Act 1974** (HASAWACT). This places a legal responsibility on employers *and* employees in relation to health and safety issues.

It is the employer's duty to provide

● safe entry and exit routes in and out of the workplace

- a safe working environment and adequate welfare facilities
- safe equipment and systems of work
- arrangements for ensuring the safe use, handling, storage and transport of articles and substances
- information on health and safety, instruction, training and supervision
- investigation of any accidents.

The employee has a duty to

- take reasonable care for his or her own health and safety
- take reasonable care for the health and safety of other people who may be affected by his or her actions
- co-operate with his or her employer or any other person carrying out duties under the Act.

In addition, if there are more than five employees, the employer must prepare a written document which states company policy on health and safety and circulate this to all employees. The Act also allows for the appointment of safety representatives selected by a recognised trade union.

CHECK IT YOURSELF

Under the Health and Safety at Work Act an employer has a duty to display details of the main terms of the Act in a notice for all employees to read. Find (and read!) this notice in your own workplace, college or training establishment. Write down the name and address of your enforcing authority and what you should do if you think there is a health and safety problem in your workplace.

TEST YOURSELF

Look at each of the statements below and identify the part(s) of the Act under which they would be categorised as an offence.

1 An employee refuses to stay for roll call after an emergency evacuation.
2 An emergency escape door has been blocked by a filing cabinet.
3 No safety stools are provided for employees to reach files from high shelves.
4 Toxic cleaning fluid is stored in an unlabelled bottle.
5 A photocopier is kept in use even though the front door has broken off.
6 An employee wedges open a fire door.

Additional regulations

HASAWACT is known as an **enabling** or **umbrella** Act under which additional regulations can be added to keep the law up to date. Since 1985 a number of these have been introduced including

- the Reporting of Injuries, Diseases and Dangerous Occurrences Regulations (RIDDOR)

- the Control of Substances Hazardous to Health (COSHH)
- Electricity at Work Regulations
- Noise at Work Regulations
- Health and Safety (First Aid) Regulations.

New regulations on Fire Precautions are scheduled to be introduced during 1994.

RIDDOR

These regulations compel organisations to notify the Health and Safety Executive (HSE) if any accidents occur which cause serious or fatal injuries or lead to a lengthy period off work. In addition, the organisation must keep records of all notifiable injuries, dangerous occurrences and diseases.

COSHH

These regulations cover the control of hazardous substances and require employers to take steps either to eliminate the substance, or control its storage and use and provide protective clothing.

DID YOU KNOW?

Many office workers are under the mistaken impression that COSHH regulations have nothing to do with them. In fact, many office machines such as photocopiers give off fumes, cleaning staff use chemicals and solvents and even felt tip pens emit gas! Whilst these may not be hazardous in small quantities they can all be classified as *potentially* hazardous.

Noise at Work Regulations

These regulations require employers to assess noise hazards in the workplace, reduce these where possible, keep employees informed of noise hazards and provide ear protectors.

The Electricity at Work Regulations

These apply to the design, construction, use and maintenance of electrical systems and installations.

SPECIAL NOTE

First aid is covered as a separate topic on page 42. Fire precautions and emergency procedures are dealt with on page 46.

European Health and Safety Law

The main force behind health and safety law today is the European Community and all EU law involves two main aspects, which are

- worker participation, and
- the assessment and monitoring of risks.

All EU directives *must* be implemented in member states and it is the responsibility of the Health and Safety Commission to produce the regulations which will apply in the United Kingdom. On 1 January 1993 six new regulations came into force in the UK as a direct result of EU directives. They are commonly known as the **six-pack**.

TEST YOURSELF

The six regulations introduced in the 'six-pack' are shown in the chart on pages 37–38. Read them carefully, then see if you can answer the questions below.

1 Your office has only one small, decrepit stapler and yet you are often asked to staple large quantities of documents. Yesterday you hurt your hand quite badly. Which regulations require your employer to provide a stapler which is more suitable to the task and keep it well maintained?

2 You work in a small office which is definitely overcrowded. There is a broken window to your left and no source of drinking water in your part of the building. Which regulations will force your employer to improve the situation?

3 A major part of your office building is being renovated and scaffolding has been erected. On a scheduled visit to the area to plan the new office area you are told you must wear a hard safety hat.

    a Which regulations compel your employer to provide you with a suitable helmet?

    b Do you have to wear it – and if so, why?

4 Your friend is employed in the printing department of a large organisation. He informs you that he is going on a course related to identifying and assessing risks in his area and minimising these. Which regulation has prompted his employer to take this action?

5 Your colleague complains that there are no trolleys on which equipment can be transported in your office. Regularly nothing can be moved until there are two or three people around to help to carry it. Under which regulations will your employers have to change this situation?

6 You regularly use a VDU in your work and your eyes often start to ache before the end of a day. You think your sight is deteriorating. When you mention the fact to your supervisor she ignores you.

    a Which regulation means she will now have to take notice of your concerns?

    b What action will your employer have to take?

The six-pack regulations

1 The Management of Health and Safety at Work Regulations 1992

These regulations are more commonly referred to as the **Management Regs**. Under these all employers must

- carry out risk assessments which assess significant risks both to employees and others affected by the business
- keep a record of the assessment and the measures which have been identified to control the risk (if there are more than five employees)
- appoint competent people to help to implement the health and safety arrangements
- make arrangements to plan, organise, control, maintain and review health and safety arrangements
- set up emergency procedures to deal with situations of serious or imminent danger
- provide full information and training to all employees plus details of any risks involved in their work.

2 Workplace (Health, Safety and Welfare) Regulations

These regulations state minimum legal standards for a range of health and safety issues including

- **Health** – lighting, ventilation and temperature; space and room dimensions; workstations and seating; cleanliness
- **Safety** – maintenance of the workplace and equipment, floors, windows and skylights; doors, gates and escalators; traffic routes, falls and falling objects
- **Welfare** – toilets and washing facilities; drinking water; changing rooms, rest rooms and eating facilities.

3 Display Screen Equipment Regulations

These regulations apply to all employees who regularly use display screen equipment (DSE) as a significant part of their work. They relate to the furniture used in relation to a VDU (called a **workstation**) as well as the equipment.

Employers must

- assess all workstations for health and safety risks and lower the risks as much as possible
- plan work activities to incorporate rest breaks at regular intervals
- arrange and pay for eye tests and pay for spectacles or lenses if these are prescribed specifically for VDU work
- provide health and safety training for DSE users and retrain if the workstation is changed or modified

- provide DSE users with information on all aspects of health and safety which apply to them and measures being taken to reduce risks to their health.

4 Provision and Use of Work Equipment Regulations

The term 'work equipment' relates to any type of machine, appliance, apparatus or tools used at work. In an office these include photocopiers, fax machines and even staplers.

The employer must

- ensure that all equipment is suitable for the task and keep it well maintained
- take into account working conditions and potential hazards when selecting new equipment
- issue appropriate information, instructions and training on its use
- restrict access when necessary

5 Personal Protective Equipment at Work Regulations

These regulations relate to the provision of protective clothing and equipment (PPE) when risks cannot be eliminated. Obvious examples are ear muffs, safety helmets and safety goggles.

It will be up to employers to ensure that PPE is provided without charge, is suitable and fits properly, is maintained in good condition, is stored safely and that information is provided on its use.

6 Manual Handling Operations Regulations

These require employers to

- avoid any manual handling operations in which employees could be injured (e.g. by using an automated or mechanised process)
- assess and reduce the risk of injury as much as possible
- provide employees with information on specific loads which will help them avoid risk.

Enforcement of Health and Safety legislation

Health and safety legislation is enforced by the Health and Safety Executive (HSE) and by local authority environmental health departments. Generally, environmental health officers are responsible for dealing with offices and shops and HSE inspectors investigate factories and other industrial establishments.

An inspector can visit any premises, without warning, either to investigate an accident or complaint or simply to inspect the premises and question the employees. The inspector may then give advice to the management and the safety representatives. However, they also have the power to issue a notice.

- An **Improvement notice** means the employer has to put matters right within a fixed time.
- A **Prohibition notice** forbids the employer to continue with any process which endangers either the workers or the general public.

If the company fails to comply with the notice then the organisation can be fined or the owner imprisoned.

DID YOU KNOW?

An employee who ignores health and safety law also risks action being taken against him or her. In addition, any claim for compensation made because of a resulting injury is likely to be reduced or disregarded altogether.

Organisational policy and procedures

Health and safety policy

Under the Health and Safety at Work Act, organisations must produce a health and safety document for their employees giving the company rules, regulations and procedures. It will also include

- details of how accidents must be reported
- where the accident book and the first aid box are situated
- details of qualified first aiders and safety training
- the duties of the official safety representatives – and their names
- the name of the manager in charge of seeing that health and safety policy is carried out
- information on safe working practices throughout the organisation.

This statement must be revised when changes occur, for instance through new legislation, staff changes or new technology.

CHECK IT YOURSELF

If you work for a company which has more than *five* employees, obtain a copy of your organisation's safety policy and identify the areas mentioned above. If you work for a very small company, try to see a copy from another organisation by asking a friend or, if you are at college, ask your tutor to show you a copy of the college policy document.

Safety representatives and safety committees

All recognised trade unions have a legal right to appoint safety representatives in the workplace. These representatives are elected by union members (not the employer). The number varies from one organisation to another depending upon the size of the company, type of work carried out, potentially hazardous areas and so on. It is usual for a safety representative to have worked for an organisation for at least two years before being appointed.

A safety committee must be formed if two or more safety representatives request this in writing.

Each safety representative is responsible for

- investigating potential hazards and dangerous occurrences
- examining the cause(s) of any accidents
- investigating employee complaints
- discussing health and safety problems with the employer
- carrying out inspections
- representing the employees during any visits from health and safety inspectors
- attending safety committee meetings.

Under the new European regulations it is likely that safety representatives will be very involved in risk assessment and reduction, and the training and information which must be provided to all employees.

The safety committee is responsible for

- monitoring local accident trends and recommending preventative action
- examining certain accident reports and looking at ways of preventing a recurrence
- making safety recommendations to management
- promoting health and safety
- promoting accident prevention.

CHECK IT YOURSELF

1 Find out the name and location of your departmental safety representative.
2 If possible, talk to your safety representative about the type of complaints he or she has received from employees over the past year and the action which has been taken.
3 Obtain any documentation which has been produced for your department in relation to risk assessment and information to employees.

Emergency procedures

All organisations need to consider the type of emergencies which may occur and the action which must be taken by staff if they do. Generally, emergency situations can be divided into two types, which are

- accidents and health emergencies which may occur to employees and visitors
- incidents which require an emergency evacuation of the building.

Accidents

By law, all organisations must take out employers' liability insurance which covers claims from employees if they are injured at work. Some organisations must also take out public liability insurance which also protects visitors, customers and the general public.

However, under the Health and Safety at Work Act, all organisations have a legal responsibility to take action to prevent accidents occurring wherever possible, take effective action if they do, record what happened and investigate the circumstances in which they occurred.

Accident report forms

All organisations must keep a record of accidents which occur on their premises. If you are involved in an accident you will be asked to complete an **Accident report form** which will give details of

- the injured person (name, address, age, department etc.)
- the injury sustained
- details of the accident (what happened, date, time and location)
- first aid or medical treatment received
- names of witnesses (if any).

Details are usually transferred to an **Accident book** and the form is then filed. If the accident is serious then, under RIDDOR, it may have to be reported to the HSE. The incident may also be investigated by a safety representative and/or the safety committee.

DID YOU KNOW?

- If you fail to report an accident to your employer and are then absent from work because you were injured, you may find that you are not allowed any DSS benefits to which you would normally have been entitled.
- In Britain accident reports must be kept for 30 years before they are destroyed. Can you think why?

Accident monitoring

The records of accidents are usually examined regularly to

- compare accident rates in the organisation with national statistics
- identify areas of particular concern
- identify improvement or deterioration in standards
- identify any areas of change which may affect statistics (e.g. the introduction of a new production process)
- check that any recommended action has been taken.

DID YOU KNOW?

Safety conscious organisations don't just record actual accidents. They also record 'near-miss' accidents as these show potential hazards which must also be rectified (*see page 49*).

(*see page 49*)

CHECK IT YOURSELF

1   Obtain a copy of your company's accident report form. Find out what happens after the form has been completed

a   if the accident is minor
b   if a serious accident occurred.

2   Find out the correct procedure you should follow in your own organisation if an accident occurs. Note that the action you should take will depend on whether you are a qualified first aider or not (*see below*).

SPECIAL NOTE

All accident forms must be completed clearly and legibly and contain all relevant information. If your handwriting is poor then *print* the information so that it is easy to read. It is also better to complete the form *promptly* – before the details have been forgotten!

TEST YOURSELF

You work for a small organisation which does not have a printed accident form. Yesterday afternoon, while your boss was away, a visitor called Mrs Moxham slipped in reception and sprained her ankle. Apparently the floor in the area was wet at the time. Your colleague, Peter Bell, took her to hospital, where her ankle was strapped, and then took her home. Mrs Moxham is talking about taking legal action against your company.

Write a brief memo to your boss, Margery Taylor, explaining the situation.

First aid

Under the **Health and Safety (First Aid) Regulations** the number of first aiders in an organisation will depend on the degree of risk. In low risk situations, such as offices, an employer is seen to need one first aider for every 50 employees during normal working hours. The number required increases in more hazardous situations. On an oil rig, for example, the number would be far higher.

All employers must appoint two types of first aid personnel, who are

● **suitable persons** – who hold a current first aid certificate (usually awarded by the St John Ambulance or the British Red Cross)

- **appointed persons** – who cover for temporary absences of trained first aiders. Emergency training is usually advisable before appointment.

First aiders who may need to treat poisoning, acid burns or give oxygen for resuscitation are required to take additional training.

First aid boxes and first aid rooms

Not every company needs to provide a first aid room. The decision to do this will depend on the number of employees and the potential hazards to be found in that particular organisation.

However, every organisation must have a first aid box or kit. The contents (and number) will vary, again depending on how potentially hazardous the workplace is, but will usually include

- a guidance card
- individually wrapped sterile dressings
- sterile eye pads
- triangular bandages
- safety pins
- sterile wound dressings in different sizes
- sterile water for eye baths (if no nearby tap water is available).

DID YOU KNOW?

Drugs are *never* kept in first aid boxes or issued by first aiders. If an accident victim had a severe reaction to a drug issued to them by a first aider, he or she could take legal action to obtain compensation.

CHECK IT YOURSELF

Investigate the contents of the first aid box at your place of work or college. List the type of dressings and number of each. Assess whether you consider these are adequate, bearing in mind the type of organisation for which you work.

Attending an accident

If you are the first person to arrive at the scene of an accident then the action to take will depend very much on whether you are a qualified first aider or not.

Whatever your status, it is important that you try to ensure that nothing is moved or disturbed as this may affect the judgement of anyone who is involved in investigating why the accident occurred.

If you are not a qualified first aider yourself, it is very important that you ensure that any injured people receive first aid or specialist attention immediately.

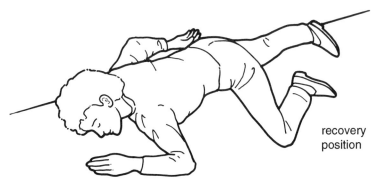

recovery
position

The basic rules to follow

1. Do not move the patient.
2. If the patient is not breathing then **immediately** find someone who can administer the kiss of life (if you cannot do so yourself).
3. Place the patient in the recovery position and keep warm and covered.
4. Do not give him or her any food, drink or a cigarette.
5. Loosen any tight clothing.
6. Comfort and reassure the patient until help arrives.

Severe burns or bleeding

Everyone should know the correct procedure to follow if a colleague is bleeding severely, has been burned or received an electric shock.

- If the patient is bleeding then raise the wound (unless there are suspected broken bones) and apply pressure to the wound with your hand or a clean dry cloth. When the bleeding has stopped apply a dressing.
- If a patient is suffering from a burn or scald reduce the heat immediately by running cool, clean water over the burn. Do not attempt to remove any clothing from the skin. Cover with a sterile dressing. If the burn is severe then the casualty must go to hospital.

 ## DID YOU KNOW?

If you touch someone who has suffered an electric shock *without* turning off the current first, then you are in serious danger of being electrocuted yourself. Always check that the casualty is out of contact with the current first. If it is impossible to turn off the electricity supply quickly then you can only come into contact with the patient if you are standing on something which will insulate you (e.g. a rubber mat). Then you should push them away from the supply using a wooden or plastic implement. Anyone suffering a severe electric shock is likely to have stopped breathing and needs the assistance of someone who can give mouth to mouth resuscitation *immediately*.

1 Find out yourself how to cope with the following emergencies.

   a Your friend opens the window and suddenly shouts that she has something in her eye.

   b A little girl who is visiting your office licks the lid of a bottle containing a poisonous substance.

2 Find out how to give artificial respiration and, if you are interested, enquire about the possibility of becoming a qualified first aider yourself.

Health emergencies

A variety of health emergencies can take place in any organisation. There have probably been days you have been ill yourself – you may have eaten something which disagreed with you, been starting a bad cold or flu, had a headache or migraine or even fainted. Most organisations have a rest room or medical room. If you feel really ill then someone will probably take you home.

It is possible, too, that you or one of your colleagues is diabetic, epileptic or asthmatic. An emergency situation can result

● if a diabetic hasn't eaten or has eaten the wrong food
● if someone with epilepsy has a fit
● if a colleague has an asthma attack.

People who suffer from these conditions are usually well aware of the action that should be taken if they become ill – and will almost certainly make sure their colleagues have this information. The main thing is not to panic if an emergency occurs. If you have no idea at all how to cope then get help – **immediately**.

Probably the most alarming emergency to witness is the sight of someone choking. The victim should be slapped sharply on the back. If this fails the correct procedure to follow is different depending upon whether you are dealing with a child or an adult. If you attend a first aid course you will be taught the correct procedure, but it is useful to find this out yourself anyway – just in case.

1 Find out the correct procedure to follow if one of your colleagues

● faints
● has an epileptic fit
● has an asthma attack.

2 Why do you think it is important to know whether any of your colleagues has serious health problems, and to what extent do you think such information should be confidential? Discuss this question with your supervisor or tutor.

3 You are eating alongside your colleague in the canteen when he suddenly starts choking on a fish bone.

    a Find out the correct procedure to follow.

    b In what way should your actions be different if you are dealing with a small child?

SPECIAL NOTE

The most important fact to remember is that of *your own scope and limitations* in dealing with emergency situations. You can actively contribute towards a disaster if you think you are more clever or capable than you really are. Equally, if you don't take some action in an emergency then serious problems can occur.

CHECK IT YOURSELF

Make a list of all the emergencies you feel you would be capable of coping with and give clear reasons why. Then write down the emergencies you couldn't cope with, why not and if you intend (or would like) to learn more.

Discuss your list with your supervisor or tutor and include any notes for self-development in your action plan you created in Unit 1.

Evacuations

Incidents which can lead to an emergency evacuation of the building include

- fire
- bomb threats
- gas leaks
- severe flooding.

The type of procedures to follow and the scale of disaster which may occur will depend very much on where you work. If you are employed in a chemical plant you are more apt to be involved in regular routine drills than if you work in a solicitors' office!

Fire

Until the **Fire Precautions Regulations 1992** come into effect the main legislation which relates to fire is the **Fire Precautions Act 1971** (FPA). This is enforced by the fire authority, which has similar powers to the HSE in that it can issue Prohibition and Improvement notices and prosecute companies which ignore these.

Designated premises each require a fire certificate – and this applies to most offices, shops and factories. All these premises need proper fire alarm systems installed and there must be **protected** means of escape. The fire certificate itself will show a plan of the premises, with the position of all fire resistant doors and the position of fire extinguishers and break-glass alarms. Even if the workplace does not need a certificate there must still be an adequate means of escape and some equipment with which to fight fires. Such equipment should be inspected and tested regularly.

All organisations should have regular fire drills and fire alarms should be tested once a week. Employees should be given instruction and training on the correct procedure to follow in case of a fire. In addition, staff should know

- they must leave the building immediately, leaving personal belongings behind
- that fire exits must be kept clear at all times
- fire doors must be kept shut
- no-one should use a lift when the fire alarm sounds
- the different types of fire fighting equipment and how to use them.

 DID YOU KNOW?

Some organisations use gas-flooding systems to extinguish fires. The gas removes oxygen from the air and kills the fire without damaging any equipment. Staff who work in such areas must be well trained in evacuation procedures and must leave the area immediately the warning sounds.

CHECK IT YOURSELF

1   In your own organisation do you know

- what to do if you discover a fire
- what to do when the fire alarm is raised
- the location of fire alarms
- the location and use of different types of fire fighting equipment (e.g. fire alarms and extinguishers, smoke detectors etc.)
- escape routes and fire exits
- how to operate a panic bar on an emergency exit door
- how to cope if you are helping someone with a disability
- where you must assemble for a roll call?

Write a check list which could act as a guide for a new colleague who has just started to work with you.

2   Discuss with your tutor or supervisor the role you would be expected to take in relation to

- helping to fight a fire yourself

● assisting others.

It is important to note that you can easily turn from being helpful into being a nuisance! Usually the experts want everyone off the premises as quickly as possible.

DID YOU KNOW?

Reception or visitors' registers are used to check that all visitors are off the premises during a roll call. For that reason, if you are assisting a member of the public, make sure that he or she knows where the assembly point is, to prevent anyone searching the building for them afterwards.

Bomb threats

The only difference between an evacuation because of a bomb threat and an evacuation because of fire is that, in the case of a bomb threat, you will usually be told to take your belongings with you when you leave. This reduces the number of items which have to be searched by the bomb squad or 'sniffer' dogs.

The important issue is not to argue but to leave immediately – regardless of whether it is pouring with rain, you were just starting your lunch or in the middle of an important job!

In all other types of evacuation, the same rule applies.

Reporting an emergency

The procedure to follow if you are the first to find out about an emergency will again vary from one organisation to another. If you are not sure of the procedure to follow then it is important to **find out** – in the meantime, your supervisor or *any* senior member of staff is your first point of contact.

In your own organisation you should know the correct action to take if you

● knock over a bottle of flammable liquid
● smell burning or see something catch fire
● smell gas
● receive a bomb threat over the telephone
● see a suspicious package in the mail
● find water pouring into a cupboard through the ceiling
● hear crackling coming from a light fitting inside a false ceiling
● witness a bad car crash right outside your building.

CHECK IT YOURSELF

1 Find out the correct procedure to follow in each of the above situations in your own organisation.

2 Talk to your colleagues about emergency situations that they have been involved in and the action they took. Add any relevant ones to the list above.

3 Find out what documents you should complete in each of the above cases (if any).

Risk assessment and hazards

There are two types of hazards in every workplace. There are those which *actually exist* and which can cause an accident and those which *could* cause a problem or have the *potential* to cause an accident.

- An employee leaves the bottom drawer of the filing cabinet open. This is obviously an **existing hazard** until the drawer is closed again.
- A filing cabinet has a faulty bottom drawer which will only close if it is kicked hard. This is a **potential hazard** as, one day, kicks won't work and the drawer will remain open until the cabinet is repaired. Potential hazards are sometimes called 'accidents waiting to happen'.

If you are involved in identifying hazards in an office then it is useful to consider

- the building itself
- the design and layout of offices
- office environment and good housekeeping
- information technology
- equipment
- working habits.

 DID YOU KNOW?

Buildings can be 'sick' just like human beings! **Sick building syndrome** is the name given to buildings which are unhealthy to work in – often through alterations to the original design. Workers may find that they suffer from headaches, dizziness, nausea, skin problems and even eye irritation. This may be because of inadequate ventilation, too much fluorescent lighting, chemical emissions from photocopiers and laser printers, dust build up from man-made carpets and soft furnishings – or even a combination of all these.

The building itself

New buildings usually have safety features incorporated into them when they are designed. Older buildings can cause more problems (*see above*). Healthy buildings have good ventilation and/or well-maintained air conditioning.

Other safety features include wide doors, anti-slip floors, non-flicker lights and emergency lights on ceilings and floors to show the routes to emergency exits if the lights fail.

Safety signs should be positioned around the buildings to show which areas are dangerous or have restricted access, or to give information.

CHECK IT YOURSELF

The **Safety Signs Regulations 1980** requires all signs to be issued in one of four colours and one of four shapes.

- red, blue, yellow or green
- rectangular, triangular, a bold circle or a circle with a cross bar.

One shape/colour denotes a **prohibition** i.e. don't do. Another is a **mandatory** sign i.e. what you must do. A third is a **warning** to indicate danger and the fourth shows a **safe condition**.

1 Identify which colour and shape has which meaning.

2 Find *at least two* examples of each type of sign and say what each one means.

The design and layout of offices

Offices may be closed or open plan. Closed offices are usually small areas situated off a main corridor. An open plan office is used by many staff. Acoustic screens may separate different areas and help to reduce noise levels. Because the actions of a few staff will affect everyone in an open-plan office there is usually a no-smoking policy in operation.

People should have enough room to work in comfort and 'walk-through' areas should be kept clear. Furniture should be well-designed and desks should be at the correct height. Chairs should be adjustable to prevent poor posture and give proper back support. Sufficient storage space should be provided for papers, files and reference books. Safety stools should be provided for reaching items stored on high shelves. Floors should be non-slip.

DID YOU KNOW?

The term **wire management** refers to office furniture which is specially designed to conceal all the cables which lead from computers, printers, telephones etc.

Office environment and good housekeeping

In addition to properly planned offices, additional facilities need to be provided in relation to eating facilities, changing rooms and rest rooms. Temperature, lighting, toilet and washing facilities are all covered under the **Workplace (Health, Safety and Welfare) Regulations 1992** (*see page 37*).

In addition, windows should be cleaned regularly and blinds should be provided to prevent glare from sunshine. Suitable lighting should also be provided – uplights may be better as there is less likelihood of glare or shadows. Noise should be kept to reasonable limits, e.g. by providing acoustic hoods for computer printers.

Good housekeeping relates to the tidiness and cleanliness of work areas and the safe storage of dangerous or flammable substances.

CHECK IT YOURSELF

Make out a checklist for your own organisation which includes the items mentioned above and any others which you consider are relevant. Then walk around your building and score each item out of 5, where 5 is the maximum score. For example, large, clean windows with clean, adjustable blinds would score 5, whereas a small, dirty window with no blinds (or a broken blind) would score 0 or 1.

Discuss your findings with your supervisor or tutor.

 ## SPECIAL NOTE

Despite the fact that the law is on your side in relation to identifying hazards and assessing risks, it is as well to remember that your supervisor may not take too readily to a junior member of staff suggesting that radical alterations should take place and that the organisation is failing in its duty! The two skills of tact and diplomacy are very important, when you point out problems or potential hazards. It is quite possible that your supervisor has noticed them before and is struggling to get someone to do something about them!

Information technology

The design of work stations is covered by the **Health and Safety (Display Screen Equipment) Regulations 1992** (*see page 37*). The term **workstation** includes the display screen, keyboard, desk and chair, software and systems used *in addition* to environmental factors such as lighting, noise and humidity. The design and position of workstations should take into account the fact that glare and reflections from light on the screen can cause problems for a VDU operator.

Two other health and safety issues related to VDU work are stress and repetitive strain injury.

Stress may be caused if an operator is under constant pressure to produce accurate work very quickly. Making the work more varied can help – in addition to the regular rest breaks required by law.

Repetitive strain injury (RSI) relates to an injury caused by constantly making repetitive or awkward movements. **Tenosynovitis**

(teno for short) may be suffered by keyboard or VDU operators who repeatedly 'strike' the keys of a typewriter or keyboard. The tendon sheaths in the hand, wrist and arms become inflamed and the first symptoms are aching, tenderness or numbness of the hand, wrist or arm. The condition can become very painful and may result in a complete inability to grip normal objects.

Good workstation and keyboard design and adequate rest breaks can help to prevent RSI. Any workers who think they may have a problem should report the problem to their safety representative and see their doctor immediately.

Computers and health and safety are also covered in Unit 6, page 233.

Computers and health and safety are also covered in Unit 6, page 233.

CHECK IT YOURSELF

How many health and safety hazards can you see here?

① DID YOU KNOW?

In a recent legal battle, the Inland Revenue had to pay £79 000 to a former typist who is now registered as disabled because of RSI. In another case, BT had to pay £6000 to two former employees plus court costs of about £100 000. Both the Inland Revenue and BT face at least another 150 claims!

1 Look through a software or safety catalogue and identify all the items sold in relation to safety and VDU work, e.g. special cleaning materials, screen filters, wrist rests and so on.
2 Are there any ways in which you think VDU workers can help themselves to prevent RSI occurring? Discuss any ideas you have with your tutor.

Equipment

Equipment can be particularly hazardous as there may be moving parts, electrical connections, sharp or dangerous parts. In the case of the latter these will usually be protected by a special guard or cover which must *never* be removed. In addition, with some items of equipment (such as duplicators and photocopiers) chemicals or additives may be required which need special care.

Whilst it is not possible to produce a list of instructions which applies equally to all types of equipment, the following key points should always be remembered.

Safety checklist when using equipment

● Do not use any equipment for which you have not been trained or received any instructions.
● Make sure you know how to stop and/or disconnect the equipment immediately in case of an emergency.
● Never operate equipment with moving parts whilst wearing long, dangling jewellery or a loose scarf or tie. Keep long hair tied back off your face.
● Never place liquids on top of, or near to, any type of equipment.
● Report any trailing leads or broken plugs or sockets.
● Make sure any equipment which can give out dangerous fumes (e.g. a photocopier) is kept in a well-ventilated, preferably separate, room.
● Buy equipment with safety features built in, e.g. filing cabinets where only one drawer opens at a time to prevent tilting.
● Only use equipment in accordance with the correct operating procedures as shown in the handbook.
● *Never* tamper with or fiddle about inside equipment which isn't working properly. Report the fault to someone who knows what to do.
● Make sure you know what to do if you splash your skin or clothing with any chemicals or additives or – even worse – get some in your eyes.
● Only use recommended cleaning agents on any type of equipment.

Under the **Provision and Use of Work Equipment Regulations** the employer must ensure that all equipment is well maintained and properly serviced (*see page 38*).

(*see page 38*)

CHECK IT YOURSELF

Here is a drawing which shows the different parts of a document shredder.

1 How many hazards can you identify?
2 Imagine a young, untrained and impulsive worker who jams the equipment accidentally. What do you imagine could be the possible result(s) if he decides to try to rectify the problem himself?

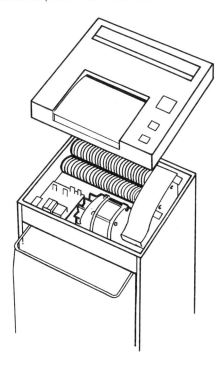

Lifting and moving equipment

Lifting and moving equipment is now specifically covered in the regulations on **Manual Handling**. You may think that these only apply to warehouses and factories but you would be wrong. Often, in offices, there are reasons why equipment, furniture or even some heavy boxes should be moved. If you do this carelessly or incorrectly then, quite apart from damaging the equipment itself, you could cause serious damage to yourself.

Key points to remember

● Always get someone to help you – even if only to lift something on to a trolley or truck.
● Disconnect any electrical equipment from the mains and remove any cables which might get in the way.
● See if the equipment can be divided into several lighter loads, e.g. a computer should be disconnected and moved section by section

- VDU first, then disk drive, then keyboard and finally the printer.
- If the weight is unevenly distributed (e.g. a typewriter), hold the heavy end closest to your body.
- Be careful of any sharp edges which could cut your hands or hook themselves onto your clothes.
- Don't lift anything which is too heavy – quite apart from the fact that this is dangerous you are likely to crash it back down on the floor rather than set it down gently!

DID YOU KNOW?

Lifting equipment incorrectly is one of the main causes of back problems. *Always* bend your knees (so that you are sitting on your haunches) and keep your back *straight*. As you lift, take the strain in your legs, *not* in your back.

Working habits

Safe working habits include

- walking (not running!) down corridors and up or down stairs
- not carrying so many items that vision is obscured
- wrapping broken glass and other dangerous objects in paper before throwing in a wastepaper basket
- closing drawers of cupboards and filing cabinets after use
- storing items safely – not piling them one on top of another
- cleaning up anything you spill and picking up anything you drop immediately
- putting all rubbish into the correct container – and emptying this if it is full by mid-day.

CHECK IT YOURSELF

No matter how many rules and regulations there are – or how much information and training is given – the majority of accidents are caused by *people* who are distracted or not concentrating for one reason or another. Nobody *wants* to have an accident – but people do – every day! Think back to the last occasion you had an accident (even a very minor one) and try to think *why*. Was it because you were distracted at the time – or because someone else wasn't concentrating on what they were doing?

Identifying hazards and taking action

The *type* of hazards which can be identified in a workplace depends very much on the industry, the nature of the organisation, the layout of the building and offices – even the age of the building.

It is easy to identify **actual** hazards – if the carpet is worn, a flex has frayed, someone has left a pile of boxes behind the door. It is far harder to identify **potential** hazards. If you identify a hazard, in some cases you may be able to rectify the problem yourself. In other cases you will need to obtain permission before you take any action. **If you are in any doubt at all, check first!** You are likely to make yourself very unpopular with your supervisor and your colleagues if you take action which is outside your authority or which is against standard practice in your company.

Above all, don't be a walking hazard yourself! Review your own working habits – and the best place to start is to carry out a risk assessment of your own working area or workstation. This can be done in several parts

  a   the area itself and layout
  b   the equipment you use or for which you are responsible
  c   fixtures and fittings which are within reach or which affect you
  d   your own working habits.

In the case of the latter, for instance, check if your desk is neat and tidy (include any drawers!), if your books and files are stored neatly (or piled on top of one another!). Do you make sure you have turned off equipment after use? Do you put away your belongings – or leave shopping bags or sports bags on the floor? In other words, do you *think* about other people? Only when you can be confident that you are fairly blameless yourself can you start to comment about other situations and other people!

TEST YOURSELF

Carry out a risk assessment of your own work area or workstation under the headings given above. Identify any actual or potential hazards in each case and say what can be done to reduce them. State the action you can take to minimise hazards both for yourself and others.

Review your list with your supervisor or tutor.

UNIT REVIEW (1)

At the end of this element you should be able to

  ● identify existing or potential hazards and put these right if authorised to do so
  ● report other hazards promptly and accurately to the most appropriate person
  ● know the correct action to take in an emergency which will also conform to organisational requirements
  ● report and record emergencies accurately, completely and legibly
  ● follow work practices which conform to organisational requirements

- report working conditions which do not conform to organisational requirements to the appropriate person
- organise your own workstation to minimise risk to self and others.

REVIEW YOUR KNOWLEDGE AND UNDERSTANDING

True or false?

1 A person who empties the fire buckets for a joke is committing an offence under the Health and Safety at Work Act.
2 A VDU operator whose eyesight is failing must pay for his or her own eye test.
3 An employee is within his or her rights to refuse to wear protective clothing which isn't comfortable.
4 All types of fire extinguishers can be used on electrical fires.
5 After an emergency evacuation, all staff and visitors should proceed immediately to the assembly point.

Fill in the blanks

6 The person who is officially responsible for investigating employee complaints about health and safety issues is called a _____ _____ .

7 VDU and other keyboard operators can suffer from a condition caused by making continual or awkward movements called _____ _____ _____ .

8 You cut your hand quite severely on a sharp knife in the mailroom. The document you will be asked to complete is called an _____ _____ _____ .

Work it out

9 Most accidents at work are caused by

- slipping, tripping and falling
- being struck by falling objects or colliding with objects or people
- electrical equipment
- handling materials and equipment incorrectly.

a Under *each* of the above headings see how many types of accident you can think of. Below are a few causes of accidents to give you a start – begin by putting them under the right headings.
  – running along corridors and round corners
  – carrying a heavy object without assistance
  – computer wires trailing on the floor
  – plug sockets overloaded

b In each case state how the accident could have been *prevented* in the first place.

10 You have recently been employed in the office of a large bakery. The building comprises a computer room with several VDU operators, a

general office area, the bakery itself and a distribution/transport area where the vans are loaded.

You are interested in eventually becoming a safety representative yourself and are accompanying an experienced member of staff as he tours the buildings undertaking a risk/hazard assessment exercise.

a State *at least four* **actual** risks you may find in *each* of the four main areas of the building.

b Identify *four* **potential** hazards which may exist in each area.

c State the action you would take, if you were the safety representative, to minimise each of these.

Element 2.2

Monitor and maintain the security of the workplace

Risks and risk assessment don't just relate to health and safety. An additional type of risk, for both employers and employees, involves security. Theft of personal and business property, vandalism, criminal damage, assaults and arson attacks can create havoc and distress for businesses and staff alike. For that reason, *all* employees have a responsibility both to co-operate with the security procedures in force in their organisation and to help in identifying and preventing breaches in security themselves.

DID YOU KNOW?

Loss through theft affects company profits and, indirectly, the number of employees the company can afford and the salaries they can be paid. In 1992 Marks and Spencer lost £30 million pounds because of crime – and spent £23 million pounds improving security procedures designed to discourage theft and make staff areas more secure.

Areas of risk

The type of security risks faced by an organisation will depend on a number of factors, including

- the type of business (compare a bank with a hairdresser's shop!)
- where it is situated (a remote location or a town centre)
- the type of building and its design
- the number of staff it employs
- the number of visitors it deals with every day
- the number and type of valuables kept on the premises
- the time of day – all organisations are more vulnerable during the hours of darkness.

DID YOU KNOW?

Most organisations keep comprehensive records on every incident of theft, vandalism, criminal damage, assaults or arson attacks which give

- the place the incident occurred
- the date and time
- details of the incident (e.g. point of entry and exit and what was taken or damaged).

In this way managers can assess each type of security risk accurately and spend company money on security more effectively.

Organisational procedures

These are likely to be designed to protect

- buildings from unauthorised entry or damage
- staff from personal attack or assault
- both the organisation and its staff from theft.

A variety of expensive equipment may be purchased including security lighting, closed circuit television and intruder alarms. Special reinforced windows may be fitted and uniformed security guards may be employed. However, in many cases it is not the most advanced piece of technology or the most expensive purchase which is the most effective but the introduction *and constant use* of basic security systems – plus the alertness and vigilance of all staff.

DID YOU KNOW?

Many security guards are also employed to monitor health and safety risks, such as a fire extinguisher missing or cars blocking an emergency exit – and to take action. If this is the case, then if you spot *either* a security or a health and safety risk then you could report it to a guard on duty.

CHECK IT YOURSELF

Many organisations install some form of perimeter security around their buildings as a first line of defence. Examples include

- metal fencing with locked gates
- landscaping which includes either banks of earth or a ditch or moat
- crash barriers
- concrete blocks, concrete flower tubs or metal bollards.

Try to find *at least one* example of each of these at an organisation in your area. Try to work out why they are used before you read further.

DID YOU KNOW?

Ram-raiding is the name given to thefts which occur when a car is driven hard (rammed) into a wall, door or display window to give rapid access to the goods. The car is then used as a get-away vehicle. In 1992 Dixons lost more than £20 million through crimes which included pilfering, lorry hijacking, violence, fraud and ram-raiding.

Access to buildings

Measures usually employed to restrict or prevent access to buildings include

- keeping entrances and exits to a minimum, both for vehicles and pedestrians
- monitoring all visitors either by security personnel, closed circuit television (CCTV) or electronic detectors (or all three)
- having external lighting which illuminates all public areas (including car parks) during the hours of darkness
- installing anti-scaling devices such as spikes on roofs and external pipes
- restricting the number of people who have keys to the building
- having laid-down procedures for locking doors and windows at night with all employees knowing their individual responsibilities
- issuing identification badges to all staff and visitors
- checking all rooms carefully at the end of each working day – especially toilet areas – to make sure no-one is left or concealed on the premises
- having clear signs which show which areas are restricted to visitors or staff.

DID YOU KNOW?

The building of the future is forecast to be 'intelligent'. Security will be built in to new office buildings, with electronic tagging of both people and property – to show where every item of equipment and even every person is positioned at any one time!

Company car parks

The increase of thefts both of and from vehicles has increased considerably over the past few years. Business car parks are often 'soft' targets because thieves can be fairly certain that the vehicle owner will be away all day. For that reason many organisations have introduced

- vehicle identity discs to prevent unauthorised parking
- security staff or CCTV cameras to monitor staff car parks
- barriers which will only open when a special identification card is inserted
- floodlighting of car parks at night (which also helps to protect staff returning to their cars in the dark).

Probably the safest car parks are those which are in full sight of busy office windows – as staff can keep up informal surveillance all the time.

SPECIAL NOTE

It is useless spending thousands of pounds on CCTV installations if no-one watches what is happening. Most organisations which use CCTV have a control room where security staff oversee what is happening around the premises.

Sophisticated CCTV systems now have multi-view images to show pictures from different cameras on one screen simultaneously. If a problem occurs then the viewer can zoom in from one camera. The video tape can be played back to show what happened immediately before the incident, and often includes a time and date portion on the frame which shows when the incident occurred.

Security control rooms usually monitor the patrol duties of security staff. At regular points the security officer inserts an ID card into a reader or trips a special alarm device. If the guard is not at a certain point when he is expected, an alarm sounds in the control office.

DID YOU KNOW?

Staff are more likely to thwart their organisation's security procedures in summer than in winter. How? By opening fire doors for extra ventilation and to keep cool – and then not closing them properly afterwards! Although special locks and bolts can be fitted, obviously staff have to be able to use fire doors as emergency exits, so their fitting is subject to Fire Regulations. Don't help an unauthorised person to enter *your* premises by leaving or wedging a fire door open – whatever the circumstances!

CHECK IT YOURSELF

Walk around the outside of your own organisation and check all the security aspects you can which have already been covered in this element. If you work for a very small company then assess the building *as a whole* – not just the part occupied by your employers.

Try to identify all the security risks you can, and the measures which have been taken to prevent unauthorised access. If it helps, imagine you are trying to gain entry yourself. How would/could you do it?

Visitors and security

Virtually all organisations have security procedures which are designed to

● prevent unauthorised people from entering the premises

- control the movement of authorised people once they are on the premises
- keep a record to check whether they have left.

Many large organisations have a gatehouse where security staff check visitors as they enter the premises and issue special visitors' badges. In other companies, this may be the job of the receptionist. Then clear notices should direct all visitors to the main entrance. The main reason that a reception area is normally sited at the *front* of a building is so that visitors do not need to walk through restricted areas to find it. The name of the visitor, reason for the visit, person he or she will see and number plate of his or her vehicle is recorded in a special Visitors' Log (*see page 145*).

Sometimes the badges are colour-coded to show which areas of the building visitors may enter and which they may not. In some organisations visitors are escorted from one part of a building to another, to prevent them from wandering into areas where confidential information is handled or valuable equipment is used.

Visitors are checked out as they leave and the time of leaving entered in the visitors' book. The visitor must also hand back the badge.

DID YOU KNOW?

Special badges can be purchased which self-destruct when exposed to sunlight. The visitor who retains the badge will find it useless after it has been exposed to light!

CHECK IT YOURSELF

1 Check with your supervisor that you are quite clear about your organisation's policy for dealing with visitors. Write this down as a checklist of 'Dos' and 'Don'ts' for yourself.
2 Many people consider that all staff should challenge unauthorised visitors or strangers found wandering around a building. Others consider this is very risky. What would you do? Discuss the correct procedure you should follow with your supervisor or tutor. (*See also the chart on page 132.*)

Staff badges and electronic access

Most organisations issue identification (ID) badges to their employees. These usually incorporate a current photograph of the wearer and have a two-fold purpose.

- They prove to security and other staff that the person is a bona fide employee. In a large organisation with hundreds of workers this is essential as not everyone can be known to everyone else.

- They help visitors to identify members of staff and remember their names.

Again, different coloured badges can be used to show the degree of access around the building which is allowed to different members of staff.

Electronic systems are more expensive and sophisticated and are used inside a building to restrict access to certain areas. Examples include

- key code security locks at the entrance to certain buildings, so that only staff who know the code to key in can gain entry
- electronic tags which trigger certain doors to open, so that staff without the tags cannot open these doors
- voice pattern recognition devices which will only open doors if the person speaking is 'recognised'.

CHECK IT YOURSELF

1 Walk around your own organisation and check which security procedures are in force to prevent or limit access to certain areas.
2 Compare these, and the system of staff IDs in use in your organisation, with those in operation in other companies, by exchanging information with your colleagues on your NVQ course.

Key security

It is pointless having elaborate security procedures to control access by visitors and staff if there are no controls over key holders. Each organisation is likely to have up to four different types of keys, which include

- keys which give access to the building itself
- master keys which give access to all rooms in a building
- departmental keys which give access to only certain parts of a building
- individual office keys which only allow access to one particular room.

Keys should only be issued to people who really need them and have been authorised to be key holders by a member of the management staff. A record should be kept in a special key book. A key which is loaned out for any reason should be signed for and a check should be kept on whether or not it has been returned.

CHECK IT YOURSELF

Imagine that you are the owner of a small business with four staff.

1 To whom would you issue an access key, and why?

2   If you trusted your most senior member of staff with an access key and she lost it, what would you do?

Violence and personal assaults

People who work alone in isolated areas of a building, stay late at night, have to walk through deserted areas to get to their cars or deal with members of the public who may be irrational or disturbed for some reason all need protection. Under the **Health and Safety at Work Act** employers have a duty to take reasonable care that their employees are not exposed to any unnecessary risks – and that includes the risk of injury by criminals or other people on the premises.

Various measures are now being implemented to protect employees from the possibility of attack including

- improving communication systems (e.g. hidden panic buttons) so staff can call for help quickly and without being seen
- installing glass screens to separate visitors from staff (especially those who deal with cash)
- changing staffing arrangements and the number of staff on duty at any one time to ensure people do not work alone in high risk areas
- training staff in how to recognise danger signals and the best method of dealing with highly emotional or disturbed visitors
- issuing staff working in isolated areas with radio communications equipment
- issuing clear guidelines which all staff should follow in an emergency.

CHECK IT YOURSELF

1   It is possible to buy panic alarms which emit a loud screech when pressed. Do you think these are a wise buy or not? Why?
2   Discuss with your supervisor or tutor the correct procedure you should follow if

- a stranger enters your office late in the evening when you are working on your own
- a visitor, who is obviously the worse for drink, starts to threaten you
- you hear footsteps following you at night, on the way to the staff car park.

Check your answers with any formal procedures or guidelines which your organisation issues to staff.

Theft

Theft is the single, biggest problem for all organisations. Billions of pounds worth of property are stolen every year, from companies *and* their employees. This may include

- cash
- stock and equipment
- valuable or confidential documents
- personal property belonging to staff
- computer data.

All these need protection, although the methods employed may vary in each case.

Cash

Criminals will take more risks and go to greater lengths to steal cash than anything else. For that reason, organisations (and staff) who deal with cash need proper security procedures in place. If possible, the amount of cash on the premises should be reduced to as little as possible, especially overnight. If cash has to be transported (e.g. from and to the bank) then this should be done by security staff or trained staff and the route and time of the trip should be varied. If cash registers are used by an organisation they should be emptied regularly by trained, protected staff. Many organisations have systems where bank notes are immediately pushed through 'no return' slots which are separate from the cash register and cannot be accessed.

Today no employee can insist on being paid in cash, and many companies have insisted that salaries are paid by cheque or directly into a bank account so that large sums of cash are not needed on the premises.

In addition, many companies are installing 'cashless' vending machines and card payphones, again to reduce the number of locations where cash is stored in the building.

 SPECIAL NOTE

It is always advisable to leave empty cash registers or safes which contain little of value *open*. An incredible amount of damage can be caused during a break-in by thieves trying to open locked cabinets and safes. The same goes for internal office doors. These, too, are usually best left unlocked overnight, otherwise it can cost the company more to repair the damage than to replace missing property!

Stock and equipment

Both stock and equipment can be protected by a variety of measures.

- Electronic tagging means that the position of each tagged item can be checked by computer. If the item is moved more than a short distance then an alarm sounds.
- Security chains and anchoring devices can be attached to valuable equipment and prevent it being moved at all.
- The most valuable equipment should be stored in the most secure buildings. A list should be kept which includes the make, serial number and model number.
- Light, easily pilfered items should not be kept in areas where there is public access.
- All property can be security marked, e.g. with the name of the company and postcode. This means it is less easy to resell. A variety of methods can be used including marking with an ultra-violet pen (the mark is invisible) or attaching a prominent security label.
- A proper system of stock control should be in operation with stock only issued against official signed documents.
- Procedures for deliveries of stock and collection of unwanted stock should be known to all staff. It is preferable if this is carried out in a separate area to prevent unknown callers arriving in a main building.

Valuable or confidential documents

You may be surprised at some of the documents which a thief would class as 'valuable'. All of the following have a value to a thief.

- cheque books and bank statements
- plastic credit or cheque cards
- blank order forms and invoices
- letter headed paper
- company stamps and the official company seal.

All such documents should be kept locked away unless they are in use. Staff should also avoid discussing financial arrangements with the bank over the telephone in a public area.

TEST YOURSELF

1 What use do you think a thief may have for each of the documents given above? Discuss your ideas with your supervisor or tutor.
2 Identify any other documents used in your organisation which a thief may find useful or valuable.

SPECIAL NOTE

Many thieves are classed by the police as **opportunists**. They don't set off with the intention to steal, but if the opportunity is presented to them then they will take it. Think of this next time you leave a pile of letter heads on your desk and leave your office.

Personal property belonging to staff

You are sensible if you limit the amount and type of personal property you take to work and, needless to say, never leave anything unattended. Key points to bear in mind also include

- not lending your bank card to anyone and asking them to get cash on your behalf – as this would mean telling them your PIN number
- never taking your passport to work (these are regarded as highly desirable by thieves)
- limiting the amount of cash you carry
- keeping your cheque book and cheque card in different places (if you need to take them at all)
- leaving credit cards at home unless you need one with you for a particular reason
- not leaving a wallet in an unattended jacket or a handbag open in a public area.

If your personal property is missing then don't panic or accuse anyone (as you would have to prove your allegation!). Look around carefully and methodically and mentally retrace your steps to think where it might be. In other words, *make sure* the item is missing before you take action.

Report the missing item, with a full description, to the correct member of staff. Don't forget to report the problem to the member of staff in charge of lost property too, in case you lost it accidentally and the item is later handed in.

CHECK IT YOURSELF

1. Read the chart overleaf. This contains the ten key points which all office staff should remember at all times.
2. Check that you know the correct procedure to follow in your company to
   a. report damage to the building, e.g. broken windows, graffiti etc.
   b. report a missing item, whether this is personal or belonging to the company.
3. Check you know the system which operates in your organisation for lost and found property.

Computer data

Computer security is important for several reasons. Valuable information may be stored on computer which would take months to replace. In addition, the confidentiality of personal data held on computers is covered by law – under the **Data Protection Act**.

LANCASHIRE PARTNERSHIP AGAINST CRIME

BSIA
THE BRITISH SECURITY
INDUSTRY ASSOCIATION

Office Security
10 Points to remember

1   NEVER LEAVE HANDBAGS ON DESKS OR WALLETS IN COATS IN YOUR ABSENCE   Take them with you or lock them away.

2   ALWAYS KEEP MONEY IN A SAFE PLACE   Even if it is only the tea money never leave it in an unlocked drawer during the day. At night put it in a safe or remove it from the building altogether.

3   BE CAREFUL WITH KEYS   Always put them in a safe place and don't put spare keys for safes etc. in desk drawers. Deposit them at the bank.

4   FASTEN VULNERABLE WINDOWS IN YOUR ABSENCE   It's easy to forget, particularly in the summer, and a thief can come and go in a couple of minutes.

5   NEVER ASSUME A STRANGER WANDERING IN THE BUILDING IS A MEMBER OF STAFF   Challenge him. Even "Can I help you?" will often deter the dishonest.

6   DON'T JUST ACCEPT THAT A STRANGER IS AUTHORISED TO BE IN THE BUILDING JUST BECAUSE HE SAYS SO   Check with someone in authority. If the stranger **is** from the Post Office or the typewriter company someone in your firm will know. And never allow anyone to remove office equipment without checking first.

7   DON'T BE OVERAWED BY CALLERS   Even if he does want to see the Managing Director make sure he is known and expected.

8   NEVER LEAVE CALLERS ALONE IN YOUR OFFICE   Use the telephone to enquire whether someone can see him.

9   DON'T DISCLOSE CONFIDENTIAL INFORMATION TO A STRANGER   No matter how important he may seem, always report any such request for information to your employer.

10   DON'T ASSUME ALL STAFF ARE AS HONEST AS YOU   Take care of your property and that of your employer.

DID YOU KNOW THAT?

Lancashire Constabulary responded to over 3,000 crimes at office premises in 1992 involving the loss of over £2 million of property.
You can reduce crime from your office environment by remembering the above 10 points.

Under this Act

- All companies who hold data on people on computer must be registered as data users with the Data Protection Registrar.
- Any information held on computer must have been acquired legally.
- Personal data must only be used and disclosed to others for reasons which are compatible with the purpose for which it is held.
- The data must be relevant, accurate, kept up to date and not be excessive for the purpose for which it is required.
- Records must not be kept for longer than necessary.
- Individuals must be given access to information held about them and this must be corrected or erased if necessary.
- Proper security measures must be taken against unauthorised or accidental access to the data or alteration, disclosure, loss or destruction of the information held.

The last point is very important in relation to security procedures.

All computer users should be aware that

- Unauthorised print-outs of information must never be given to anyone.
- Precautions must be taken to prevent unauthorised people from being able to read confidential information on screen.
- User IDs and computer passwords must be kept confidential.
- Security systems in place to prevent accidental erasure of information on disk must always be followed.

 ## DID YOU KNOW?

All employees have a right to see all computerised information held about them. They may be able to claim compensation if this information is inaccurate.

Computers and the public

If computers are used in public areas then VDUs must be positioned so that the screen cannot be read by visitors or passers-by. If you work on a computer in an office which has a large display window then you may find your organisation has a special covering over part of the window to prevent people outside from being able to look into the office.

If you work in an office where visitors may be able to read your screen, then when someone approaches it is a simple matter to

- scroll up the page quickly, *or*
- turn down the brightness control, *or*
- switch off the VDU, *or*
- save your work and log out.

In the same way don't leave confidential print-outs lying around your desk for anyone to read. If anyone asks for information check with your supervisor before you give it to them.

DID YOU KNOW?

In areas which are also used by the general public, many computers have small alarms fitted which will sound if they are moved any distance, to alert employees to possible theft of equipment.

Computers and passwords

Most organisations have a system of user identification (IDs) and passwords to prevent or restrict access to important or confidential information. Each user will have his or her ID which will determine the level of access for that particular person. For instance a director of the company may have full access to all files, a supervisor will have access to most files but a junior employee will have access to only certain files.

In addition, each user will have his or her own password. This has to be used in conjunction with their ID and enables the computer to check whether the person logging on is the genuine user. All passwords should be

● kept confidential
● changed frequently
● remembered – not written down
● original words rather than obvious ones (e.g. do not use the word 'Xmas' in December or 'holiday' in the middle of July).

A final precaution may be to make certain files completely inaccessible unless a specific password is known. This may only be given to high ranking people in the organisation or those in charge of computer maintenance who may need to be able to access operating files not available to anyone else.

DID YOU KNOW?

1 When you type in a password it doesn't show on screen. If it did, anybody standing near you would be able to read it and use it themselves later!
2 A **hacker** is a person who illegally gains entry into a computer system by working out the password.

Computers and disk security

One of the biggest headaches for computer maintenance staff is not hackers or unauthorised access to information but **viruses**. A virus is a rogue program which is introduced into a computer system and which can create untold damage. This may include blanking screens, blanking hard disks or even making the whole system inoperable. Floppy disks can carry the virus. If a floppy disk becomes infected then it can pass on the virus to every other computer in which it is used.

Floppy disks which are suspected of carrying viruses are **swept**. This is a process that checks if any virus is present. If there is a virus, the disk must be wiped clean. This not only gets rid of the virus but also any other information on the disk, even if this is important or irretrievable.

You should therefore

- always take back-up copies of your work (even if it is saved on hard disk)
- store both these *and the original disks* in a secure place (and never leave them lying on your desk!)
- never take to work any borrowed programs or disks from an unknown source or outside computer and load them on your machine.

SPECIAL NOTE

Many of the most valuable items in an organisation are not the most expensive! Whilst computer disks are very cheap to buy, the information they contain may cost a considerable amount of time and money to replace.

For that reason, copy disks should be stored in special boxes inside heat resistant safes so that, in the case of fire, the contents will not be damaged.

DID YOU KNOW?

Disk manufacturers will only guarantee information on disks up to 52° C. Beyond this it is probable all information will be lost. If such disks contained all the company's records and there were no back-ups stored in a separate place, it could be weeks – if not months – before the organisation is operational again.

How reliable and honest a worker are you?

You may think it insulting that either your reliability or – even more important – your own honesty can be questioned. But before you become indignant honestly answer the quiz below!

Quiz – How reliable and honest a worker are you?

1 If you noticed a window was broken on your way in to your office would you

    a assume someone else had reported it
    b mention it to a colleague
    c report it to your supervisor immediately?

2 You leave the petty cash tin open on your desk one day – although this is strictly against company rules. When you return £10 is missing. Do you

    a keep quiet, fiddle the books and hope no-one notices
    b tell your friend and ask her to cover for you
    c own up to your supervisor?

3 You have three urgent personal letters to send one evening. Do you

    a put your mail through the franking machine
    b take three stamps from the emergency supply kept in the mail room and put the money in the drawer
    c buy some stamps when you take the firm's mail to the post office?

4 Your friend moved to America last year. Phoning him costs a fortune but you try to contact each other four times a year for a chat. It is now your turn and you are broke. Do you

    a phone from work when no-one is about
    b phone from home and borrow the money from your parents
    c write a letter instead explaining your poverty-stricken situation?

5 You work for a building society and key in account details on computer. A good friend of yours is keen on a girl who is a customer at your branch. He asks you to let him know her name and address so that he can send her a card on St Valentine's Day. Do you

    a bring up the information on computer and give him a print-out
    b say you will check with your supervisor first
    c tell him to ask her himself?

6 Some new computers have been stored in a stockroom until the new office extension has been completed. On your way to meet a friend for lunch you see two men in overalls loading all the computers onto a trolley. Do you

    a do nothing, you're late enough already
    b ask them what they're doing – and accept their story that they are cleaning out the stockroom
    c find a senior member of staff and tell him or her what you've seen?

7 You are given the job of preparing the staff newsletter but the program installed on your machine is difficult to use and the job will take you ages. Your brother says his friend has an easier program and lends you the disk. Do you

    a load it on your machine and do the work
    b take it to work and see your supervisor
    c politely refuse his offer?

8 You walk into the rest room and find someone has written in felt pen on the wall. Do you

a add a witty reply with your own felt pen
b do nothing
c report the matter to the security staff?

9 During your supervisor's absence you are trusted with a key to the main office. On the last day of her holiday you find you have lost it. Do you

   a pretend it was taken off your desk
   b say nothing, and hope she will forget to ask for it back
   c own up?

10 An hour after leaving work you remember that you left the window open in your office on the ground floor. It is dark and cold. You know your supervisor is out that night and you haven't anybody else's telephone number. Do you

   a curl up by the fire and forget it
   b go to the building and push the window shut as much as possible from the outside
   c telephone the police?

11 You work for a very small firm and have an access key. When you arrive for work one morning there has been a break-in. Do you

   a tidy up and ring the local paper for the publicity
   b tidy up and wait for your supervisor to arrive
   c touch nothing and ring the police immediately?

12 Your friend is taking a college course and needs two assignments photocopying. He says he will pay for this. Do you

   a photocopy the assignments at work and keep the money
   b photocopy the assignments at work and tell your friend it's free
   c ask your supervisor if this can be done and offer to pay for the copies?

Score yourself

Score 0 points for each **a** you chose, 1 point for each **b** and 2 points for each **c**.

23–24 points How honest were you when you completed the quiz?

17–22 points With a little more thought you'd make an ideal employee.

12–16 points You may often be full of good intentions but you can cause quite a few problems for people!

6–11 points Re-read the chapter and make a few resolutions!

0–5 points You're a walking security hazard yourself – and virtually unemployable.

There are very few people who can say, honestly, that they have never taken a pen from work, done any private photocopying or made the odd private telephone call from a company telephone. However, whilst you may consider none of these actions to be breaches of security, they all add to a company's costs and there is a fine line between 'borrowing' without permission and stealing. There is little point in trying to help your company to monitor its security if you are quietly ignoring these procedures yourself!

It is also alarming that so many people ignore potential security problems. This is clearly highlighted by the lack of response from people to a ringing burglar alarm. Very few will call the police and inform them. Most people consider it is none of their business.

If you see potential security risks at your place of work, then it *is* your responsibility to notify someone in charge. If a person wandering around has no business to be there, and is ignored by you and everyone else, you cannot really complain if staff personal belongings start to go missing.

No-one is expecting you to take unnecessary risks. Indeed, knowing when *not* to get involved can be as important as knowing when you should! The important thing is to know the correct reporting procedures so that you can take action without taking any risks yourself.

CHECK IT YOURSELF

1 Discuss with your colleagues the best way to approach a stranger in your building. Write out *at least three* statements which would challenge him or her without causing alarm or a violent reaction. Check these with your supervisor or tutor.
2 Decide which explanations he or she could give you which would be acceptable and which would not.
3 Check that you have a copy of any security guidance documents issued by your organisations and that you can state the procedure to follow if you identify any type of risk or breach in security.

 ## UNIT REVIEW (2)

At the end of this element you should be able to

- carry out your own organisation's security procedures correctly
- correctly identify security risks in your workplace
- take action to correct identified security risks or report these to the appropriate person
- deal with breaches of security in accordance with organisational procedures.

CHECK YOUR KNOWLEDGE AND UNDERSTANDING

True or false?

1 All organisations employ uniformed security staff.
2 Under the terms of the Data Protection Act, personal data must be made freely available to enquirers.
3 Many thieves are opportunists who will take advantage of breaches in security to steal.
4 Emergency exit doors should be kept closed, even in summer.
5 It is quite acceptable to allow a person to remove office equipment if he says he is from a local company.

Fill in the blanks

6 A person who gains unlawful access to a computer is called a _____ .

7 Driving a car into a building to gain access is called _____ ,
8 Staff ID badges usually contain a _____ so that the wearer can be easily identified.

Work it out

9 Your office has many outside callers every day – delivery people, visitors, maintenance workers and so on. You are concerned that a new office junior has no idea of the systems to follow to check people are who they say they are. Your organisation issues visitors' badges – but not to people who are only calling in for a matter of minutes.

   a Type out a list of instructions to help the junior to cope with this problem
   b What system can you suggest your company adopts to check the identity of all callers?

10 Carry out a security check of your own office area and workstation. Look for any obvious risks and any potential risks. Carefully reassess your own actions before you start looking at other people.

   Discuss your findings with your supervisor or tutor.

3 Contribute to the effectiveness of the workflow

This unit is concerned with workflow. Everyone knows some people who seem to cope with dozens of jobs quickly and easily – and other people who delay everything whenever they become involved. It will do your career prospects no good at all to be thought of as a **bottleneck** – someone who hinders the work rather than helps it to progress.

Dealing with a range of jobs at work every day isn't easy. You need to be able to prioritise those which are urgent, and then be prepared to change the order over and over again during the day to cope with constant changes and new demands. Being able to plan (even for problems!) helps, as does being well organised. These skills, and the systems you can use to help, are dealt with in the first element.

To cope with many jobs you need information – quickly, accurately and from a reliable source. Selecting this, obtaining it and storing it properly are all dealt with in the second element. You may like to note that there is a considerable amount of overlap between this element and Element 5.2. In this element, therefore, you will find several references to help you if you want to read about information sources in more detail in Unit 5.

The third element is concerned with resources. Even to make a few simple notes you need paper and a pencil, plus an eraser to rub out any errors. If you have to search for what you need for ten minutes then you are lengthening the job you are doing. To keep work flowing smoothly you need to be able to identify your resources beforehand, have these to hand and in working order.

This unit is not one which you can do in five minutes and then forget. It suggests methods which will change and improve the way you do your job. For these changes in routine to work for you, they must be put into practice all the time, and adjusted to fit your own particular circumstances. The aim is to make you more effective and more efficient, without having to work longer hours or do without your lunch!

Element 3.1

Plan and organise own work schedule

Whatever job you do in an office it is likely that you can divide your daily tasks into different categories, such as

1 non-routine tasks which should be done occasionally and which are not particularly important

2 routine tasks which should be done regularly

3 urgent jobs which are not vital but need to be done fairly quickly

4 urgent jobs which are very important and must be done immediately.

From that list it is obvious that given one job from each category you should do them in the reverse order to that listed (i.e. 4 through to 1). In reality, however, life is not so simple. Problems lie in

- working out (correctly!) the category in which each job falls
- coping with interruptions when you want to get on with a routine job which needs care and concentration
- wanting to do the jobs you *like* doing
- deciding which to do first from three urgent and important jobs
- having routine work left over from the previous day which is becoming more urgent by the minute
- having conflicting priorities (especially if you work for more than one person).

Prioritising is one of the most difficult skills to learn and is mainly developed through practice (and making a few mistakes!). You can make a start by working out whether a job is important, urgent or *both*. Tasks which are both should be done first, those which are neither come last. In between will lie those which are more difficult to schedule. As a rough rule of thumb, something which is important will come before something which isn't – even if it's urgent. The monthly sales report, for instance, should always come before watering the flowers – even in a heatwave!

 ## SPECIAL NOTE

Beware of jobs which *seem* to be routine but then become critical. Filing is the obvious one! If you ignore the filing for days on end because you hate it, the chances are that a document in the middle of a horrendous pile of papers will be needed at a moment's notice. You then have to scan dozens of papers quickly with your fingers firmly crossed while your boss paces the floor and becomes more and more annoyed.

Tips to help

- The more organised you are the easier it is to schedule time to deal with routine work promptly (*see below*).
- Try to allow for emergencies in your schedule, e.g. your boss suddenly interrupting you with an urgent job.
- In your schedule allow *more* time rather than less for each particular job (to allow for having to answer the telephone, talking to people, waiting at the photocopier etc.).
- If you are doing a job for the first time, allow 20 per cent longer for completing it.

TEST YOURSELF

1 Write out a list of the tasks you do at work or at college. To help, think back over the things you have done over the past month. Try to categorise these into

a urgent and important
b important
c urgent but fairly trivial
d neither urgent nor important.

Check your list with your supervisor or tutor.

2 Read the following list of tasks and decide which

a *must* be done
b *should* be done
c *could* be done if you are really well-organised.

● receiving visitors
● producing six business letters
● filing
● ringing a hotel to check the date of a business conference
● checking the telephone answering system
● ordering some new fax rolls from your local supplier
● sending three fax messages
● opening and distributing the mail
● watering the flowers
● making arrangements for your boss's trip to Scotland next month
● clearing out some old files
● sending out three catalogues in response to general enquiries
● adding two new customers to your customer name and address list on database.

DID YOU KNOW?

A famous management writer, called Peter Drucker, said that a person was efficient if they did the task right, but only became effective if they did the right task!

Being able to select *which* tasks are important and those on which your performance will be judged by your boss is therefore often more important than spending ages concentrating on the details of a routine job.

Organisation skills

How well organised are you? Do you

● always find what you put away
● have a place for everything – and everything in its place

- know what you did yesterday – and what you will do tomorrow
- know which jobs you completed today and which are still outstanding
- go home at night feeling a sense of achievement – and leave a tidy desk behind you?

To be an organised worker you need to concentrate on three main areas

- your working area and the layout
- your scheduling systems and 'memory aids'
- your own working methods and procedures.

Working area and layout

Every office worker needs a desk, preferably one with drawers at both sides. Alternatively you may have an L-shaped desk with a typewriter or computer on one side, or a custom-built workstation for IT equipment. Again there should be at least three drawers for personal items and stationery.

The equipment, furniture and other items you use regularly, such as filing cabinets, telephone and directories, noticeboards or planners, computer printer, cupboards and so on, should be near to you. You cannot work quickly and efficiently if you have to walk half a mile every time you need to do some photocopying. Unfortunately, though, there may be little you can do about the siting of major pieces of equipment, except have a quiet word with your supervisor if you have a real problem.

Ideally, if you use a telephone frequently then you should have one on your desk, but again this may not be possible. What *is* possible, however, is to make sure that your own desk area is as clear and uncluttered as possible. Desk accessories such as pen holders, paper clip holders and filing trays are very useful, but don't have so many of them that you've nowhere left to work. Generally, the larger your working area the better.

You need a comfortable, adjustable chair which gives you proper back support, particularly if you are keyboarding. Usually office chairs don't have arms as these get in the way. A swivel chair is particularly useful if you have an L-shaped desk. Make sure your chair is at the right height and right position for *you*. You have no right to complain about backache if you can't be bothered to make sure your chair is adjusted correctly! Note that your workstation and chair are particularly important if you are a VDU operator (*see Element 2.1*).

Remember that your desk is a working surface, not a storage space! You can't work on it properly if it's cluttered with paper. Similarly you can only work on one job at once. This is the *only* paperwork which should therefore be in front of you. The rest should be in one of your storage trays. Make sure these aren't too deep, otherwise you'll use them as a hoarding spot for papers and you'll struggle to find anything quickly. If you're not sure whether yours are the right depth do the flick test – see if you can quickly flick through all the papers it contains to check work outstanding at a glance.

DID YOU KNOW?

You should train yourself to answer a telephone by lifting the receiver with the hand you *don't* write with, and having a pen in the hand that you *do* write with – and *always* have a notepad close by. This saves time transferring the telephone from one hand to the other to take a message and irritating the caller by having to look around for something to write on or with!

Organising your desk area

- Clear your working area of any non-essential items and find another place to store them.
- If you have a telephone on your desk, put it towards the back at the left or right hand side (depending upon which hand you write with).
- Organise your drawer space properly. If you have a lockable drawer than this should contain personal and confidential items and anything of monetary value, e.g. postage stamps or petty cash.
- Store office stationery properly so that papers do not become creased and unusable.
- Clearly label any filing trays. The most popular headings are 'in', 'out', 'pending' and 'filing'.
- Make sure everyone knows where to leave 'new' work, preferably in your in-tray rather than on top of your desk where it could get confused with your active papers. If this isn't possible then try asking people to leave them on your chair if you're away from your desk.
- If you have certain 'regular' jobs then make sure work relating to each of these is kept in a special folder or file which is clearly labelled. Use different coloured folders (or labels) for easy identification and store these in a suitable cupboard or drawer.

DID YOU KNOW?

Many desks have a large bottom drawer at one side which will hold a series of vertical files. These can be ideal for keeping on-going work folders as they are always close at hand. When the work is completed then the documents can be transferred to the main filing system.

You have just been allocated a desk in the sales office. The top right hand drawer is lockable and the bottom right hand drawer will hold vertical files. You have the following items to store.

a Identify which items you would keep on top of your desk.

b State which drawer you would choose to store the others and why.

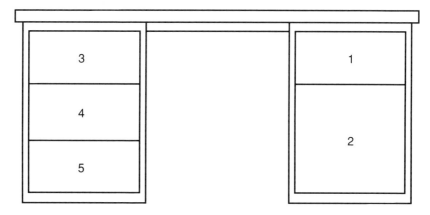

shorthand pad
letter headed paper
spare file folders
sellotape
stapler
spare staples
staple remover
pens and pencils
pencil sharpener
ruler
file containing representatives' names and addresses
scissors
paper clips
postage stamps
file containing reps current monthly sales reports
ruled writing paper (A4)
computer printer paper

DID YOU KNOW?

You should *never* leave a desk cluttered at night – it's most offputting the following morning. Put papers away in their files or in your trays, with the most urgent on the top, and leave your working surface clean and tidy.

Scheduling systems and memory aids

The worst thing in the world is leaving work feeling quite content and then, about 9 pm, realising with a sickening feeling that you forgot to give someone an urgent message at 4.30 pm or to send an important fax before you went home. You then spend the rest of the evening trying to work out how best to rescue the situation – and what to tell your boss.

Whilst no system is completely infallible (especially if you don't use it properly), there is much less chance of causing a disaster if you plan and organise your own work schedule by

- using the best system for you – and *sticking to it*
- writing down *everything* that you are asked to do
- remembering that you must do jobs in order of urgency and importance – not in the order in which you wrote them down!

Work schedules

In some organisations these are written on a pre-printed form. For instance, service engineers often use a **job sheet** which lists the calls they must make each day, with the name and address of each customer. There is usually a column for action taken. This is useful for writing down 'exceptions' e.g. if no-one was at home when the engineer called.

You can, of course, use a similar system for yourself and make out a schedule for each day or week. If you have regular routine jobs to be done on certain days then you can enter these on one week's sheets and photocopy your schedules to add your non-routine jobs.

Using this system means that you can easily identify when a day is going to be very busy or when you will have some spare time. If you are then asked to schedule a new job you will be able to do this properly, by looking for an appropriate day when you have enough time available to do the job you have been asked to do. It can often be useful to write in the 'notes' column how long a new job took you to do, then you know how much time to allow for it in future.

If you use this system, file your sheets and keep them for several months after use. That way you can use them for reference or to check when you actually did a particular job.

Making lists

An alternative to making out formal schedules is to make a straightforward list of jobs you have to do. Shorthand pads are ideal, both for writing down lists and making notes for yourself. The ideal method is

- to date the page clearly (some people prefer to write the date at the bottom so they can see which page relates to which date when they flick through the book)

- to write down the jobs you have to do in a list
- to tick each one as you complete it
- at the end of the day, to carry forward any outstanding jobs to the top of the next page.

This system is good because it is simple and you obviously don't have to do the jobs in the order in which you wrote them. You should skim up and down your list, and clear urgent and important work first.

The only snags to the system are that

- you are unlikely to write down routine jobs you have to do (which you then may forget about)
- you may forget to add jobs to your list if you're asked to do something when you haven't got your shorthand pad with you.

However, the system does show up which jobs you keep putting off – as you will find yourself transferring these to the next page day after day! At this stage you must be firm with yourself and resolve to do them before any problems arise.

DID YOU KNOW?

Many people consider the best way to start a day is to do one or two jobs which they don't like doing! They can then have a 'reward' such as a cup of coffee. If you do this you will find that afterwards you will feel quite pleased with yourself and look forward to doing the jobs you prefer doing – rather than spending all day dreading the fact that you have something awful on your list! (Or, even worse, keep ignoring it in the hope that it will go away!)

Planners and schedules

Offices which have regular events or targets to meet may have large planning boards on the wall on which to record them. A simple illustration of one type is shown below, although there are many different systems on the market.

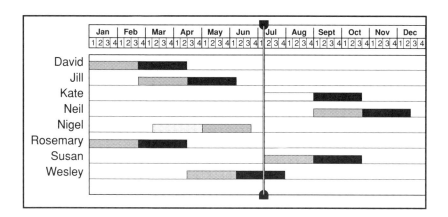

The top of the board usually shows the **time scale** and is divided into weeks or months. Down the left hand side, jobs, events or people can be listed. A vertical, movable marker is used to show the current date. Most of these systems are colour coded so that different jobs or events can be easily identified.

The benefit of these systems is that they are clear to see and it is easy to change and update information. However, to be any use at all they must be kept up to date, otherwise they will give misleading or incorrect information which is worse than none at all!

CHECK IT YOURSELF

Look through a catalogue from an office supplies company and identify the different planners which are sold.

1 Which one would you buy if you were responsible for scheduling the use of six meeting rooms by different groups of staff in your organisation?
2 Find out what the term 'perpetual planner' means, and how this differs from an ordinary planner.

Action plans

You have already met action planning when you prepared your own in Unit 1. However, action plans are used for many reasons, not just for self-development. Their main benefit is that they show the time scale over which a series of events will take place.

Imagine you work for an organisation which holds a sales conference for all sales staff once a year. On the action plan you would show

- all the different jobs which have to be done
- the date by which each one has to be completed
- the name (or initials) of the person responsible for doing each one.

When each job is complete it should be ticked off on the plan. This system is useful because you can easily tell if you are on schedule. However, it is less easy to change than a wall planner as you normally list the jobs in date order. If you want to slot in another job then you may have to redo the whole list.

Action plan for sales conference September 199-

Task	Date of completion	Action by	Tick when complete
Obtain quotes from 3 hotels	end May	JL	√
Select venue and draft programme	mid June	PN	√
Contact visiting speaker	20 June	JL	√
Finalise date	25 June	JL/PN	√
Book venue	30 June	JL	
Notify reps	early July	JL	
Finalise programme	end July	JL/PN	

Diaries

There are many types of diary on the market, the most usual being either a 'page a day' or 'two-days a page'. Usually they contain additional pages with useful information such as public holidays, foreign currencies etc.

You *can* use your diary to list your 'jobs to do today' rather than use your shorthand pad, provided you have enough space. The main advantages of using a diary are that you can use it to enter

- timed appointments and visits
- jobs carried forward to a future date
- jobs which must be done on a specific date
- regular events
- jobs listed on an action plan
- important events you mustn't forget
- provisional jobs and events (write these in *pencil* until they are definite).

This is where using a diary can be better than making a list. However, be careful you don't clutter up your diary with masses of information so that it becomes a hindrance rather than a help.

You can cope with this problem more easily if you use a 'page a day' diary and divide each page into two sections. Use one section for events and appointments, and the other for jobs which must be done that day. The size of the sections (and which is used for what) will depend upon your job and your own personal requirements.

Many organisations have electronic diaries available on their computer systems. These allow you to bring up a particular date and enter information. The system warns you if you have a clash. There is space for making notes and listing work to do each day, as well as recording appointments and events.

Recurring events (e.g. a Friday morning production meeting) only need to be entered once and can then be set to appear as often as required. Most systems also link with a database so that if you need to telephone someone, you can automatically call up their address or telephone number as well.

Using an electronic diary does radically reduce the amount of paperwork likely to be on your desk at any one time but obvious problems occur if the computer system fails and no-one knows what they are supposed to be doing. Remember, you can't carry the diary around with you from one office to another – or take it home at the end of the day to get your jobs straight!

Putting it all together

The main thing to avoid is having schedules, lists, diaries, wall planners and action plans, all containing different information and all combining to give a very confusing picture. Whatever systems you use there must be *one* book, diary or file in which all your information is brought together and you can clearly see where you are now and what you have to do in the future. You should refer to it constantly throughout the day.

Which you select will most likely depend on

- the procedures in use in your own organisation
- your own particular job – and the ratio of routine versus unexpected jobs you have to cope with.

This scheduling aid will be so valuable to you that it may be a good idea to have a photocopy of important pages in the future – just in case you lose your original!

CHECK IT YOURSELF

Discuss with your supervisor or tutor the type of procedures which are used in your organisation, and discuss the type of planning aids you could use to help you. It may be useful to list the jobs you regularly have to do and to indicate whether these are routine or not, and to note down the number and type of unexpected jobs you are asked to carry out.

Your own working methods

If you gave six people the same job to do, the chances are that each of them would go about it in a different way. At one extreme, the most organised worker would

- plan and schedule the work properly
- tackle it methodically
- keep all related documents neatly
- complete the job on time *or* notify his or her supervisor of possible delays and state why these are occurring.

At the other extreme, a disorganised worker would ignore any one of the above points (or even all of them!) or – even worse – not do the job at all.

Only you know how near you are to meeting the ideal. However, if you are some way off, the following hints and tips should help you.

- Make sure you start a 'work-in-progress' file for *each* new, special job you are asked to do.
- Label the file clearly.
- if the job has several stages, make out an action plan for yourself and put this in the front of the file.
- Tick off jobs as you go on your action plan – then if anyone asks you can tell them immediately where you are up to.
- Don't clutter the file with non-essential papers. Sort it regularly and throw away anything which is out of date or which you don't need.
- If you are in the middle of a job and are called away to do something else, put the papers back in the file and put the file away.
- Keep a close eye on your deadline dates for completion. If you are having problems – or even start to suspect there may be a problem – then *tell your supervisor immediately*.
- Don't be frightened to ask for help if you cannot cope. This is far, far better than either getting so behind that no-one can rescue the situation or cutting corners (and trying to hide the fact) by not doing the job properly or missing bits out!

 DID YOU KNOW?

One boss always used to say to her staff, 'don't bring me problems, bring me solutions'. This can be useful advice, no matter what level you work at in an organisation. If you see a problem but think you know how it can be solved then you should say so!

Team working

On many occasions you may be asked to do a job with the help of someone else – or even to work as one of a team of people. Indeed, in all offices, work is done more efficiently *and* more effectively if the group of people employed there work together to help and assist each other. The supervisor's job is to allocate work between them according to their skills, abilities, experience and strengths – and to develop and train new staff to take on different tasks.

Working in a team is different from working on your own. Every member of a team is different, and you have to take into account their strengths and weaknesses as well as your own! A management writer called Dr Meredith Belbin argued that an individual can never be perfect but a team can be. He meant that, given a good team, you can have a mix of people who collectively have qualities which balance each other and result in more 'strengths' than can ever be found in one person. To be effective, the team must get on well together, support each other and be able to rely on one another to get the job done.

DID YOU KNOW?

Another term used in conjunction with teamwork is **synergy.** This is the idea that the collective efforts of a team are greater than the individual efforts added together. Discuss this statement with your supervisor or tutor if you do not understand it.

TEST YOURSELF

How good a team worker are you? Do the quiz below and discuss your answers with your supervisor or tutor. If you are brave enough, you can also ask other members of any group in which you work for their views on your performance, too!

How good a team worker are you?

Answer 'always', 'rarely' or 'never' to each of the following.

1 If I have a problem I prefer to discuss it with someone else.
2 If something goes wrong, I prefer to ask someone for advice or help.
3 I like to work in a group.
4 I am happy to make suggestions to a group, and don't mind if a better one is thought of later.
5 I can be relied to do a job to the best of my ability.
6 I take account of other people's views.
7 I like helping other people.
8 I don't mind sharing my possessions or my time.
9 I say 'thank you' if someone helps me.
10 I take responsibility for my own actions.
11 If someone is being difficult I will think carefully before making a response.
12 I will defend a member of my group if he or she is criticised.
13 I will support other people's suggestions if I think they are helpful.
14 I can work with all sorts of people.
15 I usually get on well with people.

Score yourself 2 points for each time you answered 'always', 1 point for 'rarely' and no points for 'never'.

The nearer your score is to 30 the better a team worker you are.

Time management

The worst jobs in the world are those which arrive unexpectedly when you are very busy and which are both urgent *and* important. If, on top of that, these include jobs you don't want to do or don't like doing then you need all your skills of planning, organising and self-discipline to cope!

If you have *several* jobs to cope with at the same time, all of which are important and/or urgent then you may have similar problems. If other people are relying on you to get these jobs done on time before they can do *their* part, then you may feel under a lot of pressure for most of your working week. You will also make things a lot worse for yourself if you are one of those people who can never say 'no', so that you end up with so much to do you don't know where to start.

A technique which has been developed to help people cope with this type of problem is **time management**. It is based on the idea that, during the course of a day, many people waste time unnecessarily. By planning carefully and reducing the time they waste, everyone can be more productive. Much of time management is concerned with developing planning and reminder systems such as those mentioned earlier in this unit. Some time management courses include the use of special filofaxes and other memory aids. Other techniques include identifying where you actually waste time and doing something about it, or working out how to schedule jobs so they take less time.

CHECK IT YOURSELF

You arrive home late at 7 pm and have to ring a friend, have a bath and be out of the door by 7.30. In addition you are desperate for a cup of coffee. Decide how you should cope with this (the answer is given at the end of this element).

TEST YOURSELF

Decide which of the following time-wasting activities apply to you and what you can do about them!

- gossiping to colleagues and friends
- chatting on the telephone
- spending time looking for papers you should have filed last week
- making unnecessary journeys (usually because you've forgotten something the first time)
- shuffling papers – because you can't decide what to do
- daydreaming – because you're not in the mood for work
- doing a job badly – and then getting it back to do all over again

DID YOU KNOW?

It is better to refuse a job (politely!) than to take it on and let someone down. Explain why there is a problem and why you will have problems meeting the deadline. Everyone will prefer this, especially the person who may otherwise have to be drafted in to help you out at the last moment!

SPECIAL NOTE

An invaluable time management tip is never to shuffle papers! On many occasions you may start to go through your work, look at several papers or jobs and simply put them to the bottom of the pile again! If you were being really efficient you should

- action them, *or*
- put them in your pending tray, *or*
- file them, *or*
- throw them away!

If you put them in your pending tray, remember you have to go through this, too, on a regular basis, without shuffling the papers!

DID YOU KNOW?

It's healthy to have a six-monthly clear out of papers and other things which are completely out of date. It's also amazing how you can accumulate multiple copies of a document when you need only one. Get a rubbish sack ready and be quite ruthless. If, however, you're unsure about anything check with your supervisor first.

Relevant legal requirements

You might wonder how there could be any legal aspects involved when studying a unit on workflow. However, in trying to schedule and complete work quickly you could overlook the legal implications of a situation.

- You could cut corners and take unnecessary risks which endanger yourself and others. For instance, if there is a serious fault on the photocopier when you are rushing to finish a job you may be tempted to fiddle about inside it yourself even though you have had no instructions on how to cope with photocopier faults.

- If you deal with selling goods or services to members of the public, there is a range of consumer protection legislation which may apply to the transaction. For instance, if you describe something wrongly or initially give a price which is *lower* than the real price charged, then the customer would be within his rights to return the goods.

- If you *receive* goods on behalf of your organisation, and do not check them properly on arrival, then you might not notice faults which mean the goods should be returned.

- if you are in such a rush to clear your desk of papers you *may* throw away some documents which, by law, must be kept for a specific period of time. (*Document retention is dealt with in Unit 5, page 166.*)

- If someone asks you for information when you are busy, you could be tempted to give this out without checking if they have any right to receive it. At best you could be giving out confidential information, at worst you could be breaking the law under the Data Protection Act (*see Unit 2, page 67*).

TEST YOURSELF

Look back to the Health and Safety regulations listed in Unit 2, page 34. Can you identify *six* actions which could be taken by an office worker who is in a hurry, which would be an offence under any of these regulations?

Compare your list with those compiled by other members of your group.

Answer to 'Check it yourself' on page 89

The best way to cope with this is to

- start to run your bath
- put on the kettle
- phone your friend (while the kettle boils)
- make your coffee and let it cool while you have a quick bath!

In other words, by doing some jobs simultaneously you get more done in the same time.

UNIT REVIEW (1)

At the end of this element you should be able to

- identify your own routine and unexpected tasks
- prioritise these according to the procedures in operate in your own organisation
- use appropriate planning aids to schedule work
- change your work schedules in line with changes in priorities
- promptly report any difficulties in meeting deadlines to an appropriate person
- ask for assistance to meet specific demands and deadlines.

TEST YOUR KNOWLEDGE AND UNDERSTANDING

True or false?

1 Whatever happens during a day, a good worker always sticks to his or her planned schedule.
2 A team of people can cope with tasks which an individual could not.
3 To be properly organised, every office worker needs a diary, a shorthand pad and a wall planner.

4 It is better to pretend you know something when you don't, than to ask a colleague for help.

5 Organisational procedures and individual preferences will affect the kind of planning aids used.

Fill in the blanks

6 A computer program which schedules appointments is called an _____ _____ .

7 A management technique used to help people to become more organised and waste less time is called _____ _____ .

8 Tasks which should be done first are those which are _____ and _____ .

Work it out

9 Your supervisor has given you a job to do which normally would be done by one of your colleagues who is away because of illness. The job involves using a mail merge facility on the word processor – something you have never done before. The job must be done by 3 pm tomorrow afternoon and you already have a backlog of work to clear.

    a Write down exactly what you would do to prevent your current problem.

    b What action could you take to solve the problem occurring again in the future, both in relation to

      ● the new task you have been asked to do
      ● the backlog of work you must clear?

10 a Design a work schedule sheet on which you could list all the jobs you do in the course of a day and which clearly shows your priority jobs.

    b Enter the jobs listed on page 78 to check if your system works.

    c Test your system by

      ● adding a new, important job – i.e. binding 25 sales reports

      ● seeing if you can cope if you now find six fax rolls in the cupboard – and want to change that job from being urgent to not being urgent (for the time being!).

Element 3.2

Obtain and organise information in support of own work activities

If you think about it, the work of every office worker in an organisation is to obtain, process, store or communicate information to the person who needs it. This may be a customer, supplier or another employee. This information may be easily found in the organisation itself, or have to be found specially for a particular task. However, obtaining the correct information – and making sure you are not drowned under dozens of pieces of paper – is essential to being able to do your job well.

Types of information

When you first start in a new job you will seem baffled by the number of things you need to learn. Slowly you start to find your way around, learn about the various people in an organisation and about the job you have been employed to do. If you can work with your predecessor for a while that is ideal – as he or she will be a mine of information about what to do, where to find things and what to remember. If you have any sense you will take lots of notes for the first few days!

You can actually divide up the information you need to do any job into these three categories

- technical information (e.g. relating to the equipment you use)
- organisational information (e.g. on policies, procedures and the structure of the company)
- personal information (that you need to do your own particular job, and that particularly relates to yourself).

As a general rule you will usually find that

- Technical information is supplied automatically, e.g. when you buy a new piece of equipment or software. However, it may be incomplete, you may not be able to understand it or you may lose it!
- Organisational information is issued by your boss, your colleagues and other offices in your company. Your biggest problems may hinge around
  - what to keep and what to throw away
  - where and how to store it
  - how to obtain copies if you lose it
  - how to find information kept in a different department.

- A certain amount of personal information is given to you when you first start work, the rest you will acquire as you do the job. Identifying what you need and knowing where to find it may be your biggest problem. You then have to decide the best way of storing it.

TEST YOURSELF

You have recently started work as an assistant in the personnel department. Into which category would you put each of the following types of information?

   1   an instruction book on the word processing package you use

2 a telephone extension list
3 company health and safety procedures
4 information on how to fit a new fax roll
5 your boss's interview schedules for next week
6 where to find the forms to be given to job applicants
7 a copy of your job description

Obtaining information

The three main ways in which you can usually obtain information are

- from people – either in your own organisation or outside
- from paper-based reference materials
- through a computer system.

People

People can be an invaluable and extremely knowledgeable source of information. All you have to do is ask! However, don't use this option as the easy way out when you should either know the answer already or be able to find it yourself! Equally, if you *keep* asking people the same thing – because you can't be bothered to write it down – they are likely to get rather annoyed.

As well as asking people within your own organisation for information, you may also want to find out information quickly by telephoning a contact in another organisation or a specialist organisation such as the AA or the Citizen's Advice Bureau.

 DID YOU KNOW?

Saying 'thank you' when someone helps you costs you nothing and can make a world of difference when you want someone to help you again!

Paper-based reference materials

These can include reference books, magazines, newspapers, periodicals, leaflets, brochures, departmental or central company files, company documentation and your own written notes.

Bear in mind that you don't need to have all this information at your fingertips all the time to be able to use it! Reference books, magazines and so on can be found in your local reference library, you can send for leaflets and brochures when you need them, you can borrow files and return them when you've finished with them. That way you don't overload yourself with paper which very quickly becomes out of date or irrelevant.

Information held on computer

This will vary from one organisation to another but may include mailing lists for customers, customer records, personnel records, stock records, price lists and sales statistics. In addition many companies now operate a computerised filing system to reduce the amount of paper held at any one time (*see Unit 5, page 168*).

Information can also be obtained from viewdata systems such as Prestel or via CD-Roms. These are optical disks on which books and past copies of newspapers are stored and which can be accessed via computer.

Finally, your organisation may have a networked computer system which incorporates electronic mail – or subscribe to an external electronic mail system such as Prestel or Telecom Gold. In both these cases you have the advantage of being able to send and receive messages to other people quickly and easily (*see Unit 8*).

Keeping up to date

Bear in mind that sources of information *change* over a period of time. The person who used to deal with customer accounts may leave and the job may be transferred to someone else. A new office supplies company may open nearby. Your company may install a computerised filing system. Your own job may change, so that the type of information you need is different.

For all these reasons is it worthwhile regularly reviewing the sources of information you use to make sure that these are still the most appropriate and the most useful. There is also always the obvious point that there may be a very useful source nearby which you didn't know about! Don't therefore assume that any source you have regularly used in the past is necessarily the *only* one, the *best* one or has the information which is the most *relevant* to your needs.

SPECIAL NOTE

Sources of information are dealt with in more detail in Unit 5, page 173.

Information overload!

Despite the vision of the paperless office, modern computer systems have actually *increased* the amount of paper in most organisations. The power of the computer to store and manipulate data has meant that much more information is readily available than ever before. However, only being able to see a document on a screen has several drawbacks – not least that you can't carry it around, scribble notes on it or look at five pieces of paper at once. For that reason, most people take a print-out of the information they need.

If, on top of this, you have a tendency to squirrel away anything which you think might come in handy some time in the future, at the end of a very short time you will find yourself needing two extra desks and three extra filing cabinets in which to store it all!

The way to avoid this is

- only to print out or photocopy information if it is going to be *really* useful
- only to save it if it is really relevant and will *definitely* come in useful again soon *or* was particularly hard to find in the first place
- to review your information regularly to check it is up to date – and throw it away if it isn't!
- regularly to prune your own files and throw away papers which you saved but have not looked at for months (and are never likely to) or which are already saved on computer disk.

TEST YOURSELF

You are clearing out a drawer in your desk when you come across the following. Which would you keep and which would you throw away?

- a leaflet containing last year's postal rates
- last month's sales report
- your action plan for last year's sales conference
- a brochure you sent for on electronic filing which your boss was interested in buying but has since decided is too expensive
- an office supplies catalogue headed 1993/4
- the instruction booklet for your fax machine
- the notes you made on your first day in the job

Storing information

Needless to say, all those items really shouldn't have been stored in your desk drawers! The only way you can keep information safely and find it quickly is to store it *properly* – and the method you will use will depend upon the items you are keeping.

To keep a range of items such as those listed above, you will probably need

- box files for catalogues, leaflets, reports and other documents which cannot or must not be punched
- lever arch files for keeping large amounts of documents on one subject *or* for keeping single copies of documents in alphabetical order
- document or envelope wallets, in different colours, for keeping small numbers of papers on one topic (especially if these will be carried around)
- file folders for documents which are going to be put into your filing system.

Develop the habit of labelling all your files and folders properly – so you can see at a glance what each one contains.

If you have a large number of reference books or directories you also need a bookcase or cupboard in which to keep them. Multi-purpose cupboards can be extremely useful as these can be used to store files as well as computer disks, books, magazines and sundry other items. Many also include large files for storing computer print-outs.

Classifying information

Unit 5 covers, in detail, filing and classification systems. Basically, however, most offices have two types of information, i.e.

- that relating to *people* – customers, suppliers or staff
- that relating to *events* or *topics*.

Information relating to people is often stored in **alphabetical** order – in the same way as they are listed in a telephone directory. In a very large organisation this may not be appropriate and a special **numerical** or **alpha-numerical** system may be used (*see page 158*).

When files are organised into events or topics, this is called **subject** filing. All the files are kept in alphabetical order of subject, and this is often the best way of organising the information you deal with every day in your job. The danger is that a document can relate to *two* (or more) topics, so that you aren't sure where to store it. The answer to this is to **cross-reference** it by either

- taking a photocopy and putting the photocopy in the file in which you are *least* likely to look (with a note on the document as to where you have put the original!), *or*
- just putting a note in the file, as a reminder to yourself where to find the original.

If you find, however, that you are regularly doing this then you need to reassess how you've organised your system – and perhaps rename your topics. (*Note that cross-referencing is dealt with in more detail in Unit 5, page 162.*)

TEST YOURSELF

If you are already employed, list *six* types of information you deal with regularly and need to store yourself in a filing system. Identify a suitable topic heading for each one and put these in alphabetical order.

If you are taking a full-time course, then either do this exercise using any work experience placement you have had as a guide, or imagine that you work in the college office and think of *six* topic headings you may find in there. Again put them into alphabetical order.

DID YOU KNOW?

Small amount of information are usually kept on cards or strips in an indexing system (such as in a card index box). A typical example is the names, addresses and telephone numbers of customers – although many companies now keep these on a database. (*Indexing equipment is dealt with in Unit 5, page 154 and databases in Unit 6 page 220.*)

If you use any type of card index system then make sure you replace the cards immediately after use – otherwise they are apt to get lost!

Organisational procedures

One word of warning is due at this stage! Every organisation has different procedures which may have to be followed when you are either obtaining or storing information. There may also be different retention policies which will affect what you can throw away and when.

In one company, for instance, you may just be able to go and help yourself to a file you need. In another you may have to order it from a central filing system and may even need your boss's approval or authorisation. A small organisation is less likely to have as many formal procedures as a large one – so do check with your supervisor if you are unsure.

Confidential information

The type of job you do will affect the type of information you handle. However, it is likely that before too long you will be involved with confidential information of one type or another. This may relate to a member of staff, a customer or client, or to you or your boss. If you are ever in any doubt as to whether information is confidential then treat it as such until you are told otherwise!

If you have been authorised to obtain confidential information then make sure that

- you keep the document(s) safely locked away and *never* leave them lying on your desk
- you only send out copies when you are authorised to do so and then in a sealed envelope marked 'confidential'
- you don't disclose the information to anyone else, no matter how tempted you are
- you destroy the document(s) properly after use, preferably in a shredder.

As a double check, make sure that you are fully aware of your organisation's policies and procedures for dealing with any type of confidential information.

UNIT REVIEW (2)

At the end of this element you should be able to

- obtain and maintain up-to-date information which is relevant to your own job
- identify which type of information is relevant and appropriate for your own job
- regularly review your sources of information for their usefulness and relevance
- organise and store your information using methods which will help you in your own job
- maintain confidentiality of information in accordance with organisational procedures.

TEST YOUR KNOWLEDGE AND UNDERSTANDING

True or false?

1 The growth in the number of computers in offices has resulted in a decline in the amount of paper handled.
2 Cross-referencing is when two copies of a document are kept in the same file.
3 Reference libraries also keep back copies of magazines and periodicals.
4 The handbook relating to your telephone system is known as technical information.
5 All documents will be out of date after twelve months.

Fill in the blanks

6 Small amounts of information are often kept on cards or strips in an _____ system.
7 A _____ file is used for documents which cannot or must not be punched.
8 When files are kept on topics or events this is called _____ filing.

Work it out

9 Your supervisor has decided to buy a shredder in which to destroy confidential documents. She has no idea of the types available or their price.

Find out this information for her and present it neatly on A4 paper.

10 You have recently moved into a new office in which you will need to keep

- your own personal files
- telephone directories and the company telephone extension list
- your computer disks
- three reference books
- lever arch files and box files containing various documents
- the names, addresses and telephone numbers of part-time staff
- instruction booklets on all the equipment in your office.

Your supervisor has asked you to let her know what equipment you will need to store these properly.

Look through an office supplies catalogue and identify the items which you think would be the most useful.

Element 3.3

Obtain and maintain physical resources to carry out own work

In the last element you were looking at large items of equipment for storage. In reality, if you look through an office supplies catalogue, the vast majority of items used in an office every day are much smaller items. These are either

- office consumables, *or*

- items of small equipment, such as staplers, hole punches, scissors and disk boxes.

What are consumables? **Consumables** are office materials and supplies which are frequently used and therefore often need replacing, such as paper clips and pens.

 DID YOU KNOW?

Items which are not consumables are usually called **capital** items and an organisation will have one budget for capital expenditure (on equipment, transport, buildings etc.) and one budget for consumables.

Which of the following items are consumables and which are not?

audio machines	audio tapes
fax machines	fax rolls
franking machines	franking machine labels
petty cash box	petty cash vouchers
notice board	drawing pins

Types of office consumables

Most office consumables are **stationery** items.

Paper

This is usually bought in **reams** (500 sheets). Today dozens of different types of paper are available, from accounting paper to tracing paper. Paper can be bought in different sizes and different weights. The heavier the weight, the more expensive the paper.

The most usual types used in an office are

- **bond** paper – used for top copies of letters and reports. Good quality bond paper is watermarked.
- **photocopier** paper
- **printer** paper. Special paper is usually purchased for laser printers as this often has to be of a certain quality and weight. Dot matrix printers are fitted with special perforated paper.
- **bank** paper – used for carbon copies. Today many organisations have dispensed with carbon paper altogether and either print multiple copies of documents or photocopy them.

SPECIAL NOTE

If you *do* have to order carbon paper you may find that this is sold by the **quire,** i.e. in boxes of 24 sheets.

DID YOU KNOW?

Watermarked paper should always be used with top (smooth) side facing you. You can tell which way round to use it because if you look through the paper from the right side you can read the watermark properly. On the reverse you would read it in reverse.

Envelopes

These are purchased in boxes of 500 or 1000. The most expensive are white envelopes with self-adhesive flaps and the cheapest are small, brown envelopes which you have to stick down yourself. Again sizes vary and so does the paper used. The larger and heavier the envelope the more it costs.

Many organisations use window envelopes as this means there is no need to type the address.

DID YOU KNOW?

Business correspondence is usually typed on A4 paper which is folded into three to fit into a DL envelope. If you do this correctly, the first thing a person sees when they open it is the letter heading.

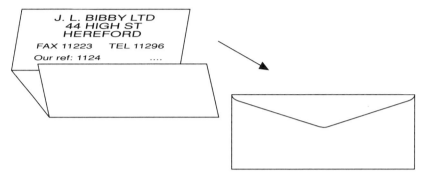

J. L. BIBBY LTD
44 HIGH ST
HEREFORD
FAX 11223   TEL 11296
Our ref: 1124   ....

Pencils and pens

These are sometimes purchased by the dozen (12) or by the gross (144). Grade B pencils are soft (9B are the softest) and grade H pencils are hard (10H being the hardest). Grade HB – of medium hardness – is the most commonly used.

Filing materials

These include filing folders, ring binders, document wallets, index cards, lever arch files, box files and so on.

Printed items

These will include letter headed paper, memos, compliment slips, business cards, invoices and statements. Printed pads of standard forms are often stocked. These are usually printed on NCR paper meaning that no carbons are required for copies to be made.

Miscellaneous items

Under this heading can be included shorthand pads, paper clips, staples, duplicating materials, bulldog clips, sellotape, rulers, rubber bands, pencil sharpeners and floppy disks.

SPECIAL NOTE

Remember your spelling

- stationery = paper and envelopes (**e** for envelope)
- stationary = not moving (as in stationary **car**)

Look through your desk *or* the bag you carry to college. Check your own 'resources'. Are they kept neatly and tidily and do you have all the items you regularly need? Or are you always having to borrow a pen or sharpen a pencil before you can use it (that's if you can find your pencil sharpener ...)?

Storage and handling of resources

A wide variety of equipment is available in which you can store stationery and other sundry items. If you keep your possessions neatly and tidily, not only will you be able to find them when you want them but they will last longer and you will need to spend less money on replacements. This is equally applicable for you personally and for any company you work for!

In some cases, incorrect storage and treatment can create real problems.

- Photocopier paper which is damp will jam in the machine.
- Crumpled letter headed paper is unusable because it looks so awful.
- A pencil dropped on the floor will have a lead which is broken all the way through.
- A floppy disk stored near direct heat or anything magnetic will be unusable – as will disks which have been crushed together in a disk box – and may have contained valuable information.
- Drawing pins and other sharp objects which are left around can be dangerous.
- Felt tips and dry markers stored without their tops will dry up and become unusable.
- Envelopes stored in damp conditions will seal themselves.
- A bottle of liquid paper which is kept without the top screwed on tightly will harden like chalk.
- Paper left in sunlight will discolour – keep it wrapped until you need it.

You can save yourself a lot of work if you plan carefully *where* you are going to store your items. Things you need every day need to be close at hand – on your desk, in your top drawer or easily accessible in a nearby cupboard.

Many consumable items are sold in boxes which are ideal as storage – or even designed as dispensers, e.g. reinforcement rings, address labels, screen wipes. For that reason it is often better to keep items in their boxes until you need them. If necessary label the box clearly so that you can easily identify the contents. Make sure all descriptive labels face outwards for easy access.

Safety first

If you are handling heavy items such as boxes of paper, lift them carefully, one box at a time (*see Unit 2, page 54*). Store them at ground level or on the bottom shelf of a cupboard to avoid unnecessary lifting.

If you need to reach items which are stored on high shelves use a safety stool.

Obtaining resources

Most organisations have a standard procedure which you must follow if you want to order any consumable items or equipment. However, this is likely to vary depending upon the size of the organisation for which you work.

Small companies

In a small company, you will need the permission of your supervisor or boss to order what you need from a local supplier. It is likely that your employer has one favoured supplier, possibly because it sells reasonably priced goods or gives a good discount.

After agreement is given, you may have to make out an official order form which your boss must sign as confirmation that the order is genuine.

DID YOU KNOW?

If you order goods urgently by fax or telephone then most suppliers will ask you to quote your official order number to confirm that the order is genuine.

Large organisations

If you work for a large company, there may be a central purchasing office which deals with all orders. In this case you will have to fill in an internal order form, known as a **requisition**, and have this authorised by your supervisor. If your organisation obtains a good discounts for ordering in large quantities, then you may have to wait a short time until the purchasing office has sufficient requests to make it worth while ordering an item.

DID YOU KNOW?

The amount of time between asking for goods and receiving them is known as **lead time**. Bear this in mind when you know you are going to require important items. It is one thing to run out of post-it notes and quite another not to be able to send out any letters because you have no letter headed paper! (Printed items are always likely to have the longest lead times.)

CHECK IT YOURSELF

1 Find out the procedures for ordering stationery in your own organisation or college. Write these out in a straightforward checklist for a new member of staff.
2 Make a list with the following headings.

Important   Average   Unimportant
items   items   items

From an office supplies catalogue identify *five* types of consumables which you would put under each heading *for your own job*. Important items are those such as letter headings, where disaster would occur if you ran out, average items are those which you need to make sure you always have, whenever possible, and unimportant items are those which are nice to have, but not really essential to do your job.

Receiving consumables

When stationery is delivered it must be carefully checked to make sure that

- the goods are correct in size, quantity and quality
- no additional goods have been included
- no goods are missing
- nothing is damaged
- if anything has been substituted for an item out of stock then the substitution is acceptable.

Packers do make mistakes and this is not always shown on the delivery note which accompanies the goods. For that reason many large organisations have the goods checked centrally and a **goods received note** is made out listing the items received and their condition. The invoice is then only paid if it agrees with this document.

If you have a problem, remember

- If goods are damaged then you have a right to a replacement or your money back.

- If goods are missing then they should be marked 'to follow' on the delivery note.
- You do not have to keep substitute items if they are unsuitable – or anything which has been sent by mistake.
- If too many goods have been received it is courteous (and honest!) to inform the supplier immediately.
- If the mistake is yours – and you completed the order form wrongly – then you have no legal right to return the goods. In this case you will have to rely on the goodwill of the supplier to take them back.

In a small company you will probably be expected to contact the supplier yourself to explain the situation. In a large organisation you may again have to refer the matter to the purchasing office – perhaps in writing.

In both cases you will be expected to store the goods safely and carefully until they are collected.

SAFETY FIRST

If you are unpacking stationery then don't leave boxes where people can fall over them!

Consumables and security

You have already learned that storing items *carefully* saves money. So does storing them *safely* because this reduces the risk of loss – either by carelessness or through pilferage.

You may be surprised to think in terms of security for small items but, if you think about it, a box of twelve computer disks or ten audio cassette tapes is very desirable and can be used in many homes. They are also a lot easier to hide in a bag or coat than a laptop computer or a camcorder!

For that reason many organisations insist that

- All items are kept in lockable cupboards.
- There is limited access to stationery stock in general – and this, too, is kept under lock and key.
- There are limits on the number of items which can be issued at any one time.
- There are limits to the number of times the same item can be issued to one person.
- Orders for all goods have to be officially authorised and those for expensive items have to be counter-signed by a senior manager.

DID YOU KNOW?

Limiting the number of items also reduces wastage. If you are issued with twelve pens at once the chances are that you will lose most of them fairly quickly because you not give them much thought or value. If you can only order three at a time – and then have to explain where they have gone if you want some more quickly – you are less likely to be quite so careless or generous with them!

CHECK IT YOURSELF

Find out the security procedures which exist in your organisation in terms of

- storage of consumables and equipment
- ordering stationery stock
- issuing stock to staff.

UNIT REVIEW (3)

At the end of this element you should be able to

- identify the resources you need in your own job
- effectively obtain the resources you need to meet the requirements of your job
- store your resources safely and securely
- locate your resources to provide easy and quick access
- obtain resources in accordance with organisational procedures
- deal with damaged or unwanted goods in accordance with organisational procedures.

TEST YOUR KNOWLEDGE AND UNDERSTANDING

True or false?

1 Even if you make a mistake on an order form you can insist on returning the goods.
2 Many organisations insist on an official order number before they will supply any goods.
3 Heavy items should be stored low down in a cupboard.
4 Pilferage only occurs in relation to expensive items of equipment.
5 A ream of paper contains 500 sheets.

Fill in the blanks

6 Direct heat and anything magnetic will ruin a _____ _____ .
7 If you ordered a gross of pens you would receive _____ .
8 An internal order form is often called a _____ .

Work it out

9 Your supervisor has calculated that during the last three months your small office has gone through

22 pairs of scissors
10 hole punches
25 small staplers.

In addition an extra ten reams of photocopier paper have been used, although no additional copies have been registered on the photocopier counter.

a Using an office supplies catalogue calculate the total cost of this wastage/pilferage.

b Make a list of *six* things you would do if you were in charge of the office to prevent this happening in future.

10 You have just started in a new job as a clerical assistant in the accounts department. The company has just moved into your area and is setting up in a new office. You will have your own computer but will mainly do clerical accounts tasks. Look at the list of standard items of office equipment and consumables given below and make out a new list which divides the items into

a those which you would need immediately
b those you would need within the first month
c those you do not need to do your job.

address book
sellotape dispenser
anti-static screen wipes and other computer cleaning materials
audio tapes
batteries (for calculator)
box files
calendar
calculator
clipboard
correction fluid
desk top accessories
diary
dictionary
disks and disk box
felt tip pens
flipchart
glue
guillotine
hole punch
lever arch files
mouse mat
paper
paper clips
pencils/pens/sharpeners
printer ribbons or cartridge

scissors
shorthand notebook
shredder
staplers
telephone answering machine
waste bin

4 Create and maintain effective working relationships

This unit is all about people. When you are at work you will deal with a wide range of people, some of whom you may not normally want to see in your private life. However, at work you are paid to get on with people, of all ages and all types.

These people are all your colleagues. They may be senior to you, the same level as you or junior to you. You may have to work with them on an individual basis or co-operate with them as a member of a team. Whether you find them easy or difficult to deal with, it is up to you to do your best to develop and maintain a pleasant working relationship so that you can work productively together. The first element of this unit deals with your working relationships with other members of staff.

The second element is concerned with people who will visit your organisation. Everyone who comes into your workplace does so for a reason and it is up to you to do your best to meet your visitors' needs – whatever these may be. Even if you can't help someone personally you should certainly be able to put him or her in contact with a member of staff who *can* help. Some visitors will be pleasant and easy to deal with – others will be less so. In this unit you will find hints and tips on dealing with a wide variety of people.

You should bear in mind that this is another unit which cannot just be studied and forgotten! You will deal with people not only during your NVQ course but throughout your life. If you gain a reputation for being pleasant, co-operative and helpful then you will find that the majority of people you meet will automatically respond. The first step lies with you!

Element 4.1

Establish and maintain working relationships with other members of staff

People go to work for many reasons, not least to earn money! However, for many people, the **social** side of work is almost as important as the **monetary** side. Indeed, the main reason many people like to go out to work is because they are lonely and enjoy meeting and talking to other people every day. It can make all the difference to someone's enjoyment of their job if their colleagues are friendly, helpful, co-operative and fun to be with. On a good day there is a cheerful atmosphere in the office with everyone working together to do their best. On a bad day, people help each other out to enable those under the most pressure to cope. In times of personal crisis, colleagues at work can be understanding, comforting and tremendously supportive. When someone has something to celebrate, the 'office do' may be a day (or night) to remember!

There are therefore several benefits to having good working relationships with other members of staff.

- You can count on them when you have a problem.
- You will gain personal satisfaction from helping them.
- You will enjoy your work more.
- You (and they) will be more productive.

DID YOU KNOW?

The key aspects of your job that make you feel good work for other people too! *No-one,* regardless of their age or status, can work well and concentrate on their job if they are upset or in the middle of a disagreement with someone else.

Your own work role and responsibilities

Your job description states the *official* list of duties you must carry out, the responsibilities you have and the name of the person to whom you are responsible. It may also indicate your position in the work team.

Whilst it is important that you know and understand your own work role and responsibilities, you should also realise that there are many *unofficial* aspects of your job, too! For instance, if there is extra work to be done there are many responses you could make.

- Wait until you are asked then
  - refuse point blank
  - refuse politely
  - refuse by making an excuse.

- Wait until you are asked then
  - agree to do it but grudgingly
  - agree to do it then make a mess of it in the hope you won't be asked again
  - agree to do it willingly.

- Offer to help when you hear there is a problem.
- Identify that there may be a problem and offer your help if it is needed.

TEST YOURSELF

As a general rule, and assuming you aren't overloaded with work yourself, which would be your response the majority of the time?

Unofficial responsibilities

At work everyone is personally responsible for their own conduct, attitude, manner and the way they behave towards other people. When you apply for a job, your interviewer will be trying to assess you in these areas, and this is far more difficult that finding out if you have the necessary qualifications to do the job.

Many interviewers complete a rating form which compares candidates on such factors as

- appearance and grooming
- personality
- attitude
- communication skills
- ability to get on with other people.

The last point is very important. An interviewer may be quite prepared to give the job to the person who will fit in with existing staff – even if that person is not the most well qualified!

Appearance and grooming

Can you honestly say you

- *always* look your best
- are *always* 'nice to be near'
- would project the *right* company image?

Good grooming has nothing to do with natural beauty but *everything* to do with attractiveness! Do the quiz opposite and see how you score. Give yourself 1 point each time you choose 'sometimes', 2 points each time you choose 'always' and no points for 'never'!

Personality

An interviewer can judge your personality from whether you

- appear interested and enthusiastic
- look pleasant and smile
- are cheerful and friendly.

No-one wants to work with someone who is depressed and miserable all the time – although if you have a very lively and outgoing personality you will have to keep it under control at times!

Attitude

Basically this can be judged by

- how you react to people in authority
- how you cope with criticism and other points of view
- how you cope under stress

Good grooming quiz

Do you:	Always	Sometimes	Never
Have your hair trimmed regularly by a professional?			
Wash your hair at least twice a week?			
Change your underwear daily?			
Have a bath, shower or all-over wash daily?			
Always have clean, well-shaped nails?			
Use an anti-perspirant all the time?			
Wear lightly fragrant cologne or aftershave?			
Refuse to eat strongly flavoured food (curry, garlic etc.) when you are working?			
Always wear clean, well-pressed clothes?			
Always carry a clean handkerchief or supply of tissues?			
Clean your teeth after every meal?			
Eat sensibly and watch your weight?			
Visit your dentist twice a year?			
Clean your shoes when they need it?			
Have them repaired when they get down at heel?			
Score			

Check your score
- 25–30 = very good
- 21–25 = good
- less than 20 = do you deserve to be employed?

- whether you always think of yourself first (and second and last!)
- how hard you are prepared to work to get what you want
- how you respond to other people.

If you take a positive approach to life, try to fit in with and consider the needs of others and realise that when something goes wrong it is not necessarily anyone's fault, then you will have a mature and responsible attitude which will be noted by any employer.

CHECK IT YOURSELF

Look back at the two quizzes you did in Unit 1 to assess your personal skills and your strengths and weaknesses (pages 7 and 8). Review your scores and try to look at the result from the point of view of

- a prospective employer
- your colleagues.

Which areas do you consider need attention?

Communication skills

The three types of communication skills which are assessed by an interviewer are

- **written skills** (how well you completed the application form or your CV, how you worded your letter, the neatness of your writing)
- **verbal skills** (how well you expressed yourself, whether you could hold a conversation, your tone and manner, how you responded to unexpected questions)
- **non-verbal skills** or body language (your posture, whether or not you made eye contact, your gestures and facial expressions).

Our communication skills have a critical effect on how we are judged by other people. You must remember that your manner and attitude are conveyed to people by the way in which you speak to them *and* by your gestures and facial expressions.

CHECK IT YOURSELF

You are quite busy one morning with several routine tasks, none of which is very urgent. Mark, a colleague of yours, is overloaded and decides to ask you for help.

1. How would you respond to each of the following approaches?
2. Which 'Mark' would you most like to work with – and why?

a Mark swaggers towards your desk, leans on it casually, glances at what you are doing and then says, 'Why don't you drop that boring stuff for a bit and see if you're capable of helping me with some real work?'

b Mark approaches your desk slowly, looking miserable. When you ask him what is wrong he sighs then starts to moan about all the work he has to do. He looks at the floor all the time. It takes you five minutes to work out that he wants you to offer to help him.

c Mark walks towards your desk positively and smiles at you when you look up. He says, 'Sorry to disturb you, I can see you're busy, but is there any chance you can lend me a hand for ten minutes? I've an urgent job to complete and I'd really appreciate your help.'

Ability to get on with other people

At an interview this is likely to be assessed by

- references on your past behaviour or work profile
- how you get on with the interviewer!

You are unlikely to get on well with someone if you can't talk to them and every piece of information has to be dragged out of you. Try to strike a balance between being too shy to talk and too full of yourself! Try, if you can, to put the needs of the other person first and forget yourself.

Establishing constructive relationships

When you first start work in any job you may find that existing staff are wary of you initially and sometimes may appear quite cool or remote. Do remember, it takes time to build up a good working relationship with people and for trust to develop – you cannot rush this process by being over-friendly!

The best way to create a good impression from the outset is always

- to be courteous and tactful to everyone
- to treat people who are senior to you or older than you with respect
- to be helpful and pleasant
- to make allowances for people having 'a bad day' or personal problems which may affect their behaviour at work
- to communicate with people using the correct tone, words and body language.

Your first test will be when people start to relate to you on a more personal level. For instance

1 Your immediate colleagues try to find out more about you over a coffee or lunch break.
2 Someone has the job of showing you how to do something.
3 Someone decides to fill you in on the office gossip.
4 Someone asks to borrow something or asks for you to do something for them.
5 Something genuinely funny occurs or someone teases you – and everyone watches for your reaction.
6 Somebody is awkward or difficult with you – and everyone else watches to see how you react.
7 You have to work closely with other people on a particular job or project.
8 Someone has to rely on you for information or to do your part of a job before they can do theirs.

The best way to start to build up constructive working relationships with people is to use these situations as opportunities where you can prove that you are reliable, trustworthy, friendly and can work as a member of a team. You don't want to be thought of as someone who over-reacts, enjoys a drama or a crisis or – even worse – creates one.

Below are *eight* responses which would be suitable for coping with the situations given on page 116. Which one would you use in which case?

A Find out exactly what it is you have to do and the date by which it must be done. Keep an open mind about suggestions you receive for how to do the work – people nearly always mean well even if their style of working isn't yours.

B Don't pass on the information to anyone else. Appear uninterested or too busy to get involved, to discourage this type of thing happening too often.

C Be prepared to laugh with everyone else – even if you're not that amused yourself. If you are the brunt of the joke people will be embarrassed if you over-react. The chances are it will be someone else's turn next time!

D Make sure you understand what you have been told and thank them for their help. As a final check, ask if you can go back to them later if you need to.

E No-one is forcing you to give away all the most personal details of your life but, even if you are very shy, you will have to satisfy people's natural curiosity to some degree. We all relate to people more easily if we know enough about them to distinguish them as individuals.

F Never let anyone down who is depending upon you. If problems start to occur, make sure you warn them in plenty of time and see what they can suggest to help.

G Don't over-react by losing your temper, speaking your mind or bursting into tears. Say nothing, walk away and cool down and then ask someone for advice on how to deal with that person. The chances are people will be volunteering suggestions to you to try to help you, and doing all they can to help you feel better!

H If you are seen as generous and willing to help, people will usually respond in the same way with you. Do as you would be done by!

Ongoing working relationships

In the course of your work you will deal with other people every day of your life. Within your own organisation these people may be

- your own line manager(s)
- your immediate colleagues
- people you deal with on related work activities (e.g. if you regularly liaise with someone from another department).

Each of these people is an individual, with his or her own hopes, fears, style of communicating and style of working, problems and personal idiosyncrasies.

You will have to deal with them over a range of matters, including

- obtaining and exchanging information
- asking for their advice and support
- consulting them on new developments
- talking about problems which affect you
- making suggestions of your own.

It is unrealistic to think that there will never be any disagreements or conflicts between yourself and someone you work with. For that reason, you will need to learn to change both your actions and reactions in different situations. The approach which is suitable for one person on one day may be totally unsuitable on another! Therefore, to make life even more complicated, there are no fixed rules which will always apply at all times to help you! Having learned the ropes, you then need to learn how to adapt your style when necessary.

 ## DID YOU KNOW?

You may not always be able to choose the person, but you may be able to choose the place and time to approach someone! Asking for a half day off, or confessing that you have made a silly mistake, when your boss is frantically busy and is just rushing to answer the telephone is obviously unwise. Even if it means staying on a bit later that day to get the opportunity to see your boss when things are quiet, this is worthwhile if it helps the encounter to go more smoothly. In other words, pick your time carefully!

Obtaining and exchanging information

Information is at the heart of most business discussions ,whether these take place at a desk, over the telephone, a cup of coffee or over a meal. If you think about it, most of your communications are related to information in one way or another. Even if you are communicating your thoughts and feelings to someone, rather than facts, this is still information to them!

One of the biggest problems you can create for people is by telling them half the story, giving incorrect information or only telling people when it is too late. The worst fault, of course, is not giving any information at all! Equally, if you are obtaining information you need to make sure you understand it well enough to be able to act upon it and pass it on accurately to someone else.

Checklist for giving information

- Make sure you understand it yourself.
- Put it into a logical order.
- Don't use words or terms the other person won't understand.
- Be precise.
- Write down information which is long, complicated or will need to be referred to over time.
- Choose a time for giving verbal information when the other person can concentrate on what you are saying.

- Check that the person has understood the information correctly.
- If information is urgent, pass it on immediately.

DID YOU KNOW?

It is useless leaving an important message on someone's desk and trusting to luck that they will see it! Someone else might cover it up with another piece of paper, it may be blown away or on to the floor or only noticed when it is too late. If you leave a message for someone then you are also responsible for checking that they have received it!

Checklist for receiving information

- Listen carefully and don't interrupt.
- Make notes if necessary.
- Check any unfamiliar words or expressions
- Check your understanding by repeating the information back to the other person.
- Take the action that was agreed, don't suddenly do something unexpected or outside your own authority without telling anyone

DID YOU KNOW?

The tone and manner someone uses can easily distract you from the message. If someone is cold or unpleasant with you then you may find you are concentrating on this rather than on what they are saying. Equally, if you give orders rather than give information, people will feel resentful and annoyed. Do bear in mind that *how* you say something is just as important as *what* you say!

Basic facts to remember

- Ask, don't demand.
- Tell, don't dictate.
- Remember the power of 'please' and 'thank you'.
- Never be too big to say 'I'm sorry'.
- Speak to others as you would like them to speak to you!

Checklist for obtaining information

- Find out the best person to contact.
- Ask them in a pleasant but business-like tone.
- Thank them afterwards.
- Make notes so you won't forget what they said and have to ask them again!

DID YOU KNOW?

Some of the best opportunities for finding out information are those which occur by chance! Don't think that the only time you can obtain information is when you contact someone formally, by telephoning or meeting them. You can ask someone over coffee, in a corridor or even on the way to the bus stop or car park! This will save you time and you can often have a better and more informal discussion at such times.

SPECIAL NOTE

You may be involved in asking for information which is confidential – or having to pass this on to someone else. (*Confidential information is dealt with in Unit 3, page 98.*) However, it is worth bearing in mind that you will usually need written authorisation to obtain such information and you should never try to browbeat someone into giving it to you if you haven't! Don't take personal offence if the person you are asking wants to check that they should pass the information on to you. Equally, you must make sure that you only pass on information to people who should have it. If no-one is available to help you clarify the problem, it is better to refuse and check afterwards than to act first and think later! If you handle confidential information then review the points made on page 99.

Asking for advice and support

This is usually easier than asking for information, as many people like to be asked for their advice. The problems occur when you don't want to do what they advise and are worried they will take offence! You should bear this point in mind if you give advice yourself.

You need to be rather more careful when you ask for people's support, as they may be worried you are trying to compromise them. As an extreme example, if you were in serious trouble with your line manager, people may be too worried about their own jobs to rush to your assistance! The best you could perhaps hope for is that someone would put in a good word for you.

There are many different reasons why you may ask people to support you.

- You may want someone to put your point of view to your line manager.
- You may want your line manager to give you a reference if you are applying for promotion or another job.
- You may want to put a suggestion to your line manager and want support for your idea.
- You may work for charity and want people to support you in an attempt to raise money.
- You may have been given responsibility for a new task and need other people's support to make it work.

Equally one of your colleagues may ask you to support them in one way or another.

Checklist for asking for advice

- Don't ask someone who is having trouble coping themselves or who constantly annoys your boss!
- Ask someone who knows what they are talking about or who knows *you* very well.
- Don't word your request in such a way that you are then honour-bound to do what they say.
- Ask at a quiet time when you can discuss the issue properly.
- Listen and don't interrupt.
- Be honest (but diplomatic) about your reaction to their suggestions – if nothing else, tell them that you will think over what they have said (and do so!).
- Thank them for taking the time and trouble to help you.
- If their advice helps you later, tell them and thank them!

Checklist for giving advice

- Don't be tempted to give advice if you don't know what you are talking about!
- Be helpful, but remember that what works for you may not work for someone else.
- Don't commit someone else to doing something without their knowledge or prior consent.
- Remember that some people just want to talk if they have a problem – if you have proved to be a good listener, this may be the most helpful thing of all.

Checklist for asking for support

- Choose who you ask carefully.
- Don't expect people to give you support if you are being unreasonable, have extreme views or if what you are trying to do will cause problems for other people.
- Explain exactly what you want each person to do and what their future commitment will be.
- Be prepared for a refusal and act graciously.
- Don't keep asking people to support you – most people have problems and commitments of their own.
- Don't expect people to support you if you never support them!

Checklist for giving support

- Find out exactly what your involvement will be – and the implications.
- Don't be frightened of asking for time to think about it before you commit yourself.
- Judge each case on its own merits. This means that it is usually better to think about each request individually, rather than letting other people or events affect your views.

- Obtain advice yourself if you are worried about a commitment or supporting someone you don't know very well.
- Don't promise support and then withdraw it at the last minute.

DID YOU KNOW?

As a general rule, you should always support your colleagues if they are criticised by someone else, and your organisation if it is criticised by someone outside. There's another word for this – it's called loyalty!

New developments and proposals for change

If you have to give people information on new proposals – or consult them – you need to bear in mind that most people respond to new ideas by thinking about them from their own point of view! If you found out that you were moving offices your first thought would be for yourself and how you would be affected. Therefore everybody's reaction is likely to be different in one way or another.

There may be times when you think of a good idea yourself and think you have found a way of solving a problem or a better way of doing a job. On these occasions it will be *you* who is proposing that a change should occur. On the other hand, your line manager may have asked staff to contribute ideas – either individually or in a meeting. How you put your ideas across may be even more important than the ideas themselves!

Checklist for receiving proposals for change

- Treat any new suggestions with an open mind.
- Think carefully before you give an opinion.
- Ask questions if you are unsure about any details or any consequences or about how it will affect you.
- If an idea is adopted, do all you can to help it to work.

Checklist for proposing a change

- Bear in mind that *very few* suggestions for change are welcomed by everyone! If a suggestion or idea will have a negative effect on someone (e.g. extra work or less or more responsibility) then they are likely to be against it.
- The best way to 'sell' an idea is to think of the *benefits* for people (other than yourself!).
- Don't get so carried away with enthusiasm that you can't consider any flaws in your plans.
- Bear in mind that people may be resentful of a new recruit telling them how to do a job! Talk to your boss in private first – when he or she has time to listen.
- *Never* compare working practices which operate in your current organisation unfavourably with those in a company which

employed you previously. Everyone likes to think their ways are the best – no matter what they may say under stress!

DID YOU KNOW?

There is a huge difference between informing someone and consulting someone! Informing means telling. It implies that you are *stating facts*. Consulting means discussing. This implies that you are *asking* and are open to receiving comments and suggestions. (*Bear in mind what was said about teams in Unit 3, page 87.*) Usually, a group discussion or a consultation with your boss will *improve* your idea or proposals, because other people can make a contribution and suggest things you've never even thought of!

Consulting people about problems

If you *consult* someone about a problem, this implies that you are, to some degree, asking for their opinion. As you should have just noted, this is different from *telling* someone about a problem!

Problems can occur in two main areas – tasks and people.

Task-related problems

These include

- not being able to do a job in time to meet a deadline
- not being able to find some information someone wants
- not knowing how to do a job
- outside influences affecting a job so that it starts to go wrong.

People-related problems

These include

- people giving you conflicting advice or information
- people make unreasonable demands on you
- people treating you unreasonably or unfairly
- people withholding information you need to do your job properly
- people who are openly disagreeable or difficult to work with.

DID YOU KNOW?

Task-related problems are always easier to deal with than people-related problems. At least with a task you can define the limits of your problem, whereas with people you sometimes don't know where the problem started or where it will end!

Checklist for task-related problems

- Define the problem properly by looking at what should have happened and what is happening – and why there is a gap between the two.

- Tell people in plenty of time for action to be taken.
- Put your problem unemotionally and factually.
- If you are responsible for the problem – or part of it – then admit to this and apologise. Don't make silly excuses or put the blame on someone else.
- Consider carefully all suggestions for solving the problem and put into effect either those your boss insists on or those you think will work.
- If the situation doesn't improve or gets worse, see someone. Keeping it to yourself or hiding the evidence will only make things worse.

Checklist for people-related problems

- Start by trying to analyse your own part in this. To what extent could you be to blame?
- Think of the problem from the other person's point of view.
- Try to analyse why the other person is behaving in this way.
- Don't lobby for support all round the office – if you are having a problem with someone deal with this on a one-to-one basis.
- Ask to see the person privately. Try to put your case quite reasonably. Don't shout or become involved in an argument. Stick to the main issue and don't try to bring in other irrelevant arguments to support your case. Don't prejudge the outcome so that, for instance, you behave negatively yourself from the outset.
- If nothing improves, have a chat with your supervisor or line manager and ask for their advice.

DID YOU KNOW?

Even if someone's behaviour seems silly and irrational to you it will always seem perfectly reasonable to them. After all, if you think about it, *you* never deliberately act in a stupid or illogical way, and yet occasionally you may be seen to be so by other people – including your friends and relatives!

Varying your approach

It has already been said that an approach that is suitable on one occasion may be totally unsuitable on another. This is particularly true with people-related problems. No two situations are identical. Even if the people and the place are the same, the time and the situation will be different.

As a general rule think about

- the size of the problem and its importance
- the status and job titles of the people involved
- the personalities of the people involved
- whether there is a confidential or personal element in the situation

- relevant historical aspects to the situation (which may give you some guidance as to why people react as they do).

TEST YOURSELF

Preferably discuss this case study as a group. Decide what you would do and talk through your response with your supervisor or tutor.

Farzana and Julie both work in the administration office of a large organisation. Their line manager is John Briggs, the office co-ordinator, though they also do work for Peter Osgood, the assistant office manager. Both John and Peter report to Diana Howson, the office manager.

Farzana is seriously considering leaving her job because she is so overloaded with work. In her view Julie is very lazy and takes ages to do even the simplest of jobs. For that reason, both John and Peter keep giving Farzana all the work – because they know it will be done well and on time.

At a recent meeting Farzana openly challenged Peter about her workload in front of several staff, and refused to do an urgent job for him. He has been very annoyed with her ever since. When she tried to tackle John in private about all his work he just laughed and said she should be flattered. Farzana is rather frightened of Diana and doesn't want to approach her directly.

The problem came to a head yesterday when Farzana told Julie she was completely idle and they had a blazing row.

1 What is your view of Farzana's handling of the situation so far?
2 If you were Farzana, *now* what would you do?
3 What do you think Farzana should have done at the outset to try to solve the problem?
4 What difference do you think it would make if

    a she and Julie were close friends
    b Diana was more approachable
    c *either* Peter *or* John agreed with her
    d she and Julie shared *one* boss
    e Farzana had only just started work with the company
    f Julie had only just started work with the company?

Equal opportunities policies and legislation

Today most organisations operate equal opportunities policies. This is shown by statements on matters such as recruitment and promotion which say

> *This organisation will not discriminate against anyone on the grounds of race, sex, age, creed, colour, religion, nationality or disability.*

The main Acts which relate to equal opportunities

- **The Sex Discrimination Act 1975** (as amended by **the Sex Discrimination Act 1980**) forbids discrimination in areas such

as employment. It also specifically forbids discrimination against married women. Amongst other things it covers
- selection for jobs
- promotion
- job training
- dismissal
- fringe benefits.

● **The Disabled Persons (Employment) Acts 1944/58** place a statutory duty on all employers with 20 or more full-time workers to employ a quota of registered disabled people based on a percentage of the total workforce.

In addition, the **Companies (Directors' Report) Employment of Disabled Persons Regulations 1980** require that every annual company report to which the regulations apply should contain a statement outlining what the company has done to give fair consideration to applications for employment by disabled persons and to arrange for appropriate training for them.

● **The Equal Pay Act 1979**, amended by the **Equal Pay (Amendment) Regulations 1983** provides for equal pay for men and women if they are employed on the same work or their work is regarded as being of 'equal value'.

● **The Race Relations Act 1976** specifically forbids discrimination on grounds of 'colour, race, nationality or ethnic or racial origin'.

DID YOU KNOW?

The **Equal Opportunities Commission** (EOC) checks that the Sex Discrimination and Equal Pay Acts are working. The **Commission for Racial Equality** (CRE) does the same in respect of the Race Relations Act.

Equal opportunities and discrimination

Both the Sex Discrimination Act and the Race Relations Act identify two different types of discrimination which are

● **direct discrimination** – e.g. if someone says, 'I'd never employ a woman in that job.'

● **indirect discrimination** – where it is more difficult for one sector of the community to meet the requirements, e.g. a job advertisement which required people to work topless in summer would presumably reduce the number of female applicants!

As an employee you should not only be aware of equal opportunities legislation, and your *own* rights in this area, but how your actions affect other people. You may not be personally responsible for recruiting staff for some time yet, but you have to work with a wide range of people who may be of different ethnic origins. Some of your colleagues may be disabled. It is both unfair and unjust to make judgements about people just because they belong to 'a group'. They should always be treated as individuals. Most disabled people are so well adjusted they don't even *think* about their disability! And no-one *likes* being treated as unusual or an oddity.

Your responsibility is to treat everyone as normal, thinking, intelligent and caring human beings no matter where they come from, what sex they are or whether they have a particular difficulty they are trying to overcome. Never feel superior or inferior to anyone else. In terms of simple humanity, this also means treating the cleaner and the tea-lady with the same *personal* respect you show the managing director!

DID YOU KNOW?

Sexual or racial harassment is against the law and both the harasser and the organisation could be held liable if nothing is done.

If you think you are a victim, look at the chart below for advice.

Equal opportunities information chart

You are being **sexually harassed** if someone

- touches you unnecessarily, repeatedly or intimately
- makes sexual comments or innuendos about your appearance or actions
- plays jokes or pranks on you which are offensive
- shows you (or circulates) sexually offensive or explicit photographs or documents
- asks you for sexual favours
- threatens you (e.g. with dismissal or a lower grade job) if you do not comply.

You are being **racially harassed** if someone

- mocks you or tells racist jokes
- uses abusive language with a racial content
- calls you a racist name
- shows you (or circulates) racially offensive material
- persistently questions you about your private life, culture, ethnic origin or religion
- gives you more work than the rest of the staff or more menial jobs
- unreasonably excludes you from normal conversation or events.

What to do

If you are being sexually or racially harassed, tell the person concerned that you find their attitude unacceptable and that they must stop this behaviour. If this has no effect then report the matter to your supervisor immediately and in confidence. If, for some reason, you cannot confide in your supervisor then see another senior person *or* a trusted colleague who has worked for the company for some time.

But

Never bring such a complaint falsely or maliciously or disciplinary action is likely to be taken against you.

UNIT REVIEW (1)

At the end of this element you should be able to

- identify and take appropriate opportunities to discuss work-related matters with the relevant members of staff
- pass on essential information to appropriate staff promptly and accurately
- maintain effective working relationships both with individuals and teams
- meet your commitments to other people within agreed time scales
- ensure that your methods of communication and support are suited to the needs of other members of staff.

CHECK YOUR KNOWLEDGE AND UNDERSTANDING

True or false?

1 The same style of approach should be used in all situations.
2 One method of establishing constructive working relationships is to tell your colleagues all about your personal life.
3 Everyone responds better if they are asked to do something, rather than being told to do it.
4 Telling half the story is almost as bad as not giving any information at all.
5 It is always better to choose a time when a person is free to listen to what you are saying.

Fill in the blanks

6 The official duties you have to undertake are stated in your _____ _____ .
7 The _____ _____ _____ forbids discrimination on the grounds of 'colour, race, nationality or ethnic or racial origin'.
8 If a person refused to employ any women in an organisation this would be an example of _____ discrimination under the _____ _____ Act.

Work it out

9 As part of your job you are responsible for maintaining personnel records in your organisation. You have recently found out that a junior member of staff in the sales department is having extended leave as she is pregnant. She is not married and it has been agreed that she needs time to decide what to do.

Yesterday, the sales administrator – who is junior to the sales manager – came in and insisted on knowing what was going on in the department. Apparently she had not been told anything about the situation and she asked you for full details. Because she has worked in the company for many years, and is senior to you, you gave her the information but now regret this.

  a What – if anything – would you do to clear yourself with your own boss, the personnel manager?
  b What *should* you have done to deal with the sales administrator?
  c Can you think of any action the management at your organisation should take to ensure the problem does not occur in future?

10 Identify one person in your life (preferably at work) with whom you find it difficult to talk or negotiate.

  a Briefly describe one incident where you feel his or her behaviour was unacceptable and you struggled to cope.
  b Try to work out *why* the other person reacted as he or she did. Don't forget to take any historical information you may have into consideration.
  c Identify an alternative style of approach you could use to cope with this person and discuss this with your supervisor or tutor.
  d If possible, try this style and analyse whether or not there is or was a difference in the response.

Element 4.2

Receive and assist visitors

Everyone who works in a business organisation has to deal with visitors. The number of visitors you meet each day, the reason for their visit and the type of needs they have will depend on your own job and the type of work carried out by your company.

- **Internal visitors** are people who call into your office but who work elsewhere in the organisation – perhaps in another department or at a branch office or even in an overseas office.
- **External visitor**s may be customers or clients, sales representatives, business associates, delivery or maintenance people or friends and relatives of the staff.

Some visitors will be expected. They will have made an appointment beforehand and the reason for their visit will be known. Indeed, the details of their visit may have been worked out very carefully beforehand. This is usually the case with important visitors who are being seen by senior management.

Other visitors will not be expected. This is often the case with internal visitors from another department or other people who call in 'because they were passing'.

Organisations which have a considerable number of visitors each day usually have a special reception desk which is the 'front office' of the company. Clear signs should lead all visitors to reception, where the staff are trained to help people promptly and efficiently. Many companies spend a considerable amount of money decorating and furnishing this area so that visitors gain the impression that meeting the needs of callers and looking after them is considered very important by the company.

Other organisations have a special customer service desk to deal with enquiries. This is often the case with retail organisations which have dozens of customers to help every working day.

DID YOU KNOW?

We are all extremely influenced by our first impression of a person or organisation. If the first time you visit a company you are virtually ignored, or made to feel a nuisance, you will dislike the idea of returning to repeat the experience.

Think how you feel in a shop, if two assistants are talking to each other and looking through you as if you are invisible!

The needs of a visitor

All visitors have one thing in common, regardless of the nature of their visit. They want to make contact, as quickly as possible, with someone who can help them. Nothing is more irritating than being passed from one person to another without making any progress with an enquiry.

- Many people will just want information – on the company, its products, services or personnel.
- Others need to make contact with a specific person or department.
- Some require immediate assistance – such as the delivery man who has parked on double yellow lines!
- Others have specific needs, but don't know who they should speak to. They may want to
    - place an order or enquire about the progress of an order
    - clarify or query details they have been given already
    - query their account
    - find out if there are any job vacancies
    - complain about a product or service they have received.

There are usually organisational procedures to ensure that routine requests from visitors can be dealt with quickly and easily. Complex requests and problems can often only be dealt with on an individual basis. Finding out *who* can deal with the matter is often the hardest part. An efficient company will have a clear organisation structure so that job roles are designated and people dealing with difficult queries are not put in the position of having to ring round five offices, in front of a client, to find someone to help!

DID YOU KNOW?

Although having a good knowledge of your organisation obviously helps you to deal with visitors more efficiently, you can *still* create a good impression even if you can't help someone personally. If you greet them professionally and find out who can help quickly, you will have dealt with them efficiently. Never be worried about asking for assistance if you don't know what to do. This is far better than annoying someone by trying to cope alone.

Creating a good impression

Whether it is your job or not, you should *never* walk past any visitor who isn't being attended to without offering to help. The same goes for visitors to your office. It is not courteous simply to go on working and ignore them just because you are busy.

It can be a nuisance if you have to keep stopping work because of interruptions, but if you give a bad impression to customers – and they go elsewhere to do business – you soon won't have any work to do!

Regular visitors will expect the people they deal with to know them by name. *Everyone* likes the personal approach because it makes them feel important. You should therefore make every effort to learn and remember the names of people you see often.

The exact procedure which is followed when visitors arrive sometimes varies, depending upon the policy of the organisation. However, the following chart should give you guidance on the action to take to create a good impression – of both yourself and your company.

The professional approach

What do you need to know before you can help someone more specifically? To be able to identify what visitors really want and need and to be able to match these to the appropriate products, services or personnel in your organisation then ideally you should know

- **your company organisation structure** – the size of your company and how it is organised, its branches, departments and location, the personnel employed and who does what, the quickest way to contact people
- **your company policies and procedures** – the main methods of communication between and among staff, policies on the community, the environment, after-sales service, dealing with complaints, giving refunds, giving donations to charity

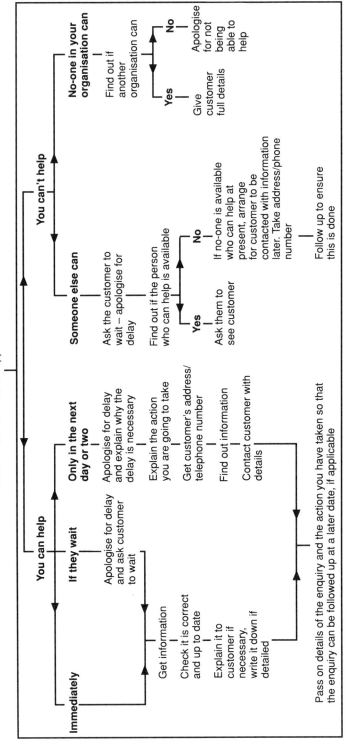

DEALING WITH VISITORS

★ Greet the visitor STRAIGHT AWAY
★ Greet the visitor POLITELY – make him or her feel welcome
★ Find out the visitor's name (and company, if applicable)
★ Find out if he or she has an appointment

You can help

Immediately

Get information

Check it is correct and up to date

Explain it to customer if necessary, write it down if detailed

If they wait

Apologise for delay and ask customer to wait

Only in the next day or two

Apologise for delay and explain why the delay is necessary

Explain the action you are going to take

Get customer's address/telephone number

Find out information

Contact customer with details

You can't help

Someone else can

Ask the customer to wait – apologise for delay

Find out if the person who can help is available

Yes

Ask them to see customer

No

If no-one is available who can help at present, arrange for customer to be contacted with information later. Take address/phone number

Follow up to ensure this is done

No-one in your organisation can

Find out if another organisation can

Yes

Give customer full details

No

Apologise for not being able to help

Pass on details of the enquiry and the action you have taken so that the enquiry can be followed up at a later date, if applicable

- **the products/services offered** – not just a broad appreciation but details of what can and can't be offered. The expertise you can gain in this area will depend very much on the type of company you work for.
  - In a retail or mail-order organisation you would probably be expected to have a good knowledge of the stock range yourself.
  - In a service industry (e.g. a bank, travel agent or insurance company) you should know the range of services offered and who to contact for further more detailed information.
  - In a manufacturing company the technical details of some products may only be known by trained sales or technical staff. In this case you *must* know the right person to contact to pass on enquiries.

  In most companies there is a whole range of leaflets and literature to promote either the organisation itself or its products or services. You can only talk about what is offered knowledgeably if you have studied the brochures yourself first!

- **the personnel employed by your organisation** – this means keeping up to date! Existing staff may leave, be transferred, promoted or take on different responsibilities. New staff may be appointed in existing or new job roles. The more you know about what people do, the more accurately you can refer difficult enquiries to the correct person.
- **regular customers and visitors** – why they call, who they see, what they buy and sell.

CHECK IT YOURSELF

Whether you are working or at college on a full-time course, you can try this exercise for yourself.

1 Obtain a copy of your company or departmental organisation chart.
2 List *five* reasons why visitors may call. Try to think of *at least two* reasons which would involve a complex enquiry.
3 From the organisation chart, identify the person you would contact to help you meet the needs of each of the visitors.
4 Check your answers with your supervisor or tutor.

Customer services

The role of customer services is to deal with general enquiries (and complaints) quickly and efficiently. In some organisations this role is carried out by the sales or marketing department. This is especially the case in a company which primarily deals with other industrial organisations.

Customer service or sales staff are usually trained to know

- where to get additional information on specialist requirements
- details of goods which are out of stock or discontinued
- the different payment methods available to customers and the law relating to credit and hire purchase
- the legal implications of describing, recommending and selling goods and services
- the procedure for following up customer enquiries and orders
- company policy in relation to faulty or returned goods.

DID YOU KNOW?

In some organisations **customer service** has a wider meaning and relates to total staff response to enquiries and when dealing with people. Such a company may set standard times within which telephone calls and letters must be answered ,and all organisational information and literature will be professionally produced and of a certain design.

CHECK IT YOURSELF

Look around your own district or town for examples of customer service designed to increase sales and customer satisfaction. Typical examples are fast food outlets which offer free meals if food is not produced on time, free delivery services and no-quibble refunds on returned goods.

If you are working, investigate the customer services offered by your organisation and the way in which these operate.

Promoting your organisation

You can promote your organisation to visitors in several ways e.g.

- by *knowing* the full range of products or services and being able to describe them accurately
- by *identifying* which product or service is most appropriate for a visitor's needs
- by *assuring* people that their needs will be met promptly and efficiently
- by *explaining* to people how a query will be dealt with and who will be responsible for contacting them.

Bear in mind that it is pointless your organisation spending thousands of pounds on marketing and advertising if you describe something wrongly or – even worse – tell someone that it isn't available when it is!

TEST YOURSELF

Visit a local bank and obtain a leaflet or brochure explaining one of the services offered.

- Note the main features.
- Ask your supervisor or tutor to clarify any points which you do not understand.
- Think about any questions people may ask.
- Pretend you work for the bank and practise explaining the service clearly and accurately to a friend or colleague.

Working in the front line

Sales and customer services staff work 'in the front line'. Their image is particularly important as they are representing their organisation to the outside world. What they say and do can directly influence the volume of business carried out.

Anyone who works on reception also has this role. This doesn't just apply to the main receptionist(s) but to anyone who ever helps out in this capacity. For that reason, staff who are dealing with visitors are usually expected to have the following attributes

- excellent communication skills
- the ability to get on with a wide range of people
- good social skills
- be well groomed
- good organisational skills
- the ability to stay calm under pressure.

TEST YOURSELF

Your organisation is advertising for a new receptionist. Your supervisor has listed the qualities she considers essential.

1 Why do you think *each* of these is important?
2 Can you identify *at least one* occasion when each would be needed?

patience	discretion	accuracy
tact	versatility	loyalty
thoughtfulness	initiative	a good memory
a good listener	dependability	neatness

The reception area

This is usually well decorated, with comfortable chairs provided for visitors, possible some low tables and reading material which may include general magazines, newspapers or technical journals. Some organisations also include their advertising leaflets and may have a product display nearby.

The reception desk usually has shelves and a generous working area *below* the height of the desk, so that papers and files are screened from view.

However, the whole image of the company is ruined if the area is dirty or untidy. If you work in reception then part of your job will be to make sure that

- personal articles are kept out of sight
- dirty cups are removed promptly and clean ashtrays are provided (if smoking is allowed)
- any stocks of magazines are tidy and the supply is kept up to date
- all record books and documents are kept neatly filed
- any flowers or plants in the area are kept watered.

DID YOU KNOW?

Organisations which have children as 'visitors' often provide 'distracters' such as a box of toys. It is usually better to do this – even though they may need tidying up regularly – than to have small children running around or tearing up magazines because they are bored!

CHECK IT YOURSELF

Find out the standard procedures which are in operation in the reception area or 'front desk' of your own organisation. In particular, find out how many people comprise the reception team and what happens when they hand over to a colleague while they have a break.

Reception activities

Many receptionists also have the job of switchboard operator – in which case there is usually a glass window which can screen them from visitors when they are dealing with telephone enquiries.

In most organisations, the activities carried out in reception include

- greeting visitors
- making introductions
- talking to visitors and other callers
- making and receiving telephone calls
- contacting staff on internal communication systems
- taking messages
- routing visitors to other parts of the organisation, which may involve directing visitors or arranging for them to be escorted to another part of the building
- following standard security procedures
- keeping visitors' records
- maintaining the reception area so that it is always neat and tidy
- maintaining general sources of information used in reception.

TEST YOURSELF

List all the activities above which fall into the broad area of 'communications'. Check your list with the ones on page 139.

Reception, security and confidentiality

Visitors and security are covered in Unit 2, page 61.

Reception staff must not only be aware of – and follow – organisational procedures in relation to security but must also ensure that

- the reception area is never left unattended
- money and confidential documents are never brought into the area
- any unattended bags or cases are reported to security
- confidential information (or office gossip!) is never discussed in reception or given to visitors.
- maintenance workers wanting access to other parts of the building or calling to collect equipment are always asked for identification
- visitors are never normally left unattended or left to wander from one department to another. If visitors need to be routed to another department it is always preferable if they are escorted around the building, not just for security reasons but so that they won't get lost!

However, in some small companies or if a visitor is very well known, it may be permissible to give directions and let them find their own way.

SPECIAL NOTE

Bear in mind that you may be asked to give a visitor directions to another office or another part of the town. If you are giving directions to a driver, always try to include information about one-way systems and which traffic lane to use. It will be much appreciated!

Escorting visitors

- Walk at a reasonable pace (bearing in mind the age and fitness of the visitor).
- Use the most direct route.
- Answer general questions or make general conversation rather than walk on in total silence.
- Give warning of hazards such as steps, swing doors and congested areas.
- Show courtesy by opening doors.
- Introduce the visitor on arrival.
- If no-one is in the office when you arrive then don't leave the visitor alone – either wait with them or find someone else to help.

Giving directions

- Be specific and clear. Refer to buildings and company signs the visitor can see.
- Make sure you know your right from your left!
- If the route is long, make a quick sketch or write down the directions as a list of points.
- Give approximate distances to help and useful landmarks to spot on the way.

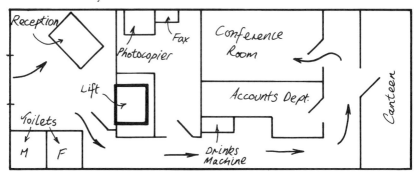

An example of a quick sketch to aid visitor.

TEST YOURSELF

Work out the clearest directions you can for

- someone arriving at your organisation and visiting someone at the opposite end of the building.
- someone *walking* from the railway station to a main hotel in the town
- someone *driving* from your organisation to a hotel on the edge of town.

DID YOU KNOW?

Most organisations have a standard pack which includes a map of the area and highlights the location of the company in relation to main roads in the area. If the company has its own car park this is usually shown. Otherwise, public parking in the area is listed.

Communication skills

It is not usual to employ a receptionist who is very shy or who finds it difficult to deal with people. Equally, it is not usual to employ anyone in an organisation who does not have some basic social and communication skills and cannot be polite and courteous to strangers. Visitors are immediately put off by a member of staff who is chewing, sniffing or scratching themselves as they speak!

When you meet with a visitor you give an impression, both of yourself, and of your organisation For the visitor you *are* the organisation.

Verbal communication skills

To be able to communicate with visitors effectively you need

- a clear speaking voice
- to speak at the right speed (too slowly and you will bore people, too fast and they may not follow what you are saying)
- good listening skills
- a good vocabulary – so that you can use the right word or expression to say what you mean (without resorting to slang!)
- the ability to put people at their ease
- the confidence to talk to strangers
- the ability to ask questions to check your understanding and/or prompt a shy or hesitant visitor.

Bear in mind that you may often be expected to take messages or pass on messages to other people. You must be able to do this clearly and unambiguously and include *all* the important points of the message in a logical order.

Written communication skills

A good written message should

- be neatly written so that anyone can read it
- contain simple, straightforward words – with no jargon or slang expressions
- include all the key facts in a logical order
- be specific about dates, days, times and figures.

TEST YOURSELF

You work for an insurance company. A customer has called in to see Mr Sharples, the office manager, unexpectedly. She refuses to see anyone else and decides to leave a message. She is rather vague – you get the idea that someone should have called her son last week with an insurance quotation. List the questions you could ask to find out more about her problem.

DID YOU KNOW?

If you fire questions at people, don't be surprised if you don't get much of an answer! Often you have to ask questions in a more gentle way and more slowly. When you think you have found out the main facts, read them back to the visitor to check you haven't misunderstood at any stage.

Methods of communication

The methods of communication which are available to you to assist a visitor quickly will vary, depending on the type of equipment available in your office or reception area. The most basic and useful piece of equipment is the telephone. If you need information from another office or member of staff, the most usual method is to phone them on their internal extension. This is also the most common method of announcing that an expected visitor has arrived and is waiting in reception.

Remember that if you can be overheard on the telephone you need to be careful what you say – and how you respond to the comments made by the person on the other end! Even if the colleague you are contacting makes a witty remark you are well advised not to laugh or joke with them over the phone – the waiting visitor could easily take offence if he or she takes your response personally!

Many modern telephones have a **loudspeaker** or **tannoy** system which will enable you to give an announcement to other telephone users if the person you are trying to contact is not immediately available. In some organisations (think of a railway station) a public announcement can be given. This is often the case in companies where members of staff may often be in different parts of the building, e.g. in a warehouse or production. It is usual to repeat an announcement *twice* (people only start to listen halfway through) and ask the person you need to contact you by telephone as quickly as possible.

In other organisations **pagers** or **radio telephones** are provided. Some pagers give out a bleep or can be set to vibrate. This is useful if the pager holder is in a meeting and wouldn't want to disturb other people. Others give a message on a small screen. The usual message is to ask the pager holder to contact you by telephone immediately (give your extension number). Bleeper holders normally know they need to contact the switchboard if their bleeper sounds.

Radio telephones are an alternative for people who walk around the building, such as security staff. You may be able to contact a radio telephone holder yourself, by dialling a special code into your telephone, or you may have to ask your company switchboard operator to do this for you.

Telecommunication equipment is dealt with in more detail in Unit 8.

 ## DID YOU KNOW?

If you speak to someone on a radio telephone it is usual to use the word 'over' at the end of your part of the conversation. Otherwise you both end up speaking simultaneously!

Support for visitors

The type of help and support you give to visitors will depend on

- the reason for their visit
- how far they have travelled
- how long they have to wait
- how long they are visiting your company
- any special requirements they have.

It is quite normal for waiting visitors to be offered a cup of tea or coffee in many organisations – though today some companies have installed vending machines and dispensed with the idea of staff actually making the drinks. Other types of support could include

- finding somewhere to store bags and cases
- giving information on local facilities and amenities
- giving special assistance to the physically handicapped or disabled
- providing visitors with maps, literature or brochures they can keep
- photocopying a document for a visitor which he or she needs to keep
- allowing them to send a fax, use your telephone or send a letter through your company mail system
- arranging transport for them.

 TEST YOURSELF

Your organisation is entertaining three important visitors from an Australian client company this week.

1 List *six* different types of support they may request. (Use the list above to help you.)
2 One of the visitors asks if you know of anywhere locally he can have his clothes cleaned. He needs an 'express' service as they leave in two days. Can you help?
3 What type of transport would you recommend they use if they wanted to do some sight-seeing on their last day?
4 If one of the visitors is blind, what additional types of support could you offer to help him on a day-to-day basis?

Difficulties in providing support

Difficulties can arise if

- you do not have the information to deal with an enquiry
- you are not certain whether it is company policy to agree to a course of action or not (e.g. making photocopies for visitors)
- you are asked to do something you *know* is not allowed (e.g. leave your desk and personally take someone to the railway station)
- a visitor is persistent and won't take 'no' for an answer
- you cannot understand what a visitor is saying or what they want
- you have asked someone to rescue you but they never arrive!

The important point is to be able to identify and acknowledge that you have a problem – and not pretend you haven't! In any of these cases you *must* contact someone in authority for assistance or advice. Watch carefully and see how they handle the situation. This may help you to cope in the future!

TEST YOURSELF

Discuss with your supervisor or tutor how you would cope with each of the following

    a initially
    b if your initial course of action didn't work.

1 A sales representative calls in and refuses to leave until the purchasing manager has seen him. The purchasing manager is out all day and no-one else in the department wants to know.

2 A visitor who has travelled some distance in bad weather asks you to find out details of what the roads will be like that evening.

3 A traffic warden informs you that the car parked outside your building is on a yellow line and the driver will be booked if it isn't moved immediately. The driver is an important visitor who is at present in a meeting with the managing director.

4 A visitor arrives in reception obviously distressed and tearful. You know she will have to wait at least five minutes to see the person she wants.

5 A visitor has been waiting to see the sales manager for 20 minutes. You have rung through to his office twice – once to tell him the visitor had arrived and the second time to remind him the visitor was still waiting. The visitor is now getting extremely impatient.

6 Two elderly visitors arrive in the middle of a cloudburst. They are soaking wet and shivering violently.

Dealing with awkward or aggressive visitors

Callers can be considered **awkward** if they don't react as you think (or hope) they will. If they are unreasonable or difficult, no matter how polite and reasonable you are, then they can be very difficult to deal with.

Aggression can be even worse to cope with. At best it is annoying, at worst upsetting or distressing. Many organisations have standard procedures which you must follow if things get difficult. These usually involve seeking help before the situation gets out of control.

A list of 'difficult' visitors is given below. The hints and tips should help you cope in most cases. However, if you ever feel frightened or threatened, get help immediately.

The chatterbox

Don't get involved in a long conversation! Be pleasant but obviously busy. Don't be abrupt or rude, just excuse yourself and carry on working.

The shy or nervous visitor

Don't become impatient or try to rush them. Don't finish off sentences for them! Speak gently, calmly and deliberately to give them the chance to absorb the information you are giving them.

The angry or aggressive visitor

Stay calm and don't interrupt whilst they tell you their problem. Be sympathetic *without* accepting the blame on behalf of your company or any of your colleagues. Be as patient, reasonable and helpful as possible. Write down the details if necessary and assure the visitor you will follow up their problem.

The flirt

Don't react – stay professional, unflustered and business-like. *Don't* let someone use flattery as a way of getting you to divulge confidential information!

Persistent visitors without an appointment

Find out your company policy for dealing with them. Often they are reps trying to sell their products. Tell them to write or ring the company next time, before calling, to make an official appointment.

The visitor who arrives at the wrong time

If they arrive too early or too late (or even on the wrong day!) see if someone can see them then rather than reschedule the appointment. If there is a long wait try to make the visitor comfortable and offer him or her a drink and something to read.

The VIP/pompous visitor/visitor in a hurry

Don't be overawed or misled into ignoring the needs of *other* visitors! If you greet all visitors in a friendly and welcoming way, deal with them promptly and efficiently and try to meet their individual needs, it won't make any difference who they are, will it?

Visitors and equal opportunities

You may dread the idea of dealing with foreign visitors who do not speak English very well or visitors with particular handicaps.

Foreign visitors

Bear in mind they may feel even more apprehensive than you do!

The following tips may help

- Listen carefully.
- Speak relatively slowly and use simple English words.
- Use short sentences.
- Repeat carefully what you think is meant to check you are right.

- Don't shout, be embarrassed, laugh or show impatience (try to imagine how you would feel in a foreign country where you don't speak the language).
- Don't be frightened to ask for help

Visitors with a handicap

Deaf people Remember, you can't tell that someone is deaf by looking at them! If someone is slightly deaf they can usually cope very well if you look at them when you speak, as this helps them to lip-read. If a person is profoundly deaf then they will gesture this fact to you and will probably signal you to write down what you want to say.

The blind Not all blind people carry white sticks. In many cases you have no way of immediately identifying someone who has a visual handicap. If you think someone cannot see very well or is blind then speak to them to enable your voice to guide them to you. *Don't* suddenly grab hold of them or drag them to a chair. If they ask you for help then lead them *gently* and give them verbal information at the same time. For instance, if you are leading a blind person towards some steps it is helpful to say how many there are and whether they go up or go down!

Other disabilities If people have difficulty walking, use crutches or are in a wheelchair then they will obviously find access to a building easier if there is a ramp, rather than steps. Be ready to hold open doors to help them. *Don't* try to rush them or appear impatient. Try to forget the disability altogether and concentrate on the person.

SPECIAL NOTE

It is surprising how many people are very keen to help all types of people and would be quite shocked if they were told that they discriminate against certain types of visitors – and yet they do. They are far more quick to react to visitors who look or sound important – and give them precedence over those who do not. Quite obviously, all companies give VIPs and very important customers special attention but beyond that it is not up to you to 'pick and choose' which visitors you think you should impress and give the rest second-rate treatment!

DID YOU KNOW?

Many people are misled by appearance and prejudge people wrongly. The story goes that in America a shabbily dressed man entered reception and asked to see one of the directors. The receptionist was patronising and unhelpful. It turned out to be the president of the company who had been gardening on his day off!

Visitors' records

The appointments book

Organisations and firms which regularly have visitors calling 'by appointment' will usually have an appointments book (think of your doctor or dentist). In this book all **expected visitors** are listed, in time order. In many companies other details are recorded, such as the name of the person the visitor will meet. There may be a comments column for making special notes. A page from an appointments book is shown below.

APPOINTMENTS BOOK				
DATE				
TIME OF APPOINTMENT	NAME	COMPANY	TO SEE	COMMENTS

TEST YOURSELF

What electronic alternative is there to an appointments book? (*If you can't remember, look back to Unit 3, page 86.*)

The visitors' book

This records *all* visitors, whether they are expected or not. It is only completed when a visitor actually arrives on the premises. It may therefore be kept by reception *or* by security staff at the main entrance. It usually shows both the time of arrival *and* the time of departure of all visitors. An example of a visitors' book is shown below.

VISITORS' BOOK					
DATE					
NAME	COMPANY	CAR REG. NUM.	PERSON TO SEE	TIME OF ARRIVAL	TIME OF DEPARTURE

Information from business visitors is often taken from a business card. Obtain *five* different examples of business cards and identify the type of information they contain. See if you can get *at least one* from a foreign visitor – sometimes the layout and information is quite different!

Visitors and Health and Safety

Bear in the mind that the Health and Safety at Work Act relates to visitors as well as employees! Visitors may be *more* likely to have accidents than employees because they are unfamiliar with the area. For this reason, special fittings are often included in public areas such as reception to prevent accidents. These include

- specially treated or covered floors so that people do not slip, even if the floor is wet
- specially toughened glass doors and windows or criss-crossed black wires in glass doors so that people do not walk into them by mistake
- swing doors marked *push* or *pull* and clear signs to show emergency exits.

Obviously there should be no trailing wires or cables for people to fall over and furniture should be positioned safely, e.g. well away from swing doors.

If any large items are brought into reception, e.g. bags, cases or special parcels, they should be moved as quickly as possible. Delivery drivers with large quantities of goods should be directed to goods inwards or the specific department which ordered the goods. It is not usual practice to have large deliveries cluttering up the reception area, for appearance as well as safety reasons.

Dealing with emergencies

Emergencies can occur for a variety of reasons, e.g.

- a visitor is taken ill in the reception area
- the building has to be evacuated quickly – none of the visitors knows the emergency procedures and one of the visitors is on the third floor in a wheelchair
- a member of staff with several appointments for that day is called away unexpectedly
- a lift full of visitors jams between floors
- a visitor has his car stolen from the car park
- a visitor starts to threaten a member of the reception staff
- the receptionist's relief is off sick and there is no-one else available to cover

- the appointment book is missing and no-one knows who is due that day
- an urgent message has been received for a visitor who arrived half an hour ago and is no longer with the person originally seen.

In some cases there will be specific organisational procedures for dealing with emergencies, especially if these are concerned with security or health and safety. In other cases it may be up to one of the members of staff, or the receptionist, to use his or her own initiative to deal with the situation.

TEST YOURSELF

Discuss with your supervisor or tutor the *type* of organisational procedures which could cover some of the problems above. In all cases, state what action you think should be taken by the member of staff concerned or the receptionist.

UNIT REVIEW (2)

At the end of this element you should be able to

- greet visitors promptly and courteously
- identify the nature of the visit and the needs of visitors and match these to the appropriate products, personnel or services of your organisation
- describe basic reception procedures and how to direct visitors in accordance with established procedures
- accurately describe and promote the structure, products or services of the organisation
- use methods of communication and types of support which are suited to the needs of particular visitors
- acknowledge when there are communication difficulties and seek appropriate help
- keep complete, legible and accurate records of visitors
- follow established procedures to deal with awkward, aggressive or difficult visitors.

CHECK YOUR KNOWLEDGE AND UNDERSTANDING

True or false?

1 An appointments book is used to record only visitors who are expected by the organisation.
2 You should always speak loudly to someone who is deaf.
3 It is important to note both the arrival and the departure time of visitors.
4 A person who calls unexpectedly cannot expect to receive much help.
5 Unless you have detailed knowledge about the products or services supplied by your company it is impossible to help a customer.

Fill in the blanks

6 Maintenance engineers who are being routed to another part of the building should always be asked for some _____ .

7 The best source of information about visitors on the premises in the case of an emergency is the _____ _____ .

8 A person who is walking around the building can be contacted easily if they carry a _____ with them.

Work it out

9 Draw up a Visitors' book with the same headings as shown in the unit but add an 'action' column at the right hand side. Date it for today and enter the following in time order, using the 24-hour clock.

3.15 pm   Mr John Barnes of Wilkins Plastics (a rep) arrives to see Joanne Pearson, buyer, without an appointment. His car registration is L298 CBP.

10.00 am   Bridget Swindlehurst arrives for an interview with Mr Matthew Webb, personnel officer. She has no car.

1.30 pm   John Penny, a joiner, arrives to start some maintenance work in the canteen. His van is registered J60 TMT.

11.15 am   Mr Tom Spibey calls in. He is the purchasing manager of Baker and Watts Ltd and wants to see Philip Jones, your sales manager, very urgently as some recent goods he received were faulty. His car registration is L390 KKY.

4.20 pm   John Drake arrives from New York. He runs the American office of your company and will be co-ordinating the visit of some important American customers due to arrive tomorrow. He has been collected at the airport by one of your company drivers.

9.30 am   Michelle Briggs, a buyer with a large company arrives unexpectedly to enquire about a new product.

10 Complete your action column, stating what action you would take for each of the following.

● Joanne Pearson never sees reps without an appointment.

● Ms Swindlehurst's interview is for tomorrow. When you tell her she bursts into tears as she has arranged to go away on holiday the following day.

● You are informed that Mr Penny cannot start work in the canteen until tomorrow – someone got the date wrong.

● Philip Jones is out of the office on business all day.

● You cannot find any copies of the leaflet containing the new product in which Michelle Briggs is interested.

5 Store, retrieve and supply information

This unit is concerned with information – how it is stored and retrieved and how it can be presented for others in a suitable form so that it can be easily understood.

All modern offices are concerned with the storage and processing of thousands of documents a year. If one important document is mislaid this can cause havoc and waste hours of everyone's time. Knowing the methods that are used for storage and being able to use them efficiently is essential for all office staff at every level. Today offices may use traditional, manual filing systems or computerised systems.

Information is not stored indefinitely without a reason. The aim is to provide a source of accessible information for a variety of purposes. Responding to requests for information requires several skills, including identification of the correct source(s), retrieval, the ability to scan large amounts of information and select only that which is relevant and then to present it in an appropriate form.

The first element of this unit examines the systems in use for storing information and how they operate. It includes the policies and procedures in operation in most organisations to control usage, unnecessary storage of out-of-date information and to protect confidential information. Both manual and computerised systems are described.

The second element of this unit is concerned with supplying information which is required for a specific purpose. It includes searching for information and the recognised sources to use, as well as the methods used for presentation. Constraints such as copyright requirements are also included.

Because information handling is a constant and continuous part of every office job the evidence you will need to prove your competence must be compiled over a period of time.

Element 5.1

Maintain and supply information

Every office in the world has at least one filing system – some have more. Why? Because this is the only way in which organisations can cope with the vast amounts of documents which have to be kept for future reference. The same applies to you at home. There are several documents which you and/or your parents need to keep safely, sometimes for many years, if not for life. Losing an important document can be disastrous and it may cost you a considerable amount of money to get a replacement.

 ## DID YOU KNOW?

If you lose a bank statement and need a duplicate the bank will charge you about £6 for a replacement! If you lost your birth certificate and urgently needed it to apply for a passport you could be involved in a considerable amount of extra work and expense, and if you couldn't get your replacement in time then your holiday abroad would have to be abandoned!

CHECK IT YOURSELF

1 Find out what system you use at home to keep the following documents safely.

- insurance policies
- bank statements
- pay slips
- guarantees for household equipment

2 Which of the following documents would you keep

a for a matter of weeks
b for about a year
c for ever?
(i)   marriage certificate
(ii)   season ticket
(iii) medical record card
(iv)   dry cleaning ticket
(v)   driving licence
(vi)   your NVQ evidence documents
(vii) a menu from the local take-away

The purpose of filing

The reasons you need to keep documents safely are obvious. However, there is a tremendous difference between filing and jamming everything in a cupboard. The reasons for using a proper system are so that

- you can find papers quickly and easily
- papers won't get torn or damaged
- you can answer queries quickly
- papers will be grouped together under common headings
- you will always have access to the most up-to-date information on a topic.

Problems can still occur, however. If someone takes a document from a file and doesn't tell you, you may *think* you have all the relevant information but this won't be true. Murphy's Law is sure to mean that the one document which is missing is the very one you need! For that reason, behind every good filing system is a series of controls to prevent anyone abusing the system and making a mess of everything!

DID YOU KNOW?

Some large organisations file on a **departmental** basis and others on a **centralised** basis. Some use a mixture of both!

- A **departmental** system means that each department or section looks after its own files. Sales will keep customer files, personnel will keep staff files and so on.
- A **centralised** system means that all (or most) of the files are kept in one place and are ordered and booked out by filing staff if other people want them for reference.
- A mixture of the two is used in many organisations. For instance, confidential files are very rarely filed centrally. As another example, in a large building society, all customer account files would be kept centrally, but the staff files and purchase orders may be kept by the relevant departments.

TEST YOURSELF

1 Why do you think that confidential files are rarely kept in a centralised system?
2 Can you think of *three* advantages to a very large organisation in keeping the majority of its files centrally?

Filing systems

Today most organisations are still coming to terms with the fact that they can *either* store the actual documents in a manual system or they can transfer to one of the new computerised systems on the market. If all the documents are kept in this way this is often called **total document management** (*see page 168*).

To set up a computerised system which can be used by everyone in the organisation can be very expensive, but if this vastly reduces the amount of paper and storage space required it can actually *save* money – especially if the company is situated in an area where office space is very expensive.

The difficulty is that people still like to hold a piece of paper, write on it and then keep it safely, so it is unlikely that *all* manual systems will ever be obsolete.

Manual storage systems

A manual storage system can require a good deal of equipment – and it is this which uses a considerable amount of expensive floor space. Equipment is required for

- actual file storage
- indexing and cross-referencing systems
- reminder and tracing systems.

File storage

Files may include

- documents fastened together in a brown manila file folder
- documents put into an envelope wallet
- A4 lever arch files
- A4 box files
- A3 computer print-outs fastened together.

There are several different storage alternatives.

Vertical filing cabinets

These consist of series of large drawers in which files are kept, one behind the other. The folders can be placed in a suspended system (which stops them from sliding down to lie horizontally at the bottom of the drawer) or be stacked one behind the other. Four-drawer cabinets are the most common.

Lateral filing cabinets

A lateral cabinet contains file pockets which face the front of the cabinet. File folders are inserted 'side on'. Many lateral cabinets are multi-purpose and can also hold other types of files, e.g. A4 box files, A3 computer print-outs etc.

Horizontal filing cabinets

This is an elaborate term for a cabinet which looks like a series of shallow drawers. Different sized cabinets are available to hold everything up to architects' plans and blueprints (though A1 drawings would have to be folded).

They are useful for storing documents which are of an awkward size, for photographs (which mustn't be folded) and for small amounts of different documents or forms.

Rotary filing

A rotary stand is used to house A4 lever arch files or box files or special file folders. The stand is rotated (like a book or postcard stand) to give all-round access to the files. Less space is used with this type of system.

DID YOU KNOW?

New filing cabinets have different features, all designed to save space and make access easier. They include

- slimmer cabinets which take up less room
- lateral cabinets with doors which slide to one side – therefore no extra room is required to allow for open doors
- deeper cabinets where the interior can rotate
- cabinets which slide on tracks to take advantage of awkward spaces or where there is restricted room for access.

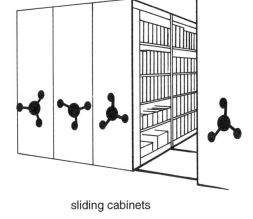

rotating cabinets   sliding cabinets

Safety features

- Modern vertical cabinets can only be opened one drawer at a time to prevent tilting.
- Use a filing stool to reach high shelves in lateral cabinets – *never* stand on a swivel chair.
- Never carry so many files that you obscure your view – especially on stairs.
- Never try to lift and carry great quantities of heavy files – use a trolley to move them.
- Steel cabinets are usually flame-proof to protect documents in the case of a fire.

CHECK IT YOURSELF

Look through an office equipment book and identify each of the storage systems mentioned.

1 Which would you buy if **safety** was your main concern? Why?
2 Which would you buy if **saving space** was your main concern?

Indexing equipment

Many manufacturers make filing cabinets in a variety of different colours to match the decor of different offices. In addition, indexing equipment can be bought to match! Some types of indexing system will be found in most offices, though the actual system used will usually depend on the type of classification system used for the main files (*see page 155*).

Card index

This is the most common system. The cards are stored in a metal drawer, one behind the other. Different sized units can be bought and some have a series of drawers, one on top of another.

Cards can easily be inserted or removed at any point and the system is easy to use as the key information is written at the top of the card. Most card index drawers have guide cards to help the user.

Visible edge

The cards are stacked one above another in separate plastic wallets in specially designed tray. The tray enables the **bottom** part of each card to be seen and this contains the key information on the card.

Rotary index

This is based on a small wheel onto which special cards are slotted. The wheel can be turned to give immediate access to any card. Most systems are quite small so can easily be kept on top of a desk.

Strip index

A small strip of card is inserted into a special holder. The strips can easily be removed and new ones added. Sometimes coloured strips are used for easy identification.

Often several holders are placed together in a circular arrangement on a central stand. Both sides of the holder can be used for different strips of card.

CHECK IT YOURSELF

1   Look through an office supplies catalogue and identify all the different types of filing and index storage systems mentioned previously.
2   What type of information do you think would be suitable for storage in *each* type of index system used?
3   Identify which of these systems are used in the organisation where you work (or visit on work experience) and state the type of information which is stored in each one.

Classification systems

The way in which files are grouped and stored will vary from one organisation to another, depending upon their particular needs. However, wherever you work you will usually find that one of three main systems is in use – or a derivation of one of them.

Alphabetical filing

This is used to describe any system where the files are stored in alphabetical order. Within the system the files may be placed

- by **name,** e.g. customer or personnel files
- by **subject,** e.g. products or projects
- by **geographical** area, e.g. branch office files.

All alphabetical systems are simple to understand and easy to use because they are **direct.** This means you can go straight to a file without having to refer to an index first.

If there are not enough papers under any one heading to warrant a separate file, it is usual to create a **miscellaneous file**. If required, a miscellaneous file can be opened for every letter of the alphabet and this is usually placed at the front of that letter section.

Filing by name

If your organisation operates an alphabetical system then you must know the rules to follow to ensure you can locate and store files properly. These are given in the chart on page 156.

DID YOU KNOW?

The best way to test if you understand the rules is to look in a telephone directory, which is simply a collection of names of people and organisations listed using these rules. However, companies may vary in the way these rules are interpreted, so your final check should be the company files.

TEST YOURSELF

All the **organisations** on the chart start with the letter 'S'. Rearrange them into one long list, using the rules given overleaf, and incorporate the organisations listed below and continued on page 157.

Social Services Department, Blackpool
The Samaritans
Serrick Marsden Ltd
Shorrock & Company, Solicitors
The Sahara Restaurant
Southampton District Council
St Mary's Rest Home

Rules for alphabetic filing

Rule to follow	Example
People	
Surname first	Clark Peter
Short names before long	Clark Peter Clarke Peter
If identical, follow first names or initials	Clark Peter Antony Clark Peter Michael Clarke Peter
Nothing always comes before something	Clark P Clark Peter Antony Clark Peter M Clark Peter Michael
Mac and Mc – all treated as Mac and filed before 'M'	MacDonald T McNulty J Marsden T
Ignore apostrophes	Obertelli J O'Brien D Oldfield C
Organisations	
Ignore the word 'the'	Sandwich Place, The Security Store, The
Numbers become words	Seven Mile Garage Seven Trees Hotel
If names are identical, follow street or town	Seven Trees Hotel, Kings Road Seven Trees Hotel, Syke Place
Initials come before full names (ignore the word 'and')	SB Animal Feeds S & J Upholstery SRA Associates Saatchi and Saatchi
Saint and St – all treated as Saint	Sainsbury J plc St John Ambulance Salford City Council
File public bodies under name or town	Sheffield City Council Social Security, Dept of Social Services Dept, Bradford Social Services Dept, Leeds

60 Plus Club
Sunway Travel Agency
SAS Tippers Ltd
John Schofield (Engineering) Ltd
Seventh Heaven Dress Designers

Filing by subject

This system is used when it is more appropriate to file under a topic than under a name. For example

- a chain store may keep files under the type of stock
- an insurance company may keep files under the type of insurance
- a manager may keep his own files under topics such as meetings, conferences, projects etc.

DID YOU KNOW?

If a topic is very broad it is usually sub-divided, e.g.

Meetings – Annual General
           Marketing
           Publicity
           Safety

TEST YOURSELF

Rearrange the following into correct subject order.

Seminars
Publicity – Open Days
Personnel – Training
Publicity – Leaflets
Travel
Publicity – Displays
Personnel – Staff Records
Publicity – Exhibitions
Personnel – Health and Safety
Personnel – Appraisals
Conferences
Publicity – Advertising
Personnel – Welfare
Personnel – Recruitment

Filing by geographical area

This system is used when the geographical area may have more significance than a specific name. For instance

- Companies which export their goods all over the world may keep customer files in name order under different countries.

- Gas and electricity boards would use a system to group files into the different regions or districts they serve.
- A head office of a large retail company with branches all over the country is likely to refer to these geographically.

The main disadvantage is that you may find yourself searching high and low if your geography is weak or you don't know where an organisation is located! To reduce this problem, large regions (e.g. counties) are usually sub-divided into smaller areas (e.g. towns).

TEST YOURSELF

You work at the head office of a large mail order company which has branches throughout the country. Rearrange the following counties and towns into the order in which they would appear in the main files. Remember that not only the main regions but also the sub-regions are always in alphabetical order.

Cornwall	**Devon**	**Cheshire**	**Kent**
Truro	Plymouth	Altrincham	Maidstone
Penzance	Paignton	Chester	Canterbury
Falmouth	Torquay	Nantwich	Sevenoaks
Newquay	Exmouth	Hale	Ashford
Bude	Exeter	Crewe	Sidcup

Numerical filing

The main disadvantage with *all* alphabetical systems is that they are unsuitable for very large numbers of files. Imagine a local hospital keeping all its patient files in alphabetical order. Very soon there would be congestion under common letters of the alphabet and the whole system would then have to be rearranged to create additional space.

To prevent this problem, organisations often use a numerical system of filing. One of two systems may be used.

- **Sequential numbering** – each new file simply takes the next number.
- **Alpha-numeric** – new numbers are allocated under the initial letter of the alphabet.

In both these systems there *must* be a separate alphabetical index – otherwise the user would not know where to find the file. Often the number used for the file is quoted in all correspondence, which saves anyone having to look up the file number when they want to file a document. They simply refer to the number in the reference. If the number is *not* quoted then you would have to look in the index and copy the number *accurately* onto the document to be filed.

Sequential numbering

This is the easiest method of creating numerical files. Each new file introduced into the system is simply given the next free number. If some earlier numbers are vacant (because some earlier files have ceased to exist) then these may be allocated to new files. This will depend on company policy.

In a large company individual departments may have their own block of numbers so that all new files still fit into one overall system.

Sequential numbering

File order		Index order	
Seymour J	749	Ashton P	750
Ashton P	750	Barrymore S	751
Barrymore S	751	Merridale J	752
Merridale J	752	Monk L	753
Monk L	753	Seymour J	749

Alpha-numerical

File order		Index order	
Crestwell T	C1	Campbell S	C7
Cunningham M	C2	Canterbury G	C6
Charnley P	C3	Cartwright J	C4
Cartwright J	C4	Charnley P	C3
Cowell A	C5	Cowell A	C5
Canterbury G	C6	Crestwell T	C1
Campbell S	C7	Cunningham M	C2

DID YOU KNOW?

Transposing two figures can create havoc in a numerical system. If a document is placed in the wrong file – or a file in the wrong place – it can be almost impossible to find.

TEST YOURSELF

Rearrange the following list *twice*. Firstly, put it into numerical order to show the order the files would be stored in a filing cabinet. Secondly, put it into alphabetical order to show the order in which the index cards would be filed.

Bryant M	482311	Gibbs P	413727
Jones R	478963	Berkovitz T	473218
Sanderson D	475712	Houldsworth S	473213
Kent G	462834	Hacking M	423314
Jallucci K	479836	Patel W	413292
Bolton T	477914	Heap S	477712

DID YOU KNOW?

Some organisations file particular papers in **chronological** or **date** order for easy access. In a sense, this is a variation of a numerical system and is used when the date has a special significance. Examples include

- travel agents – who usually file clients' travel documents under date of departure
- school departments – which store past examination papers according to the date on which the examination took place.

Alpha-numeric filing

As its name suggests, this is a combination of both alphabetical and numerical filing and is simply a method of sub-dividing numerical files using the letters of the alphabet.

Instead of each new file being given a new number, files are divided into 26 groups, A-Z and each of these groups has its own numbers. Therefore the first file under A would be given A1, the second A2 and so on.

DID YOU KNOW?

If an index card is mislaid, no-one will be able to find a file without searching through every file under a particular letter! Never remove an index card when you are using it for reference. Note down the number and leave the card where it belongs!

TEST YOURSELF

The following is a series of index cards for files in an alpha-numerical system. Rearrange this list into the order you would find them in the filing cabinet.

Hargreaves T	H12	Holden D	H14
Harper L	H6	Holt G	H3
Harris B	H1	Hopwood T	H7
Harrison M	H8	Horner M	H12
Haworth J	H2	Horrocks A	H4
Heyes P	H13	Howarth L	H10
Hill C	H9	Hussain M	H5

SPECIAL NOTE

Subject files can also be sub-divided using an alpha-numerical system. In this case each subject is given a special number, and the files are kept in this order, e.g.

50   Footwear
    50.1   Boots
    50.2   Shoes
    50.3   Slippers

Operating a manual storage system

Once a filing system is in operation, many people may be involved in using it. Unless *each one of them* knows exactly what to do the system will very quickly become chaotic. The cabinets may become jammed with old documents, files may get lost, papers may be in the wrong place and so on. It is therefore important that

- there are clear rules and procedures laid down which everyone knows and follows
- people are trained to file *properly.*

Rules and procedures

These should include clear instructions on

- the general rules of filing – and how to handle documents
- how to cross-reference documents
- how to control the lending of files and tracing these if they are overdue
- how long to retain documents and files
- how to deal with confidential documents
- company security procedures
- what to do if a problem occurs and the person to whom this should be reported.

The general rules of filing

Do ...

- File daily – to avoid a backlog and staff having to refer to outdated information.
- Pre-sort documents *first*. A concertina file can be useful for this as documents can be stored in here temporarily if you are interrupted.
- Remove paper clips and pins (as these may hook other papers). Staple related documents if necessary. Repair any which are torn.
- Punch documents *squarely* by aligning them with the guide rule on the punch, or line up the centre of the papers with the centre arrow so the holes are *always* in the same place.

Don't ...

- *Guess* where something should be filed. *Always* check with your supervisor if you are unsure.
- Squeeze too many papers into one folder. Split into two folders and write the dates on each, e.g. Dec 92 – June 95, June 95 –.

- Pull out folders by the tabs at the top, or they will break off!
- Remove individual documents from a file. Follow the official procedures for lending out the file itself (*see page 163*).
- Start a new file every time you see a new name. Check if the document should be stored in a miscellaneous file temporarily.
- Overload a filing cabinet so that the folders jam together. Follow company procedures for removing 'dead' files or extending the system (*see page 165*).

CHECK IT YOURSELF

If you don't know what a concertina file is, find out by referring to an office supplies catalogue. Then check that you understand how it could be used for pre-sorting documents by talking to your supervisor or tutor.

DID YOU KNOW?

Many organisations use a system of marking documents they have received to show that they are released for filing. When the person who was dealing with the document has finished with it, he or she may make a small mark at the top, such as a tick, to indicate that it can now be filed.

Cross-referencing

Cross-referencing is used in *all* filing systems to help staff to locate and find files or documents which could logically be placed under two (or more) names.

If you look in a telephone directory for a number, and look in the wrong place, you will often find a special entry which guides you to the correct place. For instance, if you wanted to find out the time of a train, and looked under R for Railways – you will find an entry telling you to look under B for British Rail. This is a **cross-reference entry**.

Cross-references may be used for the files themselves or for individual documents.

Cross-referencing files

Imagine you are asked to open a file for Berkeley Trading Company. The trading company has an associate company called Priory Producers but both organisations operate from the same address. Your supervisor wants all documents filed under the name of the trading company.

Your job is broken down into stages like this.

- Make out the cross-reference entry *at the same time* as you make out a new file.
- Store the cross-reference in the *opposite* place to the actual file.

- Put the cross-reference entry into the filing system itself (if an alphabetical system is used).

- Put a cross-reference card into the card index (if a numerical system is used), as shown on the right.

> **PRIORY PRODUCERS**
>
> **See under BERKELEY TRADING COMPANY**

Cross-referencing documents

Frequently documents are received which could be stored under more than one heading. This is particularly true if a subject system of filing is used. For instance, a letter from a printer may refer to publicity material for a specific conference and to a rise in printing costs in general. You may wish to file the document both under 'conference' and under 'printing'. You have two choices. You can

- photocopy the document and put a copy in *both* files
- store the document in the main file to which it belongs and put a cross-reference note in the *other* file.

CHECK IT YOURSELF

Yellow Pages is a marvellous example of listing entries under subject headings. Cross-referencing is required for people who look in the wrong place for an entry. Look through *Yellow Pages* and find *six* examples of headings with cross-reference information underneath.

Lending and tracing files

A clear system must be established for lending files. Documents should *never* be taken from files as these easily get lost. If only one document is required then it may be permissible to photocopy it for the person concerned.

Several systems can be used.

- The borrowed files may be entered in a file diary in which the files are usually listed under the date by which they must be returned
- A card index system may be used. A card is made out for the borrowed file and again filed under the date of return.

At the same time, an absent card or OUT marker should be placed where the file is usually kept, to save people searching unnecessarily for a borrowed file. Large cards may be used with different colours to indicate the date of return.

Name of file	Date Borrowed	Borrower	Date Returned
R. Jones & Co Ltd	24 April	R. Taylor	26 April
J Woodstock plc	27 April	M. Cowell	27 April
Berry & Wilson	28 April	J. Barnes	

An example of a file diary.

If a proper system is followed, it is easy to trace files when they are overdue.

- Both a file diary and a card system should be checked *daily* to ensure no files are outstanding.
- Holders of overdue files must be *reminded* to return them *or* to specify a new date for their return.

You must, of course, re-file any borrowed files immediately you receive them, and update your records accordingly.

DID YOU KNOW?

The latest method of tracking files is by computer using a system combining bar codes and special software.

System failure

A manual system may fail if

- a file has been borrowed and no card has been made out
- the person who borrowed the file has passed it on to someone else
- the borrower is away from the office
- the borrower cannot find the file.

For these reasons, most companies have control mechanisms to prevent people abusing the system, e.g.

- files may only be booked out through one person or at certain times
- cabinets are kept locked outside normal office hours
- a borrower has personal responsibility for a file until its return
- files which cannot be traced – or which are not returned despite several reminders – are immediately reported as missing to a supervisor.

DID YOU KNOW?

Many people panic when they can't find a file – which doesn't usually help! If a file is missing then try the Sherlock Holmes approach before you do anything drastic.

- Check any logical place it could be (an 'in' tray waiting to be re-filed, an 'out' tray waiting to be collected etc.).
- Check the tops of filing cabinets and desks.
- Check under any cross-reference names which may apply.
- Think of any other headings in which the file might be stored, or any other cabinets which may have been used.
- Ask other people in the office if they have used it or when they last saw it.

Retention policies

Quite obviously files can't be kept for ever or all organisations would eventually run out of space. Most companies operate a retention policy. This means that after a certain length of time documents are

- retained in the current files, *or*
- transferred to a dormant file, *or*
- transferred to long term storage (often in the basement), *or*
- destroyed. Confidential files should always be destroyed by being put through a shredding machine so that they become completely unreadable.

How long a document should be kept will depend on

- what it is or what it relates to
- whether there is a legal requirement covering the time for which it must be kept. The chart below shows the main statutory requirements in the UK.

Document retention chart

Retention time	Document
3 years	Sick pay records Bank statements (private company) Accounts books (private company)
6 years	Bank statements (public company) Accounts books (public company) Tax correspondence Customs documents Pay slips Clock cards Purchase orders
12 years	Tax assessments Sales orders Quotations Dividend payments
30 years	Accident reports
Indefinitely	Certificate and Articles of Incorporation

DID YOU KNOW?

You should never take matters into your own hands and clear out any files without specific instructions from your supervisor. Generally, even ordinary correspondence is kept for a year or two and in some cases for even longer.

CHECK IT YOURSELF

The type of retention policy in operation will often depend on the type of business an organisation undertakes.

Discuss with your supervisor or tutor how the retention policy will differ for

- a solicitor
- a travel agent
- a school
- a hospital.

Confidentiality and security

Many files in an office are confidential. These can range from personnel and wages records to files kept by the managing director about new contracts or organisational developments. Confidential files are usually kept locked away and are accessed only by those people who have the authority to read the contents.

Confidential files should *never* be left on desks or taken into public areas such as reception.

The procedure for borrowing confidential files will be different. So will procedures for the photocopying any documents. Usually there are much stricter controls on access and return.

DID YOU KNOW?

The **Data Protection Act** relates to all information held on computer, including computerised filing systems. (*Confidentiality and computerised systems are covered on page 233.*)

Problems and reporting procedures

The way in which problems are dealt with and the person to whom you are responsible will vary depending upon whether your company operates a centralised or departmental filing system.

There should be fewer problems with a centralised system as this is usually controlled by a supervisor who is specifically responsible for controlling the filing system in operation. If you work in that section you will be made fully aware of the procedures to follow.

More difficulties are likely to occur if you work in a smaller organisation with each department operating its own filing system. If there are no official procedures and staff do not know what they are doing there may be serious problems controlling files. This may not matter to you unless you are being blamed for problems which are not your fault. If this occurs, ask to talk to your line manager and suggest that some basic controls on usage are introduced quickly.

CHECK IT YOURSELF

Decide what action you would take if each of the following occurred. Discuss your answers with your supervisor or tutor.

1 A senior manager frequently borrows files but doesn't tell anyone. You do not have the authority to stop her doing this.
2 Your colleagues usually photocopy documents which need placing in more than one file. However, one member of staff is taking this to extremes, making up to six copies of documents and filing them under any heading to which they may even slightly relate.
3 A senior manager borrowed a file last week and is now abroad until Friday. The file is wanted urgently for an important meeting.
4 A temporary member of staff who was employed last month to cover for staff holiday absences didn't bother filing at all. You are getting the blame for this and have at least a week's backlog of work to do.
5 An important file you had in your hands yesterday morning is now missing. You know you put the file back in its proper place just before lunch.

Computerised filing systems

If you use a word processor then you already use one form of computerised filing! You give each document a title and store it on a disk. The title is a method of identifying the document so that it can be retrieved if you look at the disk directory, which shows the contents stored on it. (If you are *really* well organised you will also have a print-out of all your disk directories filed neatly in a folder!)

Computerised filing is really an extension of this system where

● documents produced internally on a word processor are stored into a centralised computerised filing system
● documents received by the company are scanned into the system using a special document scanner.

The main components of a computerised system are shown in the chart on page 168.

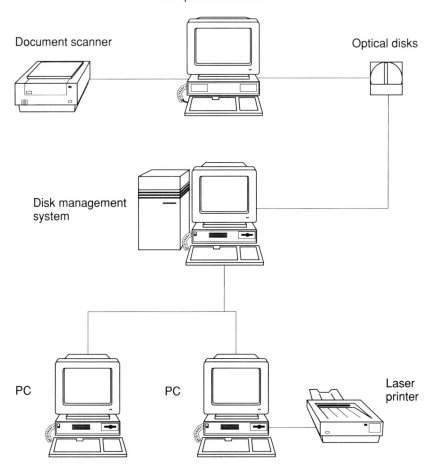

File management computer
with special software

Document scanner

Optical disks

Disk management
system

PC

PC

Laser
printer

 DID YOU KNOW?

Some manufacturers of computerised filing systems offer a scanning service as well. This may be used by companies which convert to computerised filing to scan in all the original documents, most of which can then be destroyed.

The pros and cons of computerised filing

Advantages of a computerised filing system

- It is space-saving. About 13 000 A4 documents can be stored on one optical disk.
- Scanning is quick and easy – at the rate of about 40 double-sided A4 pages a minute.

- Different people can access the system at the same time via their own personal computer, so there is no need to borrow or return files.
- Documents can be indexed under several headings so that they can be retrieved quickly and easily.
- Confidential documents can be given special codes so that they are not generally accessible.
- The contents of a file can be scanned quickly before certain documents are selected for viewing or printing.
- Documents can be electronically cross-referenced.
- Back-up files are created automatically.

Disadvantages

- The system is expensive.
- Computer failure would mean that no documents were accessible.
- A lot of time is required to convert from the old system to the new and to retrain the staff.
- Many people will still insist on taking a print-out of a document – which they may then store in a manual system!
- Any storage of information on computer is subject to the restrictions of the Data Protection Act (*see Unit 2, page 67*).

DID YOU KNOW?

The European Commission is at present considering extending data protection legislation to include *all* files, whether they are manual or computerised.

TEST YOURSELF

Look back to Unit 2, page 67, and review the details of the Data Protection Act. Then state in which of the following cases the information stored on computer would contravene the Act.

1 Your boss hears on the grapevine that a member of staff is in debt. He asks that a note be added to the personnel file.
2 A client company goes into bankruptcy and notifies you by letter. The letter is scanned into the computerised filing system.
3 Your boss decides to start a black list of all companies who do not pay their debts on time. He scans this into the computer.
4 Staff files held on computer are open to access by all members of the organisation.
5 Staff files are retained on computer for up to two years after the person has left the organisation, in case they later apply for a reference.

UNIT REVIEW (1)

At the end of this element you should be able to

- describe the difference between manual and computerised filing systems
- describe different methods of classifying information
- put new information into a storage system following organisational procedures
- maintain stored material in good condition
- monitor and record the movement of files accurately
- identify overdue files and implement the system for their return
- deal with out-of-date information as directed
- identify opportunities for improving established systems and take the appropriate action
- ensure that your own work practices conform to the requirements of the organisation for which you work.

CHECK YOUR KNOWLEDGE AND UNDERSTANDING

True or false?

1 Personal data held on computer is controlled by the Health and Safety at Work Act.
2 A computerised filing system takes up less space than a manual filing system.
3 Alpha-numeric filing means a person's name is replaced by a number.
4 A lateral filing cabinet consists of a series of drawers, one upon another.
5 Accident reports must be kept for a maximum of five years.

Fill in the blanks

6 An index is always required when a _____ classification system is used.
7 Documents scanned into a computerised filing system are stored on an _____ disk.
8 A cross reference card should always be filed in the _____ place to the actual file.

Work it out

9 You start work in the office of a local garage company where the filing system is chaotic. Files are overfull and stuffed into six old cabinets. There are many outdated documents in the files and the whole system is a mess.

Your boss wants to start a new system and has asked for your help.

a Look through an office supplies catalogue and identify the type of filing equipment you think would be appropriate.

b Draft out a memo giving your boss your ideas on

- sorting out the system
- the cost of new equipment
- procedures required
- document retention.

c The following three types of documents are kept in the system

- customer service files
- supplier files for car parts and accessories. (Sometimes the same part may be bought from several different suppliers and prices need to be compared easily.)
- MOT certificates issued (for sending reminders to customers).

State clearly what classification system you would suggest for each type of file, with your reasons.

10 Your boss is considering spending a large amount of money converting from a manual to a computerised filing system. Apart from saving space he also thinks there will other obvious advantages. To help him, he has asked you to prepare some notes.

a List all the control systems which are currently required but which will no longer be needed if the filing is computerised.

b Briefly state the benefits in terms of the health, safety and security aspects of the change.

c State any other aspects of the change which you think he should consider carefully.

Element 5.2

Supply information for a specific purpose

The importance of information

There would be absolutely no point in any organisation storing vast amounts of information if nobody ever needed it! If you think about it, information is the basis upon which most organisations operate and upon which many decisions are made, e.g.

- a company is refused credit because previous information shows they are bad payers
- a person is given promotion because their record shows that they are a hard worker, are punctual and rarely absent

- a new supplier is given a contract to provide new office equipment because information on that company shows they are reliable and the goods are competitively priced
- your company changes its procedure for the lifting and transporting of goods because information on new legislation shows that they need to change current practices
- your organisation only offers a two per cent pay rise to staff this year because information shows that is all it can afford to offer given falling sales – and this is also the current rate for pay awards in the UK.

Up-to-date, relevant information is crucial as it influences everyone's actions. You wouldn't set off to see a film at 6 pm if the information in the paper told you it was cancelled, or that it didn't start until 8 pm or thick snow was expected by 9 pm! Equally you wouldn't go if your friends gave you the information that you'd be on your own as no-one else wanted to see it! We all rely on accurate information – and need to receive it in time to use it effectively. (Think how annoyed you would be if you only found out when you arrived at the cinema that everyone else had decided not to bother!)

TEST YOURSELF

Look at the four situations above and see if you can say *where* and *how* the company could have obtained each type of information, i.e.

- information on poor payers (both previous customers and/or new customers)
- information on personnel (existing and potential), including that on punctuality and attendance
- information on suppliers' goods, prices and reputation
- information on health and safety
- information on company finances and sales to date
- information on current pay rises being offered in the UK.

Understanding information requirements

You may receive requests for information from people inside the organisation *and* from people outside the organisation. Some of them will be entitled to the information – others will not. If you are ever in any doubt about who should receive information *check first* – before you say anything you shouldn't!

If you are going to supply correct, relevant information you must be able to understand exactly what people want. An ambiguous request or one which is unclear in any way must be clarified. You also need to know how much (or little) information is required. If you start spending hours searching for detailed figures, when all your boss wanted was a quick overview of the current situation, then you have wasted time unnecessarily. *Check* if you don't understand a request. Equally, if you haven't a clue where to start looking, then *ask!* It is far better to do this than spend two hours preparing the wrong information – which will irritate both yourself and the recipient.

Interpreting someone's instructions accurately all of the time is only likely if they

- are always very specific and clear about what they mean (and don't ask you something important when either you or they are in a hurry!)
- check with you the best sources to use if you are ever unsure or if the information required is not easily found
- are well known to you – so that a misleading request is easily understood because you know them or your job so well.

Bear in mind that you *can't* be expected to be psychic but you *can* be expected to check carefully what is meant if you are ever unsure!

CHECK IT YOURSELF

1 People outside the organisation may include customers, suppliers, competitors, shareholders, government offices and service organisations (e.g. banks, accountants etc.). Make a list of the types of information you think

   a could be given to each of these people
   b could be requested by each of these people
   c must not be given without checking beforehand.

2 Identify which of the following requests is ambiguous or difficult to understand and state how you would clarify the request.

   a 'Find out what it says in the blue folder I used the other day.'
   b 'Have you got the train times for that trip next week?'
   c 'How much do you know about Mary Brown?'
   d 'How far have we got with the holiday rota?'
   e 'What's the state of play with the Brown account?'

Check your answers with your supervisor or tutor.

Information sources

The four main sources of information are

- official paper-based information, e.g. books, newspapers, journals, company documentation, brochures, leaflets and the company files
- data held on computer
- people – at your own workplace or in other organisations
- your own memory and/or written notes.

Paper-based information

Reference books – general information

The type of reference books bought by your office will depend very much on the kind of information you are expected to find regularly. As an example, every office has a telephone directory but only a solicitor would keep a copy of *The Law List* or books on specific aspects of the law.

Reference books which are useful to many organisation include

- telephone and fax directories (including *Yellow Pages* and *Business Pages*) plus a telex directory if appropriate
- a good dictionary, not just for the meanings and spellings of words but also for their pronunciation and the meaning of many abbreviations
- road maps and A–Z street guides for towns which are often visited by managers or representatives
- *AA/RAC Handbooks* which give details of towns and cities in Britain, mileage charts, names of recommended hotels and garages as well as maps of different areas and towns/cities
- *The Good Food Guide/Hotels and Restaurants in Great Britain* if managers in the organisation often entertain guests
- A good general reference book, e.g. *Whitaker's Almanack* which gives information on world organisations, populations and statesmen plus many useful names and addresses and details of how to address important people correctly.
- *Mailguide* which gives information on all postal services (information on current rates is printed in individual leaflets).
- *British Telecom Guide* which gives information on telecommunications services
- postcode directories.

 DID YOU KNOW?

Several sources of basic information are now computerised. Companies can buy a Postcode Address File which is a database of every private address in the UK with its appropriate postcode. Even *Yellow Pages* has an electronic version (called EYP – electronic yellow pages). Details of any type of business are stored on computer. This information can be accessed free of charge by organisations which have a linked terminal.

Reference books – specialist information

Your organisation may keep only a few books which contain specialist information – in which case you may need to use your reference library. Do remember that many books cannot be removed so you will have to take with you a notebook and/or enough money to make some photocopies – but be careful about copyright restrictions (*see page 187*).

It is often better to keep a range of up-to-date leaflets rather than to buy expensive books. However, you may need rather more detailed information on a regular basis on a particular topic. The main specialist areas for books are given below, with the most common sources of information listed in each.

Travel

ABC Railway and World Airways Guides give detailed timetable information. However, it may be better to keep timetables for services you frequently use and telephone British Rail or your travel agent to confirm times and availability.

Hints to Businessmen booklets are invaluable for anyone travelling abroad as they give details of customs, holidays, climate and other regulations for specific countries. They are regularly updated and are available from the Department of Trade and Industry.

Travel Trade Directory is really of use only if you do a lot of work arranging travel. It contains details of different travel operators and specialist services (e.g. air taxis!) plus the addresses of all passport and visa offices. There's no need to buy this book if your organisation uses a good travel agent – ring and ask them for information instead!

English usage/general office work

Roget's Thesaurus gives alternative meanings (synonyms) for a wide variety of words.

Black's Titles and Forms of Address gives the correct form of address for someone who is highly ranked or holds an official position – from the Queen to the Lord Mayor. It includes both the correct wording for when you are speaking and/or writing.

The Hamlyn Guide to English Usage gives guidance on difficult points of grammar and punctuation.

A good secretarial desk book (from the wide range available) provides information on documents, typing layout and abbreviations.

Who's Who and *Who Was Who* provide information on famous people in Britain. The first book relates to those who are still living and the second to those who have died.

Vacher's Parliamentary Companion gives details of MPs and members of the House of Lords.

Books on specific professions include *The Medical Register* (for medical practitioners), *The Directory of Directors* and *Kemp's International Music and Recording Industry Yearbook*.

Business

Kompass UK is a very useful book, containing a detailed guide to products manufactured in the UK and detailed information on companies. A European version is also available.

The Stock Exchange Official Yearbook gives details of UK public companies including a short history and description of each.

Guide to Key British Enterprises (Dun and Bradstreet) gives information about prominent British companies.

Croner's Reference Books on various topics are available, e.g. for exporters, importers and small businesses.

DID YOU KNOW?

Many libraries keep Extel cards. These are produced annually and contain details of British public companies. Because they are updated each year you can be sure that the information you are using is up to date. Remember that using an outdated reference book is not only misleading but can even be dangerous! You could be reading about a company which no longer exists or giving totally wrong information to your supervisor.

Current affairs

Britain, An Official Handbook gives information about all aspects of British industry and the economy.

Hansard gives daily and weekly verbatim reports of proceedings in Parliament.

Keesing's Record of World Events is a monthly newsheet, for insertion in a binder, and consists of reports and statistics summarised from the world's press and news services.

General reference

Willing's Press Guide lists all British newspapers and publications and gives details of advertising rates and circulation figures.

Kelly's Business Directory lists all manufacturers, merchants, wholesalers and firms in the UK and gives details of international exporters and services relating to different products.

DID YOU KNOW?

Details on parliamentary papers and other information published by the Government (including Health and Safety) are published by Her Majesty's Stationery Office (HMSO) and sold in Government bookshops in many large towns and cities. A variety of statistical books are also published which show how we live today and spend our money; they include the *Family Expenditure Survey* and *Social Trends*.

TEST YOURSELF

From the books listed above, can you identify which book you could use to find out the following:

1 the cost of a full page advertisement in the *Sunday Times*
2 an alternative for the word 'premonition'
3 the correct way to address a letter to the Duke of Westminster
4 a list of the directors of Marks and Spencer
5 details of how much people spend on food out of the family budget
6 the name of a good hotel in Edinburgh
7 public holidays in Venezuela
8 the name of the MP for Finchley
9 details of how to pack special items for the post
10 details of daily flights from Manchester to New York

Journals, newspapers and magazines

Many organisations take at least one daily newspaper and also subscribe to several business magazines. A good newspaper will not only give information on current affairs, share prices and exchange rates but may also contain information about road works in progress and other useful travel details.

The type of magazines taken by an organisation will often vary according to the type of business undertaken in the company. Many trades have their own specialist magazines. Companies which have many foreign visitors may keep a supply of foreign language journals and periodicals in reception.

General magazines purchased by many companies include

Business Equipment Digest which gives up-to-date information on business equipment

Business Traveller which contains articles of special interest to executives who travel frequently

Magazines such as *Management Today*, *Personnel Management* and *Management Accounting* all contain articles of specific interest to these managers.

DID YOU KNOW?

Reference libraries also keep copies of periodicals and newspapers and many have back copies available (though these may be stored on microfiche). Bear in mind that your local reference library will have a vast amount of other useful information, e.g. local maps dating back many years, local Council reports and surveys etc.

Other paper-based sources of information

Leaflets

These are often more useful than books as they contain specific information, e.g. on consumer law, tax information, postal rates, bank services and so on. They are usually very up-to-date because they are cheap to produce so organisations can afford to update them frequently.

Brochures

Brochures and catalogues are more expensive than leaflets to produce but are often used for advertising goods and services. There is often a separate price list which can be updated regularly when required.

General company information

Bear in mind this may relate to your own company or another organisation! All public companies have to publish their report and accounts each year and these are available to anyone. Within your own company you will have access to all sorts of information in the form of handbooks, charts and other documents.

Company files

The main source of information within your own company is your company files. These will contain a wealth of information on customers, suppliers, financial accounts and staff – though not all of it may be generally available to you.

 ## DID YOU KNOW?

You can save yourself a considerable amount of time if you keep a **personal file** in which you keep information you regularly need in the course of your everyday work.

If you work in sales you may need to keep a catalogue of your company's products and a price list in your file, plus a list of company representatives and their home addresses and telephone numbers. If you work for a small organisation you may have a variety of contact names and numbers, e.g.

- maintenance contacts, such as the name and telephone numbers of an electrician, plumber, heating engineer, locksmith, glazier, office equipment service engineers and burglar alarm company.
- office suppliers and printers, for re-ordering consumables such as stationery and letter headed paper
- agencies used by your company for travel, express delivery, translations, advertising etc.

TEST YOURSELF

Below are given several queries which can be answered by referring to internal sources of paper-based information. Match each query against the most appropriate source

1 extension number of the chief accountant

2 details of your own work responsibilities

3 the dates your supervisor is away on holiday

4 the VAT number of your company

5 the price of one of your products

6 the price of a filing cabinet you bought last year

7 the postcode of one of your customers

8 the terms and conditions of your employment

A company brochure and price list

B a company invoice

C customer files

D job description

E internal telephone list

F holiday rota

G contract of employment

H accounts files

Data held on computer

This category includes information held on your *own computer* and information you can access via a computer.

Your own computer

If you regularly use a computer then you will use it for a purpose. You may produce word processed documents, access a database, create a spreadsheet or design the company newsletter each month on a desktop publishing package. In the majority of cases you will save your work for future use, either to edit and update it or for later reference if required. Being able to access such information quickly means

- having a sensible 'filing' system for your disk(s)
- knowing how to access the directory
- using rapid search techniques to locate and retrieve information.

All these operational aspects of using a computer are covered in Unit 6, pages 201 to 257.

Your computer *may* be **networked** (linked) to a sophisticated computer system in your organisation so that you can use an in-house electronic mail system or appointments schedule. Equally you may be able to access customer records, stock records, price lists or even sales statistics on your computer.

DID YOU KNOW?

The content of books, journals and newspapers can be purchased on optical disk as well as in paper form! A company with a networked system could buy such a disk (called a **CD-ROM**) and store it centrally so that all users could access the information simply by typing in the key search words. For instance, 'world' and 'football' would bring up any articles on that topic. Similarly, 'health' and 'safety' would bring up any suitable articles!

Databanks

A CD-ROM is just one form of databank. A databank is the name given to a large database which holds a considerable amount of information. Most databanks require the user to pay a subscription as well as own a computer, VDU and modem which links the in-house system to the outside world.

Companies with a special requirements can pay to have access to the databank of their choice. For instance, specialist databanks are available for those in the legal profession and many travel agencies are linked to Gallileo, which not only gives them travel information at the touch of a button but enables them to make a booking and print out the tickets immediately. Such a system is known as an **interactive** system.

New Prestel

The most common interactive computer information system is New Prestel – known as a viewdata service because the information can be viewed on screen. The system links computer based information to micro-computers (or adapted television sets) over an ordinary telephone line.

The information on New Prestel is organised in 'pages' – a page being a screenful of information. Through New Prestel you can call up these pages to be displayed on your computer screen.

An easy-to-follow index shows lists of information headings with a route number to be followed until you find the page you want.

Information provided includes

- travel information
- financial information
- export information

- tax guides
- company information
- government statistics.

This is in addition to sports and entertainment information (similar to that found on Ceefax and Oracle).

Because New Prestel is interactive not only can you call up basic information but you can also ask for more details by inputting a request on your keyboard or special keypad.

Companies which pay additional subscriptions can gain access to more specialised information through New Prestel by means of a 'Gateway'. Paying the fee means you can go 'through' the Gateway to other specialised areas.

DID YOU KNOW?

If you use New Prestel you will be well advised to make a note of the numbers of the pages you use regularly. This will save you continually searching for information and – because time is money when you use New Prestel – it will be cost-effective in reducing your company's bill!

CHECK IT YOURSELF

Many libraries have access to databanks – some of which can provide you with summaries of journal articles. Visit your own library and find out

a what library databanks are available

b how you can institute a search for a specific piece of information – and how much this will cost.

People as an information source

Within your own organisation

Probably your best source of help on a regular basis is people. Your colleagues at work will know a tremendous amount of information about your customers, products, recent events and so on. Therefore, in many cases, your first option may be to

- ask someone if they know the answer
- ask someone if they know where you can find the answer!

DID YOU KNOW?

There is a tremendous difference between asking people for help or information and becoming a nuisance! The difference lies in

- asking politely

- not asking unless it is necessary (i.e. if you could easily find the information yourself by looking in a file or the telephone directory)
- not asking the same question twice (i.e. remembering or noting down the answers for future reference)
- saying 'thank you'!

CHECK IT YOURSELF

Discuss with your tutor the type of information the following people in your organisation may be able to give you.

- a safety representative
- a wages clerk
- a personnel assistant
- the sales manager
- a member of the security staff

Within other organisations

Other organisations with whom you may deal include

- your customers
- your suppliers
- service providers, e.g. accountant, bank, solicitor, insurance broker
- government offices, e.g. Inland Revenue, VAT and Department of Social Security.

All of these will be able to provide information on specific topics or occurrences – and making one telephone call may save you a lot of time.

Other types of information can be obtained by contacting specialist organisations either locally or nationally, e.g.

Local organisations

Police	Local radio station
Reference library	Local paper
Local council/town hall	Post Office
British Telecom	Citizen's Advice Bureau
Chamber of Commerce	Trading Standards Office

National organisations

The Consumers' Association	Trade Associations
Tourist Information Offices	AA or RAC
English Tourist Board	Foreign embassies
Health and Safety Executive	Equal Opportunities
Consumer reference agencies	Commission

● Discuss with your supervisor or tutor the type of information which could be supplied by *each* of the above sources.

● Make a note of any occasions when you have contacted a local (or national) source for information – and why.

DID YOU KNOW?

Do be aware that no matter who you contact you cannot expect to be given confidential information. For instance, you cannot ring a bank and find out about someone's account!

Important points to note about confidential information

● Try to avoid asking for information which is confidential as a refusal can be embarrassing for both of you.
● If your boss gives you specific authority to access confidential information in your organisation – and clears this with anyone else involved – do not repeat what you find out to other people, or leave any written notes lying about.
● *Never* try to breach (or get round!) your organisation's standard procedures for obtaining information or their security policies. If you can't find something out officially then tell your supervisor – don't try to get the information in an unorthodox way.

You as a source – plus your own notes

Don't forget that you probably know more than you realise. How many times have you thought you had no knowledge on a topic until somebody prompted you into remembering? Often, if you think something through carefully before you start you can save yourself many hours. The best sequence to follow is

● plan what you are going to need
● work out what you know already
● look back at past files and notes you have made which may help you (*see below*)
● work out a logical way of searching for the information you need
● think of any options you may have, i.e. alternative sources of information you can access.

So far as your own notes are concerned, it is silly to spend hours finding out information that you may need again, only to give this away without keeping a copy! Your notes *may* be roughly jotted in a shorthand pad. However, a more sensible approach is to type out the information in a logical order and keep a copy yourself. In a similar way, if you make notes on any topic to which you may need to refer in the future, type them out neatly and file them in a place where you can find them again easily!

TEST YOURSELF

Below are several queries, each of which you could probably answer by making one telephone call. In each case, state the source of information you would use. Then write down as many *alternative* sources as you can think of, i.e. other people you could contact if your first choice was unavailable for some reason.

1 Road conditions in another county on a snowy day in winter.
2 The current rate of statutory sick pay.
3 The names of three 4-star hotels in Brighton.
4 The date of a forthcoming major event in your own town.
5 The correct procedure to follow if a suspicious package is received in the mail.

DID YOU KNOW?

The best procedure to follow, if the person you ask at first cannot help you, is to ask *them* what they can suggest you do. You might find that, even though a contact does not have the information you require, he or she may be able to make very good alternative suggestions you would never have thought of on your own.

Coping with problems

You will encounter problems if

● you cannot find the information you need
● the information you have found isn't suitable
● you identify an alternative source but this will take longer.

As an example, imagine that you have been asked to find out the latest information on health and safety legislation by this afternoon. Where do you start?

● Internal sources – you could contact a trade union representative or a safety representative. They say they cannot help you but suggest you try contacting the TUC (Trades Union Congress) in London. They don't know the telephone number.
● External sources – you visit the local library to try to read it up in a journal or an up-to-date textbook. The woman is new, unhelpful and doesn't think they have anything other than the Health and Safety at Work Act 1974.
● Your local Town Hall – you ring and get through to the Environmental Health Office. They suggest you try the Health and Safety Executive.
● The HSE – you ring and are told to contact their supply section. When you try them this section is closed until Monday.
● The TUC – they inform you that they can send you some material but this will not arrive until the middle of next week.

What do you do?

You have thought of several options and each one has drawn a blank. You go to see your supervisor who agrees to wait until the union material arrives next week. When it does, you find out that the leaflets you have been sent are union commentaries and opinion – not details of the regulations themselves. Where did you go wrong?

- If you thought of *all* the alternatives i.e. is there an HMSO bookshop in your area, are there any other libraries (e.g. college or central reference libraries) or ordinary bookshops which might have had the correct material? Are there any specialist suppliers of health and safety materials which your local environmental health office might have known about?
- explained *exactly* what you need to the people you have spoken to – and persisted with your request if necessary?
- *discussed* the problem with your supervisor, rather than just telling him or her about the one source?
- ordered material from more than one source, if necessary, just to be on the safe side?

If you have a serious problem finding material, don't panic. Think the problem through and talk to the person who made the request in the first place. Always make sure that you

- keep them informed of progress or problems
- discuss possible alternatives with them
- warn them if there is likely to be a delay – so they can make contingency plans to cope if necessary.

DID YOU KNOW?

Working to a deadline puts pressure on everyone. It helps, however, if you know when information is definitely required for a certain date. If necessary, you would have to drop everything to get what is needed. For instance, an important visitor is arriving at your organisation from America to stay one day. Information is needed for the visit – any delay and it will be useless. If this is the case then your manager will no doubt be very supportive if you have a problem – and you will be given additional resources (time, help, money, permission to travel somewhere) to get what is needed in time.

TEST YOURSELF

Imagine that the request for health and safety material *cannot* be delayed as it is required for a Management Meeting at 9 am on Monday. It is now Friday morning. Given the problems encountered above, what could you do to get the material in time?

Discuss the problem with your colleagues and then test out your ideas on your supervisor or tutor.

Interpreting and compiling information

Getting hold of information is only the first stage. You then may have to change its format in some way so that it is in a more appropriate form. For instance, your boss would not want to take a ten-page document on health and safety to the meeting if all he needs is a summary. To be able to do this properly you need to

- understand what you are reading
- know the best form in which it should be produced for the purpose for which it is needed
- create the required document – so that it is in a suitable layout with correct spelling and punctuation!

Understanding what you read

Nobody understands complex or unfamiliar material the first time they read it. If you just scan through it then you are likely to find it totally incomprehensible.

- Read it once to get the main idea.
- Read it again, slowly, to try to take in more detail.
- Look up any unknown words in a dictionary.
- Go through it a third time, underlining the main points. (If it is an original document, take a photocopy before you do this!)
- Read through it again and check nothing has been missed out.
- If necessary, check your understanding of the main points with someone else.
- Reword them into a language you understand easily.
- If your spelling is poor, try to copy as many words as possible from the original text.
- Make a draft summary of your main points, then check this against the original.
- Add or delete information as necessary before writing out a final version.

TEST YOURSELF

Read the following information on copyright below.

   1 Answer the questions below with 'True' or 'False' to check your understanding.

      a Schools can copy anything they like.
      b Some books have no copyright restrictions.
      c A student photocopying a document in a library will have to have a licence.
      d All licence fees are paid to the Performing Rights Society.
      e 'Incidental inclusion' means the play is based on the book.

f An author's work may be used by a journalist providing the author's name is quoted.

2 Make a list of the key points in the article.
3 Write out a brief summary of the article in your own words and check your work with your supervisor or tutor.

Copyright

Anyone who uses a photocopier must be aware that they can break copyright law if there is unrestricted photocopying of certain documents. **The Copyright, Designs and Patents Act 1988** protects anyone who creates an original work from it being copied by anyone else.

In law, every time anyone writes a book, composes a song, makes a film or creates any other type of artistic work, this work is treated as their property (or copyright). If anyone else wishes to make use of it they must get permission to do so, and, on occasions, must be prepared to pay a fee.

A number of collecting agencies exist which collect payments on behalf of authors and performers. For instance, the Performing Rights Society is involved in collecting payment when records are played to the public. However, a disco or radio station will not pay a separate amount each time a record is played. Instead they will obtain a licence to do so instead. The licence fee is paid to the Society.

In a similar way, licences can be obtained to allow certain establishments to photocopy limited numbers of some publications. Educational establishments such as schools, colleges and universities can obtain one.

In addition, copies of an original document can be made for certain specific purposes e.g.

- research and private study
- criticism or review of a work providing the author and title of the work are both acknowledged
- the reporting of current events providing the author is acknowledged
- incidental inclusion in another artistic work, e.g. a television play where a book is lying on a chair with its title visible
- educational use.

However, if a licence has been granted, such exceptions do not apply. Note from the above that if an article is summarised or

---

quoted, then the author and title of the original work *must* be acknowledged (as with the reference at the bottom of this article).

A different type of exception is a book or magazine article where the normal rules of copyright do not apply. The tutor pack which accompanies this handbook is covered by special copyright conditions so that tutors can photocopy anything they need without breaking the law.

Taken from Administration level 3, *Carysforth and Rawlinson, published by Heinemann.*

Appropriate ways of supplying information

You can present information in several different ways, including

- in text form, such as a composition or summary – as above (sometimes called a **precis**)
- in graphical form, such as a diagram or chart
- in pictorial form, such as a drawing, photograph, cartoon or pictogram
- in tabular form, used for numerical information (and known as 'tabs' to typists).

The method you use will depend on the information required, the source of your original material and the purpose for which the material is now required.

 ## SPECIAL NOTE

Bear in mind that you can *receive* information in any of these formats as well! For that reason, the next element tests your ability not only to create different formats yourself, but also to understand information presented in that way.

Text form

Writing out a composition or precis is not that simple – as you have probably already discovered – but does get easier with practice. Don't make yourself look unprofessional by doing a fairly good job of summarising and then make a mess of it with the display of your document or your spelling or punctuation. The contents of Unit 7 in this book should help you with all of these points!

Bear in mind that sometimes brief note form is acceptable. For instance, if you were asked to summarise recent events with a customer for your boss you could write:

J & J Stott Ltd

18/4   Request made for representative to call

20/4   John Barker rang, made appointment for 10.30 am 25/4 with Sarah Wells

25/4   Arrived 10.15, waited until 11.15. Informed Sarah Wells out. Had to leave for next appointment.

28/4   Letter received from Sarah Wells, complaining about poor service.

This is easier to follow than a long continuous paragraph. It contains all the main facts in a format that is easy to read and follow. Remember, though, that if your boss then writes to J & J Stott he or she would *not* use note form – as this is not acceptable in a business letter (*see Unit* 7).

Do remember that if you copy anything word for word (whether you photocopy it, write it neatly or type it out) then you should always acknowledge your source(s).

Graphical form

If you were asked to explain the organisation structure of your company it would probably take several sheets of paper to try to write it properly. As an alternative, you could supply an **organisation chart**. This is the same information, in graphical form. It is easier to understand at a glance and creates a 'picture' for the person receiving the information.

In many cases this is a more appropriate way of presenting information. Other types of graphical format used in business include

- line graphs
- bar charts
- pie charts
- flow charts
- diagrams.

Many of these can be produced on computer. They look more professional and are quite easy to do if you have the right software.

Line graphs

A line graph may be composed of either a single line or several lines. If there is more than one line it is called a **multiline graph**.

Use a line graph if you need to illustrate a **trend**. Because the lines go up and down the increases and decreases can be seen at a glance. Line graphs are therefore used to show various types of statistical information such as profit figures, population growth or decline, crime rates, imports and exports, prices of goods, purchases and sales.

Creating a line graph

- The horizontal or *x*-axis goes across and the vertical or *y*-axis goes up and down. (To remember which is which remember a cross = *x*.) *Both* axes must be labelled clearly.
- Work out the spacing for your *x*-axis – starting from the extreme left. The *x*-axis almost always represents the **time** period.
- Work out your spacing for the *y*-axis. Work in units which will correspond to the squares on your graph paper.
- Remember your spacing must be even throughout.
- Insert your labels so they are centred on the mid-point which represents each one.
- Decide on either different colours or different types of line for each line of a multiline graph.
- Insert dots in pencil to mark the points, join them up in pencil using a ruler. Only ink in or colour in your lines when you are sure they are right.
- Don't forget to add a key so the reader of a multiline graph knows which line represents what.

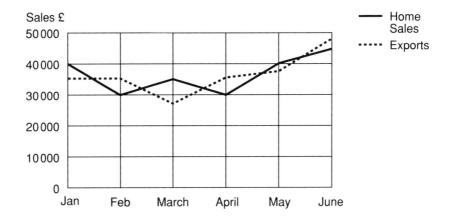

TEST YOURSELF

1 From the graph above, can you answer these questions?

   a In which months were home sales at their lowest?
   b By how much did export sales rise between March and April?
   c Between which two months did home sales rise the most?
   d By how much did home sales rise between March and June?
   e This company manufactures sunglasses and ski goggles. What trends on the graph support this?

2 Construct a graph to show the number of visitors to two tourist attractions in the summer months. The figures are as follows.

Location	May	June	July	Aug	Sept
Theme Park	5651	7290	10416	12080	4186
Water Gardens	2530	3210	3800	4020	3865

To help you, your boss has suggested that you *round* the figures to the nearest hundred in each case. Check with your supervisor or tutor if you are not sure how to do this.

DID YOU KNOW?

Graphs do not have to start at zero. If you are recording very small differences, e.g. between 52 and 78 then you could start your *y*-axis at 50 and end it at 80.

Bar charts

In this case individual bars are used instead of continuous lines. The effect is the same as in a line graph – increases and decreases are shown clearly.

A bar chart can be made up of single bars or multiple bars. A multiple bar chart compares more than one item. Shading or colour can be used but you *must* include a key. The axes are drawn in the same way as for a line graph.

DID YOU KNOW?

Bar charts can be vertical or horizontal. In the case of the latter, the lines are built up *across* the page from the *y*-axis, rather than drawn *up* the page from the *x*-axis.

TEST YOURSELF

1 The following bar chart shows the sales made by two representatives between January and June. Studying the chart and then answer the following questions.

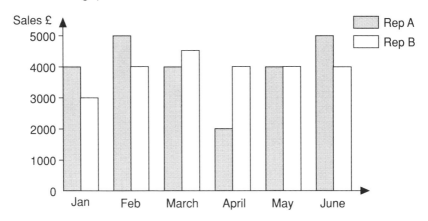

a In which two months did Rep A sell the most?

b Which was Rep B's worst month and which was his best month?

c How much did Rep B sell in his worst month?

d In which month was Rep A on holiday for two weeks?

e The company gives an award to the Rep with the best sales figures. Who is the winner?

2 Convert the graph you constructed in question 2 on page 190, showing visitors to two tourist attractions, into a bar chart.

Pie charts

A pie chart is always drawn as a circle with each wedge showing the portion of the whole that it represents. The size of the wedge is therefore proportional to the percentage it represents.

The example below shows advertising expenditure for an organisation during November. Note that a clear key is *vital*.

November advertising expenditure by type of media

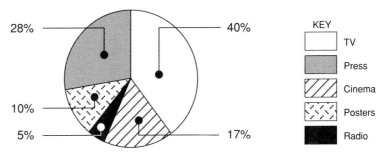

To construct a pie chart easily

- Start by marking off your circle into quarters (like a clock). Each will equal 25%.
- Then sub-divide one of these quarters if you want smaller amounts – as a rough guide aim for 10%, 10% and 5% and work from there.
- Always remember that your wedges *must* total 100%!

DID YOU KNOW?

For a better effect you can show one wedge slightly separated from the whole or – if you are really artistic – even draw a 3D pie chart such as this one.

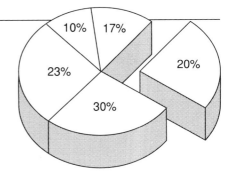

TEST YOURSELF

For the same organisation as above, expenditure in December had changed as follows

52% – TV
26% – press
8% – posters
3% – radio
11% – cinema
Construct the pie chart for that month.

Flow charts

Flow charts are used to show the way in which a procedure or system operates or is followed from start to finish. They are commonly used in designing computer programs. Flow charts are also used in production departments, to show the stages through which goods are processed and/ or stored. In this book, an example of a flow chart is given on page 131.

Drawing a flow chart is not easy, as you have to try to work out step by step what is needed or what is done. Often a flow chart may loop back on itself to show where an action has to be repeated.

In this book, an example of a flow chart is given on page 131.

CHECK IT YOURSELF

Try to draw a simple flow chart to show a novice how to make a cup of tea. Don't be put off if you make a mess of it! Compare your attempts with those of other people in your group and see who can manage to do it successfully.

Diagrams

Diagrams are often used to present information. A car user's handbook will contain diagrams showing the controls on the dashboard and parts of the engine. Electronic circuit diagrams and those showing the components of a machine are common in industry. A diagram is also a useful way of indicating the layout of something, e.g. furniture in a room. In this case it should be drawn to scale so that the size of the furniture is accurately represented in relation to the size of the room.

TEST YOURSELF

Draw a diagram which could be included in a visitors' handbook and shows accurately the route from the main car park for your building to the office of your supervisor or tutor. Bear in mind that this is not a map, if we are being really accurate, because you can use artistic licence. For instance you could illustrate key landmarks so that they are easy to spot, as in the diagram overleaf.

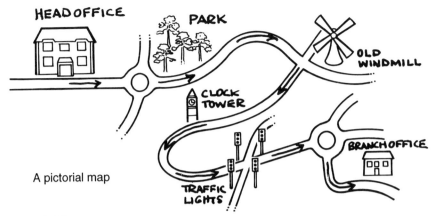

A pictorial map

Pictorial form

'A picture says a thousand words' and is sometimes more effective. The term **pictorial form** simply means the use of pictures rather than words. In fact newspapers often use pictures to illustrate situations and reduce the amount of words needed. They may also use different shots to make a special point. A proposed motorway route could be drawn on to an aerial picture of a town to show residents how they would be affected. A new building may be illustrated by an artist to show people what it will look like.

Therefore any type of illustration can be described as a pictorial representation – whether it is a sketch, a cartoon, or even a diagram. In fact, you may argue for weeks whether a diagram is a graphic or a picture but it doesn't really matter! All that matters is that you don't spend hours writing text when an illustration can do the job more easily.

It is rarely that a cartoon would be used in business. However, it is very common to see information pictorially represented in **pictograms**. These use pictures to represent one or more items and usually illustrate statistics which do not have to be interpreted very precisely and which may be seen by young people or those not familiar with the type of figures being presented. An example of a pictogram is shown below.

Each picture represents a certain quantity, with parts of pictures used to show smaller amounts. It is essential to include a key.

DID YOU KNOW?

Many signs contain pictures. We quickly learn what these represent and act accordingly. Think of road signs.

TEST YOURSELF

Safety signs are also often represented in pictures.

1   Can you think of *two* advantages of using pictures rather than words?

2   Can you identify the meaning of each of the *twelve* signs shown below
    – if not, then find out!

3   Can you remember the meanings of the different shapes? *If not, look
    back to Unit 2, page 50.*

DID YOU KNOW?

Some retail organisations make sure that the shop window displays in their regional stores are the same across the nation by sending a photograph of the desired display to all stores. This is a much better way of giving this information than writing out a three-page list of instructions for them to follow!

Tabular format

Frequently a table is a much easier method of imparting information than detailed written information. Try to imagine a publisher preparing information about the number of different books sold. Text would be difficult to understand and comparisons between sales of different books would be almost impossible to make. In tabular form, however, it would be easy to prepare this – perhaps using a 'top twenty' format.

Look at the information presented in A and B below and then answer the following questions.

1 Which do you find the easier to understand?
2 If you were asked to state the percentage increase for home sales in March, which document would you look at?
3 To which document could even more figures be added, e.g. totals, quickly and easily?

A Both home and export sales have shown continuous growth to date this year. The January home sales were £125 000, an increase of 3%, in February this increased a further 2.4% as sales reached £128 000. In March we touched £130 000 for the first time, showing an increase of 1.56% on the February figure.

Export sales in January were £75 000, an increase of 1%. In February they were £78 000, a further increase of 4% and in March they were £82 000 – yet another increase -this time of 5.13%.

B

	January		February		March	
	Sales £	% +/–	Sales £	% +/–	Sales £	% +/–
Home sales	125 000	+3%	128 000	+2.4%	130 000	+1.56%
Exports	75 000	+1%	78 000	+4.0%	82 000	+5.13%

TEST YOURSELF

1 From the following written information compile a table which will be more easily read by your representatives travelling on the Continent.

Temperatures vary throughout Europe. The average monthly figures in Celsius for four cities and for four months of the year are given as a guide. In Hamburg it is 2° in January, 13° in April, 23° in July but 13° in October. In Munich it is only 1° in January but this increases to 14° in April, then to 23° in July and back to 13° in October. In Vienna it is the same as Munich in both January and April but reaches 25° in July and then falls to 14° in October. In Zurich it is the same as Hamburg in January, then 15° in April, and the same as Vienna in July and October.

2 Look at the opposite table and answer these questions.

a Where is the water coldest?
b When is the best month to go swimming in the Atlantic?
c How much hotter is the South of France than Paris in June?

Temperatures in France

Average air temperature (Celsius)

	Mar/Apr	May/June	July/Aug	Sept/Oct
Brittany	12.9°C	18.9°C	22.6°C	19.6°C
Loire Valley	13.9°C	21.8°C	25.4°C	18.9°C
Paris	13.2°C	21.1°C	24.3°C	17.8°C
Southern France	16.8°C	24.8°C	29.7°C	22.7°C

Average sea temperature (Celsius)

	May	June	July	Aug	Sept	Oct
Channel Coast	10.8°C	13.3°C	16.2°C	16.9°C	16.2°C	14.4°C
Atlantic Coast	13.9°C	15.4°C	17.4°C	18.9°C	17.8°C	16.4°C
Mediterranean	14.4°C	15.6°C	18.9°C	19.9°C	19.4°C	16.7°C

d During which month is there the greatest different in water temperature between the Atlantic and the Mediterranean?

e Which region has an average air temperature of 20°C between March and October?

f During which two months does the sea temperature on the Channel coast change the most, and by how much?

UNIT REVIEW (2)

At the end of this element you should be able to

- understand and interpret requirements for information
- plan and search for information
- correctly identify and access information sources
- be able to offer alternative options if available information does not match requirements
- correctly interpret, transcribe and compile information
- present information pictorially, graphically, numerically and textually
- identify the most appropriate form in which to present information
- supply essential information within required deadlines
- disclose confidential information only to authorised persons.

CHECK YOUR KNOWLEDGE AND UNDERSTANDING

True or false?

1 Reference libraries also keep back copies of magazines and journals.

2 A CD-Rom is an optical disk containing information which can be accessed by computer.

3 The x-axis of a graph usually shows time.

4 A good dictionary will show the meanings of common abbreviations.

5 If you want information about National Insurance rates you should contact the Department of Health.

Fill in the blanks

6 _____ is an interactive viewdata system.

7 _____ _____ is a book which gives lists of words with similar meanings.

8 A suitable book in which to find the name of a hotel in Leeds would be _____ .

Work it out

9 Your boss has asked you to find out the following, quickly. What sources are available to you in each case?

a the exact time

b the up-to-date exchange rate of pounds sterling into American dollars

c the price of a car road fund licence

d the date(s) of next year's Motor Show

e the inoculations needed for visitors to Nigeria

f the name of a good restaurant in York

g the times and connections of suitable trains from Preston to Portsmouth

h the opening times and days and names of historic buildings in your own area

10 You work for a chocolate manufacturer which is preparing a leaflet for children who visit from local schools.

a Sales of the two main chocolate bars for the first six months of this year are given below. Select a suitable graphical form of presentation for this information and prepare this neatly and clearly. Round the figures to give the general trends, rather than exact information.

	Chocobar	Chocdeluxe
January	102 382	84 797
February	94 827	65 029
March	97 291	68 900
April	101 382	70 302
May	98 400	75 080
June	88 642	77 505

b Your company also makes Easter eggs which are on sale from February to April. In February 2000 eggs were sold, in March 6500 eggs were sold and in April 10 000 eggs were sold.

Illustrate this information in a pictorial form.

c Find out how chocolate is made and its main ingredients. Write a short paragraph for the leaflet explaining the steps in manufacturing chocolate and draw a chart which shows the main ingredients and the approximate percentage quantities in which they are used.

6 Maintain data in a computer system

This unit is about computer systems – how to use them to input, store and retrieve data and how to print out documents. It covers the type of computer systems and software you will be expected to use in business and the main features of each. Being able to use a computer effectively is virtually essential in any office. Today *everyone* is expected to be computer literate, from the managing director down to a junior clerk.

Information technology has transformed the working world over the last 20 years. In your private life you may shop and see your purchases processed by means of a bar-code reader at an electronic cash register, linked to a computerised stock control system. You may ask for a printed balance of your bank account at the cash machine. This is simply a form of computer output as the machine is linked electronically to the central bank computer.

In an office, a wide range of equipment such as microcomputers, photocopiers, telephone switchboards and fax machines, is controlled by microchips. Some of these may also be linked to a networked computer system so that employees can do many jobs without moving from their workstations.

In addition, computers are used to process, store and communicate a vast amount of information every hour of the working day. It is therefore impossible for you to work effectively in any organisation unless you have some knowledge about computers or how they work. A very basic knowledge will only make you a very average employee. To be *really* effective you need to know enough to be able to think for yourself, set your own (high!) standards and to use your own initiative when you come up against a problem.

This unit aims not only to give you the basic information you require but also to help you develop the skills you need to become a valuable employee.

DID YOU KNOW?

It is forecast that by the year 2000 the IT industry will comprise ten per cent of world economic activity and will be able to produce machines that can recognise and understand human speech and reasoning!

The layout of this unit

The order of information in this unit is slightly different from most of the others in this book. You will see in your scheme that this unit is divided into three elements

Element 6.1   Inputting data and text
Element 6.2   Locating and retrieving data and text
Element 6.3   Printing documents.

Obviously, as a first step, you need to know the basic facts about computer systems and the software which is used. In reality, when you use a computer to do a task you will not do each NVQ element separately. You may retrieve data from disk, edit it and then print it, and you would be expected to do this in one operation on one type of software.

For that reason, this unit starts by introducing you to the common features of computer systems and the software you will be expected to use. This means that some information relating to *all three* elements is often included in the different types of software covered in Element 6.1.

The additional knowledge you need for each element, plus specific information on disks and printers, then follows under each of the subsequent elements.

Element 6.1

Input data and text into a computer system

The basics

What do you need to know before you start? As a first step you need to be familiar with

- computer equipment or **hardware**
- the different types of **computer systems** to be found in business
- business application packages or **software**
- the main features of business software, and how to use it
- confidentiality and security systems
- health and safety and IT.

Computer hardware

The hardware of a computer system consists of

- **input devices** – used to put the information into the system
- **the central processing unit (CPU)** – the 'brains' of the system which carries out all the instructions received (either from the operator or from the program)
- **storage devices** – used to save both data and programs
- **output devices** – used to display the end result.

The link between these can be seen on the diagram overleaf.

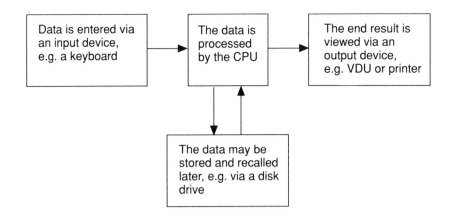

| Data is entered via an input device, e.g. a keyboard | → | The data is processed by the CPU | → | The end result is viewed via an output device, e.g. VDU or printer |

The data may be stored and recalled later, e.g. via a disk drive

Types of computer system

The exact type of equipment you will find in an office will depend on whether the organisation has stand-alone microcomputers, a networked system or a mainframe computer.

Stand-alone system

In this case your equipment will consist of

- a keyboard
- a screen (called a visual display unit – VDU)
- a central processing unit (CPU)
- a disk drive
- a printer.

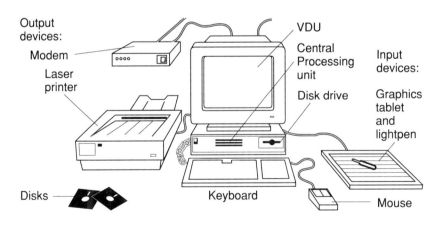

A stand-alone system

The term **stand-alone** is used because the system is self-contained and is not dependent on any other piece of equipment to operate. Such a system is sometimes referred to as a **workstation**. One advantage of a stand-alone system is that it is easily transportable and can therefore be used in different places (especially if it is very small, such as a laptop or notebook computer).

Although the system is stand-alone, there may be a telecommunications link between a workstation and other central computing facilities.

A networked system

In a network all the microcomputers in an organisation are linked together, so that they may all have access to the same information. This may be in the form of

- software programs, which are available on all or specified machines
- information which is useful to most or all of the staff (e.g. a customer address list).

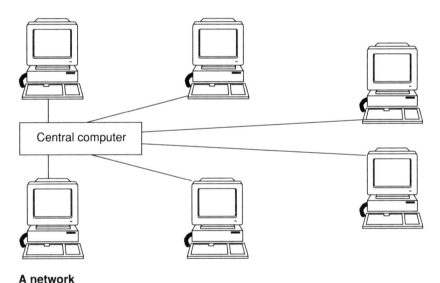

A network

If an organisation links its computers over a small (geographical) area then this is known as a **local area network (LAN)**. If the system is over a greater area this is referred to as a **wide area network (WAN)**.

Users **log on** to a network by means of their own user ID and a personal password. On most networks users must change their password regularly as a security precaution. Some users may have access to **higher level** (i.e. more confidential) information than others (*see also page 233*).

You should note that on some of the more sophisticated networks, more than computers are linked. A wide variety of office equipment can be incorporated into a network, including fax facilities and telex machines.

Using a networked computer

As mentioned above, each user of a network has to log on to gain entry to the system. When the user has finished working on the machine he or she must **log out** so that access has been officially ended. Computer staff can keep a record of the number of users and this can be useful for several reasons, including determining the main periods of use, whether the system is becoming overloaded and so on. It is important that, as a user, you use the correct procedure for logging in and *never* switch off the computer without logging out of the system properly.

DID YOU KNOW?

If you leave *any* computer switched on for a long period, with the same text or graphics showing on the VDU, this can create **screen burn**. This means that the image will be burned on to the screen and can be seen even when the computer is switched off. For this reason many computers are designed to blank the screen automatically after a few minutes of non-use. Pressing any key on the keyboard usually restores the image to the screen.

Mainframe computers

A mainframe computer is a computer which is capable of handling and processing a vast amount of information. These machines are very costly and are sometimes only leased or rented by large companies who have special computer departments and employ their own programmers and operators. Because these machines can be used by a number of people simultaneously, staff will each have a **terminal** on their desk – sometimes just a keyboard and a VDU – which is linked to the mainframe.

The software may have been individually written for the company by their own programmers and will probably include payroll, stock control and invoicing. In addition there may be some bought-in packages, such as spreadsheets and word processing.

There will be a security system in operation so that confidential information is only available to specified staff.

A large mainframe computer will have a very large memory and a high processing speed. Despite this, much of the routine work (e.g. processing invoices) is done overnight so that the computer is not overloaded during the daytime. For this reason, many companies with a mainframe computer operate a shift system so that computer staff are on duty 24 hours a day.

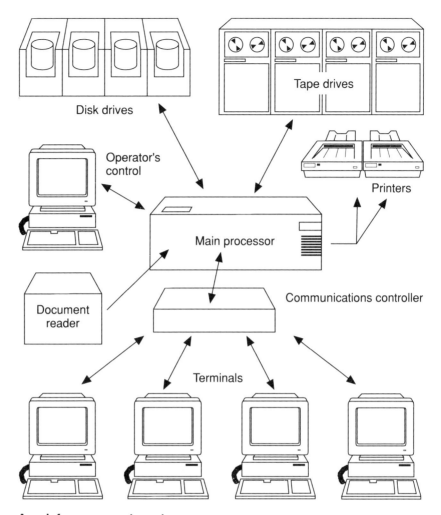

Disk drives

Tape drives

Operator's control

Printers

Main processor

Communications controller

Document reader

Terminals

A mainframe computer set-up

 DID YOU KNOW?

Executives who travel can take their computers with them if they have a **laptop** or **notebook** computer. Both of these machines are small, portable, self-contained units which incorporate a keyboard, floppy or hard disk drives and a screen. The laptop is the slightly larger version (but small enough to be used on the operator's lap). The notebook is as small as its name suggests.

A laptop computer

The latest computers are known as **palm top** or **pen computers**. Palm tops can be held in the hand and the latest only measures 7" by 4"!

It is possible to communicate with the office by means of a portable computer and both download and receive information. This is done via a telephone line and a **modem**, which may be built in to the machine. (*Modems are covered on page 208.*)

(*Modems are covered on page 208.*)

CHECK IT YOURSELF

For virtually all organisations it would be disastrous if a fire destroyed the company's computer system. Discuss as a group

1 the **costs** involved if such an event occurred (and try to think beyond the costs of the equipment!)
2 the precautions a company could take to prevent this type of occurrence.

If necessary, refresh your memory by looking back to Unit 2, Element 2.2.

DID YOU KNOW?

Computers vary in the speed at which they can process an instruction. The faster they operate the more powerful they are and so the more they (usually) cost. Faster computers are usually required for more complex programs and graphics packages. For character-based software, such as word processing, databases and spreadsheets the processing speed is less important. However, if you use an applications package which is linked to a graphic operating system, e.g. Windows, then you will find it much easier if you are operating a computer with a high speed processor.

Memory

The size of software programs a computer can run and the amount of data which it can handle without access to a storage device is determined by the size of its **memory**. The memory size is measured by the number of characters or **bytes** which the computer can store at any one time.

The memory capacity of microcomputers is measured in kilobytes, abbreviated to K, or megabytes, abbreviated to M (kilo = 1000, mega = 1 000 000). Therefore a small games computer with a 64K memory can handle approximately 64 000 characters at once.

Most business microcomputers have a base memory size of 640K with optional extended memory of usually 4 or 8 megabytes.

The memory capacity of main frame computers is measured in

● megabytes (mega = 1 million), and
● gigabytes (giga = 1000 million).

RAM

The proper term for a computer's working memory is **random access memory – RAM**. You can access any part of this data as you are working and replace it with something new if you want to.

RAM only operates on a temporary basis. When the computer is switched off any data held in RAM is lost. For this reason you need a **backing store** – usually a disk drive – so that data can be saved until it is next required.

ROM

Computers also have a **read only memory – ROM**. In this part of the memory you can read the information but cannot change it. A typical example is the basic operating system of the computer. When you switch on the computer it already knows how to operate, because a systems program telling it how to do this is already stored in ROM. You can therefore use this information, but cannot change or delete it.

Storage devices

These are dealt with in full in Element 6.2, page 237.

Care of hardware

1 Never switch a computer quickly off and on again.
2 Never move a computer without permission and without parking the heads on the hard disk first (*see page 237*).
3 Never switch off a networked computer without logging out properly.
4 Never try to take out a disk while the disk drive light is on.
5 Never leave a computer or a printer switched on for very long periods when you have finished using it.
6 Never put food, drink or other liquids on or near a computer.
7 If your machine shows an unknown error message, check with your supervisor, tutor or user manual before pressing any keys – or you may make the problem worse.
8 The machines and the screens should be cleaned regularly but *only* using the special products made for the job.

 DID YOU KNOW?

It is amazing how many people will stare at a computer which does not work without checking obvious faults! If your kettle did not work at home, presumably the first thing you would check is whether the appliance was plugged in! So start there.

A basic check list

● Check everything is plugged in.
● Check the equipment is switched on.

- Check there isn't a power cut.
- Check the power source by plugging in something else to the same socket.
- Check the connections (e.g. between VDU and computer and keyboard and computer).
- Check the brightness control on the VDU (you'll look silly if this is all that is wrong and you've called out a technician).

CHECK IT YOURSELF

1 Obtain a copy of a computer supplies catalogue.

a Find out how much you would have to spend to buy a notebook computer.

b Note down the products which are concerned with health, safety and security.

c List the type of products used for cleaning computers and price of each.

2 You are operating a stand-alone microcomputer which has a base memory of 640K and an extended memory of 8M. You are told it has a 40M hard disk.

a How many characters can be stored simultaneously in its base memory?

b How many in its extended memory?

c How many characters will the hard disk hold before it is full?

Peripherals

This term is used to describe any item of equipment which is attached to or controlled by the computer. Strictly speaking, it includes the disk drive. However, it is more usually used to describe the range of input and output devices which may be used by a computer operator, as well as communications devices, e.g. a modem.

 DID YOU KNOW?

A modem is a device which links two computers over a telephone line. A modem converts the analogue signal of the telephone line to the digital signal required by the computer, and vice versa, therefore two are required to link two computers, and so on. Modem stands for **mo**dulator **dem**odulator.

Input devices

In offices the main method of inputting data is by keyboard. However, in some organisations alternative methods may be preferred e.g.

Bar code reader used to read the bar code on goods to input sales information into

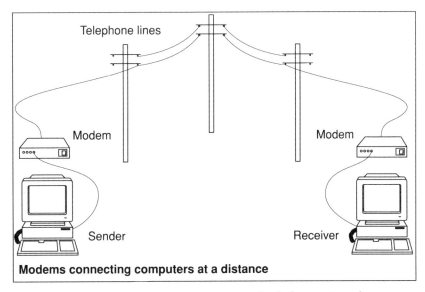

Modems connecting computers at a distance

	computerised electronic cash registers.
Touch sensitive screens	used by personnel who are not trained typists to input data – the operator simply touches the VDU screen at the required option. Found in organisations such as banks and hospitals.
Mouse	a small box moved around on the workstation desktop to change the position of the cursor on the screen. Often used by non-typists and with graphics programs.
Light pen	used to wipe over bar codes in a similar way to a bar code reader.
Graphics tablet	shapes can be drawn on these with a special stylus, like a pen.
Digitiser	used to create sophisticated graphics on computer by converting drawings, photographs and video stills to a series of digital impulses which are displayed on the VDU screen.
Document reader or scanner	a device which automatically reads text or graphics and puts this into a computer. This may be a machine into which is fed a sheet of paper or

else a hand-held device which is rolled over the required information. Some systems store just a pictorial image whereas others can store it as correct text characters. These are used in computerised filing systems to input information from documents which have been received by the company.

Magnetic ink character readers used by banks to identify cheques automatically by the numbers on them which are printed with special magnetic ink.

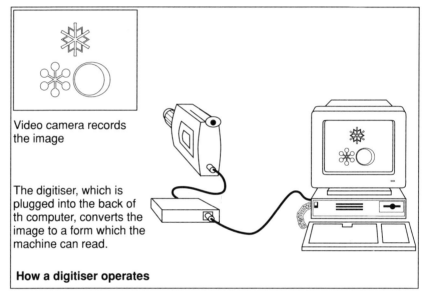

Video camera records the image

The digitiser, which is plugged into the back of th computer, converts the image to a form which the machine can read.

How a digitiser operates

Output devices

The main output device is the printer. *Printers are dealt with in Element 6.3 on pages 244 to 250.*

Operating a computer system

A computer is simply a device which enables you to process information quickly and easily. It has no in-built intelligence but simply follows instructions. It is therefore impossible for it to make mistakes on its own – if an error occurs it is because you made it! If you think of it as being a rather clever slave, rather than having a life force of its own, you will be more likely to take responsibility for your own actions!

To be able to operate one efficiently you need to know how to use the equipment correctly *and* understand how the software is meant to operate and the functions it can carry out. Failure to understand how to use it can result in expensive and time-consuming problems, if you inadvertently damage part of the system. Ignorance of how the software works can mean you waste hours of everyone's time, including your own. To be really effective you also need to take a pride in your work, so that the documents you produce are of consistently high quality and you gain a reputation for reliability and conscientiousness.

This usually pays dividends as you will be rewarded with progressively more difficult and challenging tasks – which will make your job more interesting and varied, as well as preparing you for a more senior position with more responsibility.

Operating a keyboard

The main input device is a keyboard. Keyboards vary from one computer to another although most have the standard QWERTY keyboard together with the following special keys. Find out where these are and learn how they work with *each* of the programs you use.

Function keys   there are usually up to twelve, and they will be either above or to the left of your character keys. Each will have a special use for each program you use.

Backspace   deletes the character to the left of the cursor.

Delete   deletes the character at the same position as the cursor.

Cursor keys   these are the four arrow keys which move the cursor up, down, to the left or right.

Page up/down   normally programmed by the software to move you forwards or backwards one page at a time.

Home key   this will either move your cursor to the beginning of the document or to the left of your screen.

End key   will either move your cursor to the end of the document or the right of your screen.

Esc key   usually enables you to escape from the option you have just chosen (useful if you choose the wrong one!).

Alt and Ctrl keys   usually have specific functions for the program you are using. You may like to note that holding down both Control and Alt together and pressing the Delete key will normally reset your computer. This can be useful to know if your screen **freezes** for any reason – but you will lose the work you were doing.

DID YOU KNOW?

Many keyboards can be locked by turning a key on the computer. You can use this when you leave your office to make sure that no-one else can input or alter information whilst you are away.

CHECK IT YOURSELF

1 Compare the computer systems you use at work and/or at college with those used by the other members of your NVQ group.
2 Find out the types of software packages used in your organisation or at college and their names. Divide these into two kinds – those which deal with **text** and those which deal with **numbers**.

Computer software

Software is the name for the programs which are loaded into the computer to tell it what to do. There are two types of program used with microcomputers.

System program

This is the operating system which controls the computer's operation and instructs it how to function. Whilst the most common is **disk operating system (DOS)**, the latest innovation is called **Windows**. Not only is this more powerful than DOS, enabling the user to work on several tasks at once, it is also more user-friendly as it relies on a system of **icons** (small pictures) and drop-down menus rather than keyed-in commands.

Applications programs

These are the actual business programs which can be loaded so that the computer can be used for a variety of business applications. An applications program is usually sold as a **package** comprising the software, a user manual and, sometimes, a tutorial disk or booklet. Applications packages can be bought which are compatible with either DOS or Windows – the same package is *not usually* compatible with both! Therefore, for instance, two popular word processing packages – Word and WordPerfect – can both be bought for either, i.e. Word or Word for Windows, WordPerfect or WordPerfect for Windows.

DID YOU KNOW?

The number after the title of a package indicates which issue it is. The latest WordPerfect package is called WordPerfect 6.0. This has improved and additional features to WordPerfect 5.0. Bear in mind when you are comparing software with someone else that you may not be making much sense if you are each talking about a different version of the same software!

Business applications packages

In business a wide variety of software is used, all of which has different uses and functions.

- **Word processing** packages are used for creating documents such as memos, letters and reports.
- **Database** packages are used for keeping records of customers, suppliers or anything else which could be kept on a manual card index system.
- **Spreadsheet** packages are based on an array of rows and columns and can be used for carrying out calculations including future plans, e.g. what will happen to our profit if we give all the staff a pay rise?
- **Graphics** packages may be used to create artwork for posters and adverts. Most spreadsheet packages also have a graphics capability to produce graphs, bar charts and pie charts.
- **Desktop publishing (DTP)** packages are used to create posters, newsletters and advertising material.
- **Payroll** packages do just that – they automatically calculate wages and print pay slips and the other statutory returns required by companies.
- **Accounts** packages are used for general book-keeping, producing invoices, calculating VAT returns and printing end of year financial documents.

At some time in your future career you may use any of these types of software. At this stage, however, you are most likely to use word processing, database and spreadsheet packages together with, perhaps, a basic DTP package. These are the packages which are described in more detail in this unit.

DID YOU KNOW?

1   The small block on your screen where the colours are reversed and often flashing is called the cursor. The **cursor** must be at the point at which you want to do something – whether this means choosing an option or changing some text.

2   Most packages are cleverly designed so that all the prompts are given to you on screen. Unfortunately, many people don't bother reading these so all this effort by the programmer is wasted! If you're stuck, before you try to find help, **always read your screen**. It is very likely that the answer to your problem is staring right back at you!

3   On most packages a standard VDU cannot show all of an A4 page at once, it only shows the area you are working on. You therefore need to **scroll** from one part of your document to another by pressing your cursor arrow keys. On many packages there are special commands to enable you to move from one part of a document to another quickly – learn them and use them!

Types of packages

The main packages for **text processing** are word processing packages. **Numerical processing** is usually carried out by spreadsheets, payroll and accounts packages. A further type of package is a **graphics** or drawing package, but in an office ready-made graphics are often bought on a disk and imported into documents produced using word processing and desk top publishing software.

 ## DID YOU KNOW?

Some packages are **integrated.** This means that the package can have word processing, spreadsheet, database and possibly graphics facilities. Data from one part of the package is compatible with any other part. Increasingly packages include translators so that files produced using a package by a different software manufacturer can also be 'imported'.

User-friendly packages

Some programs are advertised as 'user-friendly' – because they are supposed to be easy to learn and use. This usually means that they will incorporate either **menus** or **windows**. A menu simply gives you a list of choices, and you move the cursor to the option you want (or key in the letter to identify this option). A window operates on a similar basis. A range of options is shown across the top of your screen. When you select the one you want, a menu drops down under this option giving you a range of choices.

 ## DID YOU KNOW?

On *any* package you *must* press your 'Enter' key (or click the correct mouse button) to select the option you want. The computer cannot know which choice you have made until you do this!

If you make the wrong choice by mistake, on most packages pressing Esc (or selecting this option with your mouse) will take you back to where you were before .

Common features

Features which are common to many different types of package include

Status line(s) which gives information on the piece of work you are creating.

Prompt line which gives information on what you can do next.

Entry line usually identified by >. You enter your command immediately after this symbol.

Help feature most packages use a special Help key on your computer. This will give you the assistance the programmer thought you might need if you are stuck at this part of the program.

Commands these vary considerably from one package to another. Learn the ones you need to use on a regular basis (make a note of them to start with on a quick reminder sheet). You can look up the more obscure commands as and when you need them. The main commands you will need to know are

- **retrieve** – how to recall information already stored on disk
- **save** – how to save information you have created on to disk
- **print** – how to print a hard copy of your work
- **quit** – how to close down the package when you have finished.

DID YOU KNOW?

To use software or disks on a particular computer they must be **compatible** with the system you are using. You cannot take a disk which you have used on an Apple machine and use it directly on an IBM machine (although Apple machines can translate disks from IBM machines, and produce disks that can be read by IBM machines). In a similar way, you must make sure that any software you buy is compatible with the hardware system you are using.

Word processing packages

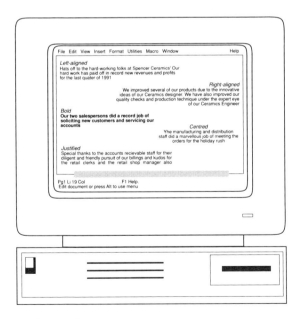

A word processing package

Word processing packages are used to produce letters, memos, reports and other business documents and have removed much of the drudgery and repetitive work this used to involve. A variety of packages are on the market, including WordPerfect, Word, Wordstar etc. You may be pleased to know that whereas the packages are obviously not identical, the type of features to be found on a word processing package are always the same. It may only be the commands and the layout of your screen which are different. Therefore if you know one package well, this should help you to learn others quickly.

DID YOU KNOW?

When you use a word processing package the text on your screen will automatically continue on to a new line. The only time you press your Return or Enter key is to make a new paragraph – when you need to press it twice.

Main features

Editing
Text can easily be inserted, deleted or amended in any document – there is never any need to have to retype pages just because some alterations need to be made.

Text enhancement
Text can be specially enhanced by using bold, underline or other options. Some packages enable you to produce text in special fonts – very large or very small, italic or other forms of typeface, such as a shadow effect. How these come out will depend very much on the printer you are using. (*See page 254.*)

Blocks
Blocks are chunks of text which you want to do something with – you may want to move, copy, delete or enhance a block. The first step is to define your block by identifying where it starts and finishes. You then give the command for the operation you require.

Reformatting
Any aspect of the layout of a document can be changed at any time. You can alter the margins, change the style of your headings (e.g. from block to centred), justify your right hand margin, change paragraphs and number your pages. You can change the design when you have seen what the finished document will look like – to improve the final appearance. (*See page 250.*)

Search (and replace)
You can search for a particular word or phrase through a document of any size. If you wish

you can replace this with another word or phase either by choice (as you look through) or automatically.

Mail merge

Mail merge is the way to produce personalised letters quickly and easily. You type in the letter and mark where the 'variable' parts will be placed. You then store it under one file name. Next you type in your 'variables' and store these under a different file name. Variables are those parts of the letter which are different for each recipient, e.g. name, address and possibly special details in the body of the letter, such as an interview time.

When you give the computer special instructions it will merge the two files in such as way that personalised letters are automatically produced.

Printing

Your print screen will usually give a variety of options, such as choice of line spacing, margin settings, justification and so on. You may also be able to print out selected pages only or multiple copies, as required. (*See unit 6.3.*)

DID YOU KNOW?

The term WYSIWYG stands for 'what you see is what you get'. This is the term used for word processing systems where you see the text on screen in the same way as it will look on the printed page.

Additional features

Headers and footers

These commands put a space (and text if you want it) at the top and bottom of documents automatically. If, for instance, you wanted to put the name of your organisation at the top of one or more pages then you would create a header with this information. If you wanted to put a special note at the bottom you would create a footer.

Pagination

This inserts page numbers automatically – an essential feature of a long document in case someone drops it on the floor and needs to sort it out again!

Spell checks

Some packages will automatically check your spelling by comparing the words you have typed with those in their electronic dictionary. Highly technical words and proper nouns (e.g. place names) will probably not be in the dictionary but can be added if you want. Bear in mind that words you have spelled wrongly but which still make a proper word will be ignored by your spell check, e.g. form/from, now/know, kind/king, work/word etc. So you still need to proofread!

Thesaurus

An electronic thesaurus will give you a list of words similar in meaning to the one at your cursor position. This can be useful to improve the vocabulary of a document or by replacing repeated words. If you use a thesaurus do make sure you know the difference between a noun and a verb – otherwise you could replace a word with one which doesn't have the same meaning at all! For instance – object (noun) is an article, a commodity or a thing, object (verb) means to protest or dispute – so be careful!

Word count

This may be included with your spell check. It can be useful if you have to complete a report or project of a certain length – as you can check your length as you go and add or delete words as required.

Graphics

This can mean actual graphics or, more usually in this context, tables and/or boxes which can be drawn (*see page 253*).

Footnotes

This option automatically numbers and places footnotes for you at any point in the text where they are required.

Switch screens

This option means you can work on two documents at once and simply switch between them, moving text as you wish.

Using a word processing package

The only way you can become expert at word processing is to practise regularly. However, some basic pointers right at the beginning will help you to do well more quickly.

1 *Don't* 'hunt and peck' around the keyboard! Really try to learn keyboarding properly at the outset – it saves hours later.
2 Learn how to move around your screen easily and quickly (usually a combination of the arrow keys and special commands for larger jumps).

3   *Never* delete lots of text and retype it when all it needs is a quick deletion or insertion at a specific point!

4   Learn the commands you need to use regularly. These will usually include

- **text commands** – bold, underscore
- **format commands** – changing margins, centring text, typing to a flush right margin, justification, inset or indented paragraphs, choosing size of paper
- **editing commands** – insert, delete, move, delete or copy blocks of text, search and replace, spell check and thesaurus
- **print commands** – number of copies, size of paper, line spacing, specific pages only.

(Formatting and editing are dealt with mainly in elements 6.2 and 6.3.)

Use the manual to look up any others you need when you want them.

5   Learn the functions you need for the job you do. For instance, if you regularly have to produce personalised letters, then learn how to use your mail merge facility. If you have to type and store standard paragraphs then learn how to do this properly.

6   Develop a sensible and logical system of saving your documents, so that you can access them easily (*see page 239*).

7   Set up directories for different types of documents – rather like you might store different types of files in a filing cabinet (*see page 241*).

8   File your print-outs in the same way using folders and files which are correctly labelled with the same names as your directories.

9   Learn the correct layout for business documents (see Unit 7). In business, each organisation may have its own 'house style' which you are required to use, no matter what you think of it! (Remember – he who pays the piper calls the tune!)

Make sure that the documents you produce are correct and professionally produced so that they won't need altering by anyone else before they can be used.

10 Use your common sense and initiative. Don't expect to be told

- to proofread your typing
- to check your spelling
- to use the correct layout (or set it out as clearly and attractively as you can)
- to save an important document
- to save the original document
- to keep confidential information to yourself
- to print out the correct number of copies.

You should do all this *automatically!*

DID YOU KNOW?

If you are inputting confidential material and are interrupted the best thing to do is to turn down the brightness on your VDU – or keep you screen angled so that callers to your desk can't read it. If you are leaving your desk then save your work and exit the package. Unless you can lock your keyboard, log off if you are on a network system, so that nobody else can use your computer under your ID.

TEST YOURSELF

Your friend has recently started work for a local charity. Money is scarce in their offices and they still use old typewriters. The manager, Mrs Thornhill, is 'anti-computer'. She thinks that

- they are expensive
- they are limited – envelopes are difficult to produce on many computer printers
- word processors are useless for filling in forms
- they are useless if there is a power cut.

Your friend doesn't agree and is desperate to buy a fairly cheap word processing system. She thinks the work could be done twice as quickly and the money would therefore be well spent.

She has asked for your help in trying to persuade Mrs Thornhill to buy a word processor.

1 List the advantages of using a word processor for standard documents such as letters, memos and reports.

2 Investigate *at least two* reasonably priced word processing systems and printers and compare their main features. Write a paragraph stating which system you recommend and give your reasons.

3 Examine Mrs Thornhill's arguments carefully. Try to suggest a solution which will keep both Mrs Thornhill and your friend happy!

4 Produce a brief report of your findings for your friend which summarises all your investigations. Use a word processor to produce this and use text enhancement features so that your document(s) are themselves a good advertisement for using a word processor!

Database packages

A database is a type of **electronic filing system** which not only stores and recalls information quickly and easily but can also sort it in various ways to suit the needs of the user.

You can keep a database on *anything* which you might record on ordinary paper records, e.g.

- a list of customers' names, addresses, telephone numbers, credit allowed etc.

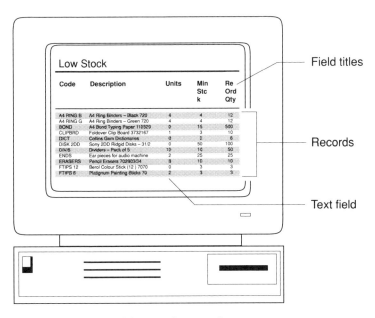

Field titles

Low Stock

Code	Description	Units	Min Stck	Re Ord Qty
A4 RING B	A4 Ring Binders – Black 720	4	4	12
A4 RING G	A4 Ring Binders – Green 720	4	4	12
BOND	A4 Bond Typing Paper 110329	0	15	500
CLIPBRD	Foldover Clip Board 3732167	1	3	10
DICT	Collins Gem Dictionaries	0	2	6
DISK 2DD	Sony 2DD Ridgid Disks – 31/2	0	50	100
DIV/5	Dividers – Pack of 5	10	10	50
ENDS	Ear pieces for audio machine	2	25	25
ERASERS	Pencil Erasers 702903/34	8	10	10
FTIPS 12	Berol Colour Stick (12) 7070	0	3	3
FTIPS 8	Platignum Painting Sticks 70	2	3	3

Records

Text field

A database package used for stock control

- a list of cars in a fleet (e.g. for a hire car company) with model, year, registration number, date last serviced etc.
- a list of books in a library with title, author, publisher, index number, year of publication etc.
- a list of students in a college or school with name, address, course attended, work experience placements etc.

The problem with manual filing is not in entering or keeping the records but *rearranging* them to find specific information. If your college or school kept student records on a card index system it would be very time-consuming to

- sort through them all to find a specific student
- sort through them to make lists under different criteria, e.g.
  - all students aged under 18
  - all students who live more than five miles away
  - all female (or male) students
  - all students who did not complete their course

and so on.

On a database system this can be done at the press of a key (or two!).

Main features

Form   This is the 'card' on screen (similar to a paper record card) which will contain the information.

Field	These are the areas for completion with specific information (the dark areas on the card in the illustration).
Data	The information to be entered in each field.
Record	The name given to a completed form.
Editing	The ability to change information in each field.
File	The name of a specific system. In the system described above the file name would probably be 'students'. When the database is completed the file will hold all the student records.

Additional features

Report	A report can be designed and printed to reorder the information and display it in a number of different ways.
Search	This command will enable you to find a record very quickly. You simply key in a 'key' piece of information and press Enter. The record you require will then be shown on screen in a matter of seconds.
Formula	These can be entered to calculate amounts at certain points (*see also under spreadsheets*). For instance, if each college student could claim bus fares for every day they attended then the record may have three fields:

Name   **Amount of fares**   **Days attended**

A formula could be entered to multiply the amount by the number of days attended and only the result would appear on the report.

Essential data On many systems you can specify whether data must be entered in a field or not. On a student record the 'name' field would be 'essential data' but details of work experience would not.

 ## DID YOU KNOW?

In many organisations, designing reports is the job of a qualified computer technician. This is particularly the case if the package is difficult to operate *or* if complicated reports are required, e.g. those requiring formulae to be entered or those where the print-out has to be listed in a certain order, e.g. alphabetically.

Using a database

1   Learn all your basic commands, e.g. load, save and print. Find out how to start to design a blank form.

2 Think about the type of file you are going to create, the design of the records and decide what fields you need.

3 Choose field title names which cannot be misinterpreted by other users and decide the length of information which will need inserting after each field name. This determines the lengths of your fields.

4 Create a record card on screen. Learn how to change and rearrange field names and field lengths and print out a copy of the blank form for reference.

5 Practise keying in data on several records. Learn how to edit your records in case you make an error and how to **resave** your latest version on disk.

6 Practise moving quickly from one record to another using the **search** command.

7 If you are operating an easy package you may be taught how to design a simple report. Think about the type of information users may want and specify reports to give them this.

8 Print out reports and check that the layout is user-friendly.

DID YOU KNOW?

1 Many database records are subject to the provisions of the Data Protection Act (*see page 67*) and it would therefore be usual to have a security system in operation so that the records could not be accessed by unauthorised personnel (*see page 70*).

2 Computerised stock records are simply another version of a database. This time the cards have been specially designed to give details of stock held.

CHECK IT YOURSELF

Discuss as a group the type of reports you would wish to see if you were operating

a a computerised stock record system

b a database containing information on each member of staff.

DID YOU KNOW?

An *on-line* database is another name for one to which users subscribe to obtain information. Ceefax and Oracle, which you can access on your television, are an example. Other well-known examples are New Prestel (*see Unit 5, page 180*).

TEST YOURSELF

Your organisation has many visitors from other parts of the UK and from abroad who are frequently entertained by your executives. It has been decided to create a database file on restaurants in your area.

1 Plan a suitable record card with field names and fields for information you think would be useful.

2 Decide on the criteria you would want to use to sort the cards to produce different reports. Produce a list for your computer technician.

3 Use your local *Yellow Pages* to make a list of *twelve* restaurants you think should be included.

4 *If possible*, produce a print-out of *at least one* report for inclusion in your portfolio.

Spreadsheet packages

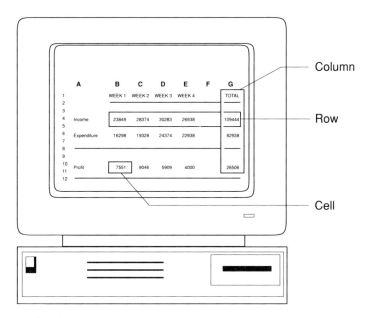

A spreadsheet package

Spreadsheet packages are used by company accountants or financial managers to assess how well the company is performing and/or how proposed changes will affect its performance. They may also be used by sales, production and personnel staff if they are involved in making calculations or predictions based on numerical information.

A spreadsheet looks like a large sheet of paper (which gives the spreadsheet its name) and is ruled off into **columns** and **rows**. Headings can be given to the columns and the rows. Figures can then be added to show income, expenditure, sales, profit etc. on either a weekly or monthly basis.

Spreadsheets are particularly useful for 'what if' calculations. If you are involved in manual calculations you will know that problems occur when

- alterations have to be made to past figures, *or*
- you want to try to predict the results of possible changes in the future. For instance, if you suddenly obtained promotion to a job which paid you an extra £25 a week but your spending increased to an average of £16 per week, can you say immediately how much more money you would have at the end of the year? And whether you would be able to afford to go abroad on holiday? If you had a spreadsheet you could enter the new figures and know the answer in seconds!

DID YOU KNOW?

The spreadsheet on which you are working is usually known as a **worksheet.** You can design this so that it is more user-friendly by using effects such as underline to separate headings from data underneath and to clearly differentiate totals.

Main features

Columns   Always go *down* a spreadsheet and are identified by a letter – A, B, C etc.

Rows   Always go *across* a spreadsheet and have an identifying number – 1, 2, 3 etc.

Cells   A cell is an individual square or box on the spreadsheet. The cell you are working on is called the **active cell**. Cells are always referred to by using the column letter first, e.g. A1, B5, W49 etc.

Entry line   This is either immediately underneath or above your spreadsheet. It is the line on which you enter text, figures, formulae or commands. Pressing the 'Enter' key moves the data into the cell on which your cursor is positioned.

Figures   These are entered by simply keying them in on the entry line and pressing Enter. Figures can be either entered in whole numbers (called **integers**) or to a specified number of decimal places (i.e. two decimal places if you are dealing in money).

Text   On some packages this must be prefaced with a special sign so that the computer knows you are entering, say, a heading and not a set of figures for calculating.

Formulae   A mathematical formula has to be entered at each point where a calculation has to take place. Normally these aren't visible on the spreadsheet.

DID YOU KNOW?

Because a spreadsheet is so large only a small part is shown on your screen at once. Therefore if you jump from cell A1 to cell W58 you are moving to a totally different part of the spreadsheet. There is usually a command to enable you to jump from one cell to another and it is well worth finding this!

TEST YOURSELF

Bearing in mind that some spreadsheets can have literally hundreds of columns and/or rows, can you suggest how columns are identified after the letter Z has been reached?

Additional features

Format
This can include the type of numbers you are displaying (e.g. integer or decimal), column width, right or left justified text. You have the choice between whether to change the format of all the cells of a spreadsheet (i.e. a **global** command) or just one specific cell, row or column.

Erase
Blanking a cell to remove the existing information.

Delete
Removing a row or column.

Copy
Copying an entry from one cell to another.

Insert
Inserting a new row or column.

Protect
Protecting specific cells and formulae against erasure.

Locking
Locking title cells in place (e.g. January, February, etc.) so that they continue to show on screen as the spreadsheet scrolls.

Graphics
Spreadsheet packages are designed to enable you to print out your finished results in graphic form, e.g. by producing a bar chart, line graph or pie chart.

Recalculating
Spreadsheet packages recalculate the answer in every column or row automatically when you make an alteration to a figure. Whilst this is useful it can be time-consuming if you have to wait for a large spreadsheet to be recalculated each time you make an entry. Therefore you have the option to turn recalculate off whilst you make several entries. However, you must remember to turn it back on again to enable the results of your calculations to be shown!

Replicating
Once you have decided on your formula (see below) it would be time consuming to enter it dozens of times. For instance, if you are trying to find the sum of 50 columns you wouldn't want to enter a 'sum' formula 50 times. If you use the replicate command this copies your command across all the other columns you specify.

Using a spreadsheet

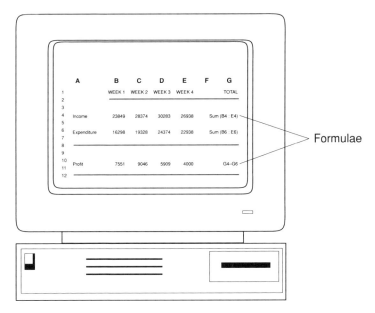

A spreadsheet showing formulae

1 Learn your basic commands (blank, edit and format) and how to enter figures and text.

2 Make sure you are aware of how to **load** a spreadsheet (from disk), **save** (to disk) and **print**. Learn how to clear your screen (which may be the command to **zap** the spreadsheet). If you are printing out a large spreadsheet on A4 paper you will need to know how to specify condensed (smaller) print.

3 Make sure you understand how to insert formulae. Simple formulae include add, subtract, multiply and divide. Bear in mind

- the answer will always be shown in the cell where your cursor is positioned
- you can identify cells or numbers for inclusion in the formula, e.g. A1+C7 or A1+18.

4 Understand the signs used for inserting formulae.

- You can add by simply specifying cell names with a plus sign in between, e.g. A1+C3. However, this would be impractical

for a large number of cells so you need to find out how to enter a sum command for your package. This means the figures in any number of cells will be added together.
● A subtraction is done by identifying the cells and inserting a subtraction sign, e.g. A1-B1.
● Multiply is entered using the symbol *, e.g. B3*D7.
● Divide is entered using the symbol /. Therefore D48/4 means divide the figure in cell D48 by 4.

DID YOU KNOW?

When professional users insert the replicate command they never specify a basic range of cells but always add one on. Then if they need to insert an extra figure later the formula doesn't need to be altered!

Graphics and spreadsheets

Most spreadsheet packages will create a variety of graphics and charts, e.g. line graphs, bar charts and pie charts. The commands for creating these will vary from one package to another. Tips to help include

● Decide on the type of graph or chart you want to produce.
● Work out
  – the **headings** and **labels** which must be included. Each heading must appear somewhere in your spreadsheet – if it doesn't then insert it in a blank cell, preferably one some distance from your main working area
  – identify the cells which you want to illustrate.

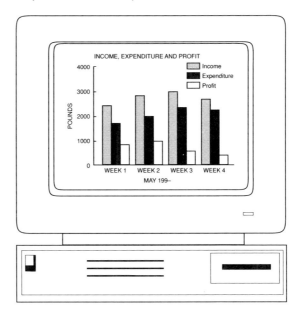

A bar chart produced on a spreadsheet package

- If you are creating a line graph or bar chart you need to know that the **vertical** axis is the **y–axis** and the **horizontal** axis is the **x–axis**, so that you can label each axis correctly.
- Information which will be shown on the graph or chart is known as **variables**. For instance, a bar chart with savings and expenditure has *two* variables, a bar chart for income, expenditure and profit has *three* variables and so on. A pie chart can only have one variable or you would need more than one circle! You will need to know the range of cells in which each variable (set of information) is contained.
- **Time labels** are only used on line graphs and bar charts. They refer to the time period the graph or chart is covering.
- **Variable labels** are used to give a bar chart or line graph its key – otherwise no-one will understand what the lines or bars represent.
- **Point labels** refer to the labels on a pie chart.

TEST YOURSELF

You work for a company which has branches in various parts of the country. You have been asked to enter the monthly sales figures for January to May and find the totals for each region and each month. Enter the data in your spreadsheet.

Adjust column widths as necessary and rule off appropriately.

Sales by region

	Jan	Feb	Mar	Apr	May	Total
South	8300	8966	9031	6890	7801	
Midlands	3898	4890	4881	3989	3991	
North	5897	5887	4789	5992	4118	
Scotland	3778	4283	4576	7503	3990	
Wales	5008	5882	5940	3082	4801	
N Ireland	3900	4800	5700	2890	4893	
Total						

Enter formulae that will add together all the figures horizontally and vertically. Ask your tutor to help you enter a formula which will check that your final total (horizontally) agrees with the total for each region when added together.

If you are able to produce graphs and charts on your package use the data to produce

- a line graph, showing the performance of each region
- a bar chart, showing the sales per region per month
- a pie chart just for one month, showing the percentage of sales per region.

Inputting text and data

If you are inputting text and/or data then you will be involved in

- creating documents
- adding text or data to existing documents
- modifying (changing) existing data
- deleting data.

If you are creating a new document then you will need to know how to set this out and format it (*see page 250*). If you are adding text or data to an existing document or changing what is already there, then you will need to know how to recall documents and amend them. *This is dealt with on page 239.*

Probably the most dangerous operation of all is deleting data! If you delete the wrong thing – or too much – you could lose precious information which could take hours to find again (or even be irreplaceable). For that reason, many software programs have a safety feature incorporated which means that you can restore *some* (but not necessarily all) of the data you deleted by accident. In addition, the latest operating systems have in-built security systems to restore whole documents or files which were deleted in error.

To prevent the problem occurring in the first place, it is sensible to have a back-up disk containing all your key documents. *This is dealt with in Element 6.2, page 242.*

Source data

Source data refers to the original sources of information you have been asked to input into a computer. These may be

- an original document (e.g. keying in details on a database from a paper record, scanning a letter into a computerised filing system)
- notes (e.g. typing a memo on a word processor from notes you made yourself).

In some cases there may be no source data – for instance if you compose a document yourself at the keyboard.

In some cases your source data will be complete. This means it does not need any additions or alterations on your part. In other cases it may be incomplete. It could be that you have to add information yourself, either by finding it first or writing it yourself. *Never* leave finding additional information until the end. Find it first, then you have assembled the tools for the job before you start. If you have to add or alter something on your own, make sure you have clarified any unclear instructions so that you know exactly what you are doing. Otherwise you may easily find you have the job of undoing all your work later!

You should only input data which has come from an *authorised* source or which you *know* to be correct. If you do not, you could be inputting data which is out of date, inaccurate or – even worse – confidential. You could even be in breach of the Data Protection Act (*see Unit 2, page 67, and Unit 5, page 167*). If you are in any doubt at all then obtain clear directions from your supervisor.

When you have accessed source data for information, make sure you return it to its proper place, according to the filing procedures laid down by your organisation. Don't leave dozens of documents lying about, with the idea that you will return them all later. Someone else may need them, too!

Coding data

Some computer systems use reference codes as a shortcut to save keying in large amounts of information. Because the information is held in an abbreviated form less computer memory is used. The same codes can often be used to search for or retrieve data.

As an example, imagine that a large company has 500 employees. Each employee has an employee code which is a combination of the first letters of their surname and department, e.g.

Nigel Williams in Sales = WILSA
Mohammed Umerji in Production = UMEPR
Carley Baker in Purchasing = BAKPU

There is, of course, the danger that there could also be a Nicola Wilkins in Sales, who would have the same code. This can be solved by incorporating a numerical system as well, e.g. WILSA1 and WILSA2.

Each of their personnel records could be made immediately retrievable by typing in the code. Even if you didn't know the particular code you could guess this from knowing their name – or there may be a master list giving all the codes. The same code may identify each user on a computerised electronic mail system (*see Unit 8, page 339*) and may also be printed on their security ID card (*see Unit 2, page 62*).

This type of code is called a **meaningful** code – each code means something because it is derived from an actual word. Another example of a meaningful code is your postcode – where the initial letters are related to the town or area in which you live. The disadvantages with this system are that it is easy to run out of codes (e.g. twelve people who fit the WILSA code!) and unauthorised people may be able to guess them.

A **meaningless** code is therefore considered safer. If you had to code colours and assigned each a number, so that 1 = black, 2 = brown, 3 = red etc. then this code is meaningless to anyone but yourself – so is therefore safer to use. Examples of meaningless codes are driving offences (e.g. SB30 is a speeding offence) and categories on motor vehicle insurance policies. Without the key you cannot understand them.

There are dozens of applications for codes, e.g.

- products purchased by the company
- products sold by the company
- customer names and addresses
- accident categories
- standard paragraphs for inserting in documents.

If you have to input a code on a set of data then you must make sure that this is keyed in accurately, otherwise you might be entering totally false information on the right record, or correct information on the wrong record!

CHECK IT YOURSELF

1 You can often tell what code you have with different organisations. Check a driving licence and look for the driver number. This is a code which includes the first few letters of the driver's surname and his or her birthdate.

2 What code is given to you by the Inland Revenue which directly affects the amount of money you take home? What does this code mean to your wages office? (If you are not sure, check the answer with your supervisor or tutor.)

Coping with problems

Problems with inputting may occur if

- your source data is incomplete and you can't find what is needed
- you have a deadline for the work and can't meet it
- you need a code but can't find it
- you make an error and don't know what to do
- your computer develops a fault when you are working.

To assist computer users, most organisations employ computer support staff whose job it is to solve users' problems where possible. If, all of a sudden, your computer stops working properly you may be able to phone a **help line** for immediate assistance.

This does not mean, however, that computer support staff will expect to solve your every minor problem. Nor may they be able to help you if you are dealing with specialised work they do not understand. Their job is concerned with the mechanics of the system, not doing your job for you!

Discuss with your tutor or supervisor the correct action to take if *any* of the problems on page 232 occurs. If you already use a computer at work, think of other problems you may have had and add these to the list, together with the correct solution.

Confidentiality and security

There are many types of security systems relating to computers.

- Most organisations have user IDs and passwords to prevent or restrict access to important or confidential information. (*See below and Unit 2, page 70.*)
- Many types of software have security systems built in to prevent accidental erasure of information.
- Some operating systems assist the user to retrieve material which was deleted in error and have special back-up features to protect important data.

In some computer installations, very elaborate security procedures exist to prevent access by unauthorised individuals to certain areas. These may include locked doors which will only respond to a key code, a swipe card or even a voice or hand print!

Most computer departments have a set of authorities for each computer user in an organisation. This may restrict or prevent access to certain files. For instance

- Category A files may be unobtainable
- Category B files may be read only
- Category C files may be read and have data input or amended.

A director of the company may have full access to all files. A junior employee may only be able to view even category C files. A supervisor may be able to view some files and have full access to others and so on.

Each user will also have his or her own password to use in conjunction with their user ID which enables the computer system to check if the person logging on is the genuine user. Needless to say, no-one is expected to tell someone else his or her password.

Computers and the law

Computer data and the Data Protection Act are covered in Unit 2, page 67 and Unit 5, page 169.

Computers and Health and Safety

People who are asked to work on computers for the first time may be concerned about health and safety implications. This does not mean that they are worried that when they plug in or use a computer they will get an electric shock! The main concerns are over

- backache
- eye strain
- headaches and migraine
- RSI and tenosynovitis
- using VDUs when pregnant.

Backache is usually caused through poor seating, bad posture or sitting for hours on end at a computer. Eye strain can be caused by flickering screens, poor lighting, glare from the screen, sunshine reflecting on a screen or by staring at a VDU for hours on end. Headaches and migraine often follow on from eye strain.

RSI stands for repetitive strain injury and is caused by making repetitive or awkward movements over and over again. A common form of this is tenosynovitis – known as teno for short. *Both RSI and tenosynovitis are covered in Unit 2, page 51.*

Some pregnant women are concerned that radiation or other emissions from VDUs may harm an unborn child. Special shields can be attached to VDUs to protect them but, as yet, there is no evidence that VDUs give off rays in enough quantity to be harmful. Modern VDUs are specifically designed to limit radiation.

Health and safety legislation

Directives issued by the European Union on IT and health and safety are now law (*see Unit 2, page 37*). The **Display Screen Equipment Regulations** lay down certain standards on equipment, seating and lighting.

Seating   All chairs must be capable of swivelling up and down on a movable base (i.e. castors). The chair should be comfortable and have an adjustable back rest to give the support which is required.

VDU desks   These must not reflect light, must be 68 cm high and be large enough to hold all the equipment plus any paperwork.

Keyboards   These must be separate from VDUs and adjustable to lie flat or slope upwards at an angle of between 10° and 15°. The keys should have a matt finish. Good keyboard design is essential to reduce or prevent the chance of teno occurring. Keys should be concave to reduce the risk of fingers slipping off them *and* to reduce the shock on the fingertips, fingers, wrists and arms.

VDU screens These must be adjustable in terms of the angle at which it is positioned and the brightness and contrast of the screen. The screen should be non-reflective and flicker-free.

In addition the Regulations include the right for VDU operators to

- have free eye tests prior to VDU work and regularly thereafter
- have regular rest breaks
- be involved in the evaluation of workstations.

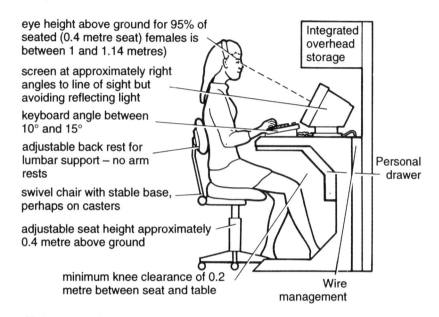

eye height above ground for 95% of seated (0.4 metre seat) females is between 1 and 1.14 metres)

screen at approximately right angles to line of sight but avoiding reflecting light

keyboard angle between 10° and 15°

adjustable back rest for lumbar support – no arm rests

swivel chair with stable base, perhaps on casters

adjustable seat height approximately 0.4 metre above ground

minimum knee clearance of 0.2 metre between seat and table

Integrated overhead storage

Personal drawer

Wire management

Sitting properly

UNIT REVIEW (1)

At the end of this element you should be able to

- explain the main types of computer system to be found in business
- explain the main types of computer software and understand their uses
- enter data and text correctly
- take the correct action if source data is incomplete or unauthorised
- follow organisational procedures for storing source material
- generate reference codes as necessary
- identify and correct errors in inputting and coding according to organisational procedures
- wherever possible produce work within agreed deadlines
- take the correct action if work is not achievable within specified deadlines
- safeguard equipment and data against damage
- follow organisational requirements for confidentiality and security of data
- follow safe working practices.

REVIEW YOUR KNOWLEDGE AND UNDERSTANDING

True or false?

1 A spreadsheet package is a type of computer software used for text processing.
2 Merging is a particular function of most word processing packages.
3 To input data using a meaningless code it is essential to have a copy of the key.
4 If your computer does not work you should immediately contact an engineer or technician for help.
5 Graphs and charts can be produced on most spreadsheet packages.

Fill in the blanks

6 A device which is essential for a computer to be able to communicate over a telephone line is a _____ .
7 The software package used to create record cards for pupils in a school is called a _____ .
8 The small block or line on a computer screen where the colours are reversed and often flashing is called a _____ .

Work it out

9 You are about to start using a computer with a 30M hard disk. Approximately how many characters can be stored on the disk before it will be full?
10 A new girl in your office is driving everyone mad. She has been given the job of helping to set up a new database system and has to input customer records from printed cards. She rarely checks her work and therefore much of the data she inputs needs amending the following day. This is delaying the work and the original deadline for completion won't be met. All the printed cards are in a heap on her desk and she now can't find where she is up to.

This morning your manager found out how behind with the work she was, sent for her and told her if she didn't improve by the end of the week she'd be looking for a new job. You quite like her and decide to take her to lunch and see if you can help. You decide to talk to her about

a how to change her working routine so that she meets her deadlines
b what she should do if the deadlines are not achievable
c how the computer can help her to find out quickly which cards have already been keyed in
d how to organise her working area and source data so that the problem does not occur again.

What would you say in each case?

Element 6.2

Locate and retrieve data from a computer system

To be able to retrieve data from a computer system, you must have stored it in the first place. The method you use to save data will depend on your software – it is usually simply a case of keying in the command. Your data will then be saved to either hard or floppy disk – depending on the storage device you are using.

Storage devices

Hard disks

Most computers today have hard disks installed. A hard disk is a fixed disk positioned inside the computer, which can hold a large number of programs and a large amount of data.

Before a hard disk computer can be moved the read/write heads must be 'parked', to avoid damaging them. This is normally done automatically when the machine is switched off, or it may be carried out through a command to the operating system.

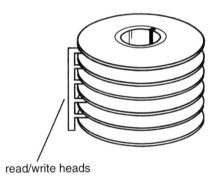

read/write heads

A stack of hard disks

Floppy disks

These are available in two sizes – $5\frac{1}{4}$" and $3\frac{1}{2}$". The amount which can be stored on a floppy disk depends on whether it is single or double sided and whether it is single, double or high density. The type of disk you use will depend on the type of data you need to store. For instance, graphics take up much more space than text, therefore if you were regularly storing documents containing graphics you would be sensible to use double sided, high density disks.

A $5\frac{1}{4}$" disk has a vinyl jacket and a dust sleeve. A smaller $3\frac{1}{2}$" disk has a hard plastic case with a metal cover which slides back when the disk is placed into the disk drive.

All floppy disks can be **write protected**, which means that no information can be added to or deleted from the disk. This can protect your work and prevent anyone else from overwriting something important by accident. On a 5¼" disk you must cover the **write protect notch** with a small piece of sticky paper (provided with the disk). On a 3½" disk there is a small plastic clip which can be slid into position.

Before you can use a floppy disk you must **format** it so that it is configured for use on your particular computer system. Remember that a disk formatted for one system will not necessarily work on another, unless you reformat it, in which case you will lose all the documents you have saved. It is usual to format disks using the disk operating system on your machine.

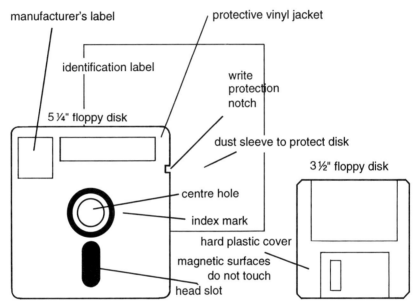

Floppy disks

Care of floppy disks

1 Handle these with care and respect at all times, or you may lose all the work you have so carefully saved!
2 Write the label for a disk *before* sticking it on. Never press on the disk itself with a biro.
3 Always keep a disk in its dust jacket or box when it is not in use.
4 Always store disks carefully in a special, purpose-made disk box.
5 Never overfill a disk box so that the disks rub against each other.
6 Keep the disks away from anything magnetic.
7 Keep the disks away from direct heat, e.g. radiators or sunlight.
8 Don't touch the exposed recording surface.

Optical disks

These are similar to music CDs and are gaining in popularity as they can store a vast amount of information, are less apt to be damaged than magnetic disks and data can be retrieved more quickly than from floppy disks. Different types of optical disks are used for different purposes.

CD-ROM disks are used for large databases. The user can access the information but cannot erase or replace it.

CD-WORM disks enable the user to write information to the disks but again it cannot be erased. They are mainly used with electronic filing systems, *see Unit 5*. (**Note:** WORM stands for Write Once, Read Many Times.)

Erasable optical disks can be used as ordinary disks. The user can store and erase data as often as he or she wishes. These are very expensive at present but as prices are falling they will probably become the floppy disk of the future.

Disk directories and searches

All systems have some type of directory which shows all the documents or files stored on a particular disk or system. However, the systems and software you use vary in the way in which you can name documents for later identification. On the best systems you can do a search for a specific document if you know any part of its content or even the date on which it was produced.

There are three methods you can use to search for documents.

Automatic searching means you can type in a key word or code which will enable the computer to find the document for you quickly. If you do not know the key word then you may have to scroll through all the titles yourself, which can be time-consuming. In this case you may find it easier to take a print-out.

Manual searching means you have to look for yourself! If you have a print-out which lists dozens of documents you may then go through it manually, highlighting the ones you want. This is the slowest method, but may be essential if you haven't enough information to search automatically.

Multi-field searching is available in most database packages, for instance, and allow the person who sets up the system to determine certain **key fields**. These are the fields which contain searchable information. The more fields which can be specified in a search *simultaneously*, the more highly targeted the information. For instance, the Vehicle Licensing Authority keeps a database of all drivers in the UK. By using multi-field searching it could immediately produce a list of all **male** drivers, **born before** 1940, with a **clean** licence, who live in **Cheshire** simply by searching under the categories in bold above.

If you have a proper system of directory management (*see below*) and/or access to sophisticated search techniques, you can considerably reduce the time you spend in searching for the document you have to recall.

Don't forget that you may be asked to recall a document from incomplete information or from a code given to you. Your supervisor or manager won't always have all the details available to help you, but will still expect you to find the right document quickly!

DID YOU KNOW?

Databases are the third most common use of PCs – after word processing and spreadsheets – and information on virtually all of us in the UK is held somewhere on a database, sometimes in alarming detail. Some central agencies receive information on individuals from a variety of sources and merge it together to get a comprehensive picture. They then sell this information to companies who want to do mail shots on their products to potential buyers. These people are found by multi-field searching. With a sophisticated database package a company which sells golf clubs, or adventure holidays for children, or car insurance for the over-50s could target its potential customers quickly and easily, and not waste time and money sending mailshots to those who have never played golf, have no children, do not hold a driving licence or who are in the wrong income or age bracket.

Directory management

Good directory management is essential if you are using a hard disk, as hundreds of documents could be held on this at any one time. Two basic rules should be followed.

- Don't keep documents on *any* disk longer than necessary – erase them.
- Set up a system of main directories and sub-directories. You may have a main directory (sometimes called the **root directory**) e.g. WPLETTERS for all the letters you type. In this you could have six sub-directories, for instance, if you produce work for six different people. These could be labelled by their surnames, e.g. WPLETKING, WPLETBROWN and so on. The directories would then hold a smaller number of documents and each would be easier to find no matter which method of searching you use.

 DID YOU KNOW?

This type of electronic filing is often known as **tree and branch filing**. Think of the main or root directory as the 'tree' and the sub-directories as separate 'branches' off the main tree. Each branch can have further divisions if you wish. In this case your tree is your filing cabinet, your branches are the

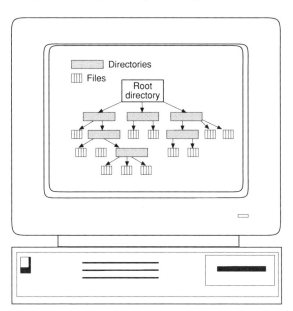

Tree and branch filing

drawers and so on. The titles of your documents are your *own* reference codes. Devise a good system *and stick to it* (or take a print-out of your directory at regular intervals). This way you will have to spend much less time searching for documents on your disk(s).

Backing up your work

If you save a valuable document to disk then you are safe, provided nothing goes wrong with your disk or system to destroy the information you have so carefully saved. The worst thing would be if your computer failed and, as part of the repair, the engineers had to wipe off all the information from your hard disk. The only way you can safeguard valuable documents is to have *two* disks – one as your working disk and the second containing exactly the same information, as a **back-up** for the first disk. This can also help if you accidentally delete any information or files from your working disk – you can restore them again from your back-up.

Do bear in mind, however, that your back-up disks need updating regularly, otherwise the information they carry will soon be out of date.

DID YOU KNOW?

If a virus is suspected in your organisation's computer system, all the disks will be **swept**. Sweeping a disk is the method used to check if a virus is present. If it is, the only solution is to wipe the disk clean. This gets rid of not only the virus but also of any other information on the disk. For that reason it is sensible to keep back-up copies of all your work – and the content of your hard disk – safely locked away. Otherwise you could lose important and irretrievable information permanently.

Confidentiality

Just because you can access certain types of information this does not mean that it should be open to all. Don't divulge what you read on screen to other people if you know it is confidential – or tell them what you are doing. Use sensible techniques to stop them reading your screen (*see page 69*). Never lend your disks to other people; not only will some of the information probably be confidential but you could find that when they give it back it has become infected with a virus from their machine.

UNIT REVIEW (2)

At the end of this element you should be able to

- use suitable computer software for the location and retrieval of data
- locate, access and retrieve requested data within specified time constraints

- use appropriate and effective search methods
- disclose confidential data only to authorised people
- safeguard equipment and data against damage
- follow safe working practices.

REVIEW YOUR KNOWLEDGE AND UNDERSTANDING

True or false?

1 Women who are pregnant should never use computers.
2 A hard disk cannot be removed from a computer.
3 Floppy disks are best stored loose in a desk drawer.
4 CD-WORM disks are optical disks mainly used with electronic filing systems.
5 Manual searching means looking through lists for information which cannot be found easily on a computer.

Fill in the blanks

6 Floppy disks are manufactured in two sizes – _____ and _____.
7 The term used for preparing a new disk for use on a computer is

_____ .

8 Searching for something on several criteria at the same time is called _____ searching.

Work it out

9 You work in a local college and have been given the job of setting up a small computer supplies shop to sell basic items to students. Your stock should include a wide range of floppy disks (e.g. double, high and quad density disks) disk pouches etc.

Use a computer supplies catalogue to identify at least fifteen useful items you would like to have in stock on your first day. Use your computer to produce an attractive price list for your shop window.

10 You use a word processing package to produce letters, memos and monthly sales reports for two managers – Mrs Swann and Mr Pansetti.

You have just been given a new computer with a hard disk and want to set up a proper directory system so that you can find documents quickly and easily.

Devise a simple code which will enable you to save and retrieve all the different types of documents you create quickly and easily.

Element 6.3

Print documents using a computer system

Computers can be linked to several types of output device – the main one being the printer. The two main types of printer are

Impact printers   which include dot matrix printers, in which mechanical contact is made between the print head and the paper.

Non-impact printers which include ink jet or laser printers, where ink is placed on the paper without any mechanical contact being made.

Other output devices include

VDU screen

Plotters   which are used to produce graphs, charts and a variety of other graphics. Colour can be used (although the number of colours is limited except on very expensive machines) and some can produce two-dimensional drawings.

COM   (Computer Output to Microfilm) – on some large computer systems the output is automatically produced as microfiche or microfilm so that large amounts of information can be stored in a small area.

Computer printers

The type of printer which is used in an office will depend on the type of output being produced. In-house documents such as payroll listings and account transactions need not be high quality and yet need to be produced quickly. A cheap but fast printer will therefore be quite suitable for this purpose.

Letters, memos and other business documents need to be printed on a good quality printer so that customers gain a good impression of the organisation. Graphic and desktop publishing packages need a very high quality printer – especially if sophisticated shading or special text effects or fonts are required.

The main types of printer to be found in offices are

Dot matrix   which are the cheapest type of printer. The image is formed by series of dots being placed on

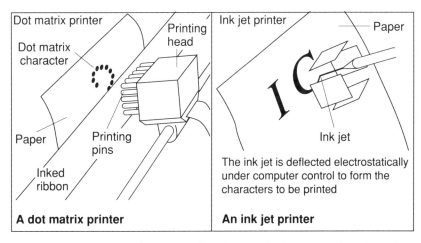

| A dot matrix printer | An ink jet printer |

Dot matrix printer — Dot matrix character — Printing head — Printing pins — Paper — Inked ribbon

Ink jet printer — Paper — Ink jet

The ink jet is deflected electrostatically under computer control to form the characters to be printed

the paper. Quality can be improved by using the near letter quality (NLQ) function which means the printer goes over each character twice to improve the density.

Ink jet or bubble jet which spray tiny droplets of ink onto virtually any surface – paper, glass, plastic or metal – through small jets or nozzles. Desktop models, including colour versions, are reasonably priced.

Laser printers which use lasers to transfer the original image onto a drum which then transfers it onto paper. Desktop models are now quite common in many offices. A Postscript laser printer can produce complex images including a wide variety of different fonts (typestyles).

DID YOU KNOW?

Large 'smart' laser printers are available which cost many thousands of pounds and are used mainly by computer centres and by newspaper publishers. Forms and headings can be memorised by the printer and printing is so rapid that hundreds of copies can be produced each minute.

CHECK IT YOURSELF

The chart overleaf shows the advantages and disadvantages of different types of printers. Which would you buy if

● you had to take long computer listings of product sales for company reps
● you had to produce quite sophisticated newsletters to send to clients
● you needed a relatively inexpensive colour printer
● you wanted a good quality printer to produce business documents?

Different types of printers

The pros and cons

Type of printer	Advantages	Disadvantages
Dot matrix	Essential for impact printing onto multi-part stationery (e.g. sets of invoices) Inexpensive to buy and cheap to run Highly reliable and last a long time Excellent for long print runs Wide carriage versions available	Only average quality print-out NLQ (near letter quality) available but still not very good quality and printing slow Most only suitable for use with continuous stationery Noisy in use
Ink jet	Very good print quality Can produce simple graphics/different fonts Quiet in operation Cheap to buy – including colour models Can print envelopes Suitable for both A4 and A3 and wide paper – both cut sheet and continuous stationery	Cannot be used with multi-part stationery Relatively slow unless in 'draft' mode Not suitable for sophisticated DTP work Only top models suitable for long print runs
Laser	Top quality documents produced	Normally only suitable with A4 cut-sheet paper

Type of printer	Advantages	Disadvantages
	Capable of printing sophisticated graphics	Not suitable for multi-part stationery
	Relatively fast	Expensive to buy
	Quiet in operation	Highest running costs
	Capable of handling long print runs	

Care of printers

1 First of all – and very important – find out how to stop the printer quickly if there is a problem. This usually means typing in a command on the computer *not* just pressing the 'off' switch! Remember that your command will vary from one computer program to another.

2 Make sure that your paper is properly loaded into the machine and correctly aligned. Continuous stationery should be positioned with the sprocket holes placed over the sprockets to keep it in position. Single sheet paper is better if it is fanned first. Make sure it is correctly aligned with the paper guides on your printer.

3 Only use the recommended paper for your printer. This is particularly important for laser printers where the quality and weight of the paper can be vital.

4 *Never* block the area where your print-out emerges. Otherwise you may find you have reams of continuous stationery backing up into the printer and jamming it.

5 Use the top of form (TOF) or form feed (FF) button to turn up the paper automatically.

6 Remember that your printer *must* be **on line** before it will print. This is the first thing to check if, for any reason, nothing is happening.

7 Look at your printer manual or the following chart to find out how to rectify basic faults and problems.

8 Read the manual to find out how to change the ribbon, ink cartridge or laser toner cartridge.

9 *Never* tamper with the printer if you are not sure what you are doing. Ask for help.

DID YOU KNOW?

An alternative form of output is to send your message to someone else's computer by **electronic mail (E-mail)**. *E-mail is dealt with in Unit 8, page 339.*

Printer problems

Printer difficulties can have many causes, ranging from simple problems, such as running out of paper, to more complex ones, such as incorrect computer-to-printer configurations (i.e. the computer and printer cannot understand one another).

To some extent the type of problem you encounter will depend on the type of printer, ribbon or paper feed system you are using. Every printer has its own operating manual which contains a 'troubleshooting' section. You should always refer to this if difficulties occur, so that you never, inadvertently, make the problem worse. Equally, you must know how to stop the printer in case of an emergency.

The most common types of problems, and the action to take, are given in the chart below – but please note that this chart is no substitute for your own user manual!

Printer problems

Fault	Probable cause	Action
No response to print command	No power to printer Printer not switched on Printer not connected to computer Printer 'off line' Wrong command given	Check plug lead Switch on Check printer lead Press 'on line' key Check software manual
Print is gibberish	Software and printer incompatiable Printer lead faulty	Call supervisor Replace lead
Poor print quality	Ribbon needs changing Ribbon too near/far from paper **Ink jet/laser –** cartridge needs changing **Laser** – paper wrong specification/internal cleaning required	Replace ribbon Adjust ribbon setting Replace cartridge Check laser manual/arrange cleaning
Print wrong size	Printer 'remembering' earlier command	Clear memory by switching printer off and on again

▶

Fault	Probable cause	Action
Characters missing	**Laser** – wrong font selected	Check laser manual
Paper jam	**Document feed** – paper wrong specification/ inserted wrongly **Tractor feed** – printed/unused sheets 'backing up' into printer **Ink jet/laser** – overfull in-tray/incorrect paper specification	Change paper and reinsert – check document feeder Stop printer. Use paper release to unjam. Clear area behind printer. Remove paper from in-tray/change paper/check manual
Crooked print	**Tractor feed** – paper dislodged from sprocket holes **Ink jet/laser** – paper not inserted properly in paper tray	Stop printer. Realign paper properly on sprocket holes Remove paper, reset paper guides
Incorrect pitch/line spacing	Software over-riding printer settings	Check software

SPECIAL NOTE

If you are ever in a position where you cannot produce urgent documents by the specified deadline – either because of printer problems or anything else – you *must* notify your supervisor immediately. Otherwise people may be standing by to receive them without knowing that they won't be available. Only if people know what is happening can they decide what emergency action to take.

Perfect print-outs

Your aim when you are producing hard copies (or print-outs) should be to

- create clean, clearly printed documents which are correctly aligned
- use the minimum of paper necessary
- use a format for the document which means it is clear and easy to read

- produce the required documents according to instructions
- produce them in time to meet any deadlines
- keep the printing area clean and tidy
- collate and distribute your print-outs correctly.

Reducing wastage

Some adverts say that a full wastepaper basket is the sign of a poor printer. To most people it's also the sign of a poor operator! You will reduce the amount of paper you need – and the time it takes (every time something has to be reprinted it takes twice as long!) – if you

- proof-read your work carefully *before* you print out
- *think* carefully when designing your document and choosing your format
- remember that if you *want* to experiment to see what a new format looks like you should either
   - find the command to view the finished document on screen, *or*
   - print out *one* copy in draft mode (it's quicker and uses less ink)
- make sure the area around the printer is clean and tidy and the printer holds the correct paper, properly aligned
- tidy up after yourself (to make life easier for those who follow you!).

Document formats

Don't get this term confused with formatting a disk (*see page 238*)! Document format is the term used when you decide what your document will look like. This means you will choose

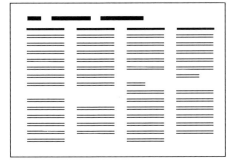

Portrait: paper short side at top

Landscape: paper long side at top

Portrait and landscape formats

- the paper size
- whether your text or graphics will be printed in portrait or landscape
- the size of your margins (left, right, top and bottom) and your page length
- line spacing
- whether or not to **justify** your right hand margin
- the type of characters to use and their size
- the number of columns you will use and the size of these
- the layout of documents such as letters, memos and reports
- the design of any tables or diagrams you are including.

Many organisations have standard settings for certain documents which you need to check carefully if you work for them (look in the files!). This is called their **house style**. The problems may start when you are left to your own devices and expected to set out a professional document.

It has been said that anyone creating a document should be something of an artist. By this it is meant that any work you produce in printed form should be visually pleasing and well balanced. In addition, if you want to be considered reliable and responsible it must be accurate in every detail (*see Proofreading below*).

 ## DID YOU KNOW?

1 If you want to set a format command which will apply *throughout* the document (e.g. margin width or justification) then you usually need to have your cursor at the **beginning** of the document when you make the command. Otherwise you will find that only the text *after* the cursor position has been affected!

2 If you put in a number of commands to create a special heading, use a certain font, set up headers and footers etc. – and need to use this format often (e.g. for a monthly sales report) – then you can store your sequence of keystrokes in **macro** on many types of software. You can then recall the whole lot by pressing just one key!

Hints and tips

1 Most office documents are printed on A4 paper – and some printers can only cope with this size of paper. You can always enlarge or reduce it later on a photocopier. However, in some cases you may have a wider printer, for instance if you were operating with large spreadsheets which would not fit on A4 paper.

2 If you are printing on standard forms, such as invoices, then it is likely that your in-house user manual will tell you which spacing to use. If not, work it out yourself and write it down for reference next time (or use your macro command to help).

Normal computer listings are usually printed out in a set format which you will be told about. Often A3 paper is used horizontally in a printer with a wide carriage.

3   If you are designing your own document, such as a report or table, it should be relatively easy to decide whether landscape or portrait format is the more suitable. Again, your printer may make the decision for you – only certain types (e.g. ink jet and laser) will print out in landscape format. Use your common sense! If you are creating a table or poster which is wide but not deep then go for landscape – if it is deep and narrow then stick to portrait.

4   A good guide for left hand and right hand margins is 1.5" or 2" each side. A document always looks better if your margins are equal. If, however, this would mean a small amount of text would be carried to another page then change your margins to 1" each side. The wonderful thing about computers is that you can change your margins several times and keep looking at the different effects, then stop when you've found the best option.

5   Top and bottom margins determine the page length. Again they usually look better when they are equal. If you only have a small amount of text on a page then you could go for wide top and bottom margins and double line spacing to make it look more effective.

6   On virtually all packages, your text or figures at the left side of the page will automatically be justified (i.e. start at the same point). Word processed documents look much more professional if you also choose right justification as well – so that they look more like the printed page.

On a spreadsheet you can choose whether you want information in cells to be left or right justified – experiment to see which looks best.

7   On *some* word processing packages you can produce work in columns. This means your finished document looks something like a newspaper.

- Two to four columns is the best format (three is often ideal). More than four means your text width is too narrow to be read easily.
- Drawing a vertical line between columns (if this is possible on your package) makes your finished work look more professional.
- As a general rule it is always better to stick to equal columns with equal spaces between them.
- Most packages have *pre-set* column widths which are standard size. Stick to these until you know what you are doing.

8 Bear in mind that you should know how to use both block and indented paragraphs and should always use headings if you are typing a long piece of continuous prose, as this makes your document much easier to read. Using numbered points and indenting your text so that it is aligned throughout will also make your work look more attractive.

9 Producing tables and diagrams is much easier if you are working with a package which almost does these automatically. On some word processing packages the outline of a table can be produced automatically. You then simply readjust the column widths to fit in with your text, e.g.

MACHINE OUTPUT – LEEDS			
	January	**February**	**March**
Machine 1	29 738	48 379	19 728
Machine 2	20 389	22 038	19 361
TOTAL	**50 127**	**70 417**	**39 089**

Note that in the table above

● the main heading has been typed in capitals, centred and emboldened for effect
● the headings and total lines have been emboldened to make them easier to read
● a space has been left after the 'thousands' column in the figures – to make the numbers clearer.

These effects are known as **text enhancement** and are achievable on most types of packages.

Any tables or diagrams you produce should be

● well-balanced
● easy to read
● clearly labelled
● well positioned
● pleasing to the eye.

DID YOU KNOW?

If you can produce tables automatically then you can also draw boxes automatically! When you create a table you will be asked to say how many rows you want *down* the page and how many columns you want *across* the page. In the table above there are four columns and five rows.

If you specify just one column and one row you have a box! e.g.

You can usually alter the size of this quite easily and type as much or as little text into it as you require.

Print characteristics

If you use an ink jet, bubble jet or laser printer, you will probably have access to different types of characters and fonts which you can use to make your document look more professional.

1 A **character set** is a particular group of characters. Your keyboard holds one character set (usually ASCII codes – pronounced 'askey'). On some packages you have the opportunity to use other sets which will include graphics or symbols not held on the standard set. For instance

- other languages, e.g. Greek (β), Hebrew (ﬡ), Cyrillic (Я) – in case you are writing to anyone in Greece, Israel or Russia and know enough to write in their language!
- mathematical and scientific signs, e.g. ÷, ≡ and ∴.
- other symbols not normally found on your keyboard, e.g. ‰, ♡, § or ✳.

The important thing is whether your printer will be able to print these out, even if you can select them in your program!

2 **Fonts** are different styles of typefaces. You can choose different fonts in many word processing packages. However, for a wide range of fonts you generally need a Postscript laser printer (*see page 245*).

Examples of fonts include

An example of Times typeface

```
An example of Courier
typeface
```

An example of Helvetica typeface

An example of Palatino typeface

3 The size of your characters will also be determined by your printer. Again if you have a Postscript laser printer you can vary these more.

Size is given in points. Opposite are examples of text showing their point size.

This is 8 point

This is 12 point

This is 24 point

This is 36 point

Proof-reading

No matter what package you are using it is important that you check your work carefully. There is little point in knowing your program backwards and being a whiz kid at formatting if your work is full of mistakes! On word processing packages you may find you have a spell check facility to help you – but this won't pick up keying-in errors if the word you have typed is still recognisable.

You need to remember that

- Proof-reading from a screen is a *skill* which must be developed.
- Generally people find it harder to read 'word by word' from a screen than a piece of paper.
- Proof-reading on a computer may mean having to scroll backwards and forwards to check that you have spelled a word the same way every time.
- The process is even more difficult – and more important – when figures are involved. The reader will *know* when the word you have typed is wrong, because the sense of the sentence will give it away. No-one can tell if a figure is wrong just by reading a document – and yet this kind of mistake could be disastrous.

If you have problems then *always* take a hard (paper) copy of your work and proofread this, with someone else as 'reader'. If necessary, you can then make any corrections before taking a final print-out.

Collation and distribution

Your final check, before giving the command to print, should be in relation to the size of the document and its distribution. How many pages are there and how many copies are required? This information will affect how you produce the document.

- If there are only a few pages for a few people then by all means give the command to print these out. Bear in mind that they will be easier for everyone to follow (and for you to collate) if they are **paginated** – which is always possible on a word processing package.
- If there are several pages or many copies required then you will usually be well advised to print out one copy and then photocopy your sets. There are three advantages to this.
  - with most printers it is usually quicker
  - someone else can use the printer while you are photocopying
  - most photocopiers can collate, printers do not.

You can therefore stack your original document (in the right page order!) in your photocopier and set it to collate – and staple too, if you wish.

Your final job may be to distribute your work to everyone concerned. The most basic method is to have a distribution list and to write people's names from this list on to the top of each document. Then, to make sure you haven't missed anyone out, do a final count of the number of names on your list and the number of documents you have written on. (*See unit 8, page 257.*)

This method, however, is *not* suitable if you are sending documents out of the organisation. In this case there may be a covering letter or compliment slip to go with them – and these will be your 'name checks'.

The main thing is to make sure you haven't missed anyone out. If you tick off the distribution list and file it with the original document, you will then be able to prove who received a copy if this is ever questioned in the future.

UNIT REVIEW (3)

At the end of this element you should be able to

- print correct and complete documents
- produce hard copies which are clean, clearly printed and aligned correctly
- minimise paper wastage
- keep the printer area clean and tidy
- achieve work within agreed deadlines
- recognise when work is not achievable within specified deadlines and report the reason promptly and accurately
- correctly collate and distribute documents as directed
- safeguard equipment and data against damage
- follow safe working practices.

REVIEW YOUR KNOWLEDGE AND UNDERSTANDING

True or false?

1 Non-impact printers cannot be used on multi-part sets of stationery.
2 The cheapest type of a printer is a dot matrix printer.
3 Printers can only be used when they are 'on line'.
4 Ink jet printers are ideal for long print runs.
5 Complicated keystroke sequences can be stored and quickly retrieved using the macro facility.

Fill in the blanks

6 The cheapest type of printer on the market is a _____ _____ printer.
7 To set a format command throughout a document your cursor should be at the _____ of the document.
8 The different styles of typeface available on a printer are known as _____ .

Work it out

9 The collator on your photocopier broke down last week and you are about to ask your office junior to help you to collate a large document by hand. There are 62 pages and 35 people on the distribution list. The document is an important survey which is going to some of your most valuable customers. It must be correct!

All the pages are numbered at the bottom and, at the moment, each page set is piled on a trolley. You and your assistant have been given a large room to work in.

Devise a working method you could use, plus a suitable checking system, so that you can be **certain** that all the collated sets are absolutely correct when you have both finished.

10 The printer in your office is frequently being jammed with paper and computer service staff are being called out unnecessarily because no-one knows what to do.

Refer to the manual of a printer you use regularly (either at work or at college) and make out a short 'help sheet' for all users on what to do if common faults occur.

7 Prepare documents

At first, you may think that there is little chance that at the start of your career you will be asked to compose and prepare documents on your own. To a degree this is true. You will not be asked to prepare complicated reports, reply to important letters or to compose memos which deal with critical matters in relation to staff or customers. However, even the supervisors and managers who do prepare such documents had to start somewhere. In addition, no organisation is going to employ you if someone has to stand over you to check how you respond to even the most basic document which lands on your desk!

You can therefore, quite reasonably, be expected to

- generate routine replies or standard letters to basic correspondence
- compose your own replies to simple memos
- prepare documents for other people (These may contain facts and figures which you have had to collect from other documents.)
- produce a range of documents using the correct layout and style expected in business
- check that the spelling, grammar and punctuation are correct in all the documents you handle – whether these were initiated by yourself or someone else.

The two elements which follow are designed to cover all these areas. Element 7.1 concentrates on documents you will compose yourself and includes a section on basic writing skills to help you to develop and improve your own abilities in this area. For this reason you should note that this is by far the longer of the two elements in this unit. Element 7.2 concentrates on the preparation of a wider range of documents, many of which will have been initiated by someone else.

Element 7.1

Respond to correspondence

Types of correspondence

Every business organisation receives a considerable amount of correspondence and other documentation through the post each day. This may be from customers, suppliers, service organisations (e.g. banks, accountants and solicitors) and even from their own associated companies or branch offices. The most common type of business correspondence received from external organisations is the **business**

letter. These need dealing with promptly and efficiently. Every letter sent out by your organisation is an advertisement for the company itself. If the layout is poor, it contains mistakes or inaccuracies or – even worse – spelling errors, then the person receiving it will take a fairly dim view of the organisation and may even stop dealing with them. Equally, if people are kept waiting weeks for a reply then they will have little confidence in the efficiency of your organisation.

In addition to the external correspondence, the company will also generate its own internal correspondence. **Memos** – (memorandum [singular] or memoranda [plural] to give them their proper name) will be sent from one department or one manager to another and, again, these will need a prompt reply.

DID YOU KNOW?

In many organisations it is more usual to send a memo about a topic than to talk it over on the telephone. This is because there will then be written evidence in the file to say what took place. This may be very important for future reference if, say, a manager is away on business and a crisis occurs, or if there is any dispute about what actually happened.

Types of response

There are basically two types of response which can be made to correspondence

- standardised replies
- an individual answer.

Standardised replies

This method saves time and money when an organisation receives many enquiries about the same topic or has to communicate with many people on the same subject. Today, word processors are often used for such documents, as the basic letter can be stored on computer and then printed out whenever it is required. Using mail merge, specific names and addresses can be inserted so that the recipient may think that he or she has received an individual reply. Some organisations even have a range of standard paragraphs stored so that a letter can be created from the most appropriate mix of these. In other cases, letters or forms are simply pre-printed and the names, addresses and other information inserted where necessary.

Individual answers

These are required when a letter or memo relates to a specific matter which needs a particular response. You may be expected to compose a reply to a simple, straightforward letter on your own. In the early days it is sensible to have this checked before you send it out. Remember that you are writing on behalf of your company, not just yourself, so the wording and layout is very important.

TEST YOURSELF

In which of the situations below do you consider that a standard reply would be used and in which do you think an individual answer would be necessary?

1　A bookshop confirming that an ordered book is now in stock.
2　A personnel department informing enquirers that there are no vacancies at present.
3　A sales department responding to a customer who has complained about a purchase.
4　The accounts department reminding a customer to pay his account.
5　A school informing parents about sports day.
6　A solicitor writing to a client about her will.
7　A travel agent confirming a holiday booking.
8　A sales director negotiating with a customer about an important contract.

DID YOU KNOW?

In some cases a standard reply is sent *before* an individual response is made. This is often the case if it would take time to investigate a matter, or if the person who should deal with it is away from the office at the time, so that the enquirer is not left wondering if his or her letter has been received.

CHECK IT YOURSELF

Do you think standardised replies are used mainly for responding to memos or letters? If you are not sure, look at the list of situations given in the *Test yourself* section above to check.

Business letters

Business letters may be sent for a variety of reasons including

● to make or respond to an enquiry
● to ask for information on goods, products or services
● to make or answer a complaint
● to provide information on the organisation, its products or methods of operation
● to sell or advertise the products
● to make interview arrangements and confirm appointments of staff.

There are standard rules which apply to all business letters and which must always be followed. These are sometimes called **correspondence conventions** and include the layout, style and phrasing used in business letters.

Correspondence conventions

An example of a business letter is shown below. This shows the layout used by most organisations today. However, this may vary slightly and it is worthwhile checking your company files for an example of one of their letters to see how it compares. Make a note of any differences and remember to vary your style if necessary. You are not in a position to try to persuade senior management to change their standard layout or house style because it is slightly different to the example in this book!

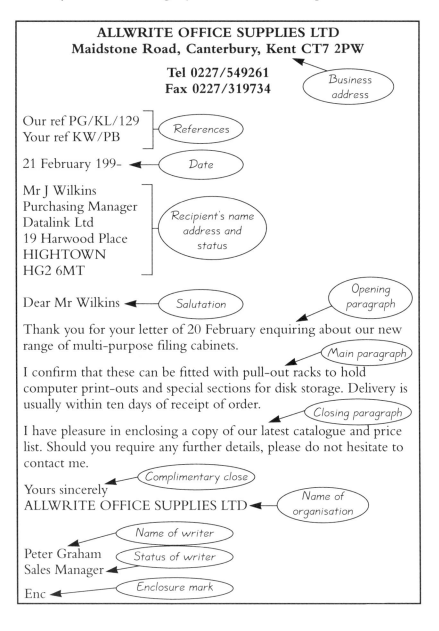

Key points to note

- The first items are usually the **references**. The **internal reference**, which comes first, relates to the originator of the letter and the typist (giving the initials of the first followed by the initials of the second). In some cases this may be followed by the file number.

  The **external reference** is the one given on the letter to which you are responding and must be quoted in any reply.

- The date comes next. It is usual for this to be written in full, i.e. 14 February 199-, *not* 14/2/199-. Nowadays it is considered old-fashioned to use ordinal numbers, e.g. 1st, 2nd, 13th etc. The date does not usually contain any punctuation.
- The name and designation of the recipient should be shown above the company name. The town or city is typed in capitals and followed by the postcode.
- The **salutation** is the 'opening' – if you use 'Dear Sir' then you must close the letter with 'Yours faithfully'. If you start with a person's name then you must finish with 'Yours sincerely'.
- The **complimentary close** is given after the body of the letter and follows the rules above. Note the spelling of 'sincerely' and the fact that *neither* 'faithfully' *nor* 'sincerely' starts with a capital letter!
- Sometimes the name of the organisation is shown immediately below the complimentary close. This confirms that the writer is sending the letter on behalf of the organisation rather than him or herself.
- Finally, after the space for the signature, the name of the writer and his or her official title is given.
- Sometimes the letters 'Enc' may be included at the end of the document. This signifies there are some enclosures. Another method is to type a row of dots in the margin alongside the line where the enclosure is mentioned, but this practice is declining because it is more difficult to do on a word processor.

SPECIAL NOTE

Business letters are *always* sent on specially printed letter headed paper. You must never send out a document on behalf of your organisation without using an official letter heading.

DID YOU KNOW?

You should *never* include a person's initials in the salutation. 'Dear Mr T Wright' is *wrong*. If you have trouble remembering this then think about it this way. You would never speak to someone and say, 'Hello, Mr T Wright,' would you? So why would you write to him like this?

Business style

The style of a business letter is different from the style you would use to write a letter to a friend and is more formal. For instance

- Abbreviated forms of words are very rarely used in business letters. It is incorrect to write *isn't, don't* or *can't*. Instead you should write *is not, do not* or *cannot*.
- Slang phrases and expressions are never used. Imagine you were informing someone they should pay their account promptly. It would be totally inappropriate to say something like

Unless you pay up straight away we're going to have to do something about it.

A business phrase (which says the same thing!) would be

We regret that unless we receive payment shortly we shall have to take further action.

- It is usual to have distinct paragraphs in a letter, each of which deals with a specific point.
  - The opening paragraph usually gives background information as to why the letter is being written.
  - The next paragraph usually gives further details (usually the information is too long to be given in full in the opening paragraph).
  - The third paragraph will usually round off the letter.

  If more than one topic has to be dealt with then there will obviously be more paragraphs.

- All the sentences you write must be *complete* sentences. This means they must have a subject and a verb. Note form is never used in business letters.
- A confidential letter has 'PERSONAL' or 'CONFIDENTIAL' typed clearly at the top (usually between the date and the name and address). The same word is also clearly shown on the envelope, above the name and address.
- If any dates are referred to in the body of the letter then these must be given properly, preferably with the *day* as well as a double-check. Your boss may have said to you, 'I'm visiting them a week on Wednesday at 2 o'clock,' your job is to write, 'Mr Blank will visit you on Wednesday, 13 March at 2 pm.'

 ## TEST YOURSELF

Identify which of the following sentences are incorrect because they are in note form, are an incomplete sentence or contain a slang expression. Write an acceptable alternative in each case.

1 Hope to hear from you.
2 Thank you for your letter of 18 June.
3 Can you call in to see us next week?
4 We can get over this obstacle if you pop in to see us for a chat when you are next in the area.
5 With reference to your recent letter.
6 Goods were sent Friday 23 March.
7 We can't prepare your accounts from the stuff you sent us as the papers didn't make sense.
8 Please let me know if you will be available to attend on that date.

DID YOU KNOW?

- Very few letters are sent out today which start Dear Sir/Madam. Many organisations try to find out the name of the correct person to whom the letter should be addressed, as this makes it more personal.

- If a woman signs her name but does not indicate whether or not she is married, you can solve the problem by using the title 'Ms' when you reply.

- If you have no idea who should receive the letter then send it to the department which would deal with it instead. For instance, a letter confirming a hotel booking could be addressed to 'Reception', one enquiring about products to 'The Sales Department' and one about an account to 'The Accounts Department'. In this case, make life easy for yourself and start your letter 'Dear Sirs' (even though this sounds sexist!).

Memos

These are more informal than business letters, but the degree of informality will depend on who is writing to whom! If you send a memo to someone at the same level as yourself in the organisation, you can be more informal than if you are sending it to someone senior to yourself. Remember this when you are writing a memo to your boss! It is also worth bearing in mind that, as your memo may be filed for future reference, silly phrases and comments may keep staring back at you for years!

The usual reason for sending a memo is to

- give information
- confirm arrangements
- make a specific request or query
- ask for or make comments or suggestions
- state action which has been taken about a certain matter.

An example of a memo is shown overleaf.

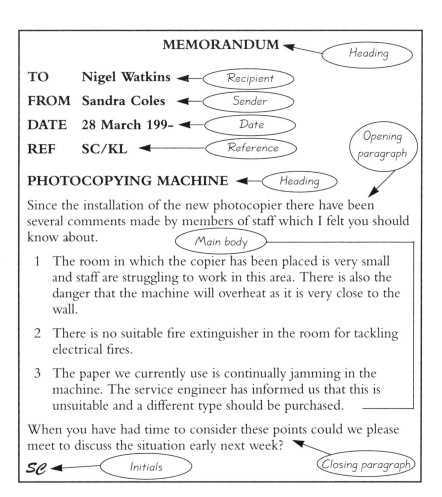

MEMORANDUM ← *Heading*

TO   **Nigel Watkins** ← *Recipient*

FROM   **Sandra Coles** ← *Sender*

DATE   **28 March 199-** ← *Date*

REF   **SC/KL** ← *Reference*

Opening paragraph

PHOTOCOPYING MACHINE ← *Heading*

Since the installation of the new photocopier there have been several comments made by members of staff which I felt you should know about. *Main body*

1   The room in which the copier has been placed is very small and staff are struggling to work in this area. There is also the danger that the machine will overheat as it is very close to the wall.

2   There is no suitable fire extinguisher in the room for tackling electrical fires.

3   The paper we currently use is continually jamming in the machine. The service engineer has informed us that this is unsuitable and a different type should be purchased.

When you have had time to consider these points could we please meet to discuss the situation early next week?

SC ← *Initials*   *Closing paragraph*

Key points to note

- Most organisations use a pre-printed memo form which may – or may not – include the name of the company. Whereas the layout of this may vary from one company to another, it nearly always includes the following printed headings.
    - **To**   (for stating the name of the recipient)
    - **From**   (for stating the name of sender)
    - **Date**   (for recording the date it was sent)
    - **Ref**   (for recording the internal reference, as for business letters)

- Memos should always start with a clear subject heading. This helps the recipient to identify at a glance what the memo is about and find it quickly when necessary.

It is therefore *not* usual to write a memo about more than one topic. Instead, separate memos would be written in each case. This also saves problems when they have to be filed.

- There is no salutation or complimentary close on a memo.
- Memos are never signed but may be initialed by the sender.
- If there is an enclosure this is indicated underneath the initials, with the abbreviation 'Enc'.
- Confidential memos may be sent. These should have 'Personal' or 'Confidential' in a prominent place (usually at the top) and be sent out in an envelope – also marked 'Personal' or 'Confidential' – addressed to the recipient.

CHECK IT YOURSELF

Look back at the list of correspondence conventions mentioned on page 263 and identify how many of these also apply to memos.

Dealing with correspondence

If you are involved in handling correspondence then you have several decisions to make before you can take action.

- Is the document something you can deal with yourself? If not, to whom should it be passed – bearing in mind that prompt action should always be taken?
- How urgent or important is it and how quickly must a reply be sent? If it is very urgent, it may be that a letter would not be the best method of response. If it is routine or totally unimportant then there may be a cheaper method of response.
- What additional information is required before a reply can be composed? Where will you find it? Is there anything which may be confidential or which must be checked by someone else?
- Are there any other points to bear in mind? For instance, will other people require copies and if so, who? Will you need to file the document and will this affect your reference and/or wording? Are there any other relevant points which the writer must bear in mind when drafting a reply?
- What is the context in which you received the correspondence and in which it must be presented? How will this affect your actions?

All these factors may seem overwhelming at first, until you start to consider them separately.

For you, or not for you?

If you are in any doubt at all then you must check with your supervisor or line manager. *Never* leave a document lying on your desk for days while you make up your mind! If you are regularly perplexed on this issue then sit down with your supervisor and talk through the type of documents you can answer yourself and those which you must pass on. The basic rule is never to take action or give information which is outside your own area of authority.

You may like to note that this problem is always worse when you have just started in a new job. The longer you work for an organisation and the longer you do a job, the easier it is to make these decisions.

Basically, you are more likely to be asked to draft a reply yourself to straightforward letters which require easy answers. You may be able to refer to past letters in the files on a similar topic to help you – or there may be an official standard reply you must use.

In other cases you may be given notes by your boss to help you – but bear in mind these may be his or her thoughts at the time and not necessarily stated in the order they should appear in the letter.

Don't be offended if your boss wants to check your work and alters it in some way. Look carefully at *why* it has been altered and make a note not to repeat any basic errors again. Remember, this is an important way in which you can learn and develop your writing skills – and it is far better it is seen and corrected by your boss than commented on by an outside organisation!

The type and method of reply

You would probably be quite horrified if you worked out how much it actually costs to send a business letter. You have to think not only of the paper and the postage costs but the *time* spent in writing the reply, filing the document and mailing the letter. Everyone's time is valuable in an organisation – if you spend two hours deciding what to write (rather than making a simple telephone call) it will have cost your company two hours of your time!

The three factors you need to consider when you are dealing with correspondence are

- how fast a reply is required
- which is the best method to use
- how much will each method cost.

An extreme example of urgency, importance and cost would be a request for an important quotation which must be received by a potential customer the same day. The quotation could result in a sale of worth, say, £250000. In that case the document would be produced immediately and either it would be faxed to the recipient or the original would be sent by courier. The company would not mind the expense as it would be worth it to win the contract.

This method would obviously be a totally inappropriate way of dealing with a routine enquiry. This could be answered by letter or, if a quick and easy response is possible, the telephone may serve just as well. This would be the case, for instance, if you received a memo from someone asking for information and you knew they had to receive it the same day. It would probably be easier to phone them with the details immediately.

There are several ways in which you can send letters quickly or more safely through the post and there are also electronic means of communications. All these are dealt with in Unit 8.

DID YOU KNOW?

If you telephone someone with information, rather than write to them, it is a good idea to type a brief note outlining the action you took, with the date and time, and place it in the file. There is then a record of what occurred for future reference if there are any queries or complications.

Additional information

It is always easier to compose a document if you collect all the information you need before you start, rather than having to keep breaking off to find something. This may mean asking people for details, checking the files and searching computer records or other reference sources.

Be wary of including financial or personal information without checking that this may be disclosed. You could be giving out details which are confidential or for which you need security clearance. If you are in any doubt at all then *ask*!

Additional facts to consider

Probably the most important of these is whether there are any other factors which may influence your reply. As an example, imagine you have received two letters on your desk enquiring about your company's products. A standard response is to write giving details and assuring the customer that, when his or her order is received, the goods will be sent out promptly. However, suppose one of the enquiries has been received from a previous customer who still has an outstanding debt with your company of over £1000. Obviously this would need a different type of reply.

For that reason, you may need to make additional enquiries to find out if there are any reasons why a standard response should *not* be made.

You must also consider if anyone else will be affected by your actions and should therefore receive a copy of your response (or information about what you have done).

Finally, check that you know where the document will be filed and that you have included any relevant references or file numbers.

The context

The context in which you are given correspondence and have to present it has already been dealt with in many of the points above. **Context** simply means the background situation. Under this heading you can include

- the importance or urgency of the document in relation to how busy you are with other work
- background details and information
- house style and rules on whether or not you are allowed to sign a document in your boss's absence (*see page 291*)
- your boss's methods of working, whether he or she has very fixed ideas about style and layout, or wants to check every document you draft before it is sent
- the amount of research and information which will be needed.

An important point to remember is that your own views will be less important than those of the person who pays you! You may have one boss who insists on commas everywhere and then another who likes the minimum of punctuation, one who has little knowledge of vocabulary, another who is very pedantic, so that every word has to be used very precisely. And who are you to argue?

DID YOU KNOW?

The hardest thing in the world is keeping your mouth shut when you know you are right and your boss is wrong! *If* you decide to point out a fundamental error your boss has made, be very careful. Suggest, perhaps, that he or she may have overlooked it rather than that he or she did not know enough to alter it! And be very sure you are right before you say anything at all!

Writing and composition skills

To write a good business communication, the skills you need include

- clear and accurate punctuation
- a good vocabulary
- accurate spelling
- a good knowledge of grammar
- a sense of order and rhythm so that the writing flows naturally from one point to the next and is never disjointed
- the ability to choose the correct phrases and tone for the person receiving the document.

DID YOU KNOW?

A good business communication contains sentences which vary in length. If you use too many short sentences, your document will seem clipped and disjointed. If you use too many long ones, your reader may not understand what you mean. Try to vary the length and yet keep the meaning throughout.

CHECK IT YOURSELF

The following section is intended to give you some of the basic skills you need to prepare business documents on your own. Note the information given in each section and apply your knowledge in the *Test yourself* sections which follow. If you find anything particularly difficult to understand, see your tutor or supervisor for additional help.

Punctuation skills

Accurate punctuation is vital for the correct meaning of a communication to be conveyed to the reader. You should already be aware that

- Any communication of any length should be sub-divided into paragraphs and each paragraph should contain a main theme or topic. When the topic changes a new paragraph should be started.
- Each paragraph is comprised of sentences which should vary in length.

Sentences – the beginning and the end

Every sentence must begin with a capital letter and end with a full stop, a question mark or an exclamation mark. Exclamation marks are the most rarely used in business correspondence but can be included to indicate humour or surprise.

CHECK IT YOURSELF

Find *two* examples of where sentences end with a question mark or an exclamation mark in this chapter. Discuss with your tutor why this type of punctuation has been chosen at that point.

SPECIAL NOTE

Full stops used to be used in abbreviations which are made up of capital letters, such as B.B.C. Nowadays it is usual to omit these and write the letters close together instead, e.g. BBC.

Sub-division of sentences

Sentences can be sub-divided by the use of commas, dashes, semi-colons, colons and brackets.

Commas   ,

Commas are used to

- clarify meaning
Mr Evans, the solicitor who is handling the case, will be in court tomorrow.

- divide a list of items
We visited Rome, Venice, Turin and Florence on our tour.

- separate a phrase within a sentence
The engineer will visit us tomorrow, probably in the morning, to mend the photocopier in the sales office.

- separate an introductory word or phrase
However, it is unlikely that we shall be able to go there on Wednesday.

DID YOU KNOW?

When you mark off a phrase in the middle of a sentence you must put a comma both *before* and *after* it. Check the examples above to see where this has been done.

Longer pauses

Dashes   –

Dashes can be substituted for commas to give a more distinct pause. Again, if the phrase being separated is in the middle of the sentence, a dash must be inserted both before and after it, e.g.

I hope to go to Edinburgh next Wednesday – provided Margaret Anderson can see me then – and return on Friday afternoon.

Semi-colons   ;

A semi-colon is used to join two closely connected sentences in place of a conjunction or joining word, e.g.

These boys are well-known for their athleticism; they play football, cricket and rugby.

If you are worried about using a semi-colon then use a full stop instead and make a second sentence, e.g.

These boys are well-known for their athleticism. They play football, cricket and rugby.

Colons   :

A colon is usually used to separate a clause which introduces a list, e.g.

We stock a variety of goods for the motorist: seat covers, floor-mats, fog lamps, anti-freeze and luggage racks.

Brackets   ( )

Brackets are used to sub-divide additional information added to a sentence, without changing the original meaning or punctuation. Occasionally an entire sentence may be enclosed in brackets if this provides purely additional information, e.g.

Three suggestions were receives last week (from Anne, Jayne and Sue) but we still need more ideas.

Information on electronic mail is given in Unit 8 of this book. (See page 339.)

Whilst brackets are used vary sparingly in business correspondence, there may be times when you want to insert a phrase in brackets *inside* another phrase in brackets! In this case a different style of brackets is normally used to show the difference. An example is given in this unit on page 259. Can you find it?

SPECIAL NOTE

If you open brackets, don't forget to close them! Check your work carefully afterwards to make sure you have remembered to do this.

Capital letters

In addition to being used at the beginning of a sentence, capitals are also used for proper nouns, e.g. Jersey, Mozart, Christmas.

Capitals are *not* used for common nouns (e.g. company, organisation, manager, government, university etc.) unless a specific example is being used – which is then a proper noun, e.g.

There are many universities in Britain.
I believe she will be going to Manchester University next year.

Which manager do you work for?
The Sales Manager of this company is Mr Watts.

Apostrophes

The apostrophe is probably the most troublesome of all punctuation marks and causes the most confusion. Apostrophes are normally used

- to show where letters are missing in a shortened word, e.g.
  can't (cannot)
  he's (he is)
  I'll (I will)
  they're (they are)

- to show ownership, e.g. *the manager's office.*

It is this second use which normally causes the most problems. Often you may know that there should be an apostrophe, but not where to put it! Try this. Change the sentence round to find out exactly *who* is the owner by adding the words *of the*. In the above example you would have *the office of the manager*. This shows there is only one owner.

When there is one owner the apostrophe goes *before* the 's', when there are several owners the apostrophe goes after the 's'. Therefore, in this case, one owner, so *manager's office*.

Compare this with the phrase *the girls' changing room*. This is *the changing room of the girls* and girls is therefore plural.

TEST YOURSELF

Turn these around yourself, add *of the,* then decide whether you have one owner or several and insert the apostrophe accordingly.

- the drivers car
- the wasps nest
- the Mayors parlour
- the members lounge
- the dogs bowl
- the students common room

Check the spelling

In many cases the spelling of a word tells you whether you are talking about one owner or several. In other cases you need to know the *sense* of the sentence before you can decide, e.g.

the company's results
(one company)

the companies' results
(many companies)

the lady's hairdresser
(one lady)

the ladies' hairdresser
(many ladies)

the boy's club
(one boy and one club)

the boys' club
(a club for many boys)

In the last example you would need more information before you could make a decision.

Special plurals

When a word changes to become plural, e.g. child and children, see whether you need an 's' once you have added *of the*. If you *don't,* then the apostrophe comes before the 's', e.g.

The childrens books means the books of the children, so *the children's books.*

If a plural word ends in 's' already (as in ladies) then simply add the apostrophe, e.g. *the ladies' hats*. However, if a *singular* word ends in 's' you need to add an apostrophe *plus* an extra 's', e.g.

We are going to St James's Park tomorrow.
(We are going to the Park of St James tomorrow.)

SPECIAL NOTE

Do beware of the word *its*. When *its* shows ownership there is **no** apostrophe. The word *it's* means *it is*. Therefore

The cat drank its milk. (Possessive) *but*
It's getting late. (It is getting late).

Time

Units of time, e.g. days, months and years can also be possessive, e.g.

a year's pay (pay of one year)
three months' work (work of three months)

The same rules apply – before the 's' if singular, after the 's' if plural.

DID YOU KNOW?

Some people who start to use apostrophes become so keen on them that they put them after every word which ends in 's'! Remember that the vast majority of words ending with an 's' are perfectly ordinary plural words, e.g. shops, cups, chairs and houses which don't need an apostrophe at all.

Hyphens

A hyphen is used to divide complex words, e.g. red-headed, part-time, ill-mannered. It may also be used at the end of a line to signify word division but this practice is becoming less common as modern printers and typewriters can automatically justify right-hand margins on printed documents.

Nowadays many complex words also remain unhyphenated, e.g. swimming bath. (Technically this is a complex word because a bath can't swim!) However, occasionally a hyphen is essential because the unhyphenated word would mean something entirely different, e.g.

It is important he re-signs the contract before the end of May.

He has said he will resign from the football team in spring.

DID YOU KNOW?

There is a fundamental difference between the abbreviations *'e.g.'* and *'i.e.'* – they are *not* interchangeable!

- **e.g.** should be used when you are giving some examples of many things – and means 'for example'. (It actually stands for the Latin phrase *exempli gratia*.). Look at the following sentence – and instead of reading 'e.g.' read 'for example'.

  The trader sold many unusual fruits and vegetables, e.g. papaya, mango and lychees.

- **i.e.** stands for 'that is' and is used to give a specific example. (It actually stands for the Latin words *id est.*) Read the following sentence and substitute the phrase 'that is' for the abbreviation.

Many legal advisers (i.e. solicitors) have free Saturday morning consultations.

TEST YOURSELF ON PUNCTUATION

1 Insert apostrophes in the correct places in the following sentences.
  a Paul, my fathers friend, is visiting the miners social club next Wednesday.
  b When its 6 pm we feed Marys goat and give the dog some water in its bowl.
  c Todays results were disastrous for us – its a long time since the companys finances were so badly affected.

2 Capitalise words which should start with an initial capital letter.
  a in autumn we intend to visit our branch office in frankfurt.
  b leaders of the british government will meet the chinese delegation on thursday.
  c many people believe that scott discovered the south pole but this is a fallacy.

3 Rewrite the following passage punctuating it correctly and dividing it into two paragraphs.

the sales managers report on the recent sales conference was interesting and informative mr owen stated that the conference had been held at the fernlea hotel near ambleside in the lake district on 26 and 27 october representatives had attended from all the uk regions including wales scotland northern ireland and eire they had been enthusiastic about the new product range for the summer especially the boys shoes and ladies sandals despite increased competition from overseas sales are expected to be above average and several firm orders have already been received from mr jamiesons region in the north of england.

Vocabulary

How many times have you been writing something and not known which word you should use next? Or found yourself using the same word over and over again? Or – even worse – using a slang expression because you couldn't think of a more formal word to use?

Although this happens to all of us at some time, quite obviously the more words you know the less this is likely to occur – and the more accurately you can convey the meaning you want.

There are various ways in which you can extend your vocabulary, for example

- by reading newspapers, magazines and books
- by playing word games, e.g. Scrabble
- by doing crosswords (Start with the easy ones!)
- by always questioning people who use a word you don't know
- by always looking up in a dictionary any new word you hear or read (including those you read in this book)!

DID YOU KNOW?

It's quite common that although you may think you have never heard a certain word, once you *do* hear it and find out what it means you suddenly find yourself hearing it over and over again! The reason is that we tend unconsciously to block out unfamiliar words and guess the sense of a sentence. (If you think about it, small children do this all the time.) Only when you are consciously aware of the word do you realise when it has been used.

Dictionaries

Dictionaries are not always useful for people who can't spell, especially if the beginning of a word starts with an unexpected combination of letters, e.g. lieutenant (pronounced left-tenant).

They are actually far more useful for giving the meanings of strange words. A good dictionary will also include information on pronunciation, abbreviations and other miscellaneous information. Another useful reference book is a **thesaurus** which gives synonyms of words (i.e. words and phrases which have the same or similar meaning).

TEST YOURSELF ON VOCABULARY

1 How quickly can you look up each of the following words and write down the meaning?

candid	escalate	charismatic
sceptical	unorthodox	rescind
sporadic	superfluous	despotic

2 Try *saying* these words – pronouncing them by following the spelling. Then check if you are correct by looking up the pronunciation in your dictionary and their meaning. Then check with your tutor or supervisor that you are pronouncing each one correctly.

epitome	vehement	rhetoric
vacillate	naive	blackguard

3 **Synonyms** are words which *have the same meaning*. The problem with the list below is that whilst the words in column B should mean the same as the corresponding word in column A, the words in column B are mixed up. Can you rearrange the words so that they are correctly matched?

Column A	Column B
pensive	outgoing
donate	emotionless
stoical	genuine
veritable	hasten
extrovert	give
expedite	fair
impartial	shorten
prognosis	thoughtful
authentic	forecast
condense	true

4 **Homonyms** are words which sound the same but which are different in meaning and spelling. Homonyms and other words which sound very similar are frequently confused. In the sentences below

● Select the word which should be used.
● Find out and note down the meaning of the other word.

The police will *prosecute/persecute* him after the *collusion/collision*. It is against my *principals/principles* to *accede/exceed* to your request.
Don't *lose/loose* that *cheque/check – draw/drawer* the money out today.
I *accept/except there/their* are problems at the building *sight/site*. Type a *draught/draft* of the document and go *through/threw* it with me.
Whose/who's the girl in *personnel/personal* who *past/passed* her exam with distinction?

Spelling

Generally, the more you read the better you become at spelling. This is because you constantly see the correct spellings of words and will notice when they are written in any other way.

You should be able to spell basic words correctly all the time. You can check in a dictionary for longer words but it is a good idea to make a real effort to improve your spelling by consciously learning new words – and the best way to do this is to write out the word two or three times, concentrating on the spelling all the time.

If you *really* can't remember how to spell a word, then choose an alternative instead!

Common errors

Errors often occur when a word can be spelt in more than one way and has more than one use. The most common areas of confusion are given below.

There/their/they're

- there – a place (e.g. *here and there*)
  It is also used before a verb, e.g. *there is.*
- their – belonging to them (e.g. *their coats*)
- they're – a contracted word – short for *they are.*

Where/wear/were

- where – a place (e.g. *where are you?*)
- wear – to put on (e.g. *will you wear it?*)
- were – a verb, the plural of 'was' (e.g. *we were here*).

To/too/two

- to – used before a verb or pronoun (e.g. *to go to them*)
- too – as well (e.g. *we will go too*)
- two – the number 2.

Be careful also of *know* and *no, of* and *off* and *your* and *you're.*

DID YOU KNOW?

Although the spelling may be correct, words which should be written separately are sometimes written together in error. Typical examples include

- thank you – which is *always* two words
- all right – *not* alright
- a lot – a poor phrase to use but still two words.

Be careful, too, of words which are sometimes written together and sometimes separately, e.g.

- may be/maybe – *maybe* written together means *perhaps.*

Changing the spelling

This, too, can cause confusion and errors. The most common are

- forgetting to change a 'y' to an 'i' for the past tense, e.g.
  pay – paid (*not* payed!)
  try – tried (*not* tryed!)
- adding 'full' to a word and forgetting to drop the final 'l', e.g.
  beautiful, careful, forgetful, successful.
- not understanding the difference between a noun (spelt with a 'c') and a verb (spelt with an 's'), e.g.

Noun	Verb
practice	practise
licence	license
advice	advise

Remember! If you can put the word 'the' at the front then the word is a noun, e.g. the doctor's practice, the driving licence, the solicitor's advice.

If you can put the word 'to' in front of it, then the word is a verb, e.g. to practise medicine, to license the car, to advise a client.

DID YOU KNOW?

Probably the most common errors are concerned with mixing up 'i' and 'e'. A good general rule to follow is

i before e unless after c or if the word has an 'a' sound. Therefore

medieval (not after 'c') *but* receipt (after 'c')

relief (not after 'c') *but* deceive (after 'c')

rein, reign, vein, veil and weight – all words which sound like 'a'.

Even then there are exceptions, e.g. leisure, neither, either, weird and height – so be careful. If you're not sure, check in a dictionary.

TEST YOURSELF ON SPELLING

1 Below are some words used commonly in business correspondence. Twenty are spelled incorrectly. Can you identify which ones?

accomodation	liason
advertisment	manouvre
awfull	miniture
alledge	noticeable
benevolant	occurrance
colleages	ommitted
committee	predecesser
competant	prestigous
courteous	questionaire
conscientious	received
consistant	referred
definate	seperate
deficient	sincerly
development	underrate
enviroment	waive

2 Rewrite the following sentences, correcting all the spelling mistakes.

a The Presidant gave a humourous speach yesterday, when he was the honorary guest at our centenery.

b She wanted to order fourty reams of paper from the stationary store but was told this was to much and the order had to be refered to the manager.

c She recieved two differant references – one said she was incompetant and unfit to join the permanant staff whilst the other described her as extremly conscientous.

d It was embarassing when the forein minister visited Parliment yesterday with all his advisors acompanying him.

Grammar

We may smile when we hear young children say sentences such as 'I is tired' and 'He learned me to do that.' We don't smile when we hear adults speak like this or make similar grammatical errors. In speech such mistakes sometimes pass relatively unnoticed; in written documents, once you know they are wrong, such errors almost seem to leap out from the page!

CHECK IT YOURSELF

Can you identify what is wrong in each of the following sentences?

1 Which boy works the hardest – Tony or Dave?
2 Neither of the flats were suitable.
3 The Government are going to debate this tomorrow.
4 Do you know who you will be working for?
5 We haven't been nowhere near his house.
6 Neither the girl or her mother had visited the shop.
7 I shall be delighted if you would come to see me tomorrow.
8 He had to quickly run to meet his friend.
9 She asked if you and me could see her in the morning.
10 I understand you met Mr Sharp yesterday. How did you find him?
11 The delay was due to Mr Parker's absence.

Common grammatical errors

Some of the errors above may have seemed obvious – others more difficult. Look through the explanations and answers below and study carefully those you *didn't* find in the list above.

Comparative and superlative

● If you are comparing two objects then add 'er', if you are comparing more than two add 'est'. Therefore sentence one should read

Which boy works the harder – Tony or Dave?

● Some words do not have 'er' or 'est' added to them, e.g. beautiful, handsome, angry. If you are comparing two objects put the word 'more' in front, if more than two, use the word 'most', e.g.

She is the most beautiful girl I have ever seen. She is certainly more beautiful than Sarah.

Agreeing singular and plural words

The verbs which follow singular words must also be singular and those which follow plural words must be plural. This is simple and we follow this rule every time we speak, e.g.

I *am* going − we *are* going
He *was* leaving − they *were* leaving

Difficulties arise when we are given alternatives to the basic pronouns, e.g. each, every, all, none, either, neither and none.

The test here is to see if you can put the word 'one' afterwards. If you can, the word is singular and takes a singular verb. Therefore

each (one) and *every* (one) − both are singular
either (one) and *neither* (one) − singular again
none means not one − another singular

Therefore sentence 2 should have read

Neither of the flats was suitable.
(Neither one of the flats was suitable.)

Confusion occurs more often because of the phrase in the middle. Try to make things easier for yourself by ignoring any words in the middle (as well as adding 'one' to help you), e.g.

None of the people on yesterday's boat trip ... over 65. means
Not one of the people (....) was over 65.

Collective nouns also cause problems. These are used to describe a group, e.g. government, committee, society, board. Although there may be many people involved it is only *one* group and is therefore singular. Therefore sentence 3 should read

The Government is going to debate this tomorrow.

Ending a sentence

When you are writing, try to avoid ending a sentence with a preposition, e.g. 'to', 'of', 'with', 'about' or 'for'. This may mean changing the sentence around e.g.

Which company are you referring to? *should* read

To which company are you referring? (or)
Which company do you mean?

You may have to alter 'who' to 'whom' when you change your sentence. For instance, sentence 4 should read

Do you know for whom you will be working?

This may seem very formal but is really correct English. If you have a problem with this then reword your sentence entirely as in the example above, e.g.

Do you know the name of your manager?

Double negatives

These are meaningless as they cancel each other out! 'He is not going nowhere' means he must be going somewhere! If you use double negatives when you are speaking then the listener will probably ignore them – *don't* use them when you are writing. By now you should realise that sentence 5 should read

We haven't been anywhere near his house.

Word pairs

Some words always go together – particularly either/or and neither/nor. Sentence 6 should therefore read

Neither the girl nor her mother had visited the shop.

Other matches include

- shall and will
- should and would.

Sentence 7 should therefore read

I shall be delighted if you will come and see me tomorrow. or
I should be delighted if you would come and see me tomorrow.

Two words which causes a lot of confusion are *'who'* and *'whom'*. The rule for this is rather complicated so if you are unsure which is right and cannot check it with anyone, try to find a way round it by rewording your sentence, e.g.

Mr Baker is the person to who/whom you should write.

can become

You should write to Mr Baker.

In other words, keep it simple!

Split infinitives

The **infinitive** is the root of a verb – 'to go', 'to run', 'to carry' etc. Wherever possible, try not to split an infinitive by putting another word in the middle. You may recall all the comment about the opening of *StarTrek* – '... to boldly go ...' – because it included a split infinitive!

Simply change the words around in your sentence, so that sentence 8 becomes

He had to run quickly to meet his friend.

'I' and 'me'

It can sometimes be difficult to decide whether you should write 'you and I' or 'you and me'. The simple way to decide this is to substitute 'we' or 'us'.

we – you and I

us – you and me

Using this test, sentence 9 would read

She asked if we could see her in the morning.

Therefore the correct version is

She asked if you and I could see her in the morning.

Ambiguity

An ambiguous sentence is one which could mean two things. If you said to a friend, 'You need your hair cutting badly!' she may reply, 'No, I need my hair cutting very well!'

In sentence 10 the second sentence is ambiguous – and also slang. We do not know if the writer meant the word 'find' in a geographical sense (as you would find something which was lost) or to mean 'what did you think of him?'

Make sure what you write is precise and accurate so that the reader knows exactly what you mean.

DID YOU KNOW?

Words to avoid (because they mean so little) are 'got' and 'nice'. Think of the sentence – *The day got nicer and nicer.* This is so imprecise it is hardly worth writing – even though you may have a vague idea what the writer meant!

Other bad errors

Word confusions which sound terrible include

- learned and taught
- lend and borrow.

You may also find it easy to misuse the word 'due'. Many people use 'due' when they really mean 'because'. This is the case in sentence 11 which should read

The delay was because of Mr Parker's absence.

DID YOU KNOW?

There are no such phrases in the English language as '*could of*', '*would of*' or '*should of*'! If you find yourself writing any expressions like this you are **wrong.**

You are using the conditional form of the verb to have, therefore you should write

could have   would have   should have

etc.

1   Retest your ability to spot grammatical errors by correcting the following sentences.

   a   The Safety Committee are using that room next week.
   b   She wanted to know where he was going to.
   c   She never has no time to talk about it.
   d   None of us were interested in his proposal.
   e   The car which developed the fault was a BMW which is unusual.
   f   She had to rapidly produce the memo he wanted.
   g   I would be pleased if you will send us the cheque immediately.
   h   Do you know whom Mr Taylor wants to see?
   i   He has asked to see you and I at noon.
   j   He is someone who I have never been able to get along with.

2   Rewrite the following passage without using the word *'got'* once and without changing the meaning. Think of a suitable alternative for the word *'nice'* every time it appears and substitute any slang expressions with more acceptable words.

   Keith got ready early for his job interview yesterday. It was a nice day and the place wasn't far away. The guy who saw him looked quite nice and had a nice big office. They chatted for a bit then got involved discussing Keith's application form. Keith got a bit lost when the bloke asked what he had been up to between 16 and 17 as Keith had taken a year out but wanted to keep this quiet. He got over the problem by referring to the nice part-time job he'd had at the time. At the end of the interview Keith shook hands with the guy who promised to get back to him soon. After two weeks Keith got a nice letter telling him he'd landed the job but got a shock when he saw the salary. He thought he could have got more and wondered whether to hang on a bit longer and see if he could get fixed up somewhere else.

Composition skills

The next stage is to put all your skills together and start to produce correspondence on your own. Remember that at all times the **tone** of your document must be correct – formal (but not too distant), business-like, concise, clear and courteous.

Before you start

Consider

   ● Who will receive the document and what tone and vocabulary should you use?
   ● What are the important facts which must be conveyed?
   ● What response do you want?

Whilst you write

Remember

- Use words you will both understand. Don't use any unfamiliar words unless you are absolutely clear what these mean.
- Use simple phrases and no slang expressions.
- Follow a logical order.
- Keep it clear and concise – don't waffle.
- Use a presentational style which will make it easier to follow – either paragraphs or numbered points if there are a number of items to include (*see page 300*).

After you have written

- Read your communication through and correct any errors.
- Be fussy – check your spelling and punctuation.
- Check your 'message' is clear.
- Make sure your tone is correct throughout.

TEST YOURSELF

Write short memos to your boss, Margaret Thompson, the Personnel Manager, to cover each of the following situations.

1   Before she went out of the office early today she asked you to arrange a meeting for her with Chris Maitland, the Managing Director. The MD's secretary has just telephoned you to confirm that the MD can see her for half an hour at 9.30 in the morning.

2   You have just received a telephone call from Mr Michael Blake, a tutor at the local college, asking if he can send a student on work experience for two weeks in May, starting on the second Monday in the month. The student is male, aged 17 and is currently taking a business studies course. He would prefer some experience in both Accounts and Purchasing. When you rang these departments to check if this would be possible, the Chief Accountant was agreeable, but worried about space in the office, but the Purchasing Manager refused. He argued they were short-staffed at present and were too busy to cope with a student.

3   You had arranged to take a personal day off in two weeks' time to go shopping with a friend. Your friend had now informed you that she will have to make it the following week – which clashes with a busy week of interviews. You obviously need permission before you can agree to this.

4   The Sales Manager rang up to speak to Ms Thompson (in her absence) about the short-list of interviewees for the representative required for his department. He is annoyed that none of the applicants seemed sufficiently qualified and he has wasted an afternoon interviewing for nothing. He wants to know immediately what action

can be taken, as the situation is becoming more critical each day, with no company being visited in the south west region.

5   You received a telephone call from John Brahms, the Production Manager. He has clear evidence that one of his operatives, John Blackstone, has been clocking in his friend, Joe Bishop, whilst the latter was off work sick. This is a disciplinary offence which usually leads to instant dismissal. He wants to discuss the situation first thing in the morning and thinks there may be strong union involvement. He does not want the information to become public knowledge until he has decided what action to take.

Check your work with your tutor or supervisor. Ask him or her to correct any errors you have made, and then make a final version of each document. Even if no obvious errors have been made, it is useful to discuss the phrases you used and the order in which you made your points.

 ## DID YOU KNOW?

Special signs can be used on corrected documents to show you what alterations to make. You don't need to learn these specially – usually they are obvious, e.g.

Correction signs	
NP	– new paragraph (Which means you didn't start one when one was necessary.)
run on or ⊇	– don't start a new paragraph (Which means you started one unnecessarily.)
trs	– transpose (You wrote or typed two letters or words the wrong way round.)
#	– an insertion mark (Which means you forgot to leave a space.)
໑	– deletion (Delete the words or letters which have been crossed out.)
⋏	– insertion (Insert the words written next to the mark.)
uc/lc	– upper case and lower case (The word should have an initial capital or should not have an initial capital!)
stet	– leave it as it was (It really means your boss changed something and then wanted it changed back again!)

 ## TEST YOURSELF

You have received the following memo back from Margaret Thompson. She has highlighted some typing and grammatical errors, plus one or two spelling mistakes. Type out a final version of the memo, incorporating all her corrections.

MEMORANDUM

TO   Brenda Sharples

FROM John Walker

DATE 10 February 199-

REF JW

 INTERVIEWS FOR WORD PROCESSOR OPERATOR

  these will be held next Mon, 15 February, starting at 2pm. There are four candidates ~~which~~ *who* have been short-listed ~~for the job~~.

 The interview schedule is as follows:

2.00 pm	Marilyn ~~Jones~~ *James*
2.30 pm	Brian Thompson
3.00 pm	Jalinda Sagermann
3.30 pm	Pauline Cox

Please go to Ms Thompson's office at 1.30 pm on that day to discuss the applications. A copy of all the application forms ~~are~~ *is* enclosed.

~~Thank you~~

Presentational style

The way in which you display letters and memos will depend on their content. It may be necessary to incorporate a table or detailed information which cannot sensibly be given in paragraph form. You therefore need to think of different ways in which you can present the information, bearing in mind that it should be clear and easy to understand by the reader.

 ## TEST YOURSELF

You have recently been doing an analytical study of clock cards for Margaret Thompson. There are 152 workers who clock in for work in your organisation. During the last month you found that 65 people were late by up to five minutes. Of these, 28 were regularly late by ten minutes and 12 by fifteen minutes. There was a considerable amount of absenteeism. During the month, 55 staff were absent for one day, 32 for two to four days and 27 for longer than four days. The major reason given was influenza.

Display this information clearly and concisely in a memo to Ms Thompson.

Composing business letters

A business letter must always be clear, concise and courteous, and must not include any jargon or abbreviations that the reader would not understand.

Preparation stages

- Check that you have all the information to hand.
- Arrange the information in a logical order – always give background information or the reason for writing *first*.
- Decide on a suitable opening and conclusion.
- Draft out the letter.
- Read it through *as if you were the recipient*. Check
  - the tone
  - the order
  - the terms and phrases you have used
  - that no key information has been omitted.
- Type it out using your organisation's house style.

DID YOU KNOW?

- Many writers leave a document for a while before reading it through. Mistakes are then easier to see.
- It is totally wrong to begin any letter with the phrase 'I am writing ...' because this is stating the obvious!

Starting and concluding a letter

Starting and ending a letter can create more problems than anything else when you first start writing letters. The following points may help you.

- If you are replying to a letter you have received then start by using the phrase 'Thank you for your letter of (date) regarding ...'
- If you are writing after speaking to someone on the telephone, start by using the phrase 'Further to our recent telephone conversation ...' but *make sure you complete the sentence!*
- If you are writing a letter of enquiry, start by saying where you found out about their organisation, e.g. 'Further to your advertisement in the Sunday Gazette, I would be grateful if you could send me details of your ...'
- If you are writing a letter of complaint, start by giving some background about your purchase, e.g. 'Last week I purchased a

stereo system from your store. Unfortunately, within two days of normal use it had stopped working.' (**Note:** In a real letter you should give details of the make and model you bought.)

- There are several standard conclusions, e.g.
  - We look forward to hearing from you.
  - Please let us know if we can be of any further assistance.
  - We look forward to receiving your confirmation.
  - We hope this information will be helpful to you.
  - If you have any further queries, please do not hesitate to contact us.

Again, do make sure you write a *complete* sentence.

DID YOU KNOW?

- To avoid writing an incomplete sentence, never start a sentence with a word ending in '-ing'.

- In some organisations staff are instructed to write 'we' and not 'I' when they compose a letter. This is because the person concerned is writing on behalf of the company and not personally. Check if this is the case where you work, by looking at existing letters in the files. What you should never do is change from one to the other in the middle!

TEST YOURSELF

The situations below all involve Mr Charles Dixon, Sales Manager of Bramley Products, Hightown. In the first two tasks you are asked to write a letter to the company, then you are asked to draft out the reply bearing in mind Mr Dixon's instructions. In the third task, you are asked to write two letters on behalf of Mr Dixon. Write out your letters neatly and ask your tutor and/or supervisor for their comments.

Task 1

a As a student write to Mr Dixon at Bramley Products Ltd, Main Road, Hightown, HG5 9TP. Explain that you are writing a business studies project and would be grateful for any information he can supply on the organisation and how it operates.

b Students often contact the Sales Department for information about the company if they are doing business studies projects. A standard information pack has been produced which can be sent to all enquirers. Mr Dixon has asked you to prepare a standard letter which can be sent with the packs which

- thanks the student for their enquiry
- explains that an information pack is enclosed
- asks them to contact the company again if they require any additional information.

Task 2

a You are Miss J Watts, the Buyer at Simkins and Dove, 14 Watery Close, Hightown, HG5 2TT. Write and ask them if they can supply you with 10 A3 sheets of blotting paper, 25 red clipboards and 40 reams of A4 white photocopying paper by the last date of this month.

b An order has been received from a regular customer – Miss J Watts, the Buyer at Simkins & Dove, 14 Watery Close, Hightown, HG5 2TT. Unfortunately one item she asked for – blotting paper – is no longer stocked by your organisation because of lack of demand. The clipboards she ordered can be supplied but not by the date requested.

Mr Dixon has asked that you write to her and explain these facts. He has also asked you to check if she still wants to receive the clipboards or to cancel the order.

Finally he has noticed that their account from last month is still overdue. As they are normally good payers he thinks this must be an oversight and has asked that you point it out in the letter and request that payment be made as soon as possible.

Task 3

a The forthcoming sales conference is to be held at the Berkeley Hotel, Union Road, Hightown, HG4 9TG. During telephone discussions, the manager, Mr J Wilkins, has promised that a conference room will be provided with full facilities. Write and confirm the arrangements. Explain that 20 delegates will be arriving at 9 am on the second Wednesday of next month. Coffee should be served at 11 am, lunch at 1 pm and afternoon tea at 3.30 pm. Also, 20 single rooms will be required. Dinner will be taken in the main dining room at 9 pm. The following day all the delegates will require breakfast but will leave at 4.30 pm. Refreshments and lunch are required as before.

A flip chart and overhead projector must be provided in the conference room. A list of delegates will be sent to the hotel three days before the event.

b The recent sales conference was held at the Berkeley Hotel but was not a success. On the day in question the conference room was being re-decorated which meant that 20 people had to be crammed into a smaller room. There was a delay in the dining room in the evening and several people had to wait to be served. The following morning there were no flip charts or overhead projectors available. The quoted rate for the conference facilities was £400 plus £100 per night for each room plus breakfast, £5.50 for lunch and £12.50 per head for dinner. Mr Dixon thinks this is too high, given the lack of facilities and the difficulties which occurred.

He has asked you to write to the manager, disputing the total amount which has to be paid and stating the problems which were encountered.

CHECK IT YOURSELF

The rules on who should sign letters vary from one organisation to another. The following are all alternatives – check which operates in your company.

- You can sign any letters you are authorised to write.
- All letters must be signed by a senior member of staff.
- Letters can be signed by staff but only when a member of the senior staff is absent.
- Any letters which are signed in a manager's absence must be clearly marked 'pp'. This stands for *per pro* or *on behalf of* and makes it clear that the letter was signed by someone else other than the writer. The letter is signed with someone else's signature but the manager's name and title are shown underneath, e.g.

Yours sincerely
DAVENPORT PLC

pp Sara Godley

Nigel Watts
Purchasing Manager

- Any letters which are signed in a manager's absence must be signed in his or her name but then noted accordingly, e.g.

Yours sincerely
DAVENPORT PLC

Nigel Watts

Nigel Watts
Personnel Manager

Note: Dictated by Mr Watts and signed in his absence.

UNIT REVIEW (1)

At the end of this element you should be able to

- identify correctly correspondence to which you should reply yourself
- identify and route correspondence which must be handled by other people to them without delay
- select the best type of response bearing in mind the importance, urgency and cost of the reply
- convey accurately the exact meaning and tone of the response using correct language and grammar
- respond in a way which is accurate, clear and in the style of the organisation

- check your work for standard punctuation, spelling and grammatical errors
- use standard correspondence conventions and select the best method of presenting the information
- store copies of correspondence, replies and other notes in accordance with standard organisational procedures
- identify occasions when security and confidentiality of data are required and take the necessary procedures in line with organisational requirements.

REVIEW YOUR KNOWLEDGE AND UNDERSTANDING

True or false?

State if the following sentences are all free from errors. If they are *not,* write a correct version.

1 In two week's time we will be visiting london to see St Pauls' Cathedrel and Westminster abbey.
2 She told me to thankyou for giving her your advise that she would be uneligible to start on that course next year.
3 We sincerely hope that when they're over there, they enjoy the attractions as much as we did.
4 Which of the following two calculations do you find the easiest to do?
5 She said it would be alright for us to state that its impossible to prove the ommission was critical to the sucess of the project.

Fill in the blanks

6 The word 'due' is often used when the writer really means to use the word _____ .
7 A confidential memo should always be sent out in a _____ _____ .
8 If a letter starts Dear Mrs Smith, then it must end with the words _____ _____ .

Work it out

9 In each of the following examples the meaning of the word is given to you, plus the first three letters. Can you complete the gaps?

able to use both hands alike	amb_____
a crime against the state	tre _____
no longer in use	obs _____
a word based on initials	acr_____
concerning the elderly	ger_____
the highest point	zen _____
going on all the time	inc_____
pompous and showy	pre_____
unstable and changeable	vol _____

10 Brian Hanson, the Sales Manager at your company, has asked you to write a memo to Tony Marsland, Chief Accountant, based on the following notes he took at a meeting he attended yesterday.

- Barbara Yates, Purchasing Director of KLS Services not happy with credit terms offered in our last letter.
- We offered terms of 30% on delivery, balance in 4 instalments.
- KLS want to pay 25% on delivery, balance in 6 instalments.
- What does Tony think? Seems OK to me – check credit rating first?
- Advise Tony terms offered in response to possible order for 2 XL10 machines – total value £50 000.

Element 7.2
Prepare a variety of documents

The previous element concentrated on the preparation of memos and business letters. In reality you will probably be asked to prepare a variety of other documents during your working life. You will also be involved in keeping records for your organisation in one form or another. Broadly, these can be categorised into documents which contain

- mainly text, e.g. letters, memos, forms, summaries, reports, internal notices or advertisements and written records
- tables
- listings (e.g. of customers, suppliers, bad payers etc. – often printed out from a computer)
- numerical information, e.g. expense claims, petty cash vouchers, sales figures and other financial records.

Basic rules to follow

- Make sure you clearly understand what you have been asked to do. You will irritate everyone (including yourself) if you spend hours preparing a document which does not contain the required information, because you misunderstood the instructions. If in doubt then *check* – by clarifying the instructions – even to the point of starting the document and then taking it to your boss for approval before you continue.

  Key facts to check include

  – any special points on layout
  – the final form in which the document should appear, i.e. typed or handwritten
  – the urgency with which it is required
  – the number of copies required
  – the distribution list

- whether your boss wants to check it before it is sent out
- any special instructions on confidentiality or security.

If you are given an unrealistic deadline or are having problems obtaining the information or doing the work in time, you must consult your boss and keep him or her informed (*see also Unit 3*).

- Don't think that because you are preparing a draft document or a simple list, or because it is for internal use only, that it can be scruffy and full of crossings-out! You should set your own (high!) standards of presentation and make sure that *nothing* which leaves your desk is a bad advertisement for your professionalism. Minor corrections may be made provided they cannot be seen. This means taking time and trouble over them – not slapping on liquid paper as if it were house paint!
- If you are collecting information from a variety of sources, e.g. merging together small amounts of information from different lists, then you will need a logical method of working, otherwise you will get confused. *This is dealt with in listings on page 302.*
- Remember that the content of a document must be consistent throughout. The best way to achieve this is to think about style and layout before you start, e.g.
  - Are you using blocked or indented paragraphs?
  - Is your spacing consistent between paragraphs?
  - If you are using numbered points, are there consistent spaces between the number and the start of the text?
  - Are you using the 12 hour clock or the 24 hour clock?
  - Are you writing figures out in full or writing them in numerical form? (The usual convention is to show one as a word and everything else in figures unless it is the start of a sentence.)
  - Are you using a comma or a space to denote numbers over a thousand – i.e. £10,000 or £10 000?
  - Should you use 'I' or 'we'?
  - Are you using initial capitals correctly and not writing the same word both ways in one document, e.g. the Continent and the continent?
  - Are you using full stops in abbreviations or not?

Once you know the style which is preferred by your organisation then stick to it. Don't make changes part-way through!

- Display your work effectively on appropriately-sized paper (usually A4). Bear in mind that you can use paper **landscape** (short side on) or **portrait**. Landscape would, for instance, be more appropriate for a table which is quite short but has several headings across the top.
- Spelling, grammar and punctuation must also be correct; you must check your work carefully before submitting a final document.

- Take as much trouble with the copying, collation and distribution of the document as you do with its actual preparation. No-one will be impressed if they receive a ten-page document with two pages missing, one back to front and stapled in the wrong place! (*See also Unit 6, Element 6.3.*)

DID YOU KNOW?

It is not usually acceptable to write any words in an abbreviated form *except* standard abbreviations, e.g. Mr, Mrs, Dr, Co, Ltd, BBC, ITV etc. Therefore words such as *Road* and *Avenue,* and the names of months, should be written in full. It is also incorrect to write the ampersand (&) anywhere except in the phrase *'& Co Ltd'.*

Text-based documents

Letters and memos were covered in the previous element. Summaries are included in Unit 5, Element 5.2. This section therefore deals with forms, reports, internal notices and advertisements and written records.

Forms

During your working life you will probably have to complete several forms, some required internally and some required by outside organisations. You may even have to design a form yourself from time to time.

Completing forms

- Always read the form through first and identify any sections which must *not* be completed.
- Note the amount of space allowed for each entry, so that you can adjust your writing to fit. If you have to include an explanation or comment in any area ,it is better if you draft it out first to find out if it will fit in the space available.
- Make a special note of the information to be provided in each space. A common mistake is to include the postcode in the space for the main address when there is a separate space provided for it.
- Identify any special instructions, e.g. whether block capitals are required, if a special pen must be used, or only certain sections completed.
- If you are worried about completing the form, take a photocopy on which you can practise first.
- Write clearly.
- Do not leave any blanks. If a section is not relevant then insert the letters N/A (for *not applicable*). This shows the reader that you did not miss out information accidentally.
- Check the form afterwards and find out whether you can date and sign it yourself or whether this must be done by your manager.

TEST YOURSELF

Obtain a form for a driving licence from the post office. Complete this with information about yourself and ask your tutor or supervisor to check your work.

Designing forms

Always try to keep it as simple as possible. Think through the information which is required and then decide upon suitable headings under which this could be recorded. Often a tabular layout is more appropriate than a questionnaire layout.

An example of a tabular layout is an appointment book (*see page 145*). An example of a questionnaire layout is the driving licence form you have just completed.

Bear in mind that if *you* are going to design a form to record information *yourself,* then you will understand what you are trying to achieve. If *other people* will be using it, it is a good idea to show it to someone else to see if it is easily understandable.

Make sure that any alternatives are easy to follow, e.g. whether only one section or another needs to be completed.

TEST YOURSELF

1   Your boss is concerned that the photocopier in your office is being used too much and wants to monitor the numbers of copies taken over the next few weeks. He has asked you to design a form on which users must write their name, the date and time the copies were made, the number of pages copied and the quantity of copies made from each page. It will be your job to calculate and enter the total number of copies taken.

Design a suitable form on which to record this information.

2   You are helping to organise your company's annual Christmas dinner dance. This will be held on the second Saturday in December at the Greenhill Hotel, Hightown, starting at 7.30 pm. Dinner will be served at 8 pm. There will be a disco which starts at 9.30 pm. Transport is available for those who want it. There is no charge to staff as this event is paid for by the company each year.

You have been asked to write a memo to all staff informing them about the event and to design a tear-off slip which staff can complete to indicate if they will be attending and whether or not they will require transport.

DID YOU KNOW?

A tear-off slip should be separated from the main text of a memo or letter by a series of hyphens which runs from *edge to edge* on the paper and *not* margin to margin.

It is usual to put a heading on the slip so that you can remember what it is about when you get it back!

If there is any blank white space, this should occur between the end of the memo or letter and the start of the slip. The slip itself should always end about one inch (2.5 cm) from the bottom of the paper, as shown below.

MEMORANDUM

TO   **All sales staff**

FROM **Sales Manager**

DATE **18 November 199-**

STAFF TRAINING DAY

This will be held on Tuesday, 28 November. The morning session will include a special section on consumer legislation and customer relations. In the afternoon there will be a demonstration of the range of new products which have been launched this year.

Refreshments will be provided in the morning and afternoon and lunch will be served at 12.30 pm.

Could you please confirm below whether you will require lunch and indicate if you will require a vegetarian meal.

- -

SALES TRAINING DAY

I will require lunch: Yes/No

Vegetarian meal required: Yes/No

Signed ....Dated.....................

Internal notices and advertisements

Notices and advertisements are a method of conveying the same information quickly to a large number of readers simultaneously. Many companies have noticeboards on which current events are shown, some use electronic mail systems to inform personnel about these matters (*see Unit 8*). Very large organisations may have their own internal staff magazines which include articles on personnel, company developments, advertisements and so on.

Some notices will be formally worded and some will be informal – depending on the content. A notice about a union meeting or a change in eating arrangements in the canteen will be worded more formally than an advertisement for a pub quiz or treasure hunt!

 ## DID YOU KNOW?

In *all* types of documents, the language you choose and your style of writing can influence the type and number of responses you receive. This is particularly true if you are writing a notice or advertisement. If you look at general advertisements you will see they use adjectives or persuasive phrases to tempt you to buy. Words such as *free, gift, exciting* and *wonderful* attract our attention much more quickly than words such as *good value* and *interesting*.

Composing notices and advertisements

- Use simple, straightforward language that everyone can understand.
- Stick to the main points and use concise phrases which people will be able to remember. ATTENTION – TRIVIA QUIZ is more eye-catching and memorable than 'I SHOULD LIKE TO DRAW YOUR ATTENTION TO A TRIVIA QUIZ TO BE HELD NEXT WEEK'.
- Keep it short. If necessary give a contact name and telephone number where more information can be obtained. Bear in mind that people read notices quickly and sometimes when they are on the move. They won't have time to stand and stare for ages.
- Use colour for impact if you want to, but keep to a maximum of two colours (black and red are effective) otherwise your notice will look childish.
- A border can be effective but takes time. Forget any ideas of wavy lines or amateurish graphics.
- Date your notice at the bottom left-hand corner. This helps the person who is responsible for keeping the notice board up to date, as he or she will know how long your notice has been there.
- Remove any advertisements promptly once the goods have been sold.

 ## DID YOU KNOW?

On some word processing packages and all desk top publishing packages, you can use different fonts, typestyles and sizes (*see Unit 6*). Again, don't mix these up too much or you will achieve an amateurish effect rather than a professional looking document.

 ## TEST YOURSELF

Your company has decided to offer free anti-flu injections to all staff this winter following a spate of absences last year through influenza. A doctor will be on the premises on the third Monday of next month to administer these in the medical room. Staff will be notified individually of the times of their appointments. Those interested must contact Personnel Department (extension 2245) no later than one week on Friday. Prepare a notice to advertise this. Discuss your notice with your tutor.

Reports

Reports are used

- to present information on a particular topic after research has been carried out
- to give details of work carried out over a certain period, with information on what still needs to be done
- to give an account of what actually happened at an event (e.g. a road accident report or a police report).

Reports vary considerably in their length, complexity and the degree of formality required. At this stage of your career you are only likely to be asked to produce short reports, probably of a relatively informal nature. Often common headings are used in a report and these are shown in the example on page 300.

Writing a report

- The **terms of reference** are simply a statement of what you have been asked to do.
- The **procedure** states the methods you used to obtain your information.
- The **findings** are what you found out. These must be actual facts and not your own thoughts or opinions.
- The **conclusion** is a general statement which sums up what you found.
- The **recommendations** are the action you are suggesting should take place bearing in mind your conclusion.

CHECK IT YOURSELF

There is a considerable difference between statements of fact and statements of opinion (i.e. personal views). In each of the following cases, can you state which is which?

1. **a** The car was black.
   b The driver was going too fast.

2. **a** The office is too cold in winter.
   b The office has only two small radiators.

3. **a** The quality of food served in the canteen is poor.
   b The canteen is unpopular with staff – only 10 out of 45 staff use it regularly.

REPORT *Terms of reference*

Report on staff reactions to the idea of introducing flexible working hours.

Procedure

1   I designed a survey, to be completed by all staff.

2   I issued this on Monday, 6 December. Staff had one week in which to complete it.

3   Questionnaires were returned by 32 staff. Two members of staff were absent on the week the survey was carried out.

Findings

1   22 members of staff were in favour of the idea but 12 wanted more information before they made a definite decision.

2   10 members of staff were against the idea. The main comments made were as follows.

   a Staff arriving late would find it difficult to park.

   b The number of hours which could be carried forward was too low.

Conclusion

It would appear most staff would be in favour of the idea if they could receive reassurance about parking and the number of hours carried forward could be reviewed.

Recommendations

I recommend that these concerns are investigated and all staff receive a full information pack about the proposed scheme as soon as possible.

Petra Sykes
Personnel Assistant
16 December 199–

Setting out a report

The clearest way to detail information is probably to make a list of numbered points. Because these may often have to be sub-divided, you need to use a system which will be consistent throughout your report. You have two options.

- A combination of letters and numbers, e.g.

    1 SALES DEPARTMENT
      a Staffing
        i) Full-time staff
        ii) Part-time staff

or

A SALES DEPARTMENT
  1 Staffing
    a) Full–time staff
    b) Part–time staff

● A decimal numbering system, e.g.

  1 SALES DEPARTMENT
  1.1 Staffing
    1.1.1 Full–time staff
    1.1.2 Part–time staff
  1.2 Location

The decimal method may seem more complicated but has the advantage that in a long report you can divide your material into as many sections as you need to, with ease.

Bear in mind that both the numbering system *and* the spacing must be consistent within your document.

TEST YOURSELF

Your company is considering installing two payphones in the building to reduce the number of private calls made on the company telephones. You were asked to prepare a brief report about this, including whether or not they should be cardphones and where they should be sited. You designed a questionnaire for staff, a summary of which is given below.

From this summary prepare the report required.

PAYPHONE QUESTIONNAIRE – SUMMARY

1a Number of questionnaires issued:.....*25*...

1b Number of questionnaires returned:...*22*...
    Notes on difference: ...*3 staff absent*..

2   Number in favour of idea of 2 payphones: *18*

3   Number against (and main reasons): *4*
    May be charged above standard rate..
    May be queues to use a telephone..

4   Ideas for siting phones:
    In exit foyer to car park..
    On main admin. corridor..
    Adjacent to canteen..

5a Number in favour of cardphones: *15*

5b Number against (and main reasons): *7*
    Cannot use them if have no card – want to know if cards.....................
    will be sold here..

Written records

There are dozens of examples of written records in every company – visit reports, customer complaints records, customer enquiry forms, filing records, log sheets and so on.

Make sure that any records for which you are responsible are neatly completed with accurate information and kept up to date.

Tabular documents

These are dealt with in full in Unit 5, Element 5.2.

Listings

Everyone knows what is meant by a **list**. Nowadays many of these are produced by computer – so many, in fact, that they sometimes make a mockery of the idea of the 'paperless office'! All databases have the ability to produce reports which are really lists giving information (*see Unit 6*).

Lists are also found in **typed** form (e.g. internal telephone lists), **printed** form (e.g. lists of share prices in a newspaper) and **written** form (e.g. notes of future appointments).

If you need a copy of a list it is usually a simple matter to obtain one. The problems can start when you have to extract only *some* information from *several* lists – especially if these have been updated so there are alterations all over the place. You may also need to do some research to find all the information you need.

If you are merging together the content of several lists and extracting only what is relevant, then it is important that you work methodically and check your work carefully.

- Start by looking at all your lists and making *absolutely certain* that you know which information you need in each case.
- If possible mark this in some noticeable way, e.g. by using a red pen.
- If you have to change the order of a list (e.g. into alphabetical order) then write a number against each entry to denote where it will occur on your final list, e.g.

4	John Watson
1	Peter Adams
3	Julie Philips
2	Joyce Long

- Take a tally of the final number you should have and your number of marks. They should agree.
- When you type out your list, place a ruler on your original document(s) so that you don't lose your place – especially if you are interrupted.

- If some of the information you are looking at does not need transferring, then cross this through so you won't be tempted to copy it. If you can't mark your original document, photocopy it first.
- If possible use a word processor – then you can change things around during the checking procedure if you've put anything in the wrong place! Otherwise draft out your list in writing and check it carefully *before* starting to type it.

DID YOU KNOW?

It is always easier to proof-read a difficult job if you have someone else to help you. One person should read aloud from the original documents and the other person should check the final version. If you created the document it is useful if you are the reader. This saves explaining exactly what is required to the checker and also reduces the temptation to see what you *want* to see – rather than what you actually wrote!

TEST YOURSELF

You have been asked to compile an up-to-date internal telephone extension list. You have a copy of the old one on which the switchboard operator has made several alterations. You also have a list of new staff from Personnel (who must be included) and a list of staff who have left. The switchboard operator has written in their extension numbers. You have also been handed a memo from the Administration Manager which must be taken into account.

From this information prepare an up-to-date list.

TELEPHONE EXTENSION LIST

Personnel Department

2114/4⁵ Personnel Manager – Tom Short
2117 Personnel Secretary – Irene Phillips
2118 Assistant Personnel Manager – Graham Browne
2119 Training Officer – John Jackson

Sales Department

2256 Sales Manager – Mark Halstead
2257/⁹ Assistant Sales Manager – Valerie Parker
2258 Sales Secretary – Joanne Baker
2260 Sales Office Manager – Imran Hussein

Accounts Department

2349 Chief Accountant – Bob Johnson
2350 Cost Accountant – Travor James
2351 Management Accountant – Jayne Foster
2352 Accounts Supervisor – Doreen Walters (Mrs)

```
                        MEMORANDUM

TO      Switchboard Operator

FROM    Personnel Department

DATE    16 September 199-

STAFF CHANGES

New staff:       Ronald Wilson (Sales Co-ordinator) ——— ext 2257
                 Sandra Adams (Wages Supervisor) ————— 2353
          ext ——— Kathleen Evans (Welfare Officer – Personnel)
          2116    Mary Holt (Assistant Sales Manager) ——— ext 2259

Staff left:      Valerie Parker (Assistant Sales Manager)
```

```
                        MEMORANDUM

TO      Administration Clerk

FROM    Administration Manager

DATE    20 September 199-

TELEPHONE SYSTEM

Please note that from tomorrow, all Sales Department telephone numbers
will start with the figure 1 and not with the figure 2.

On the updated list can you please make sure the departments are listed in
alphabetical order and that staff within each department are also listed
alphabetically, followed by their title and then by the extension, as the
example below:

Accounts department

Sandra Adams     Wages Supervisor     2335
```

Numeric documents

Numeric documents are those which contain numbers rather than text.
The most obvious numeric documents are the company accounts: both
the Profit and Loss Account and the Balance Sheet contain very
important financial information. These final accounts are compiled
from company records such as the cash book, sales ledger, purchase
ledger etc. which nowadays may be kept on computer.

You may have little involvement in actual accounts but may still be
responsible for completing some of the documents which contribute to
these, e.g. checking or producing invoices, making out receipts or petty
cash vouchers or helping your boss to complete an expenses claim. In

some of these cases you will be expected to insert information from the details given to you and, probably, to carry out some basic calculations.

Another obvious numeric document is your pay slip! If you are involved in working with wages, time sheets or clock cards then you will be recording numeric information which must be accurate if people are to receive the correct amount which is owed to them.

Some listings may also be mainly numeric, e.g. sales figures for a period, payments made, bank statements and so on. So might some travel itineraries if they contain times, dates and flight numbers (*see Option Unit 11*).

Compiling numeric documents

- Make sure you have all the information you need, that it is accurate and up to date.
- If you have to complete any forms or records, be certain that you understand exactly where each type of information should be entered.
- Write all figures very clearly. *Don't* alter any figures or cross them out without making absolutely certain that the correction is unobtrusive and the correct figure is easy to read.
- Proof-read *very* carefully. This time it is even more important to have a reader and a checker. **Remember** – typographical errors are relatively easy to spot because your sentence won't make sense. Numeric errors are impossible to spot as any number *might* be acceptable (within reason!)
- Check and *double-check* all your calculations.

CHECK IT YOURSELF

The consequences of incorrect numerical information can be disastrous. Can you think of the worse possible outcome in each of the following cases?

1 A quotation is sent out for £3000 rather than £3500.
2 A cheque is completed for £281 rather than £218.
3 The wrong year is inserted on a cheque.
4 The number of hours on a time sheet is transferred as 14 rather than 41.
5 Two sales are not entered on a customer's record card.

TEST YOURSELF

You work for an organisation which employs five representatives. There are also two technical staff who sometimes visit different organisations. All the representatives have company cars and are paid expenses at the rate of 10p a mile for every journey they make. Technical staff use their own cars and are paid 29p a mile.

Representatives have to state their mileage at the start and end of each month. Technical staff simply state the mileage covered on company business.

Your job is to calculate the expenses for each person and the total mileage for each representative's car.

1 Draw up your own copy of the form below on which to enter the information.

2 From the information given in the memo which follows, complete the form and carry out the necessary calculations. (**Note:** enter N/A in the columns for start and end mileage for technical staff.)

MILEAGE CLAIMS

Month...

Name	Miles at start of week	Miles at end of week	Total miles	Rate paid	Total payment due
		Total amount owing		£	

MEMORANDUM

TO   **Sales clerk**

FROM **Sales secretary**

DATE   **2 April 199-**

MILEAGE EXPENSE CLAIMS

The following are the details for the month of March.

Name	Miles as at 1 March	Miles as at 31 March
Representatives		
Ken Ashcroft	50283	51841
Justine Campbell	21340	22223
John Davies	45091	46492
Sharon Lewis	49903	51101
Ken Sharples	60423	61865
Technical staff		
Christine Hawkins	– total company mileage = 265	
Simon Wilkins	– total company mileage = 561	

UNIT REVIEW (2)

At the end of this element you should be able to

- clarify any instructions given to you in relation to document preparation
- produce completed documentation which meets the requirements of your workplace and current conventions in terms of layout and style
- proof-read your own work, check your spelling, grammar and punctuation and make unobtrusive corrections where necessary
- maintain security and confidentiality where necessary
- collate and route both copies and originals of your document(s).
- understand the importance of meeting deadlines and consulting with others when the work is not achievable in the time stated.

TEST YOUR KNOWLEDGE AND UNDERSTANDING

True or false?

1 All notices should be produced using two colours.
2 Different types of numbering systems can be used in reports to sub-divide information.
3 A statement of fact is the same as a statement of opinion.
4 The fewer words used in a notice or an advertisement the better.
5 Many listings today are produced by computer.

Fill in the blanks

6 When a tear-off slip is included in a letter, the hyphens which separate it from the main text should be typed from _____ _____ _____ .
7 The best way to proof-read any document is to have both a _____ and a _____ .
8 If you are compiling a list from several sources, then it is sensible to use a _____ on any original documents so that you will not lose your place.

Work it out

9 Your company employs six representatives who send you visit reports each week. Your job is to collate the information and pass it to your boss. Basically the reps report on the companies they have visited, who they saw, what was discussed, any queries upon which they need information and follow-up action – plus the date of the next proposed visit.

   a Design a form which will incorporate this information.
   b *Summarise* the information on the representative's report overleaf on to your form to check that it works.

```
REPRESENTATIVE'S REPORT FORM

Date of visit:              10 May 199-

Name of company:           P T Lawson & Sons Ltd

Person seen:               Mr John Lawson

Main points discussed:

Current stocks of equipment:

    4 desktop fax machines
    2 XL20 machines
    1 XL30 machine

Sales to date:

    XL 20 machines selling well - received an order for 2 more to be supplied.
    Wants to know if XL40 machine can be supplied on sale or return basis.

    NB informed Mr Lawson about new advertising campaign

Recommended action:

    Inform Mr Lawson if XL40 m/c can be supplied on sale or return

Proposed date of next visit:     15 June 199-

Signed....Mary Woods...................Dated ...15 May..........................
```

10 You work for a travel company which is compiling an information booklet for customers. Your boss wants to start with one which concentrates on European destinations. On one page she wants to include average temperatures of the main resorts.

a List the capital cities of all the countries in Europe.
b From a national daily newspaper, enter the current temperatures of all the cities on your list which are covered by the newspaper. Delete the rest.
c Note the month in which you obtained the information. Now visit your local library and find out the average temperature of each city in three months' time, six months' time and nine months' time (by referring to information given *last* year!).
d Present the information clearly in the form of a numeric table.

8 Receive and transmit information

This unit covers the transmission and receipt of information electronically and by using the standard postal systems. Bear in mind that some companies operate an internal mail system between their associated offices, as well as using the services of the Royal Mail or private companies.

During the course of this unit you will read about a variety of different methods used to send and receive information. After completing it you should be able to select the most cost-effective and suitable method for each document you handle, bearing in mind the needs of your organisation and the equipment you have available.

Element 8.1 is concerned with receiving and sending information electronically. These methods are becoming more and more popular today as speedy and cost-effective alternatives to traditional methods. Transmission systems today can incorporate voice, data, text and images which can be sent and received very rapidly all over the world. All the current methods available for use by business are included in this section. In addition, at the end of the element you will find an A–Z directory on telecommunications which you can use as a quick reference guide.

Element 8.2 concentrates on receiving and sending mail by both internal and external mailing systems. The services offered by the Royal Mail are constantly changing and it is important that you are up to date with both the services offered and the charges made. The size of your organisation and the type of documentation produced will influence the services which are used by the company as a whole. Even so, even the smallest firm can benefit if its employees have a good knowledge of the different methods of sending mail which are available today.

Element 8.1

Receive and transmit information electronically

The need to transmit information quickly and accurately to people all over the world has never been so strong as it is today. Many businesses operate on a global scale or are in constant contact with customers and suppliers in different locations. The emphasis is on speed of service and a constant need for up-to-date information. You, as a consumer, are part of that revolution.

- You phone several holiday companies during the winter months for brochures and expect to be able to ring them *at any time*, to receive a prompt response and to be able to leave a message if necessary.
- You visit a cash machine and expect to be able to order a statement, a new cheque book or obtain the balance of your account – at the press of a few keys.
- We are all used to seeing television pictures and receiving news reports from all over the world – reported almost as they happen.

In all these cases, information – in one form or another – is being processed electronically. Your verbal message will be recorded on an answering machine, your bank has a data link between the cash machine and its central computer to give you the services you require and your television picture is a visual image – backed up by written information which has been transmitted by fax or computer and beamed to this country via satellite.

DID YOU KNOW?

The basic difference between **data** and **information** is one of context. The number 20 – out of context – is simply meaningless data. It could refer to anything. However, if that figure is printed out on a cash machine as '£20 balance' then to you it is information – because you know the context in which the figure 20 is meant.

Telecommunications systems

The telecommunications system you use in business will depend on

- the type of information you are transmitting, i.e. voice, data or text
- the distance involved
- the time of day
- whether the person you are trying to contact is likely to be available or not
- the cost of using each system
- the importance and urgency of the information
- the equipment available in your organisation.

Transmission systems

For voice

The most obvious method is the telephone, but bear in mind that in addition to standard telephones and company switchboards there are also pagers and mobile telephones, additional equipment such as answering machines and special services offered by several private organisations.

One of the newest innovations is **voice messaging systems** or **Voicemail** which is rapidly becoming as popular as **electronic mail** (*see page 315*).

For data

Data communications may be over a small geographical area (called a **local area network** or **LAN**) or over a large geographical area (called a **wide area network** or **WAN**). Data is transmitted digitally (i.e. by pulses) at a very rapid rate from one computer to another. Nowadays data can be transmitted globally, often using satellite links.

For text

The most popular system in use today is facsimile or **fax**. Fax machines are falling in price and yet the range of facilities available on them is continually increasing. Text can also be transmitted by computer, usually by electronic mail or **Email**.

DID YOU KNOW?

In the UK the number of fax users in the mid-1980s was less than 500 000, today there are well over a million machines in operation.

CHECK IT YOURSELF

1   Suppliers of fax equipment say that machines are falling in price because of advanced technology and increased sales. Discuss with your supervisor or tutor why these two factors affect prices.
2   Consider why an organisation may prefer to send certain types of information in written form, rather than verbally. Try to list *at least five* occasions when it would be better for the information to be written down.

Your own organisation and its procedures

Wherever you work, it is important that you identify the range of electronic equipment available for sending information and how it works. This includes

- your telephone (or telephone extension)
- the type of switchboard installed and the facilities available
- voice messaging systems, pagers and mobile phones
- any answering machines in use
- computer networks and fax machines (and whether these are linked)
- internal or external electronic mail systems
- any external providers of specialist services.

Before you use any of these you need to know exactly

- how each one works
- any specific operating instructions laid down by your organisation *in addition to* those specified by the manufacturers or suppliers of the equipment or service

- any organisational requirements in relation to their use, e.g. how to answer a telephone, how to set out fax messages
- any special security or confidentiality procedures which are in force.

This element will point out certain factors you can look out for in this area, but these are only a general guide. It is important that you check with your supervisor or manager *before* you use anything for the first time, to see if there are specific points you should know.

Voice transmission systems

Telephone systems

There are four types of telephone system available for businesses.

- **A PABX (private automatic branch exchange) system** is controlled by a switchboard operator, who deals with all incoming calls on behalf of the organisation. Users normally have an ordinary touch telephone with gate (#) and star (*) keys and can make their own outgoing calls by keying the figure 9 before the number.
- **A key telephone system** comprises a number of linked feature phones (*see below*). Any user can answer an incoming call and transfer a call to another extension.
- **A hybrid system** has one feature phone of a key system programmed to be the operator's phone and the other users (or some of them) are equipped with ordinary telephones. This is a cheaper option than buying expensive feature phones for everyone.
- **An Automatic Call Distributor (ACD) system** routes calls to the first free telephone extension. If all the extensions are engaged the caller is placed on hold – to hear either 'music on hold' or recorded information. As soon as an operator is free the call which has been on hold the longest is answered automatically.

CHECK IT YOURSELF

Which system do you think would be most suitable in each of the following organisations?

- A small company with open-plan offices where everyone knows enough about each other's work to answer any call.
- The sales centre of a large mail order company in the months before Christmas.
- A computer consultancy with a receptionist, three consultants and five other staff. Each of the consultants has their own office.
- A large public limited company which employs 500 staff.

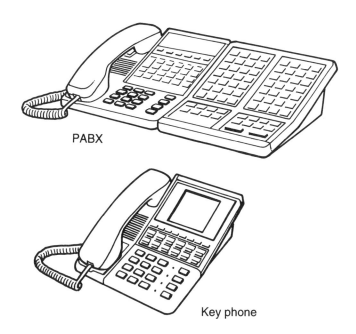

PABX

Key phone

Telephone systems

PABX or key system?

Whereas there used to be a noticeable difference between the type of features to be found on each system, this is no longer the case. The introduction of feature phones, which are pre-programmed with microchips, has meant that many functions which were once only obtainable if a PABX switchboard was installed, are now available to everyone. (On a PABX the features are programmed into the switchboard so that users can access them automatically.)

There is, however, a considerable difference in terms of size. It is possible for a PABX system to support hundreds of exchange lines and thousands of extensions, whereas the maximum size of a key system is 1–36 exchange lines and 2–96 extensions. In practice, however, the system would become inoperable before its maximum size was reached – and very expensive if feature phones were supplied to everyone. For that reason, small businesses may have one (or a few) feature phones, with one designated as the switchboard. Everyone else has an ordinary telephone.

Telephone features

The following features are available on most telephone systems today.

Abbreviated dialling Provides a shortened version of commonly used numbers.

Automatic call routeing Will automatically select the cheapest call route between BT and Mercury.

Callback (sometimes called 'camp-on busy') Automatically recalls an engaged extension when it is free.

Call barring Prevents certain extensions making certain types of call, e.g. IDD, directory enquiries etc. Only the number 999 cannot be barred.

Call forwarding (also called 'call diversion') Routes all calls to a specific extension or to another if the user is away from his or her office.

Call logging A telephone management system whereby all calls from extensions are recorded, together with the units used (*see A–Z Directory, page 348*).

Call pick-up Allows the user of one extension to answer another phone from his or her own extension without having to move!

Call sequencing This system greets callers with a pre-recorded message and then queues them automatically. A further message is given after a few moments if the caller is still holding.

Call waiting A tone or light tells an extension user another incoming call is waiting.

Conference calls Enables several users to speak to each other simultaneously.

Direct dialling in (DDI – PABX only) Allows outside calls to be connected directly to an extension rather than via the operator.

Distinctive ringing The difference in the ringing sound differentiates between external calls, internal calls and the diverted ringing signal.

Do not disturb Temporarily shuts down an extension.

Group hunting Enables a call to be connected to a group of extensions. The first one free will ring.

Hands free The user can make or receive calls without picking up the handset – he or she speaks and listens through a loudspeaker instead. (NB not suitable for confidential calls!)

Intrude Enables the switchboard operator (or boss!) to break into a call if something urgent occurs. There is normally a warning bleep.

Last number redial Automatically redials the last number called.

Memory protection A back-up battery system protects numbers programmed into the system from being erased, even during a power cut. In addition several phones will continue to work without power so that the company is not cut off completely.

Message waiting The user's telephone has a special light (or gives out a bleep) to indicate if a message has been taken in the user's absence or left in Voicemail.

Music on hold Today many companies use pre-recorded 'proper' music rather than electronic music. However, copyright material cannot be played without a licence from the Performing Rights Society.

Night service The system operates out of normal working hours. Calls can be routed automatically to one or several extensions, an answering machine or bells can ring in different locations.

Paging General announcements can be made on systems with speaker phones so individuals can be paged.

Secrecy button Pressing this stops the caller from hearing what is being said (e.g. to a colleague).

DID YOU KNOW?

A system becoming more and more popular is **Voicemail**. Under this system a user calls an electronic mailbox and leaves a message for callers in their **Voicebox**. The person called can then leave a message in reply. The original idea was to enable people to contact someone easily even if that person was often away from his or her desk. However, it can also be used as an alternative if a person is too busy to receive calls for a time. He or she presses 'do not disturb' on the extension. All callers are then routed to Voicemail, where they have the opportunity to contact another extension instead or ring back later. Some companies prefer Voicemail to electronic mail since it is quicker to use because people leaving messages do not need to key in their information.

A company operating a Voicemail system will often have two numbers – one to call for Voicemail, the other to the switchboard. Once through to Voicemail, a computer voice will tell the caller what to do to leave a message, collect a message or contact a different extension.

CHECK IT YOURSELF

Research has shown that the majority of telephone users only use a quarter of the features available on the system they have installed. Is this true where you work?

1   Make a list of the features mentioned on the previous pages which are available on your telephone system at work (or your college system).

2   Ask *at least four* people which features they use

   a regularly   **b** sometimes   **c** never.

3   Discuss as a group why you think this is the case and what, if anything, should be done about the situation.

Using your company's telephone system

Even if you know *exactly* how the telephone equipment in your organisation functions, this does not necessarily mean you will be marvellous at receiving incoming messages or transmitting information yourself! When you use a telephone on behalf of your company, you have several responsibilities

- to give a good impression of yourself and the organisation by being friendly, helpful and polite
- to receive or convey information *accurately*
- to respond quickly to urgent information
- to prove you are trustworthy when dealing with confidential information
- to keep the cost down!

DID YOU KNOW?

If you dread answering the telephone at work then you are not alone! It is one of the jobs most feared by new employees or people on work experience – mainly because they are worried that they will not know what the caller is talking about and will make fools of themselves. The following section should make you realise that it is perfectly possible to sound competent and efficient *and* give a good impression, even if you can't offer specific help to a caller.

Giving a good impression

Even if you have never received any formal telephone training at work, you can learn a lot from listening to other people and noting how the most effective people in your organisation deal with calls. The main points you need to consider vary slightly, depending on whether you are receiving incoming calls for your organisation or just for yourself or your department.

Receiving calls for your organisation

In this capacity *you* are the first person an outside caller speaks to, and therefore you are the invisible receptionist for the company. You will be judged on your voice, manner, speed and efficiency. Although you really need proper training and a good knowledge of your organisation to do this job properly, the following may help you if you have to take on this job unexpectedly.

- Answer all calls promptly with the official company greeting, e.g. 'Good morning' and the name of the company.
- Give priority to incoming calls rather than extension users.
- Direct incoming calls to the correct extension. If an extension is engaged, give the caller the choice whether to hold or call back later.

- Keep callers who are holding informed as to what is happening by regularly going back to them.

On most systems today you will find that extension users make their own calls. The only time you would be involved is to obtain an operator service or specific information.

If you deputise for a switchboard operator, check that you know where any special records are kept, such as fault reports or other call logs, and that all the directories and reference books you may need are close to hand.

 DID YOU KNOW?

Many companies with a customer service department arrange for calls to be routed directly to this section and for staff to answer far more informally and always include their first name, e.g. 'Good morning, Faxline Service – Paul speaking, how can I help you?' Staff are also trained to sound cheerful and speak with a 'smile in their voice' to welcome the customer.

CHECK IT YOURSELF

Can you think of *at least two* reasons why many companies insist that staff give their name when talking to customers?

Receiving calls for yourself or your department

This is one of the tasks regularly carried out by *all* members of staff. Even if the telephone is not on your desk, if no-one else is available to answer it then you shouldn't just ignore it and hope it will go away! You have a responsibility both to your company and to your colleagues to answer the phone and deal with whoever is calling. Some golden rules to follow are given below.

- Answer all calls promptly (the caller can't see how busy you are!).
- Always answer with a pen in one hand, and have some paper or a telephone message pad nearby.
- Greet callers properly, either with the name of the department (or office) or the extension number and, preferably, your own name.
- Never answer the telephone while you are eating or drinking.
- Always sound pleasant and helpful.
- Find out who is calling and either the name of the person to whom they want to speak or what the call is about.
- If the call is for someone who *is* available then the caller should be asked to 'hold the line a moment' (*not* 'hang on!') whilst you pass on the call to this person. *Don't* just dumbly wave the receiver in their direction! Explain who is calling and what it is about.

- If the call is for someone who is *not* available then you have four options
  - see if someone else can help
  - offer to help yourself
  - take a message
  - ask the caller to ring back later or say that the person they wanted will ring them back later.

- If the caller wants information which will take you some time to find, *don't* keep them holding on, offer to ring back when you have it to hand.
- *Never* promise to ring someone back and let them down.
- *Always* check with your supervisor if you think you are being asked for information which may be confidential.

 ## DID YOU KNOW?

Telephone receivers are very sensitive and may transmit information you don't want overheard! Be careful what you say when you leave a receiver on a desk or are handing over a call to someone else: 'It's that stupid woman from Sales again,' may well make you an enemy for life!

CHECK IT YOURSELF

1 Some callers with an enquiry need transferring to another extension. Can you *confidently* say that you can do this easily on your telephone system and never cut anyone off?

2 Find out your company procedure as to whether you should ask a caller to ring back later *or* whether you should arrange for someone from the office to call them back later. Discuss with your tutor or supervisor the occasions when the first option is preferable and times when the second option is better.

Additional hints and tips

If you really want to impress callers with how professional you sound then develop a good telephone technique.

- Use a person's name during the conversation (this makes them feel important and helps you to remember who you are speaking to!).
- End a call by saying 'thank you for calling'. This makes everyone feel good.
- Avoid using slang, no matter what the temptation (and this includes OK!).
- Say figures in *pairs* – they're easier to understand.
- Let the person who made the call conclude it (if you can!).
- Check all the main details of the call *before* ringing off – names, figures, dates and other key facts.

- Ask a caller to spell out difficult names. This does not make you sound stupid – it is much more silly not to check and then to write down a word which makes your colleagues laugh for weeks or a name no-one can understand.

DID YOU KNOW?

If you are cut off in the middle of a conversation, remember that the person who made the call should be the one to attempt the reconnection.

Message taking

It is always helpful to use a standard telephone message form to record a message, as the headings help you to remember all the information you need. A typical form is shown below.

Telephone message form

MESSAGE FORM		
TO	**DEPT**	....
DATE	**TIME**	....
CALLER'S NAME		
ORGANISATION		
TEL NO	**EXT NO**	....
Telephoned	☐	
Returned your call	☐	
Called to see you	☐	
Left a message	☐	
Please return call	☐	
Please arrange appointment	☐	
Message:		
....		
....		
....		
....		
....		
....		
Taken by:	**Dept**	....

You should always

- use simple, straightforward words
- keep your sentences short, but vary the length a little so that your message flows
- include all the key facts
- leave out irrelevant information
- be very specific about days, dates and times. If you give a non-specific time (e.g. tomorrow) then add the day and date – in case your message isn't read immediately
- mark urgent messages *clearly*
- be polite – if you are repeating a request to your boss to do something, phrase it like a request *not* an order!

Don't forget that your responsibility doesn't end when you place the message on the right desk – it only ends when the person has read it and understood it! For that reason, check later if urgent messages have been seen by someone – and see your supervisor or someone senior if they have not, so that the correct action can be taken. *Never* take a message and then forget it – the results can be disastrous!

Identifying key facts

Every message contains a number of key facts. If you miss these out the message may not make *complete* sense. Business callers are normally quite good at giving you the key facts in an ordered way and checking them with you afterwards. Private callers may be less helpful and some may like to chat so that it is difficult to sort out what is important from what is not. A good way to check that you have the message clear in your mind is to read back your summary to the caller at the end.

You may have to develop the skill of questioning people to find out additional information which you think is important, or facts they have forgotten to tell you (e.g. their telephone number). Use your telephone message sheet as a guide to help you and don't be put off asking a question, even if the caller sounds abrupt or nervous.

 TEST YOURSELF

1 Identify the key facts in the following message.
2 Identify any additional information which would be helpful but which the caller hasn't offered, and which you should ask for.
3 Write out the message clearly and check it with your supervisor or tutor.

Good morning. My name is Philip Bryant of the *Hightown Gazette*. I wonder if you could tell your Sales Manager, Margery Tyler, that we're doing a 4-page feature soon on insurance and thought your company would like to advertise in it. The feature will include articles on house, motor and travel insurance for the general public. The last date for us to receive your advert would be a month today – but if she's interested I'd like to know what size advert she'd be thinking of, then I can book the space. Can you ask her to give me a ring on Hightown 405928, extension 3420. Thanks.

Initiating a call

There will be occasions when you have to make a call, either on your own behalf or on someone else's. If you prepare well in advance then there is far less chance that you will make a mistake or forget to say something important.

- List all the facts you must mention. Then rewrite your list so that the facts are in a logical order with a generous space opposite each one (in which you can write your contact's comments).
- Make sure you have written down the correct number to call.
- Dial the number carefully and, when the telephone is answered, check you are through to the correct place. Then ask for the person you want.
- Be prepared to give your own name and that of your company in reply to the question, 'Who is calling?'
- Greet the person properly when they come on the line and introduce yourself. If you are calling on behalf of someone else, make this clear.
- State the facts you need to mention in the correct order. Don't speak too quickly in a desperate attempt to get the call over quickly!
- Note the person's responses in the spaces on your list. Write legibly so that you can read back your notes clearly afterwards.
- At the end, summarise the main points the other person has made, so that you are clear you haven't misunderstood them or missed anything out.
- Remember that as you made the call, you should be the one to conclude it – properly!
- If you made the call on someone else's behalf, be prepared to write up a brief summary of the call. In some organisations this is usually done in the form of a memo.

 ## TEST YOURSELF

You work in the Personnel Office and do a considerable amount of work for Nick Brown, the Security Officer. He has recently seen an advertisement in the local paper for a self-defence course for women. He thinks it could be a good idea to run this within the company *or* to tell employees about it, in case they would like to attend. He favours the first option because he thinks there will be a good response from female staff.

He asked you to telephone the organisers to find out more information. The conversation you had is shown below.

You: Good afternoon. My name is _____ from Yates and Barlow Ltd. I'm ringing on behalf of our Security Officer, Nick Brown, who has seen your recent advertisement for a self-defence course for women.

Them:	Is that the one on the 16th of next month? If so, I'm sorry, but all the places are taken.
You:	I see. Do you know if there are any plans to run another course?
Them:	There may be, if there is enough demand. I won't be able to tell you for at least a fortnight.
You:	If you do run another course, how much will it cost to attend?
Them:	The price for this one is £35 per person and the course lasts three hours.
You:	Our Security Officer was interested in the possibility of running the course here. Do you know if this could be arranged?
Them:	Yes, provided you have at least 15 people interested. We could then do it at a cheaper rate – £25 per person because we're using your facilities and not ours. However, I can't arrange a date with you now. Sally Thomas, who runs these sessions, is out of the office until next week.
You:	I don't know if Mr Brown has thought of any dates yet – he just wanted basic information at this stage. Perhaps he could contact Sally Thomas next week? By the way, is that Miss Thomas or Mrs Thomas?
Them:	Miss Thomas. Yes, that would be fine. We'll wait to hear from you then.
You:	Yes. Thank you for your help. Goodbye.

Summarise the information you have received in a memo to Nick Brown.

CHECK IT YOURSELF

Not all calls are as straightforward as the one above. Sometimes you will have problems finding a number, getting through to the person you want or obtaining the information for when it is required. On other occasions you may answer the phone and find that the caller has a strong foreign accent, doesn't know who they want to speak to, can only give you a hazy idea of what they want, or is angry or annoyed about something.

Discuss with your colleagues occasions when you (and they) have had problems dealing with a caller and decide the correct action to take in each of the above situations.

SPECIAL NOTE

Information on equipment and line faults, charges, directories and telephone services is given in the A–Z Directory, *see page 345*.

Other types of telephone equipment

Mobile phones

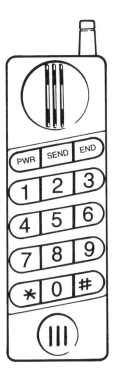

A mobile phone

These are used extensively by people whose work takes them out to different locations. The smallest types available are hand-portables which can be carried in a pocket or handbag. They work on rechargeable batteries, but the smaller the phone the smaller the batteries, and therefore the more often they must be recharged.

Carphones are fitted permanently into a vehicle; transportables can be used either as a hand-held portable phone *or* installed in a car.

Most mobile phones also have a variety of features, such as stored numbers, a notepad (for storing a number whilst talking on the phone), a background light (so that calls can be made in the dark) and either a security code or call locking device to prevent a thief from using the phone to make calls.

Calls made from and to a mobile phone are charged at a higher rate than calls to an ordinary telephone. Different rates are offered by most service providers, depending on whether the phone is for personal or business use and the number of times it is likely to be used in a given period.

Mobile phones communicate via the Cellnet system (*see A–Z Directory, page 345*). There are base stations all over the UK, each controlling a cell network with its own transmitter. A car travelling up the M1 or M6 would travel through several cell areas.

Calling someone on a car phone is easy – you just dial the car phone number. If the person has the phone switched off, or is travelling out of range, then a pre-recorded message tells you that the person you are calling is not available at present. There may be a facility for you to leave a message yourself, asking the holder to return your call.

CHECK IT YOURSELF

What businesses do you think use mobile phones most and why? Have you seen someone use such a phone in a public place such as at an airport or on a plane? If so, were you impressed, or did you have a different reaction?

Bleepers and pagers

These are an alternative for people who are frequently away from their desk so that they can be contacted quickly and easily. They are supplied

- as a sound bleeper only
- to show a numeric display
- to show an alpha-numeric display.

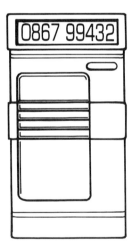

A pager

Sound bleepers are used by employees who work from a fixed base. If the bleeper sounds they know they need to call base immediately (usually the switchboard operator).

The display types give more information. A user of a numeric bleeper will know which each code number represents, e.g. 01 could mean 'call the office immediately'. Numeric pagers are mainly used in conjunction with a PABX switchboard. Extension users can signal the pager direct from their telephone and the pager displays the number the pager holder should call.

Alpha-numeric pagers can show both text and numbers, so no codes are necessary. However, the number of words per message is likely to be limited, so all messages should be kept short and to the point.

Pagers being used away from the office can be accessed

- by contacting the appropriate paging bureau and giving them the pager number and the message (in words or code numbers as appropriate). The message is then relayed via a central computer.
- directly via a touch tone telephone (with * and # keys). In this case the user is talking to the computer directly and is prompted by a computer voice.

The cost of a pager is related to the regions and zones in which it will be used: the wider the area, the higher the cost (in which case a mobile phone may be a better option).

DID YOU KNOW?

There are several private organisations which provide paging and voice messaging services. Some offer a personalised answering service by an operator on behalf of a pager user who is not available to respond to calls, and also send out regular information on travel and news headlines to all pager users.

Answering machines

Most organisations use answering machines to take calls when the office is closed. Sometimes an answering machine may be used when an office is open, to deal with routine enquiries or to give a pre-recorded message (e.g. cinema or surgery times). This saves the main telephone lines becoming congested.

Answering machine features

Most answering machines hold two tapes. One tape holds the pre-recorded message and this automatically rewinds after every call. The second tape holds the incoming messages (normally up to a maximum of 90 minutes in total) and stays in position after each message, ready for the next call.

The tape for the pre-recorded message is only short – about three minutes – so lengthy messages cannot be recorded for callers.

DID YOU KNOW?

Answering machines can be programmed to contact a bleeper holder or a specified telephone number automatically if a message has been left for them on the machine.

Similarly, the owner of an answering machine can access messages from any touch tone telephone if he or she is away from the office. A small device called a **keytone** can be used to convert any phone into a touch tone phone. The owner calls in to the home phone and holds the keytone device to the mouthpiece and plays it. The owner can then listen to messages, from any country.

CHECK IT YOURSELF

Most answering machines have the following features. Check which are available on any answering machines in your organisation and that you know how to use them.

Announcement-only Just gives the announcement – no message can be left.

Call screening The owner can listen in and decide whether to answer personally.

Handset listening Allows the owner to retain privacy when listening to messages left on tape.

Two-way recording Both sides of a telephone conversation can be recorded.

Speaking to an answering machine

If you are connected to a business answering machine you will often find yourself hearing specific instructions on how to speak, e.g.

- speak slowly and clearly after the tone
- give your full name and company name
- state your address or telephone number
- spell any difficult words.

In addition it is important to remember to keep your message short and to give only the essential facts.

TEST YOURSELF

Your boss, Jerry Adams, has arranged to go to Glasgow on Monday to see a demonstration of a new electronic filing system. He thinks Peter Briggs, the computer services manager, would be interested in joining him. If so, he thinks they should both travel by train and meet at the station at 8 am. He can book the tickets in advance if he knows if Peter will be going.

Jerry Adams has tried to contact Peter by phone but has been informed that he is away from the office until Friday. Apparently Peter can be contacted at home, where he has an answering machine. Jerry has asked you to ring on his behalf and leave a message. Jerry Adams can be contacted at work all week or at home in the evening. His home number is 203982.

1　Prepare a suitable, concise message you could leave on Peter Briggs' answering machine which includes all the key points mentioned above.
2　Record your message on tape, listen to it yourself and comment on your own performance!
3　Now record it a second time, trying to improve any faults you had.

Transcribing messages left on tape

In every office, someone has the job of listening to the tape on an answering machine and listing all the calls and messages which have been left. This is relatively easy as you can rewind the tape to listen to any tricky parts more than once.

- Have a pad and pencil ready.
- Do one message at a time.
- Listen to it all the way through first.
- Note the key points when you listen the second time.
- Play it through a third time and check you have everything down correctly.
- Don't erase the message from the tape until you are certain there will be no further queries.

Problem messages

Not all the messages you receive will be easy to transcribe.

- Some callers may be nervous and there may be long pauses.
- Some may talk too quickly and be difficult to follow.
- Some may miss out important information.
- Others may talk a long time – and may even be cut off part-way through.
- Some messages may require urgent action.

CHECK IT YOURSELF

Discuss with your supervisor or tutor what you should do in *each* of the above situations to ensure the message is dealt with as efficiently as possible.

Data transmission systems

On the most basic of these systems, data is transmitted directly from one computer to another, using a telephone line. The basic requirements for such as system are

- two computers
- two modems (*see Unit 6, page 208*)
- two telephones
- communicating software in each computer.

To send or receive data 'down the line', one computer calls the other; the computer operator may do this or the procedure may be automatic. Transfer of data or complete files can now take place quite easily – or the operator can access programs on the external computer that he or she does not have on his or her own computer.

The applications of this are almost endless.

- Teleworkers (who work at home using a computer) can send updated files to their companies directly.
- People working at home can access their work computer for files and other details they need – or read electronic mail messages left on a central computer.
- Supermarkets can send details of stock movements directly to their head office computer.
- Banks can update customer accounts on the main computer directly from branch offices.
- Travel agents can access tour operators' computers to find out holiday details and vacancies.
- Representatives can send details of orders received to the company computer for processing.
- Programmers and other computer personnel involved in software development can work at home, on their own PC, and test out their programs on the main computer.

Companies may use standard British Telecom lines for data transfer *or* rent their own private circuit between two locations. This is likely to be the case if the line is used constantly, as the private line rental is cheaper than the cost of many standard telephone calls.

More advanced systems use special data networks to link the computers and additional specialist equipment which acts as a back-up data storage system and regulates the speed of input and output. Data networks range in size from a local system (a LAN) up to a global system where data is transmitted worldwide (*see also A–Z Directory on page 345 and 347*).

If you are involved in communicating with an external computer, you will be shown how to do this with the computer and software communications package used by your company. Basically, you just need to make sure you send the correct information to the right place! You will also find that this system can be popular for confidential information: as this can be protected by a password it is inaccessible to anyone else (and much more reliable than sending floppy disks through the post!)

DID YOU KNOW?

Sending data and information to customers and suppliers electronically is known as **electronic trading**.

CHECK IT YOURSELF

Check the A–Z directory to find out what types of documents are transmitted using **Electronic Data Interchange (EDI)**.

ISDN

Imagine making a telephone call to someone, seeing their video image appear on your computer screen as you talk and discussing a fax you are

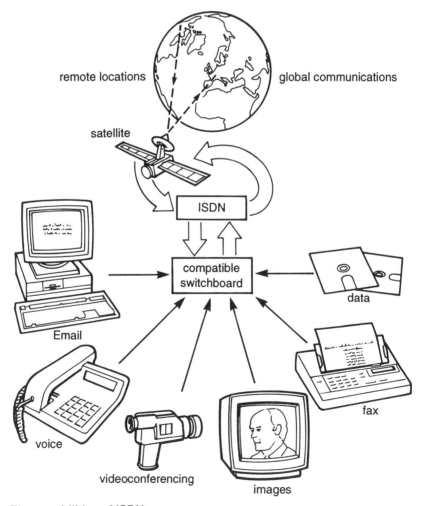

The capabilities of ISDN

sending at the same time! All this is possible using **Integrated Services Digital Network (ISDN)**.

ISDN is a new development which enables voice, data, text and images to be transmitted down one digital line very rapidly – an A4 page can be faxed via ISDN in just two seconds! A computer file which would normally take 60 seconds to send is transmitted in only 15 seconds. Therefore call charges are lower (*see also A–Z directory, page 347*).

A company wishing to use ISDN must have a special switchboard installed which is linked to one of the ISDN services. Two services are available, one for small to medium-sized companies and one for large firms. As yet, only a few telephone systems are on the market which will link with ISDN and these are quite expensive, though prices are expected to fall in the next few years.

The aim is that eventually ISDN will be a completely global network so that businesses can use it to communicate to any country rapidly, reliably and efficiently.

Text transmission systems

Fax machines

Even in many very small businesses, one item of telecommunications equipment considered an essential is the fax machine. For virtually the price of a telephone call, documents containing text, graphics and even photographs can be sent easily to almost anywhere in the world.

A fax machine scans a document, converts the dark parts it sees (the text and graphics) into digital pulses and transmits these pulses down a

telephone line to another fax machine. The second machine then repeats the pulses it receives, to create a replica of the original document.

The process is quick and easy and the users can discuss the document on the telephone if they want to – usually immediately it has been transmitted.

Fax machines have been falling in price, yet the features they offer have become more and more sophisticated. There is a wide range of machines on the market, ranging from simple desktop models to much larger machines designed for almost constant use.

DID YOU KNOW?

The smallest fax on the market incorporates a telephone as well as acting as a copier and is only 11.4" × 7.2" (29 cm × 18 cm)! Measure that if you're not sure of the size! The price is currently under £300.

Facts about fax

One of the main developments with fax machines is the number of cheaper models on the market which use plain A4 paper. You will know if this is the case on your machine – if you have to buy special fax rolls then your machine uses specially coated paper. There are several disadvantages of this.

- Fax rolls are more expensive than plain paper.
- Faxes are apt to be received from the machine tightly curled – especially if the roll is nearly empty.
- The fax roll can run out overnight or when there is no-one in the office.
- Messages can fade if they are not photocopied before filing.

All fax machines have some type of display panel to prompt the operator, a key pad and – usually – a telephone handset. It is better to have a separate telephone line installed just for faxes, but many small businesses do not. It is quite to easy to switch between telephone and fax communications if the usage of either is only small.

All fax machines both transmit *and* receive messages. They must be left in receive mode when not in use; virtually all machines do this automatically.

Fax features

Many features are now common to almost all fax machines and new developments are taking place all the time. However, there are still differences between the type of features you will generally find on a small machine and those you will find on a high volume machine.

Basic functions on most machines

Activity log The machine automatically prints out a report on the document(s) sent/received and the result of each (e.g. OK or not OK).

Anti-curl device Straightens out the paper from a fax roll.

Automatic dialling Transmission is automatic once the connection has been made.

Document carrier Holds important or flimsy originals.

Document feeder Holds originals yet to be transmitted.

Fax header Automatically prints the company name, fax number, date and time on the top of all documents – plus the page number.

Loudspeaker The operator can hear what is happening as he or she tries to make a connection, *without* having to lift up the handset.

Number memory Stores the most frequently used fax numbers so that the operator can dial using a short numeric code.

Paper-out warning Warns the operator to refill the paper tray or replace the fax roll.

Repeat dialling Automatically keeps trying a number if the other fax is engaged.

Transmission report Printed out after each fax, this gives details of time, date, sender, receiver, number of pages, duration and result (e.g. OK or not OK).

Verification mark A small mark is printed at the foot of each transmitted page.

Voice contact Enables sender and receiver to discuss the fax. On cheaper machines this is only possible once transmission is complete.

More sophisticated functions

Broadcast facility A document can be sent to several faxes automatically.

Collator Automatically re-arranges a multi-page document so that the pages are transmitted in the correct order.

Deferred dialling The fax can transmit overnight

Duplexing The machine has the ability to transmit two-sided documents.

Network capability The machine can be linked to a computer so that faxes can be sent or received via PCs.

Memory capability Messages can be stored in memory. On some machines these messages can be transmitted at the same time as incoming faxes are being received. Some 'memory' machines print out a longer transmission report when documents have been sent from memory, showing part of the document, so it is easy to match with the original.

Polling The fax can call another machine and collect messages left for it. Some machines can do this automatically after having sent a message to another fax.

Resolution settings These may be standard, fine, superfine or for photographs. Using these wisely can save money (*see page 337*).

Transmission reservation Enables a fax which is receiving an incoming document to be programmed to send a fax as soon as it's free.

White line skip The machine ignores white spaces which speeds up transmission.

DID YOU KNOW?

- Faxes of the future will be in colour. The technology already exists for this but, as yet, the machines are too expensive to be worth marketing.
- In ten years' time many business people on the move will have fax machines in their cars. Faxes may be integrated with PCs in special workstations and may also act as printer and copier all in one!

Using a fax machine

The easiest way to learn how to use a fax machine is to watch someone else who knows what they are doing. Instruction manuals vary from very good to very poor and you may easily forget what to do if you don't use the machine regularly. Watch, take notes and ask questions if you are unsure. Then write out a 'help sheet' for yourself which will remind you what to do next time.

The three basic things to learn are

- how to prepare material for transmission
- how to send faxes
- how to deal with incoming faxes.

You will also be more popular if you learn what to do to speed up your messages and reduce the costs of transmission.

Preparing material for transmission

In some cases you will receive messages to send from other people, on other occasions you may be preparing your own messages. The main factors to consider in either case are

- the type of paper used in your organisation to send faxes. Some companies use letter headed paper, others specially printed fax forms. Some use plain paper and type the words **FAX MESSAGE** at the top.
- whether there is any particular format that you should use. Sometimes faxes are set out similar to a memo (*see below*).
- whether any important or original documents have to be faxed. If so, and these are valuable, coloured, very small/large *or* poorly

printed then you will have to take a photocopy and make any size and print adjustments. Bear in mind faxes print only in black and white – so coloured print on an original comes out very poorly. Photocopy any doubtful documents first.

● the length of the fax. Word your message carefully – the shorter it is, without being too brief, the more quickly it will transmit and the less this will cost. Normally fax messages are quite informal but, like most communications, this really depends upon the importance of the person you are faxing. Bear in mind that, unlike memos, fax messages are often signed.

● how many pages you are sending. Bear in mind that faxes are numbered differently to other documents, e.g. page 1 of 3, page 2 of 3 and so on. This tells the receiver how many documents to expect, so they can check at the end of the transmission that all of them have been received.

J BAXTER & CO LTD
15 Bridge Street
HIGHTOWN

Tel: 0892 585728   **Fax: 0892 449922**

FAX MESSAGE

TO: Tony Barnes, Advertising Department

FROM: Sarah Goodison

DATE: 14 July 199–   **Page 1 of 3**

ADVERTISING PROOFS

The only error I can see is in the contact name on the last line of the advert. Name should be Sandra Gray, not Sarah Gray. We have also made some alterations to the chart on page 2 – amended text follows this message.

Please can you confirm the date the adverts will appear and, if possible try to place them as near the front of the paper as possible.

Thanks

Sarah

DID YOU KNOW?

Some faxes have the ability to store signatures and then print them on the appropriate documents. Obviously there must be a security system linked to this, or someone could easily send a message in someone else's name.

Sending faxes

- Check the document guide is set correctly for the width of your paper.
- Check you have the right number to call, if you are unsure then use the *UK Fax Book* to find out.
- Check which way your text should face otherwise you will simply transmit blank pages!
- Check you know how to
  - dial the number, check it is correct and cancel it if you make a mistake (normally it is shown on a small display)
  - remove the paper quickly if it is crooked or starts to jam in the machine
  - cancel a call if you can't get through or set the machine to redial automatically.
- Dial the number, check your display, and press 'send' or a similar key when you are connected (unless this procedure is automatic).
- If your fax feeds the paper into the machine, leave the machine to push it out again – it doesn't need any help!
- The display screen will usually prompt you and inform you if there is any fault on the line or problem with the transmission (*see below*).
- Either the display screen or a bleeper will warn you if the other operator wants to speak to you.
- Check you have a verification mark on each page transmitted and that the transmission report says 'OK'.
- Fasten the transmission report to your fax and return it to the sender (or store it safely if it's your own document).

SPECIAL NOTE

Either file your fax immediately *or,* if you are waiting for a reply, put it in your 'pending' tray to remind you.

Receiving faxes

On some machines, incoming faxes are automatically stacked in a special paper tray. On cheaper models they may come out as cut rolls of paper (very tightly rolled up if the roll is nearly at an end). Make sure you don't mistake any of these for rubbish if the fax is sited on a nearby desk – especially if the paper falls on the floor!

Check who should receive each fax and deliver it *quickly.* Remember, faxes are used for urgent information! If the recipient is absent or away from the office then find someone else to deal with it, *don't* just put it on someone's desk if you have no idea where they are or when they will be back.

DID YOU KNOW?

- All faxes can be used as copying machines when not in use as faxes.
- The *UK Fax Book* is the fax directory for the UK. Directory enquiries for numbers not listed and overseas subscribers can be contacted by dialling 153.

Fax faults and problems

Below are given the main faults which can occur and what you should do. However, remember that each fax machine is sold with a manual which clearly states the basic procedures to follow in the case of equipment problems. Check this for your machine – especially the 'trouble-shooting' guide (probably near the back).

- **Transmission failure part-way through**
  Check the verification marks to see where the transmission failed. Write a short note saying what happened. Go back one page and reconnect – faxing your note first.
- **Blank sheets faxed**
  The paper was in the machine upside down or the printing ribbon or cartridge ran out.
- **Machine cut off part-way through**
  This was probably because the paper ran out. Refill – and next time don't ignore the warnings that the paper is running out. The red stripe which appears towards the end of a fax roll is not a new type of design – it's telling you to replace the roll!
- **Fax printing wrong day/date**
  Reset the time and date.
- **Display poor or dull**
  The batteries need changing (this may be shown on your screen).
- **Overheating**
  A low volume fax is being used too much, or for a very long transmission, or for sending a page which is very black. Wait a short time and then try again.
- **Paper jam**
  Instructions on how to solve this will be in your manual. Don't panic if an alarm sounds when you open the machine – there is usually a reset button to stop this.
- **Message unreadable**
  This is probably because of the poor quality of the original. Photocopy (preferably with ink density set higher) and/or enlarge it and try again.
- **Dirty marks on messages**
  The machine needs cleaning – particularly the rollers. Use methylated spirits *not* water!
- **Top or bottom of document missing**
  Either the text starts too high or low or the operator did not feed

in the original correctly, or pulled out the original before transmission was finished.

- **Fax sent to wrong company**
  Faulty dialling or wrong number.

CHECK IT YOURSELF

Discuss with your tutor the action you should take in each of the following cases.

- You receive a fax which was meant for another organisation.
- You receive a fax which was meant for you but which becomes unreadable half-way through transmission.
- You receive a fax with a page missing.
- A manager in your company gives you a note to fax and asks you to type it out first. You can hardly read a word that he has written.
- You cannot transmit an urgent fax within the deadline given to you because the line is constantly engaged.
- You receive a fax marked 'Urgent – to whom it may concern' – but don't know who to give it to.

Fax costs

The machines themselves are very cheap. Small machines start at about £300 and even quite sophisticated machines are well under £1000. Transmission costs are the same as if you were making a telephone call. It is therefore cheaper if

- you send faxes overnight
- transmission time is short.

The speed of transmission is determined by

- the type of machine you have
- the resolution mode being used
- the length of the message
- the amount of detail and its density
- its destination.

The average time taken to transmit an A4 page with a modern machine which has a 'white-line skip' facility (*see page 333*) is about 20 seconds. If you are linked to ISDN the time is much shorter. Faxing in standard resolution mode is much more rapid than if the machine is set on fine or superfine mode – and standard mode is perfectly acceptable for most general documents.

Because the machine is reading black lines, the fewer there are, the less it has to read and the more quickly the fax will be transmitted. Similarly, if you have a few lines of text top and bottom, and a line drawing in the middle, this will fax more quickly than a long printed document. A very dark or intricate diagram or a lot of solid text will take the longest.

CHECK IT YOURSELF

1   Which of the faxes below would take the longest to send? Which the shortest?

A

B

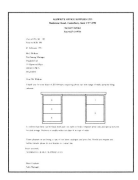

C

2   See if you can explain to your supervisor or tutor why a document sent to the company across the road will take (virtually) the same length of time to transmit as one to Australia.

DID YOU KNOW?

It can cost less to fax a one-page document overseas than to post it by airmail. You can work this out by comparing the cost of, say, an airmail letter to the USA (*see Element 8.2*) and the cost of a telephone call which lasts, say, 30 seconds cheap rate. (But bear in mind the cheap rate period is different than within the UK!)

Fax machines and security

You may think that because messages simply arrive on a fax machine, there is no way in which confidential information can be sent by fax. On the smaller, desktop models this is usually the case. However, the larger machines often have a range of security features, which may include passwords or pass codes. Incoming messages are stored in memory and only the person with the correct password can print out a copy.

DID YOU KNOW?

Faxes can be used to transmit messages to electronic mailboxes. *See below.*

Electronic mail

Electronic mail, or **Email** as it is more usually called, is a system of preparing and transmitting messages from one computer to another by using a system of mailboxes. All users have their own mailbox in which their electronic mail is stored until they are ready to read it. The user can reply, store or delete messages, print them out, redirect them and even check if a message sent previously has been read by the recipient.

The advantages of electronic mail are that

- all types of data can be transmitted – graphics, text, spreadsheets etc.
- there is complete confidentiality as only the user can access his or her own mailbox by using the password or ID
- Email messages can be sent and retrieved from virtually anywhere in the world
- messages can be sent to several mailboxes at the same time
- a recipient who wishes to incorporate the information received by Email into other computer files does not need to key it in for a second time.

Internal electronic mail

Many companies operate their own electronic mail system on computers which are linked by a network (*see Unit 6*). This saves people having to make telephone calls, send memos or other internal messages. The network can be in just one building, in several buildings in one area, throughout the UK or even international! Therefore a network can link a head office with all the branch offices and other subsidiary companies.

External electronic mail

The two main Email services are **Telecom Gold** and the **New Prestel Mailbox** service. **Telecom Gold** is the more popular of the two.

To use an external Email service you will need

- a computer
- a modem
- a telephone line
- special communications software.

Users who subscribe to either service have a mailbox ID *plus* a password (which can be changed at any time).

Email features

Whether you are using an internal or external service, the following features are likely to be available.

Blind copy The ability to send a copy of a message to other users without anyone else knowing that you have done so.

Carbon copy Sends a copy of a message to someone else.

Cancel Discontinues a message you were going to send.

Delete Erases messages you've read and don't need again.

Envelope A line on a screen summarises an incoming message, and usually changes colour when the message has been read.

Forward Sends a message you have received to someone else – you can attach your own comments if you want to.

Information The usual command for finding out whether the recipient has read your message yet – and at what time on what day!

In mailbox Contains incoming messages in date/time order.

Message The message screen on which you compose a message.

Out mailbox The mailbox which stores outgoing mail.

Print Enables you to print the contents of messages.

Read The option which enables you to read a message.

Reply The option chosen if you want to reply to a message you have received – both your name and the recipient's name are usually included automatically.

Scan (External systems only) condenses information so that you can read several messages quickly.

Send Transmits your message to the recipient's mailbox.

User group A group of people, with a common title, which is set up so that you can send simultaneous messages to all members of that group.

Using electronic mail

If you have never used the system yourself, you will find it far easier if someone demonstrates it to you the first time. Internal mail systems are usually easy to use, external mail systems are a little more complicated and Telecom Gold can be quite difficult for a beginner.

- Concentrate on the commands you need to know *first*, i.e. read, delete, message, send and cancel.
- Learn to read your screen properly (there are many prompts if you know where to look!) and know how to access the 'help' facility.
- If you are listed as a user, check your mailbox *daily*. People use Email for urgent messages and it is annoying if someone hasn't read their mail three days later!

- Look at the files to check the layout (or ask someone) if you are sending a message for the first time. Usually the top of the message is pre-set (and will include your name as sender and the date and time automatically). You enter the name of the recipient and give your message a title (which will appear in the recipient's envelope). Keep this short and to the point.
- The message is usually informal. It is your choice whether or not to include any informal salutation (e.g. Regards) or your name at the end (as it is printed on the top anyway – see example below).
- Check it first before you send it – many are the Email users who rue the day they sent an Email to everyone on the network which included a very obvious spelling error!
- Only print out a message if you *know* you are going to need to action it later or file it. The idea of the system is *not* to create piles of paper!
- Regularly delete any unwanted messages in your **In mailbox** and **Out mailbox** – otherwise it will take you ages to search through everything if you want to find a specific message again.

From	Alana McCabe (MCCABE.A)
To	Simpson.J
Date	Tuesday, 14 June 199- 9.35 am
Subject	Furnishing Fabric

Simon Foster called quite late yesterday and left some samples for us to look at. Think these could be useful in relation to the Hudson job. I left them in your office and locked the door so no doubt you found them first thing this morning!

Could you take a look at these and also show them to Melinda for her opinion? If you're interested I'll work out quantity required and get a firm price from Simon later today.

Thanks

cc SHAW.M

DID YOU KNOW

On all Email systems you can save or store messages you may want at a later date. You can then delete them from your mailbox but will know that they haven't gone for ever!

Faults and problems

If everything is functioning properly you should have few problems. However, here are some you may encounter.

- **Unknown user ID**

  You are trying to send to an unlisted user. Your system may allow you to list all users, then check the spelling of their name/correct initial. On most systems you can flag a user from the list and transfer this to your message so that you can be sure it is copied correctly.

- **No response**

  It may be that the system failed during transmission and this often isn't known or signalled to the user. Check your information screen to see if they have read the message. If not then send a reminder and/or telephone them.

- **Cannot read received message**

  This is often due to a temporary system problem, e.g. maintenance work was being done on the system when the message was sent. If you can identify the sender, Email or ring them to tell them your problem. If it happens often, contact your internal computer service engineer or help desk.

- **System failure**

  If this happens partway through a message, your screen may freeze on you, which can be extremely annoying if you are halfway through a very long message! On an internal system you should phone your computer service engineer or help desk. If you are using an external system, remember that *you are still connected via the phone link* (so still being charged!). *Either* press the relevant button on your modem to cancel the call (if there is one) or switch off your PC (if you can't log off properly) and re-enter. Then instruct your telephone to hang up. Both Telecom Gold and New Prestel operate a help line for users who are having problems.

 DID YOU KNOW?

On some internal systems, routine maintenance work or systems failure can mean that messages you have read are deleted – perhaps before you wanted them to be. On other systems this happens automatically after a certain time period to save space in the system. Check if this is the case in your organisation – otherwise you will lose messages you perhaps should have considered saving or printing for future reference.

Email costs

Internal electronic mail may be free – because the company already has the network and computers in place. Email may be simply an additional, useful facility on a local network. However, to communicate over a large area, or to company employees in remote locations (e.g. working from home) the basic internal system will have to be extended by one of the special services available, e.g. BT's Message Switching Service or Mailbox Service. For this the company will pay a registration fee, plus a monthly standing charge and then additional charges for usage and special services.

External Email users have two bills to pay each time they access the system – one for the phone call and the second for the connection time and any additional charges. These can be quite expensive, so it is important to know what you are doing and to keep the connection time as short as possible. Telecom Gold users pay a membership fee which varies depending upon the type of service they require. Club membership gives the user one mailbox. Corporate membership is designed for organisations which require unlimited mailboxes. On both systems there is also a standing charge – monthly for Telecom Gold and quarterly for New Prestel – so using external Email can be quite costly.

Email and security

There should be no problems unless someone guesses your password – or you tell someone what it is! Try to avoid doing this even in an emergency because this means the person you give it to can send out messages in your name as well as read your mail!

Probably the biggest security problem is accessing Email and then being distracted or interrupted, leaving your computer on and walking away from it. At that point anyone can use it – and it will appear to be you!

UNIT REVIEW (1)

At the end of this element you should be able to

- select the most appropriate transmission system for voice, data and text, in relation to urgency, cost and security
- use equipment correctly and in accordance with standard operating instructions and organisational requirements
- accurately prepare material for transmission
- transmit information correctly within required deadlines
- deal with outgoing and incoming communications in accordance with approved organisational procedures
- promptly route incoming information to its correct location
- ensure that security and confidentiality procedures conform to organisational requirements
- promptly rectify or report any equipment or system faults.

CHECK YOUR KNOWLEDGE AND UNDERSTANDING

True or false?

1 All fax machines can be used as copiers.
2 A touch tone telephone is one with * and # keys.
3 Every Email user has their own private password.
4 Your responsibility for taking a telephone message ends once it is on the recipient's desk.
5 Multi-coloured documents fax very clearly.

Fill in the blanks

6 The system which stores verbal messages for later access is called
_____ .

7 The document which is printed, which confirms if a fax was sent without any problems, is called the _____ _____ .

8 People who work in different areas of a building, or even outside, may carry a _____ which is linked to the switchboard.

Work it out

9 a Draw up a chart with the headings as shown below. Then look through the element again noting any comments which relate to these headings to complete the chart for reference.

b Identify *one* item which you would transmit using each system and justify your decision.

COMPARISON OF TRANSMISSION SYSTEMS			
System	**Urgency**	**Cost**	**Security**
Telephone			
Answering machine			
Voicemail			
Electronic data systems			
Fax			
Email			

10 Use the A–Z guide which follows to answer the following questions.

a When and what is Phoneday?

b What is the new emergency number and will this replace 999?

c What is daytime rate?

d Which company is BT's main competitor?

e What number do you dial to report a fault on a business line?

f Where would you use a Skyphone?

g Who can access directory enquiries free of charge?

h What would you use to decode a dialling code?

i How can a foreign visitor, who speaks very little English, arrange to make a reverse charge call to his home?

j How can people hold meetings with others far away, without moving from their office?

k State *four* ways in which people can make a call if they have no money.

A–Z of telecommunications

Answering machines Common in many offices today these may be bought or rented. Some models are stand-alone, others have a telephone combined. Usually two tapes are used – one to give the pre-recorded announcement, the other to take the message.

Bleepers An alternative to a mobile phone for someone who is often on the move. (*See under pagers.*)

British Telecom The main public telecommunications operator in the UK.

Business services High volume users can often take advantage of special schemes to reduce telephone costs.

Call rates The price of telephone and fax calls. **Daytime rate** is charged for local and national calls between 8 am and 6 pm on weekdays, at other times **cheap rate** is in force. On international calls cheap rate times are often different.

CallStream The BT service which uses 0891 and 0898 numbers. Callers pay maximum rates with the tariff shared between BT and the organisation. Used for sales promotions and charities who are fund raising and want to help customers to respond easily.

Cellnet A UK wide radio network for mobile telephones. A **Callback** messaging service is also available which takes messages if a cellphone is in use or switched off and then relays them. Developments are taking place to extend Cellnet over most European countries.

Cellphones Mobile telephones which use the Cellnet network. Different types are available – hand-portable, mobile carphones and transportable phones.

Chargecard Issued by BT so that customers can make calls from anywhere in the world with the cost being billed to them (or their company) at their main address.

Cohort 500 A BT service which supplies on-line directory information to switchboard operators as well as other services.

Data communications This can range from transferring basic data within one building to complex and integrated systems which transmit both voice and data all over the world (*see also **GSN** and **ISDN***).

Digital exchanges Digital technology has meant that different types of information such as voice, data, text and pictures and be transmitted at high speed over one network. Today most local exchanges are digital so that **network services** are available to all subscribers in that area. The system transmits information in pulses which are quickly understood by a wide range of equipment.

Directories Five different directories are available from BT

- **Business Pages** – which is a classified directory of business users
- **Electronic Yellow Pages (EYP)** – information on national Yellow Pages listings is available on computer
- **Phone Books** – issued for different geographical areas
- **Talking Pages** – a classified information service through which customers can find details of businesses and services throughout the UK
- **Yellow Pages** – regional directories which list subscribers according to the type of business or service offered.

In addition a **Phone Book Companion** is available from BT which lists all UK and international dialling dodes and a **Code Decoder**, which gives the location of all UK codes.

Directory Enquiries A chargeable service which can be accessed to find information on telephone numbers. Calls made from a payphone are not charged, neither are those made by disabled or blind customers.

Electronic Data Interchange (EDI) A system which enables businesses to transmit business documents (e.g. orders, invoices and VAT returns) set out in a standard format electronically by computer. An additional service (**EDI★NET**) enables businesses to send documents to different locations in one transmission. In conjunction with **GNS** the data can be sent almost worldwide.

Emergency services Can be accessed by dialling 999 **or 112**. This number has been introduced *in addition* to 999, as it is the same as the European Community emergency number, so you can dial the same number wherever you are in Europe. Six services are available – police, ambulance, fire brigade, mountain rescue, coastguard and cave rescue.

Facsimile machines The official name for fax machines. A wide range of machines is available to suit both private users and large businesses.

Freephone A BT service which enables companies to offer their customers free calls. The customer dials the operator and quotes the Freephone number and the company pays for the call.

Faults Telephone line faults should be reported promptly by dialling 154 (for a business line) or 151 (private line). Equipment faults should be reported to the manufacturer *after* the customer has checked the manual to make sure the problem isn't something simple he or she can sort out themselves!

Global Network Services (GNS) A BT service which allows businesses to communicate data all over the world via a 24-hour network. Security systems including special passwords are available for sensitive data. Users of some GNS services can also access business information on database, including financial information, business information and flight schedules.

Home Direct The BT service which foreign visitors can dial if they want assistance to arrange a reverse charge or credit card call to their own country.

Integrated Services Digital Network (ISDN) Probably the most rapidly growing facility for business users. ISDN enables customers to send large amounts of voice, data, text and images on one digital line. The service is being made available on a global basis and can be used by businesses to send data from one computer to another, for high-speed faxing, for video-conferencing and for voice messaging – simultaneously if required. Telephone equipment can now be purchased which enables instant access to ISDN.

International Direct Dialling (IDD) Most countries in the world can now be dialled directly. The codes are given in the blue pages of the Phone Book.

International 0800 Enables callers from abroad to call a British company with a LinkLine number free of charge (*see below*).

LinkLine The BT service which enables customers to call a company free of charge. The customer dials 0800 or 0345 followed by the company's LinkLine number. The company pays for the call. A more sophisticated service is Advanced LinkLine. This enables callers to leave a message if no-one is available on the number to take the call.

Local Area Network (LAN) Computers inter-connected over a small geographical area.

Malicious calls The official term for hoax callers and 'dirty' phone calls. Because the latter can be extremely distressing to receive BT now has an Adviceline available on 0800 666700. Many telephone switchboards can record these calls automatically to give the police additional information.

Mercury The second largest public telecommunications operator in the UK and BT's main competitor.

Mercury compatible Means a telephone is compatible with both BT and Mercury systems and routed by the cheapest service.

MultiLink A variation of the LinkLine service where the company can play a pre-recorded message to callers giving them information.

Multifax A service which enables fax users to send the same message to a number of different fax users very rapidly.

New Prestel BT's viewdata service (*see Unit 5, page 180*).

Oftel The department responsible for supervising the UK telecommunications industry and promoting consumer interests.

Operator services In addition to directory enquiries, the operator can also be contacted for assistance or information in relation to telephone accounts, telephone faults and difficulties making a call. Check the Phone Book for the number as these can differ, depending on whether they come from a business number or a residential number.

Pagers Different types of pagers can be purchased, some of which simply bleep, others store and display messages. Most can be set to vibrate rather than bleep if this is more convenient. Pagers can be contacted directly or via a bureau.

Phoneday Set for Sunday, 16 April 1995, the day when all UK area codes change.

Private Circuits Available to businesses who wish to have their own private lines connecting telephone extensions, PABX switchboards, computers, fax machines etc. Used by companies who want to set up their own electronic mail system or send high speed communications within the company (e.g. the link between a bank computer and its cash machines).

SatStream A service which enables business customers to communicate globally via satellite.

Security Telephones can be used as part of a security system. When an alarm is activated an electronic signal is sent to the alarm company or to a special BT operator to indicate an emergency.

Skyphone Telecommunications service for aircraft which will enable passengers and crew to make telephone calls whilst on board. British Airways are scheduled to introduce these soon on domestic routes. Telephones will be fitted in the seat armrest and can be activated by using a credit or charge card.

Telecom Gold BT's electronic mail service (*see page 339*).

Telephone management Different systems available to enable business users to monitor the cost, quantity and duration of their calls plus obtain listings of the numbers called.

Telephone meeting equipment A range of equipment which enables business customers to link to each other by voice and visually.

Timeline Originally called the Speaking Clock and available by dialling 8081.

Videoconferencing A two-way sound and vision link which enables meetings to be held *either* at BT videoconferencing centres *or* on business premises which have hired or bought the necessary equipment.

Videophone A telephone which also incorporates a screen on which the caller can be seen.

Voicemail A system of leaving messages in voice mailboxes so that another user can access messages when free (*see page 310*). BT's **Voicebank** service is available so that small businesses can take advantage of this facility.

Wide Area Network (WAN) Computers inter-connected over a small geographical area.

Yellow Pages – The Business Database A BT database which lists the UK *Yellow Pages* on disk with a special search facilities.

Element 8.2
Receive and send mail

Despite the tremendous growth of electronic mail systems, vast numbers of documents are sent out every day by more traditional methods, especially by the Royal Mail service. Many large organisations use direct mail shots to advertise their goods and services – so much so that many people complain about the amount of 'junk mail' they receive. Even the smallest company will probably send the majority of its letters and invoices through the post.

Dealing with mail is an important skill which is often ignored. Yet, if incoming information is delayed people may be taking action when they shouldn't – or not taking action when they should. Equally, if outgoing information is delayed, there could be serious consequences, e.g. the loss of an important order. Therefore every employee's effectiveness may depend on the efficiency of the incoming and outgoing mail service in the company.

Mailroom systems and equipment

These will obviously vary depending upon whether your organisation deals with six letters a day or 6000!

Incoming mail

At the very least, even in the smallest firm, you should have a paper knife with which to open the envelopes! However, you can probably hope for rather more than this!

Automatic mail opening equipment

The basic models simply make a slit in the envelope, very close to the edge so that the contents cannot be damaged. Such a machine will usually deal with different sizes of envelopes and even padded envelopes. The operator then removes the contents.

At the other end of the scale are sophisticated machines which

- automatically detect the number of sheets of paper, cheques, credit cards and other important documents
- can either hold the envelope apart for easy extraction by the operator or automatically extract the documents and stack them
- can automatically send cheques through equipment which processes all remittances (*see page 356*).

However, don't expect to find this type of machine unless you work in a company where vast amounts of mail, often containing money, are received daily (e.g. a credit card or mail order company).

Work table or workstation

This should be organised with clearly labelled trays for each department or recipient – preferably within easy reach of the operator. There should be a clear, large working surface.

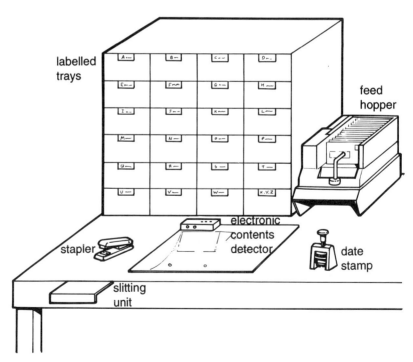

A workstation for incoming mail

Date stamp

All incoming mail should be stamped with the date it is opened, in case of later queries. Date stamps can vary from small, hand-held stamps to small machines which sense an inserted document and stamp it automatically.

 DID YOU KNOW?

Wise mailroom operators keep the empty envelopes for at least 24 hours. There may be queries relating to missing enclosures and, before contacting the company concerned, it is sensible to make sure the document has not been left in the envelope by mistake.

Outgoing mail

Again the variety of equipment, its size and complexity will depend on the volume of outgoing mail regularly handled by your organisation.

Electronic postal scales

These weigh all envelopes and electronically calculate the correct postage rate in each case. There are normally simple keys to press to indicate special services and destinations. The machines work by means of a microchip which is programmed with the current postage rates. When these change, the manufacturers supply an updated chip which the operator fits into the machine.

The main difference between the basic and more sophisticated models is the maximum weight they can handle and the range of destinations and services which can be selected.

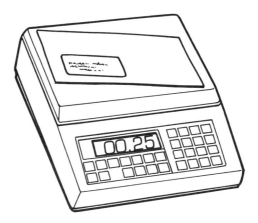

 DID YOU KNOW?

Some of the latest models will

- link to a franking machine so that the mail is weighed and franked correctly automatically

● memorise all the amounts spent on postage and then display these on the machine or link to a computer to print out the postal accounts for each day.

Franking machines

Franking mail is much faster than sticking on stamps, and odd amounts of postage are never a problem. There is no danger of pilferage of stamps and franked envelopes look more professional and can carry an advertisement for the company as well.

All the envelopes are fed through the machine which automatically prints a postal impression on each item. Most machines produce labels which can be stuck to large or bulky envelopes or parcels.

Franking machines are bought, rented or leased from a supplier. The company must then contact the Royal Mail Customer Service Centre before the machine is used. The machine must be inspected at least once a year (usually by the supplier) to check it is operating properly.

Franking machine users pay in advance for postage units which are programmed into the machine. A display on the machine shows when the amount of credit is running low. More units must then be purchased. There are various ways of doing this, from taking the machine to the post office to telephoning a recrediting centre.

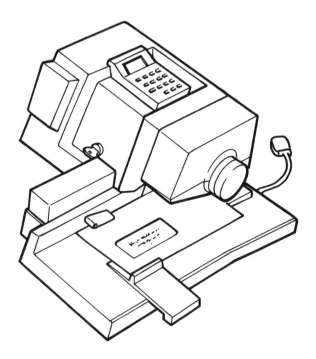

The operator must ensure the date is correct and the impression is clear (and replenish the ink as necessary).

Franked mail is usually placed in special pouches – red for first class and green for second class. These must be handed over the counter at the post office and not posted in the normal way. Bulky items are placed in special coloured mail bags. Companies with large quantities of mail can arrange for it to be collected by the Royal Mail service.

The record of units used is obviously a check on the amount being spent on postage. In addition, the more sophisticated machines can separate postage into different departments and give itemised information for checking expenditure.

Solving problems during franking

Envelope franked with wrong date   Either refrank a new envelope and save the spoiled one for recrediting by the post office *or* add a second label for 'zero' postage (showing the correct date) and put this on the reverse of the envelope.

Envelope franked with too low an amount   If you do nothing about this the letter will either go by second class post *or*, if the postage is still too low, the recipient will have to pay a **surcharge.** Again either refrank a new envelope (and save the old one) *or* add a label showing the outstanding postage.

Envelope franked with too high an amount   Keep all these envelopes and return to the post office for recrediting.

Only part of the impression showing   This can happen if an envelope is an odd shape or contains items which don't reach right to the top. The envelope has gone through on two levels and only the higher one of these receives the impression. Again, refrank with a different envelope, save the old one, and remember to print out a label next time instead!

CHECK IT YOURSELF

Try to see at least two franking machines in operation and to use one of them yourself. Bear in mind you can practise by setting the dial at 0p.

Check the type of features available on the machine(s) you see.

- Does the operator set the date manually or is there an automatic clock on the machine?
- Does the machine seal envelopes too?
- How are units purchased for the machine?
- What is the maximum value which can be franked on one envelope or label?

- Has the machine any safeguards to warn the operator if he or she mistakenly sets the postage for £60 instead of £6?
- Can the machine be linked to electronic postage scales so that mail can be weighed and priced automatically?

DID YOU KNOW?

Instead of using stamps or a franking machine, companies can

- buy prepaid envelopes for first class, second class or registered post from the post office
- order envelopes and postcards pre-printed with first and second class Postage Paid symbols from Royal Mail
- order stationery pre-printed with Printed Postage Impressions (PPIs). These are used for bulk mailings both to the UK and overseas.

Addressing machines

There are many different computerised addressing machines available, the majority of which can be linked to computers containing databases of addresses. Labels and wrappers, cards and envelopes are printed quickly and accurately.

Special programs can be bought either from the Royal Mail itself (The Postcode Address File) or from other suppliers, which enable addresses to be keyed in and checked quickly and easily.

Additional equipment

Other equipment will automatically fold forms and other documents and insert them into envelopes.

DID YOU KNOW?

A completely integrated mailing system, designed for organisations dealing with thousands of documents a day, will link all these machines together and the whole system will be controlled by computer. This will check that all insertions are fed into the mail in the correct sequence, put into the correct printed envelope and franked with the correct postage.

Mailroom and organisational procedures

An important point to remember is that although there are certain standard mailroom procedures in relation to processing mail, these may vary from one organisation to another. You therefore need to know any special requirements which operate where you work – and be prepared to adapt your methods when you change your job!

Incoming mail

Standard procedures

1. Mail is pre-sorted into different categories

   - **urgent** – which is opened quickly and delivered immediately or collected by the recipient if this arrives after the morning mail has been dealt with
   - **personal or private and confidential** – left unopened
   - mail containing **remittances** or payments, e.g. cheques, postal orders or even cash. A record is usually kept of these.
   - **recorded delivery and registered mail** which has been signed for on delivery. This may be recorded in a special book.
   - **wrongly delivered mail** – usually stacked to be reposted unopened and with any additional postal instructions marked on the envelope, e.g. 'Not known at this address' or 'Try Bath Street'.
   - **routine mail (i.e. first and second class mail)** – first class mail is normally opened first.

2. All enclosures are checked, then stapled or clipped to the main document. Any omissions are noted on the main document after the envelope has been checked.
3. All documents are usually date-stamped unless they are financial or legal documents, e.g. cheques, postal orders, contracts etc.
4. The mail is sorted into departments and placed in mail baskets for distribution or collection. The order in which the documents should be placed is

   - urgent documents (on the top)
   - private and confidential or personal letters
   - first class mail
   - second class mail
   - circulars and magazines.

Procedures to check in your own organisation

- Does your organisation have a mailroom which opens incoming post for the whole company, or does each department open its own?
- What time does the mailroom start work and what is the scheduled time for completing the task of sorting incoming mail?
- Is mail delivered to recipients or collected by them?
- Is the mail pre-sorted into departments before delivery, by the Royal Mail, using the Selectapost service?
- Who deals with envelopes which are marked 'personal' if the recipient is away from the office – especially if the envelope is also marked 'urgent'?

- Are there any procedures for recording remittances and/or special mail, e.g. recorded delivery and registered items?
- How long should envelopes be kept after they have been emptied?
- Are parcels opened in the mailroom or sent to the recipient unopened?
- What systems are used to circulate documents or other material which must be seen by several people?
- What should you do with items which have obviously been damaged during delivery?
- What organisational procedures are in force for dealing with suspect items?
- What happens to mail which is delivered by hand or special courier during the day?

DID YOU KNOW?

If you receive any parcels, you will be expected to sign for them – and remember these may be delivered at different times to the main post. It is usual to sign for unopened parcels by writing 'Contents not checked' as the person delivering them will not have time to stand and wait whilst you unpack everything. If the parcel is obviously damaged then it may be refused or if accepted, should be signed for as 'Damaged on delivery'.

A general guide to incoming mail requirements

Remittances

A record of money received in the mail is either made manually in a **Remittance book** or recorded on computer (sometimes automatically – *see page 350*).

Any discrepancies are also noted and the entries are usually countersigned by a supervisor. An example of a Remittance book is shown below.

Date	Name	Method of payment	Amount £	Account Number	Comments
5 Feb	J Bryant	Cheque	152.20	683970	
"	T Cook	Cheque	22.50	483092	
"	J McNulty	PO	6.00	330940	
"	K Hussein	Cash (reg)	15.00	220839	
"	J Palowski	Cheque	180.00	408507	cheque not dated
"	L Ellis	Cash (reg)	16.00	682201	
Cashier's signature ....K Watson........... Date ...5/2/94........					

Circulating mail

Mail which has to be seen by several people is usually dealt with differently, depending on the type of item. A letter, or set of documents, may be copied and a copy sent to each person who has an interest in it. However, it is important that each recipient knows who else has received a copy, and for this reason it is usual to

- Write a neat distribution list at the top of the document.
- Count how many people must receive the documents in addition to the addressee, and make this number of photocopies.
- Tick the appropriate name on each one. Make sure the addressee (or the most important person listed) receives the original.
- Put each document in the correct mail basket.

A bulky document, such as a multi-page bound report, a brochure or a magazine, obviously cannot be photocopied and in this case a **circulation** or **routeing** slip is completed.

CIRCULATION SLIP		
Name	Date received	Date passed on
Please return to		

![CHECK IT YOURSELF]

1 Why do you think it is necessary that each recipient knows who else receives a copy of a document? If this information was not given, what might happen?
2 Why do you think it is advisable to put 'Date received' and 'Date passed on' on a circulation slip – rather than just a list of names?
3 If a report or brochure was important, why might it be useful to keep a copy of the routeing slip?

Suspicious items

Organisations which work in sensitive areas, such as military establishments and high security installations, may invest in expensive screening equipment which scans all their mail before it is allowed to be opened. These machines are similar to the ones used at airports to check hand-baggage. The Post Office also routinely scans mail.

Smaller organisations and companies which are involved only in general business trading may not feel there is a need to invest in such equipment. Nevertheless, staff who work in mailrooms should know the signs to look for in case anything suspicious is received. If they have any doubts about the correct procedure to follow, they should contact their local Crime Prevention Officer for information.

Signs to watch for include

- grease marks on the envelope or wrapping
- the smell of marzipan or almonds
- visible wiring or tin foil, especially if the package or envelope is damaged
- an envelope or package which feels unusually heavy for its size
- uneven weight distribution in a package or rigid contents in a flexible envelope
- excessive wrapping
- poor handwriting, spelling or typing
- an incorrect address or an unusual postmark
- too many stamps for the weight of the package
- a postmark which is outside Great Britain
- delivery by hand from an unknown source.

What to do

1 If you are at all suspicious then tell your supervisor immediately.
2 If you are on your own then

- Immediately isolate the item in a locked room, away from windows and thin partition walls. If possible, put the item on a table in a fairly central position.
- Do not mess about with the package or interfere with the wrapping in any way.
- Do not place it in water or sand.
- Leave the building and telephone the police from a different place, as some devices can be activated by telephone signals.
- Dial 999. Be prepared to give your name, your company name and location and details of the problem clearly on request.

TEST YOURSELF

1 You are half asleep one morning after a hectic night out with some friends. By mistake you open an envelope for a senior manager, clearly

marked 'Personal'. It is from his bank, complaining about the non-payment of a large loan. Your immediate urge is to throw the letter away so the manager will never know you have read it. What would be the correct procedure to follow?

2 In the middle of the afternoon a large parcel marked 'Valuable/insured' is delivered by a private courier. The addressee is away from the office for the next two weeks. What would you do?

3 Your supervisor has decided to keep a record of all damaged items which are received. What headings would you suggest and why?

Outgoing mail

The range of procedures actually carried out in the mail room itself, or in individual departments, varies from one company to another.

Standard procedures which may be carried out centrally or within each department

1 Letters are checked to ensure that

- they have been signed
- the address on the letter matches the envelope
- all enclosures are attached.

2 Documents are folded the minimum number of times and placed in the envelope.

3 All envelopes are sealed. Bulky items may be fastened with sticky tape for extra security, but never try to squeeze too much paper into too small an envelope!

Standard procedures carried out in the mailroom

1 Internal mail is sorted and placed in the appropriate baskets.

2 External mail is sorted into the following groups

- special items
- foreign mail
- routine items
- parcels.

3 All items are weighed and the correct postage rate is calculated. This is usually done automatically using electronic postage scales (*see page 351*). Otherwise the weight is written on the envelope or parcel in *pencil* and then calculated from Royal Mail postage charts.

4 Any forms which are required for special mail are completed, and any special records made (*see below*).

5 The mail is franked or stamped and either delivered to the post office or collected at a pre-arranged time.

 ## DID YOU KNOW?

Nowadays many organisations use window envelopes routinely for most items as this saves typing addresses twice. It is important, however, that all documents placed in these envelopes are correctly aligned so that *all* the address is clearly visible and will remain so even when the envelope is held at one corner and shaken.

Procedures to check in your own organisation

- Is mail processed all day, or does the mailroom operate only from a certain time each afternoon?
- What is the deadline for completing the work so that the post will leave on time?
- Does the organisation have a standard policy in relation to posting mail? (Some organisations will only send documents by second class mail, others refuse any post which is not in an 'organisational' envelope unless it is pre-stamped.)
- Are parcels wrapped in each department or in the mailroom?
- What special services are used the most, and do these items of mail have to be referred to a supervisor?
- What methods of recording special items are in force?
- Are any private organisations used for urgent items?
- Does the organisation have any special contracts with the Royal Mail service which will affect the batching and sending of mail?

CHECK IT YOURSELF

1 Some organisations won't let any documents be sent by first class mail on a Friday. Can you think why?

2 Look up *at least three* private organisations which provide a delivery or courier service in your area. Give two examples of when each of these may be more useful than the traditional methods.

A general guide to outgoing mail requirements

In addition to knowing the correct procedure to follow, you also need to know

- what materials to use, and when
- what services to use, and when.

This will enable you to maintain the company image, keep costs down and select the best mailing service for each item.

Materials

Each mailroom will have a variety of materials available including envelopes (in various sizes), sticky tape (in various sizes and strengths), brown paper, jiffy (padded) bags and packing material (*see below*) and Royal Mail labels for special items. Special Royal Mail stationery may also be available for overseas mail, e.g. Airpacks and Swiftpacks.

Note the different sizes of envelopes and how these match to the various sizes of paper. Some envelopes are A4 size and are useful if several A4 documents have to be sent as they do not need folding. If only one or two pages of A4 paper are being posted, these can be neatly folded into three parts to fit into a DL envelope (*see page 102*).

Envelopes are available in brown and white. White envelopes are usually kept for correspondence (as they are more expensive). Self-sealing envelopes are the most expensive, especially if they are also of high-quality paper, and are designed to open on the longer side. These are known as **banker envelopes**. Pocket envelopes have the opening on the shorter side and are cheaper.

The mailroom may also keep a stock of compliment slips. These are usually sent out with advertising literature or in answer to general queries.

CHECK IT YOURSELF

- Check the materials available in any mailroom in which you work.
- Find out the cost of different types and sizes of envelopes and jiffy bags by visiting the post office, a local stationers' or looking through a stationery catalogue.
- Obtain a variety of different envelopes and practise folding A4 paper the minimum of times to fit into each one.
- The three sizes of envelopes recommended by the Royal Mail are C5, C6 and DL. Identify each of these in your collection of envelopes.
- Some companies use special envelopes which are reusable for circulating internal mail between departments. See if you can obtain an example of one of these.

 ## DID YOU KNOW?

Although addressing an envelope correctly is a skill you should already know, many people make basic mistakes and do not follow the Royal Mail guidelines. Apart from anything else it should be *neatly* written if it has not been printed or typed. Other important points to remember are

- start writing half-way down the envelope
- start with the name of the addressee and his or her title (e.g. Mr, Mrs, Ms, Miss, Dr)
- start a new line for each line of the address
- *always* put the town or city in *capitals*
- put the postcode as the last item, preferably on its own line, with *no* punctuation
- special mailing instructions, e.g. 'By hand' or 'Urgent' should be put at the top left-hand side
- special addressee instructions should be put two lines before the rest of the address, e.g. 'Personal', 'Private and confidential' or 'For the attention of ...'

- letters going abroad should have *both* the city (or town) *and* the country in capitals.

DID YOU KNOW?

- The Royal Mail service prefer it if *no* punctuation is used in *any part* of the address.
- If you don't know a postcode you can find it by either looking in the telephone directory or phoning the Royal Mail Postcode enquiry line on 0345 111222; you will be charged at the local rate for your telephone call.

SPECIAL NOTE

Letters to overseas destinations may seem to have the address in the wrong order! Don't worry about this – in some countries the town and the street are in the reverse order to ours. Simply do what you are told or copy the address carefully from the letter heading!

Wrapping parcels

These must be wrapped securely so that the contents are not damaged. Special labels are available, e.g. FRAGILE or DO NOT BEND and these should be used where appropriate.

A range of wrapping materials is available, e.g.

- strong boxes
- corrugated paper, bubble wrap and polystyrene chips
- paper which has been through a shredder.

It is important that the parcel cannot be damaged if it is knocked from outside and that it cannot rattle about inside a box. Packing material is used to pad the parcel inside the box and fill any gaps.

The parcel must be labelled clearly and include both the sender's address and the recipient's address. The sender's address should, preferably, be put on the reverse side so that there is no confusion.

SPECIAL NOTE

If you use staples of any kind to secure the package, make sure the points are flattened, covered, or all face inwards so that they do not injure anyone.

CHECK IT YOURSELF

- Obtain a copy of the Royal Mail leaflet *Wrapping up well* and find out how to wrap fragile, heavy, delicate and sharp items. Make a note of what you can do if any item you send is damaged in transit.
- Look at the address label which follows. There are *four* errors. Can you find them?

Mrs P Hanson, Personnel Manager
Briggs & Saunders Ltd
Fountain Road
Reading
RD7 JXL

Royal Mail services

The type of service you will choose for special items will vary, depending on

- whether it is routine, urgent, valuable or important
- whether the item is a letter or parcel
- whether it is for the UK or abroad.

The explanations below summarise each of the most important services. However, choosing which one would be the most appropriate also depends on the cost of each service, and the rates often change. This is where you have some work to do (*see below*).

Routine mail

This may mainly be sent by second class mail. You can obtain proof of posting easily by obtaining or completing a **certificate of posting** which is free. The certificate is stamped at the post office.

In business very few documents are sent abroad by surface mail, which is usually too slow. Remember that all documents sent to Europe go by airmail. Lightweight mail goes at a special rate to countries in the EU. Mail for other countries will need an airmail sticker (or a special airmail envelope). An alternative is to write the words 'PAR AVION – BY AIRMAIL' clearly on the top left of the envelope.

Small parcels can be sent by the **packet service**, otherwise the standard **Parcelforce** services may be used.

Urgent mail

The cheapest way of sending documents quickly within the UK is to use the **Special Delivery** service which guarantees next day delivery for a small charge. There is a limited amount of compensation if the item is lost or damaged so the service is not suitable for valuable items.

The equivalent service for documents being sent abroad is **Swiftair Express**. You can make life easier for yourself by buying a pre-paid envelope for this, called a Swiftpack.

Datapost provides a rapid *and* safe delivery service but costs more. Datapost can be used for parcels sent within the UK and abroad.

Valuable and important

You need to understand the difference between these two types of item. A **valuable** item is one which is worth a lot of money. An **important** item has little monetary value but you would suffer a lot of inconvenience replacing it if it was lost or damaged. Examples are passports, credit cards, legal documents.

If you need monetary compensation then use one of the **Registered** services and, if necessary, **Consequential loss** as well. However, the protection of consequential loss is not related to the item itself but to the consequences of its loss. Therefore, if a company lost business as a result of a registered item not being delivered, they could claim under this service.

Although you can send documents abroad using registered post, the consequential loss service is only available within the UK and does not apply to the Channel Islands or Isle of Man.

Important documents being sent within or outside the UK should be sent by recorded delivery.

Parcelforce **Datapost** services within and outside the UK offer high levels of compensation plus the option of consequential loss cover. The usual compensation available on the **Parcelforce Standard** service can be increased to £150 or £500 by paying an additional fee.

DID YOU KNOW?

If you require proof that a registered or recorded item has been delivered then you can either complete an **Advice of Delivery** form when you post the item or telephone 0645 272100, quoting the number on your receipt. If you need a copy of the delivery signature you will have to pay a small charge.

TEST YOURSELF

1 Photocopy or copy out the chart on pages 366–367 neatly and find out the cost of each service listed. Enter the price in the appropriate column.
2 Give *two* examples of when you would use each service and check your answer with your supervisor or tutor.

DID YOU KNOW?

● The Royal Mail Service runs special courses for mailroom staff to teach them about the full range of Royal Mail business services so that staff have the knowledge necessary to choose the best method of sending items through the post cost-effectively. Details can be obtained from any Royal Mail Customer Service Centre.

- If you regularly send items abroad, and need information on customs regulations and special packaging, it is worth buying the Royal Mail *International Service Guide.* This is available either in book form or on a floppy disk which will run on any IBM compatible PC. The disk is free and the book is very reasonably priced.

Recording outgoing mail

Many organisations do not keep manual records of outgoing mail because they can obtain these direct from other sources, e.g. franking machine or electronic scale displays or computer print-outs.

However, you may work for a small company or firm which needs to keep manual records. This is particularly true if, for example, you work for a solicitor or accountant where each item sent to a client may be billed to his or her account. In that case, the following procedure usually applies.

- Routine mail is not recorded (because the time taken to do this would mean the job was not cost-effective). Instead the mail is batched and the details recorded in one entry.
- Special services are recorded, particularly expensive parcels and Datapost items.
- Receipts for such documents are kept, as the company will claim such expenses against its tax at the end of the year.
- The items are recorded in a postage book which is balanced each day (*see below*).

Postage book

Date	Details	Cost £	Special items	Special fees £
4 Nov	36 × 1st class mail	9.00		
	52 × 2nd class mail	9.88		
	J Shorrock Ltd	.25	Special delivery	2.70
	Mr John Taylor	.19	Recorded delivery	.55
	Mrs Sarah Briggs	.25	Registered Plus	3.30
	Samco Inc. NY	.60	Swiftair	2.70
		20.17		9.25

 DID YOU KNOW?

All organisations need to keep some records of postage costs and this information is given to the company accountant on a regular basis. Postage costs are only one of many expenses which will be listed to reduce the company's tax liability.

Type of mail	United Kingdom			Overseas				
	Mail service	Delivery/comments	Price	Mail service	Delivery/comments	Price A	B	C
ROUTINE Letters	1st class 2nd class Certificate of Posting	Delivered next day Delivered in 3 days Gives proof of posting		Airmail Surface mail (not Europe)	3–4 days Europe 4–7 days other Up to 12 weeks			
Parcels	Parcelforce 48 Parcelforce Standard	Delivered in 2 days Delivered in 3 days		International Standard International Economy Surface mail	5 days Europe 7 days other 10 days Europe 20 days other Up to 12 weeks			
URGENT Letters	Special Delivery Datapost	By 12.30 pm next day Next day		Swiftair Express Datapost	Priority service to most countries Next day Europe 2 days most other			
Parcels	Parcelforce Datapost 10 Datapost 12 Parcelforce 24	By 10 am next day By noon next day By end of next day		International Datapost	Next day Europe 2 days most other			

Type of mail	Mail service	United Kingdom Delivery/comments	Price	Mail service	Overseas Delivery/comments	Price A B C
VALUABLE OR IMPORTANT Letters	Registered	Next day by 12.30 pm max compensation £500		International Registered	Compensation up to £500 or £1000	
	Registered Plus	Next day by 5.20 pm max compensation £2200		International Recorded	Compensation only up to £24 – for **important documents only**	
	Consequential loss	Extra compensation to £10000				
	Recorded delivery	1st or 2nd class – **important documents only**				
	Advice of delivery	Gives proof of delivery				
Parcels	Datapost 10 or 12	Max compensation £5000+ consequential loss to £10000 if required		International Datapost	Compensation up to £10000 depending on fee paid	
	Parcelforce 24 or 48	Max compensation £10000		International Standard	Compensation up to £250	
	Parcelforce Standard plus compensation fee	Compensation up to £500 depending upon additional fee paid				

UNIT REVIEW (2)

At the end of this element you should be able to

- process and direct all incoming mail correctly to its destination
- follow organisational procedures for identifying and dealing with suspect items
- prepare outgoing mail correctly for dispatch
- select the most appropriate mailing system to use, in relation to cost, urgency and security
- process incoming and outgoing mail within the required deadlines.

 ## CHECK YOUR KNOWLEDGE AND UNDERSTANDING

True or false?

1 Recorded delivery items can be sent by first or second class.
2 Letters marked 'Personal' must always be opened if the addressee is absent.
3 A catalogue which arrives in the mail, and must be seen by several people, would be photocopied.
4 It is not possible to obtain proof of delivery on any Royal Mail service.
5 Datapost can be used for inland and overseas parcels.

Fill in the blanks

6 The most cost-effective priority service for letters abroad is _____ _____ .

7 Many electronic scales can be linked to a _____ _____ so that items are weighed and processed for posting in one operation.

8 The service to use to send important documents is _____ _____ .

Work it out

9 Which Royal Mail service(s) would you choose to send each of the following through the post?

   a the deeds to a house
   b a passport, if it was vital this was returned promptly so that the owner could go on a business trip to negotiate an important contract
   c a sample of metal, worth £5000, to a laboratory in Paris
   d an urgent letter to a company in New York
   e an urgent letter to a woman in York

10 The following are all popular business services which are not included in the chart on pages 366–367.

- Mailsort
- Business reply
- Airstream

- Freepost
- Printflow

Your boss wants to know something about each of these services, including whether they are for inland mail, overseas mail or both.

Use either the *Mailguide* or leaflets from your local post office to find out about each service and write a brief description for your manager.

9 Maintain and issue stock items

This unit comprises two elements. Element 9.1 refers to your ability to order, monitor and maintain suitable stock levels. Element 9.2 relates to your ability to issue stock items as and when requested, cope with emergencies and keep the necessary records up to date and accurate.

Element 9.1

Order, monitor and maintain stock

The skills you will need

You will need to prove that you can

- maintain sufficient stocks to meet current and anticipated demands
- order stock in accordance with organisational procedures
- handle and securely store stock in line with organisational requirements
- carry out stock checks and inventory reconciliations and report any discrepancies to the appropriate person
- check incoming deliveries against orders and report any discrepancies to the appropriate person
- keep up-to-date, legible and accurate records.

The knowledge and understanding you will need

You will need to know

- the importance of stock costs, how to store stock correctly and rotate it
- relevant health and safety issues, e.g. how to lift and handle stock and how to handle and store hazardous materials
- how to work out and maintain suitable stock levels
- how to order stock and check deliveries
- your legal rights in returning damaged or incorrect stock
- how to dispose of surplus, damaged and out-of-date stock
- how to report or record discrepancies.

What counts as stock?

In this case you are concerned with

- office consumables
- small items of office equipment
- other materials.

If you work for a large company, you may have a centralised purchasing office which makes out all the orders for the organisation. You will therefore put your requests **internally** – to the purchasing office. Equally, there may be specialist suppliers, within the organisation, of certain items, e.g. computer disks and paper. Goods bought for the organisation as a whole are usually cheaper because suppliers give discounts for large orders.

If you work for a small company, or need a special item, then you may deal with an outside supplier yourself. In this case you would be expected to get several different quotations so that you can select the cheapest or most reliable supplier.

 ## DID YOU KNOW?

Stock is usually ordered internally by completing a **requisition form**. Stock is ordered from an outside supplier by completing an official company **order form**.

CHECK IT YOURSELF

1 *Office consumables and small items of office equipment were dealt with in Element 3.3, page 100.* Look back at these pages now and refresh your memory on the different types of supplies used in an office. You are advised to re-read all of this element as much of the contents apply to this unit.

2 Look through an office stationery or computer supplies catalogue and identify *at least ten* other items which you use at college, at work or have used on work experience.

3 Discuss with your supervisor or tutor the type of items which would be ordered internally in your organisation or college, and those where individual staff may deal with a supplier direct.

Stock levels

All organisations are keen to minimise the amount of stock they keep – otherwise money is tied up unnecessarily. If stock goes out of date or perishes then the money is wasted. Additional costs are those of storage and people's time in finding items. Therefore there will be a **maximum** level set for each item. This is the most stock which can be held at any one time.

However, if stocks are too low, supplies may run short or even run out. If people have no paper clips for a week the situation is annoying but not desperate. If there are no envelopes or letter headed paper then there are real problems! In certain cases, allowance has to be made for the time for delivery. A few boxes of paper clips or envelopes could be bought immediately from a local stationers. Letter headed paper needs to be printed and this takes time. Therefore, when the **minimum** level of stock is decided, the three main factors to be considered are

- the type of problems which would occur if the stock ran out, and their severity
- the amount of time taken to obtain new supplies, often referred to as **lead time**
- the demand for the item. **Active** stock, e.g. pens and paper needs a higher level of buffer stock than inactive stock items. **Buffer stock** is the amount of stock you need to have in hand to meet requests whilst new supplies are being delivered. The more buffer stock that is needed, the higher will be the minimum level of stock required.

TEST YOURSELF

You work for a small firm of accountants. There are three partners who run the firm, each has an assistant and there are four other office staff besides yourself.

1   Look through your catalogue of office supplies and select *14* common items of stock, e.g. paper, envelopes etc. List these according to their correct catalogue description.
2   Bearing in mind the size of firm you work for, allocate a maximum and minimum amount for each item, taking into account all the factors mentioned above.
3   Assuming the firm has just opened its offices, calculate the cost of ordering all your items for the first time. Remember you will be ordering the maximum amount in each case, and don't forget to add VAT if applicable!
4   Compare your total with the rest of your colleagues and discuss your answers. Ask your supervisor or tutor to comment on the levels you decided and the cost factor involved.

Note: Keep your lists from this activity safely – you will need them again later in this element.

Storage of stock

On the basis that organisations want to minimise the cost of buying stock, there is little point in going through all the procedures mentioned above and then throwing the stock in a cupboard and ignoring it! All stock must be

- checked carefully when it is delivered (*see Element 3.3, page 105 and this element, page 376*)
- stored in a dry, well-ventilated, lockable cupboard to prevent deterioration through damp or pilferage

- stacked with the new stock **at the bottom** so that the oldest stock is always used first (This is called **stock rotation**.)
- stacked with the descriptive labels facing outwards so that it is easy for people to see what it is.

The cupboard should have a series of slatted shelves (which allow the air to circulate) and it is also sensible to

- label all the shelves and have a room plan which other people can follow, if they are also authorised to store or issue stock
- keep fast moving items where they are most easily accessible
- keep large and bulky items low down (or on the floor under the bottom shelf) to avoid heavy weights falling down on top of you
- keep paper wrapped (otherwise it discolours)
- keep pens and pencils in boxes to stop them rolling about or getting knocked off the shelf
- break down items supplied in large quantities, e.g. paper clips, to avoid wastage.

Safety first

Health and safety is important in relation to the storage of stock.

- All dangerous substances must be clearly labelled. Under COSHH certain items, e.g. acid, must *not* be stored in a stock room but in a special chemical safe or a bonded store.
- Flammable liquids must be kept well away from heat.
- The **level** of any dangerous or flammable substances stored must be kept to a minimum.
- People must **never** smoke in a stock room.
- All boxes must be removed once they are emptied.
- Full boxes must not be stored where people could fall over them.
- A safety stool must be provided for reaching items stored on high shelves.
- Potential accidents can be avoided if items such as drawing pins are kept in boxes and paper is kept wrapped. Remember that paper can give a nasty cut!
- There must be a trolley for transporting heavy items and anyone working in the stock room must be given instruction on how to lift items correctly, bearing in mind the requirements of the Manual Handling Operations Regulations.

DID YOU KNOW?

Most dangerous and hazardous substances stored in offices are associated with reprographic equipment. Offset-litho machines use blanket wash and etching fluid, both of which are flammable. Methyl ethyl ketone (MEK) is also used as a blanket wash and is even more hazardous. Toner (used in a photocopier), which is a special form of powdered ink, can be messy and dangerous. If it gets onto your hands or clothes it must be washed off with cold water – hot water makes it set. If it gets in your eyes you need to take remedial action quickly (*see Unit 2*).

Cleaning fluids (e.g. to remove graffiti), and some types of adhesives can also be hazardous because they give off dangerous fumes.

All dangerous substances are marked with hazard warning signs and clear instructions on how they should be stored. Additional information can be obtained on request from the manufacturers.

CHECK IT YOURSELF

1 Look back at Unit 2, and note how many provisions of the Health and Safety at Work Act and the European Regulations apply to a stock room. Note also what is said about COSHH and what these letters stand for.
2 Look back at Element 3.3, pages 103–4 where additional information is given on the storage of stationery items and safety (including lifting).
3 Visit the stationery stock room (or cupboard!) at your workplace or college and note how the items are stored and how many of the storage and safety factors given above have been considered. Find out if any dangerous substances are stored on the premises and if so, how they are kept and what precautions are taken when they are handled.

Make a note of any additional useful information you obtain, for future reference.

Stock control systems

Having a stock control system means that the store room is not an 'open access' area. Otherwise people would simply help themselves and there would be no control over the amount of stock taken or used. You can guess what would happen – and the cost of buying and replacing stock would be enormous!

This would be even worse if there was no control over the type of goods which could be ordered – people would order things on impulse, use some of them, not bother with the others and this would add to the cost.

There is therefore usually a set system in place.

● People wanting stock must complete an official requisition or order form and pass this to the stock control clerk.
● This document must be counter-signed by someone in authority.
● All stock is issued by a stock clerk who then adjusts the records kept for those particular items.

- When the level for any item is approaching the minimum figure, the stock clerk re-orders the required goods from the official supplier.
- At regular intervals the stock records are matched with the actual amounts of stock. These are called **stock checks** or **inventory reconciliations**.
- A note is made of any surplus, damaged or out-of-date stock and these are disposed of according to certain procedures.

DID YOU KNOW?

Stock records can be kept manually or on computer. *These are dealt with in more detail in Element 9.2.*

Ordering stock

Many organisations have lists of their official suppliers. If you work for a large company you will probably have little choice about which supplier to use. If you work in a small company then the situation may be rather different. Often a supplier is chosen who is local, reliable and provides a good range of quality products at a reasonable price.

When you order an item, the supplier will want confirmation on an official order form which will have a unique number. This number must be quoted on any enquiries you make.

You must complete any order form *correctly* by

- clearly specifying the amount you require bearing in mind the **units** in which the goods are sold (see below)
- clearly writing or typing the reference or catalogue number of the goods
- giving a brief description of the items
- stating the unit price.

The order does *not* give any details of the total price, VAT or delivery charges. However, you may be able to specify how soon the order is required and if it is very urgent you could fax it rather than sending it by post.

Remember that you will probably have to have the order signed by someone in authority before it can be sent.

DID YOU KNOW?

Paper is sold in **reams** (500 sheets) or in **quires** (24 sheets). Pens are sold in **dozens** (12) but may be sold by the **gross** (144). Envelopes are usually supplied in anything from packs of 50 to boxes of 1000! Bear in mind, therefore, that you will have to order goods in multiples of the basic unit sold and cannot order part amounts.

This may mean that the amount actually ordered is slightly different from the exact difference between the amount currently in stock and the maximum amount allowed.

TEST YOURSELF

Refer to the lists you prepared earlier as a result of the 'Test yourself' on page 372. (Remember, you were warned to keep these sheets safely!) Also refer to the catalogue you used to prepare these.

Photocopy the order form given at the end of this unit and complete it to order the maximum amount you decided of *the first five* items on your list, your order number is 4876. Ask your supervisor or tutor to check the form has been completed correctly.

Taking delivery

In a large organisation deliveries may be made at a central point and checked by specialist staff. At this point a **goods received note** may be completed, which lists the contents of the order and any items which are damaged.

The actual delivery of goods, or the goods received note, must be checked against the order which was sent to the firm to make sure that all items have been sent in the right quantities and are in good condition. If an item is temporarily out of stock it may be marked as 'to follow' on the **delivery note** which accompanies the goods. The delivery note should also be checked to make sure that it matches the goods received.

DID YOU KNOW?

Make sure, if you are checking off goods, that anyone who handles the documents afterwards can clearly see that they have been checked. For instance, insert clear ticks opposite each item, write clear entries if there are any discrepancies and initial your work – so that if there are any queries people know who to come to for information.

CHECK IT YOURSELF

1 Look back at Element 3.3, pages 105–6 where detailed information is given on receiving consumables.
2 Visit your local Trading Standards Office and obtain some leaflets on the

- Sale of Goods Act 1979
- Trade Descriptions Act 1968
- Consumer Protection Act 1987.

If there is no local Trading Standards Office then you can research this information in various books at your local library. Ask for a simple consumer book, such as those published by the Consumers' Association.

3   Find out what your legal rights are if you

- receive a packet of damaged files and the company refuses to let you return them
- buy 100 floppy disks in a sale and find none of them work
- buy a hole punch which doesn't work
- buy a disk box which is advertised as containing 50 disks but only holds 20.
- buy an electric stapler which gives you an electric shock the first time you use it.

4   Investigate the procedures for ordering stock at your organisation or college and try to obtain a copy of their official order form.

DID YOU KNOW?

Stationery, equipment and other items are a recognised business expense. The total amount of expenses is deducted from the company's **gross** profit to calculate the **net** profit and it is on this figure that the business tax is calculated. It is therefore important that all orders, invoices and records of payments are kept for the company accountant.

Stock checks and stock inventories

At regular intervals, a check is made to ensure that the stock records and actual physical amount of stock are the same. A note is also made of any items which cannot be used for any reason – and the cost of these may be **written off** by the accountant.

The procedure is normally as follows.

- Each item is counted and the total is checked off against the stock record for that item.
- If the count is correct then the stock sheet is ticked for that item.
- If the count is incorrect then the stock is recounted as a double-check. The discrepancy is then noted on the sheet.
- All discrepancies are reported to the supervisor or manager.

The supervisor will look at the size of the discrepancy and the item involved. Finding that two pens are missing is rather different (and probably due to carelessness) from being unable to account for 20 audio machines and 50 reams of paper! A full investigation may be made if pilferage is suspected.

At the same time, stock is listed which is

- damaged
- obsolete
- surplus to requirements.

Damaged stock

Damaged stock *may* have to be thrown away, although some investigation should take place into *how* it was damaged if a large amount is involved. Sometimes, however, the stock may be resaleable to staff at a discounted price, or used for another purposes. For instance, slightly discoloured paper may be made into scrap pads.

Obsolete or out-of-date stock

This is stock which has been ordered but which is now out of date. Examples include

- letter headings which show a telephone number with an outdated code (Remember Phoneday?)
- computer disks which are the wrong size for the disk drives now installed in the company machines
- business cards printed with the name of a representative who has now left the company.

Again, there are three choices – throw it away, sell it to staff cheaply or find an alternative use for it if possible.

Surplus stock

This is stock which was ordered for a specific purpose and, possibly because the quantity had to be estimated, some is still in stock but no longer required. An example would be a special project where special folders or coloured files were used. If too many were ordered and the project has now ended, there may still be a supply in the stock room.

The obvious answer is to find out if anyone else in the company has a use for them or, if they were only ordered recently from a supplier who is used regularly, whether the supplier will be good-natured enough to take them back (though he has no obligation to do so).

DID YOU KNOW?

- A final check should be made regarding the **activity** of different items. If some items of stock are rarely used, it may be more economic to stop keeping them on the premises and order them (or buy them locally) only when they are required. A less drastic measure is to review the maximum and minimum levels of stock which are kept for each item under review.
- The total amount of items which are unusable is called **wastage.** All companies try to keep wastage to a minimum.

CHECK IT YOURSELF

1   Find out what items of stock kept in your organisation (or college) are surplus to requirements or out of date.

2 Find out what procedures are in place to deal with these items.

3 Discuss with the stock clerk what happens if goods are missing or damaged. What records are kept and to whom is the problem reported?

4 Obtain as many examples as you can of documents which relate to this element – stock records, delivery notes, copies of orders, stock inventory checklists, any reports relating to damaged or missing stock.

 Note: The 'Check Your Knowledge and Understanding' section for this unit is on page 385.

Element 9.2

Issue stock items on request

The skills you will need

You will need to prove that you can

- issue stock in accordance with organisational procedures
- respond to requests promptly and accurately
- handle and securely store stock in accordance with organisational requirements
- keep up-to-date, legible and accurate records
- promptly and accurately report damage to stock to the appropriate person.

The knowledge and understanding you will need

You will need to know

- the issuing and recording systems used in your organisation
- where materials are located and stored
- the stock control procedures in force in your organisation
- how to handle hazardous materials
- your organisation's procedures for issuing and recording stock
- how, and to whom, to report problems
- the levels at which stock must be re-ordered
- the procedures in force for dealing with emergency orders.

Facts you already know

If you have worked your way *properly* through Element 9.1 then you should already have a good understanding of your organisation's procedures in relation to stock control. You should know where stock is stored, how it is stored and why. You should know who is in authority and deals with stock problems. You should also have a good appreciation of stock levels and why these are set.

This section therefore concentrates on actual stock control and compares two systems – **manual** stock control and **computerised** stock control. It also looks at emergency orders – and how to deal with these.

Manual systems

The most usual system is for a series of stock record cards to be made out, one card for each item. An example of such a card is shown below.

STATIONERY RECORD CARD

ITEM: *A4 white photocopying paper*   **MAXIMUM** *100 rms*
MINIMUM *25 rms*

SUPPLIER: *Copynational Ltd*   **UNITS** *reams*

Date	Received	Issued	Department	Order No	Balance
1 Nov					*35 reams*
3 "		*6 reams*	*Sales*	*548*	*29 reams*
5 "		*10 reams*	*Personnel*	*183*	*19 reams*
7 "		*2 reams*	*Production*	*221*	*17 reams*
10 "	*80 reams*				*97 reams*
15 "		*5 reams*	*Accounts*	*371*	*92 reams*

The information may be held on a visible edge record card, so that the main details are recorded at the bottom.

The cards are usually stored in alphabetical order. When an item is issued it is recorded clearly on the card and the new balance calculated. This balance should be compared with the minimum amount of stock allowed *each time goods are issued*. When the stock gets near its re-order level the card may be flagged with a special coloured clip or symbol as a warning.

When the re-order level is reached then the item must be marked for re-order. Only when the goods are received, checked and unpacked is the card updated. Whilst the goods are actually on order the card may be flagged with a different coloured clip or symbol to denote that you are now waiting for new stock to arrive.

TEST YOURSELF

1   Draw up *three* record cards (or use prepared cards provided by your tutor). Complete them for the following items.

shorthand notebooks
Supplier: Ace Office Products Ltd
Max. – 200 books   Min – 50 books
Units – 10 books

A4 white bond paper
Supplier: Copynational Ltd
Max. – 100 reams   Min – 20 reams
Units – reams

DL white banker envelopes
Supplier: Ace Office Products Ltd
Max. – 3000 envelopes Min – 500 envelopes
Unit – packs of 50

2   Your opening balances should now be entered as at 1 December 19—

Shorthand notebooks – 80
A4 white bond paper – 35 reams
DL white banker envelopes – 1250

3   You issue stationery against authorised requisitions weekly. Your
December requisitions are as follows. Book out the stock issued in
each case.

Date	Dept	Req. No	Items required
3/12	Sales	105	5 reams bond paper 4 shorthand books 6 packs envelopes
3/12	Personnel	217	10 shorthand books 6 reams bond paper
10/12	Accounts	521	3 reams bond paper 2 packs envelopes
15/12	Purchasing	307	5 reams bond paper 3 packs envelopes
17/12	Personnel	218	8 shorthand books 4 packs envelopes

4   Consult the final balance on each of your stock cards and decide
which items you need to re-order before the Christmas holiday.

5   Bearing in mind that management will keep a check on how much is
ordered by each department, examine each of the requisitions you have
received carefully. Think why each of the items may be required. Do
you consider any department is using any item to excess? If so, which?

Discuss your answers with your supervisor or tutor.

The advantages and disadvantages of manual systems

Advantages

● Cards are easy to complete and store.
● Cards can be updated in the stock room, in an office or even at home!

- The information on all items is available at a glance.
- The system is easy to follow.

Disadvantages

- Cards are difficult to analyse, e.g. suppose you had to tell your boss, in five minutes, which items are the most 'active' and which the most 'inactive'.
- Excessive ordering by one department may be difficult to spot.
- A manual stock check sheet must be made out, listing all items and their current balance, for each stock inventory carried out.

Many of these problems can be solved if the company operates a computerised system.

Computer stock control systems

If the system is computerised, the stock control clerk will use a form of database package which has been specially designed for stock.

Stock record cards are brought up on screen and information is inserted under headings such as

- name of item
- cost of one unit
- description of unit, e.g. kg, dozen, gross
- quantity in stock
- minimum stock
- re-order quantity
- quantity on order (required to stop the computer repeatedly giving reminders that this item is low)
- supplier's name and address.

There is also usually a brief **code** field. This is so that you can enter a short code for each item. The code is used to find a specific record very quickly. (*If you have forgotten about codes, look back at Unit 6, page 231.*)

TEST YOURSELF

From the information given above, design a suitable record card for a computerised system. Bear in mind that alongside each heading you will need a **field** for the data. Show the length of fields you think you would need in each case.

Booking stock in and out

One the system has been set up, and a record completed for each item kept in stock, the system must be kept up to date by recording all stock issued and received.

On most systems this is done by searching for the appropriate record and then instructing the computer whether the stock should be booked *in* or *out*. You will then usually be prompted to enter the quantity.

The computer then automatically recalculates the 'Quantity in stock' field to show the current amount.

Stock control reports

The main advantage of having a computerised system is that a variety of reports can be produced to show the state of current stock, e.g.

- a print-out of all the stock at cost price, which gives an instant valuation of all the stock held
- a list of all stock which needs to be re-ordered (*see illustration page 221*)
- a stock check list – which can easily be completed during a stock inventory (*see example below*)
- a stock turnover analysis – which shows the quantity issued over a certain period and therefore shows you your most active items.

STOCK INVENTORY CHECK LIST			
Code	**Description**	**Current Stock**	**Actual Stock**
A4RINGB	A4 Ring Binders – Black	52	
A4RINGR	A4 Ring Binders Red	27	
A4RINGG	A4 Ring Binders – Green	18	
BOND	A4 Bond typing paper	60	
CLIPS	Foldover Clipboards	25	
DISKS3	Floppy Disks – 3 ½"	50	
DISKS5	Floppy Disks – 5 ¼"	12	
DIV5	Dividers – packs of 5	68	
DIV10	Dividers – packs of 10	35	
ERASERS	Pencil Erasers	80	

Adjustments and audits

After a physical stock check it may be necessary to make adjustments to allow for damaged goods, loss, obsolete items and so on. On most packages, when you make an adjustment you also have to give a reason for doing so!

These reasons are required if you run an **audit trail**. This is a comprehensive report which shows every computer entry which has been made over a given period (normally since the last audit trail was made). Explanations are printed alongside any unusual items, such as adjustments.

The accountant or manager in charge of stock would normally require to see this report at regular intervals.

DID YOU KNOW?

Some stock control packages are linked with computerised accounts packages so that the value of stock ordered and issued is automatically transferred to the main accounts.

TEST YOURSELF

Draw up a list of advantages and disadvantages of a computerised stock system, similar to the one shown for manual systems on pages 381–2. Check your notes with your supervisor or tutor.

CHECK IT YOURSELF

Find out about the type of stock control system used in your organisation. If a manual system is in operation obtain copies of a blank record card and practise inserting information from the exercise you did earlier. Find out if any additional information is required and, if so, what this is and where you would find it.

If a computer system is used, take a print-out of a stock record. Find out what reports can be printed and, if possible, obtain some examples.

Time periods and emergencies

The frequency with which stock is issued will depend on the size of the organisation, its standard procedures and the amount of flexibility which is allowed.

In some companies stock can be accessed virtually **on demand** provided the correct forms have been completed. This means people don't have to think in advance about their needs.

At the other extreme is the company which issues stock at fixed time periods, e.g. once weekly. This may be because the stock clerk does another job on other days. In this case people submit their orders each week, knowing that they will receive their goods on a specific day the following week.

Emergencies are more likely to occur under this system because people have forgotten an important item, or something is needed unexpectedly.

The other type of emergency is, of course, that there is a sudden increase in demand for a popular item and stocks run out – or someone forgot to re-order something in the first place!

Dealing with problems

It is quite possible that your company has a standard procedure for dealing with emergencies. If so, it is important that you find out what this is and do not make decisions outside your own area of authority. Always check if you are not sure what to do.

Issuing stock 'outside hours'

If someone has a *real* problem because of an unexpected requirement then you will be considered most unhelpful if you do not assist them, and you will hardly be helping the work flow! (*Remember Unit 3?*) However, this is totally different from coping with someone who never follows the official system and expects you to drop what you are doing immediately they have one of their regular crises! If you suffer from this problem discuss the matter with your supervisor.

Obtaining emergency supplies

You may be out of stock of an item because

- it wasn't ordered
- the supplier is out of stock
- it was never required before.

Don't start ringing around suppliers without obtaining permission beforehand! If this is acceptable, a good policy is to try several suppliers to see who could deliver the item the soonest (or have it ready to be collected). Bear in mind that you may be offered a substitute item and you should consult the person who requires the goods to see if this would be acceptable. Finally, remember to check the price and make sure that this is acceptable with your supervisor!

CHECK IT YOURSELF

Find out about the system used in your organisation for dealing with emergency orders. If you can, find out specific examples of when goods have been required in a hurry, why, and what was done to obtain them.

CHECK YOUR KNOWLEDGE AND UNDERSTANDING

True or false?

1 Stock which is used regularly is known as active stock.
2 Heavy items should be stored on the top shelf.
3 COSHH stands for Containers for Substances Harmful to Health.
4 A gross is 124.
5 An order form includes the price of the product, the addition of VAT and any delivery charges.

Fill in the blanks

6 The amount of time allowed for delivery is often referred to as

_____ _____ .

7   The total number of items which are damaged, out of date or surplus to requirements is known as _____ .

8   The amount of stock kept to allow for the time taken for delivery and to keep pace with current requests is called _____ _____ .

Work it out

9   List *six* measures a company can take to minimise expenditure on stationery requirements.

10 You are surprised to find that a delivery you have received from one of your suppliers contains 24 fax rolls – your company has two fax machines, both of which use ordinary plain paper. When you check your order you find that you transposed two figures when you wrote the order number. You actually intended to order fax message pads and, under description, you simply wrote 'fax supplies'.

   a   What would you do *immediately?*
   b   Can you legally insist that the supplier takes the goods back?
   c   What suggestions would you have for minimising your losses if the goods cannot be returned?

BRIGGS AND WATSON LTD
14 Castle Parade
HIGHTOWN
HG4 9KF

Tel: 0678 498203   VAT Reg No: 829/38297/75

ORDER

To: Date:
                                     Order No:

Please supply

Quantity	Description	Cat No.	Unit price

Delivery:

Signed:

Order form for 'Test yourself' on pages 376 and 397.

10 Process documents relating to goods and services

This unit comprises two elements. Element 10.1 relates to ordering goods and services from different suppliers. Element 10.2 involves processing claims for payment – these may be invoices received which relate to goods and services *or* expense claims which have been submitted by staff.

Element 10.1

Order goods and services

The skills you will need

You will need to prove that you can

- understand your instructions completely before you order goods and services
- order goods and services in accordance with authorised procedures
- complete documentation for ordering goods in accordance with specified procedures
- obtain competitive prices, prior to placing an order, where this is applicable.

The knowledge and understanding you will need

You will need to know

- how to order goods and services (and the documents involved)
- the various sources of reference you can use
- what contractual arrangements are in force within your own organisation
- your organisation's policies and procedures
- the procedures required by different suppliers.

What counts as goods and services?

Every organisation purchases a variety of different goods and services. These include

- capital items, such as new buildings, vehicles and expensive equipment
- consumable items, such as stationery and food
- raw materials, which are used in the production of other goods (Think of all the different raw materials used in the production of a car!)

- a variety of services, from window cleaning to repairing all the photocopiers.

DID YOU KNOW?

A company which itself provides a service (such as a bank or insurance company) will not buy raw materials. These will only be purchased by companies which manufacture goods for sale.

CHECK IT YOURSELF

Identify *ten* items which are purchased by your organisation which can be classified as capital items, consumables or services. Try to find examples of each. Check your answers with your supervisor or tutor.

Organisational policies

These will vary considerably depending upon whether the organisation is small or large and, often, whether it is in the private or the public sector.

- In a large organisation, or one which is in the public sector (e.g. a hospital or local authority) there may be very formal procedures for ordering goods. There may also be a list of recommended or specified suppliers of goods and contracts in force with suppliers of certain services, e.g. cleaning or security. The buying of goods may be **centralised** and in this case all orders are dealt with by the purchasing department.
- A small organisation can be more flexible. Suppliers may be changed quite frequently so that the best deal can be obtained. This is because a small organisation cannot buy in bulk so has to **shop around** more. There may be fewer contracts in force, except for essential services.

In *all* organisations there will be procedures in force to prevent staff ordering goods as they please. This is obviously necessary, otherwise staff may duplicate orders and spend money without considering the consequences.

Every organisation has to work to a **budget**. This is the total amount scheduled for purchases over a certain period, usually a year. To make sure the company doesn't overspend, a senior manager is usually in charge and has to approve or **authorise** all orders sent out in the company name. The larger the amount of money being spent, the more senior the person who will authorise the expenditure. A supervisor may be able to order five reams of photocopying paper but the managing director would be involved in authorising a contract to build a new warehouse at a cost of £6 million!

All goods and services must be ordered on official company order forms. Each of these will have a unique order number. The order will have to be signed by the manager who has the authority to authorise the expenditure. The manager can then keep a check on the total amount being spent, and the type of goods being ordered.

DID YOU KNOW?

If you order goods over the phone, most suppliers will ask you for your official order number. If you cannot quote this, they will not process your order. If you give the number, this is confirmation to the supplier that your company will pay for the goods, but they will still expect a copy of the signed official order or a **confirmatory order** to be sent to them by post or fax as soon as possible.

CHECK IT YOURSELF

Find out the official procedure for ordering goods in your organisation. Check

- if this is carried out centrally or by individual departments
- the name(s) of the manager(s) who can authorise orders, and the amounts they are allowed to spend before referring the matter to more senior management
- the procedure you would have to follow to
  - obtain an official order number
  - order urgent items over the telephone
  - obtain permission to buy an expensive item, e.g. a new printer for a computer.

Sources of reference and information

Before you buy any item you should check whether

- there is a specific supplier you must use
- you can compare prices from different suppliers yourself.

If you can compare prices, there are various ways of obtaining the information you need. If you needed three new computer printers, for instance, you could

- obtain catalogues and price lists from computer equipment suppliers
- arrange for representatives to visit you and tell you about the features available on their printers and the prices
- look through business equipment magazines, read the advertisements and send for further details about the printers which interested you
- visit a computer trade fair or exhibition

- keep a file of advertisements and mail shots about computer equipment received through the post
- telephone computer suppliers listed in *Yellow Pages*
- write a letter of enquiry to suppliers in your area.

DID YOU KNOW?

Price lists are often issued *separately* from catalogues so that a new price list can be printed easily whenever prices change without the expense of reprinting the catalogue.

Most price lists are shown in *page order* to match the catalogue but you must be very careful to

- Check the correct catalogue number in the price list against the one shown in the catalogue, as the numbers will vary for different models, colours or sizes.
- Write the number *accurately* when you order. If you transpose the number and the wrong goods arrive, the supplier is under no obligation to take them back!

SPECIAL NOTE

Remember that you cannot easily check the quality of goods from a catalogue, although price may be a guide.

Purchasing procedures

1 When you have obtained the information you need, you need to compare

- the **type** of goods and range stocked by the supplier
- the **price** and **discounts** available
- **delivery times** and **charges**
- length of **warranty** or **guarantee** (if equipment)
- **servicing** or **maintenance** agreements (if applicable).

2 You may be able to order the goods you need directly from the catalogue by completing an official order form and quoting the reference number and quantity of the goods you require.

However, in many cases, you may need a specific **quotation** from the supplier. The quotation states the price at which the goods or service will be supplied and any discounts which are offered. These may include

- **trade discount**, given as an allowance to people in the same type of business or because the buyer is placing a large order
- **cash discount**, given to encourage people to pay promptly. A percentage is taken off the price if payment is made within a certain period. Therefore *5% – one month* on a quotation

would mean that the buyer can deduct five per cent from the price if he or she pays within one month.

Remember that **value added tax** (VAT) is added to the total cost of the goods *after any discounts have been subtracted*. The current rate is 17.5%.

The quotation will also show the delivery date and any delivery charges.

- **Carriage paid** means that the *supplier* will pay for delivery.
- **Carriage forward** means that the *buyer* must pay for delivery.

If the quotation is for a service, then full details of the work covered, or service provided by the quotation will be included.

PARKHURST CONTRACT CLEANERS LTD
Centenary Way
HIGHTOWN
HG5 6TG

Tel 0689-582978   **Fax: 0689-729387**

Q U O T A T I O N

Varey and Makepeace
Accountants
4 Ivory Place
HIGHTOWN
HG2 1AZ   16 February 199-

To: Cleaning of carpets in reception and
    two directors' offices   £46.00

    Plus VAT @ 17.5%   £8.05

                               £54.08

All work to be carried out on Saturday, 10 March.

Signed: *Jane Marchant*

Sales Manager

---

3 You should compare quotations in terms of quality of goods, price and discounts, delivery and after-sales service (if applicable) and then choose the supplier you think would be the most suitable. You should also consider several other factors.

Reputation	Is the company well-established or new? Have you dealt with them before or heard any reports about them?
Location	Is the company situated locally? This might be useful if goods are needed quickly or if they may need to be returned or if after-sales service may be required.
Relationship	Some organisations have a policy of keeping to a few regular suppliers to build up a good relationship with them so that they receive a personal service and priority treatment. Find out if this would affect the range of suppliers you could use.
Credit	A supplier who offers three months' credit would usually be more attractive than one who requires payment in full within one month.

 ## SPECIAL NOTE

Remember that the cheapest is not always the best! It very much depends what you are buying. A hundred cheap pens may be an excellent buy, a cheap photocopier may be quite the opposite, if it keeps breaking down and the company which supplied it goes out of business in two months' time!

 ## DID YOU KNOW?

When you check the price of goods you should do this in the following way.

a Find out the total price of the goods you require.
e.g. 3 × £1000 = £3000

b Deduct any trade discount.
e.g. 10% discount = £3000 – £300 = £2700

c Deduct any cash discount.
e.g. 5% cash discount = £2700 – £135 = £2565.

d Add on the VAT.
e.g. £2565 + 17.5% = £2565 + £448.87 = £3013.87

e Add VAT on to the delivery charge to find the total price of delivery.
e.g. £10 + 17.5% = £11.75

f Add the price of the goods and the price of the delivery charge together.
i.e. £3013.87 + £11.75 = £3025.62.

Notes

● If you decide not to take advantage of the cash discount quoted, then you simply add this figure back on again. If, in the above example, the goods weren't paid for promptly, then the figure of £135 (Step **c**) would have to be added on again. The total price would then be £3160.62.

- If you don't take advantage of the cash discount the VAT figure does not change.
- If certain items don't apply, e.g. no cash discount or no delivery charges, simply omit that stage from your calculations.

Check anything you do not understand in this section *carefully* with your supervisor or tutor, as you will need to check that you can do this properly in Element 10.2.

TEST YOURSELF

You have received *two* quotations for your three computer printers.

- The first is from A1 Supplies Ltd. They have quoted £399 each less 5% trade discount, plus VAT. Delivery is free.
- The second is from Print International Ltd. This quote is for £410 each less 7.5% trade discount and there is an additional 2.5% cash discount if you pay in 14 days. Delivery is £10.

a Which company is offering the better deal?
b What price would you have to pay Print International if you didn't settle the account until after 14 days?

Variations to standard procedures

Tenders

Some companies advertise that they want to buy certain goods or need a certain service providing and ask suppliers to submit **tenders.** A tender is a written offer which states the price at which a supplier is prepared to provide a service or supply certain goods. The buyer will have a closing date for tenders to be received and, on that day, will open them and choose the best one, bearing in mind price, quality, service and time of delivery. The tenders are all opened at a specific time and date *and* at the same time. If they were not, one supplier might find out information which would help to undercut the competition. See below for an example of an advertisement for tenders.

HIGHTOWN EDUCATION COMMITTEE
Education Offices
Railway Road
HIGHTOWN
HG1 3MT

Tel: 0689-627386

TENDERS required for the external painting of 12 primary schools between June and September. Full details and tender forms available on application. Final date for tenders: 16 March 199-.

Estimates

An **estimate** is an alternative to a quotation. However, instead of giving details of the goods or service, an estimate usually gives just a total estimated price. It is therefore much less precise and the buyer cannot complain if the final invoice is slightly different from the original estimated figure. See below for an example of an estimate.

BRIGGS BUILDERS
Openshaw Road
HIGHTOWN
HG5 4TM

Tel: 0689-372862

E S T I M A T E

Parker and Yates Ltd
14 Dewsbury Road
HIGHTOWN
HG9 2JJ   16 March 199-

To rebuilding brick wall at front of
office block   Approx £120.00

A. Briggs
Proprietor

Writing out the order

There are usually **four** copies of an order form.

- The **top** copy is sent to the supplier.
- The **second** copy is kept by the department which ordered the goods (or person who requested them).
- The **third** copy is sent to the accounts department.
- The **final** copy is kept by the purchasing department or staff who ordered the goods.

The order does *not* show details of VAT, delivery charges or total prices but must contain a complete description as well as a reference or catalogue number of the goods.

ORDER
Coombes & Webb Ltd

**15 Devonport Way
PORTSMOUTH
PR6 9KR
Tel: 0705–482937**

TO: Business Supplies Ltd
14 Docklands Parade
SOUTHAMPTON

ORDER NO: 2948/90

DATE: 15 October 19—

Please supply:

Quantity	Description	Catalogue Number	Unit price
250 Reams	A4 white bond paper	K/38279	£3.50 per ream
24	Red lever arch files	K/02938	£1.30 each

Delivery.....as soon as possible..............................

Signed...J Taylor...

Routine orders

Routine orders for repeat goods from regular suppliers are usual in every organisation. If you are responsible for ordering goods then you should check that

- the quantity ordered allows for
  - current stock levels

- lead time (i.e. the gap between order and delivery)
- availability (i.e. whether the goods are in short supply)
- demand (whether it is increasing, static or decreasing)

- the price is unchanged or still within acceptable limits
- discounts are still in force
- credit facilities are unchanged.

Tell your supervisor about any changes; a major change may mean a change of supplier. This is particularly the case with service suppliers, as their prices may change quite considerably from one year to the next.

Special orders

If you are involved in a special order then make sure you understand what is involved before you contact any suppliers or complete any documentation. The more complicated the requirements, the more careful you need to be to ascertain what, exactly, is required. It is far more difficult to obtain suitable quotations to furnish a new office than it is to buy ten new calculators!

If you get it wrong, then at best you will have wasted your own time and those of the suppliers you contact. At worst you could complete an order form for the wrong goods, and if this is not checked by anyone, or signed in a hurry, you could be faced with serious problems when the goods are delivered!

Chasing up orders

If you are responsible for ordering any type of goods it is useful to keep a master list of items which are on order and tick each item when it has been delivered. This will show you at a glance if any items are outstanding. You can then telephone the supplier to find out what has happened. Possibilities are that

- they never received the order
- the goods are out of stock.

If the order was lost in the post (or in their office!) you should fax them a duplicate immediately and ask for the goods to be delivered urgently.

If the goods are out of stock then you must check when the suppliers next expect a delivery, then find out from the person who needed the goods if the delay is acceptable. If it is not, you may need permission to contact alternative suppliers to see if the goods can be obtained more quickly.

CHECK IT YOURSELF

Obtain a copy of the standard order form used by your organisation. Find out

- what checking procedures are in force to chase up late deliveries

- your organisation's policy if your usual supplier is out of stock of urgently required goods.

TEST YOURSELF

1 Write a letter of enquiry to be sent to office equipment suppliers in your area about a plain paper fax machine. Your organisation is considering buying two of these machines and wants them to have the following features.

- activity logging
- page memory so that messages can be stored in memory and sent out later
- polling
- the ability to transmit photographs

The machines should be suitable for quite frequent usage.

Check your final letter with your supervisor or tutor.

Note: *Check back to Unit 8 if you are unsure what some of these features mean!*

2 Your organisation has a standard list of suppliers for most of its consumables. Your ink jet printer takes special cartridges which cost £13.50 each from the company you have been told to use. You are allowed to order up to six each month and need this number for the amount of work you produce.

Recently you have been having severe problems with this supplier. On two occasions they were out of stock and you very nearly ran out of cartridges as it took nearly a month for them to be delivered. There is poor customer service when you phone to enquire about your orders and now you have found that they have increased the price to £15 per cartridge and a minimum of 12 must be ordered at any one time.

You want to talk to your supervisor about changing to a different supplier.

a What information would you obtain before seeing your supervisor, to help to persuade him or her to use another company?

b Write a memo detailing your problem and giving your suggestions for the future.

3 Assuming your supervisor agrees to a change of supplier, in a computer supplies catalogue find out the price of six cartridges, one mouse mat and a disk box to hold at least 20 3 ½" disks. Make out an order to the supplier for the goods you need *either* on a copy of your official company order form *or* on a photocopy of the order form on page 386 of this book.

Note: The 'Check Your Knowledge and Understanding' section for this unit is on page 410.

Element 10.2

Process claims for payment

The skills you will need

You will need to prove that you can

- verify claims in accordance with organisational procedures
- check calculations for accuracy and validity
- investigate and resolve discrepancies yourself or refer these (if they are serious) to an appropriate authority
- refer and pass on claims you have verified to those people who are authorised to deal with them
- keep accurate, complete and legible records.

The knowledge and understanding you will need

You will need to know

- how to check and verify documents which relate to goods and services ordered by yourself and other people
- how to carry out and check basic calculations – additions, subtractions, multiplications, divisions and percentages
- how you should record the result of your checking procedures
- your organisation's procedures for processing claims for payment
- your organisation's procedures for reporting discrepancies.

What are claims for payment?

Basically, the two types of claims for payment you may have to deal with are

- invoices
- expense claims.

No organisation can afford to pay claims without checking them first, and querying any discrepancies. However, the type of checks which are carried out and the variety of discrepancies which may be found will vary, depending upon the type of document being handled.

Checking invoices for payment

After any goods have been delivered or services provided, the supplier wants payment. He or she will therefore send an invoice which lists the goods and the amount owing. This must be checked by the buyer before it is paid. The checks that need to be made include

- that the goods were actually delivered
- that the goods were as ordered in terms of description, quality and quantity

- that the goods are priced according to the original quotation (or suppliers' catalogue)
- that any agreed discounts have been included
- that all calculations are correct.

When goods are delivered they are accompanied by a **delivery note**. This document lists the goods but does not show the price. In some companies the person who unpacks the goods simply ticks them off on the delivery note and makes a note of any problems, e.g. if any goods were missing or marked 'to follow'.

Other organisations have a central point where all goods are received and the staff make out a **goods received note**. This lists all the items in the package and notes any problems or discrepancies.

Both the delivery note and the goods received note are usually sent to the accounts department where they are checked against the invoice when this arrives.

There is usually a seven-stage process involved in verifying invoices and this is given in the chart below.

	Verifying invoices for payment
Stage 1	Assemble the documents you need – quotation, copy order, delivery note and goods received note.
Stage 2	Check the invoice against the quotation/copy order. ● Is the quantity correct? ● Do the descriptions match? ● Are all the prices as quoted? ● Is the discount correct? ● Do the terms of payment match? ● Were you/are you liable for transport charges?
Stage 3	Check the invoice against the GRN or delivery note. ● Were all the goods delivered? ● Were they all in good condition on arrival?
Stage 4	Check the figures. ● Are all the calculations accurate? ● Is the date correct?
Stage 5	If this is a VAT invoice ● Is the supplier's VAT number shown? ● Is the tax point the same as (or before) the date the goods arrived?
Stage 6	Check the file. ● Is this a duplicate invoice sent by mistake?
Stage 7	Approve invoice for payment.

Service invoices

Invoices for services may be more difficult to check as you may not know whether the service was provided at the right time and whether it was carried out properly or according to the original request. The procedure in many organisations is for specified managers to be responsible for authorising the payments for services which relate to their departments.

Again, however, calculations and the risk of duplication must still be checked before the invoice is approved for payment.

DID YOU KNOW?

Many organisations have a reference system which clearly indicates the person who ordered the goods or service. This means that it is an easy matter to check with the person concerned that everything is in order, without having to hunt high and low throughout the organisation.

VAT invoices

Most invoices will include an amount for value added tax. However, you should note that only companies who are registered for VAT, and quote their VAT number clearly on the invoice, are allowed to charge VAT.

VAT invoices need special care as your organisation can **reclaim** some of the VAT it has paid when it completes its **VAT return**.

On a VAT invoice you will see the term **tax point**. This usually corresponds to the date of the invoice and indicates the date that the ownership of the goods was transferred from the seller to the buyer. VAT must be charged in the same period in which the goods are delivered. It is not legal to hand goods over and then defer invoicing them so that VAT is due much later.

DID YOU KNOW?

The letters **E & O E** at the bottom of an invoice stand for 'errors and omissions excepted'. This means that if the supplier has made a genuine mistake when the invoice was produced and charged you too little, they have the right to send you a supplementary invoice for the difference.

Processing invoices for payment

Ideally a variety of people should be involved in checking an invoice, especially if it is for a large amount of money. It should not be the responsibility of just one person.

Usually the document is stamped with a rubber stamp showing the stages it must pass through. As each person carries out their function they initial the appropriate box.

ACCOUNT VERIFICATION		
Item	**Status**	**Verified by**
Goods received		
Invoice details match order		
Invoice details match GRN		
Invoice correct		
Payment approved .... (signed)		

DID YOU KNOW?

In very large companies it may be uneconomic to employ someone to check every invoice, especially those for very small amounts. In this case invoices over a certain figure, e.g. £100, would be checked and smaller totals would be **batch checked**, i.e. certain invoices would be checked at random.

Types of discrepancy

Below are some reasons why an invoice would not be passed for payment.

- The invoice may have been incorrectly completed, e.g. with the wrong goods, price or quantity.
- Items may have been delivered at different times (in a split order) and so more than one GRN would have to be found and checked.
- The GRN could have been incorrectly completed and contain inaccurate or insufficient information.
- The person receiving the goods may not have checked them properly e.g. some may have been reported damaged and returned at a later date.
- Invoices are often printed by computer or typed. GRNs are more likely to be completed by hand. If someone's handwriting is illegible it may be impossible to check the GRN against the invoice.

Problem solving

If you find a mistake or discrepancy on an invoice you must know how to deal with it. The procedure is often different in small and large organisations. In a large organisation the problem would be referred to a supervisor. In a small organisation the clerks in the accounts department may have to sort it out themselves.

- If the discrepancy is small and the organisation is one which is dealt with regularly, it is normal to telephone them to point out the error. They may issue a replacement invoice, but are more likely to send a **supplementary invoice** or a **credit note** for the difference.

● If the discrepancy is large it is better to write to the organisation, as any correspondence will then be on file and can be referred to later if there is a dispute.

● If there are regular discrepancies from a particular organisation then a more formal **letter of complaint** may be sent by the manager.

DID YOU KNOW?

A **reputable** company points out errors whether they are being overcharged or undercharged! Most companies would rather keep their reputation than save a few pounds by keeping quiet about a mistake which will probably be discovered by the supplier at a later date.

Paying the account

When the invoice has been authorised for payment, the accounts department will pay the supplier, usually by cheque. In many cases the company waits until a **statement** has been received from the supplier showing the balance owing to date. This document is also checked before the cheque is sent. However, if a company can take advantage of cash discount terms by paying more promptly, it is more likely that payment will be made before the statement is due.

CHECK IT YOURSELF

Find out about the procedure in your organisation for verifying invoices. In particular, check

● whether *all* invoices are checked or only those for large amounts
● the stages through which each invoice must pass before it is allowed to be paid
● how discrepancies are reported, and to whom
● to whom you should pass invoices once they are correct
● what records are kept to record discrepancies or problems.

TEST YOURSELF

1 Study the order and GRN opposite carefully and the invoice on page 404 and then write down your answer to the following questions.

 a Can payment of the invoice be authorised? If not, list the discrepancies you have found.
 b What action should now be taken?

2 Brainstorm other reasons why someone checking invoices against orders and GRNs may not be able to authorise payment. Write a list of your ideas and check this with your supervisor or tutor.

QUALPRINT LTD
22 CARNEI WAY
GLENDALE
NEWSHIRE
FE1 8CA

TEL 032 745612   **ORDER**   VAT REG NO: 680/73842/88

TO   Business Supplies Ltd   DATE: 23rd October 199–
     14 Docklands Parade
     GLENDALE   ORDER No. 121/934
     FE2 8DJ

PLEASE SUPPLY

QUANTITY	DESCRIPTION	Ref No	Unit price
10 Packs	A4 Superlux Card Blue	SL/3	£11
3 Boxes	Blue ball pens	BP/4	£3.20
50 Sheets	A3 Card White	C/A3/W	20p

DELIVERY   As soon as possible

SIGNED   *G. Gaston*

QUALPRINT
Goods Received Note

Supplier:

Business Supplies Ltd
14 Docklands Parade
Glendale.
Fe2 8DS.

GRN No.: *1081*
Date: *31 OCT 199–*
Delivery Note *121/934*

ORDER NO.	QUANTITY	DESCRIPTION	REF NO.
121/943	*3 Boxes*	*Ball pens*	*BP/3*
	10 packs	*superlux card Blue*	*SL/B*
	40 sheets	*white A3 (card)*	*A3W*

Received by _____

```
              BUSINESS SUPPLIES LTD
              14 DOCKLANDS PARADE
              GLENDALE
              GE2 8DJ

  TEL 032 782943                          VAT REG NO. 483/28372/75

  FAX 032 212 314

                        INVOICE

  To:  Qualprint Ltd                      Deliver to:
       22 Carnie Way
       GLENDALE
       NEWSHIRE
       FE1 8CA
```

Your order no.	Invoice date/tax point	Invoice no.	Despatch date
121/934	I Nov 199–	1293	31 Oct 199–

Quantity	Description	Cat. no	Unit price	Total price	VAT rate	VAT amount
10 PACKS	A4 SUPERLUX CARD BLUE	SL/3	£12.00	£120.00	17.5%	£21.00
3 BOXES	BLUE BALL PENS	BP/4	£3.20	£9.60		£1.68
50 Sheets	A3 Card White	C/A3/W	20p	£10.00		£2.75
		Delivery charges		£2.00	17.5%	0.35
		Sub-total		£139.60		
		VAT		£25.43		
		Total amount due		£167.03		

```
  Terms:
  E & O E
```

Checking expense claims for payment

Expense claims are completed by many employees, on either a regular
or occasional basis. Employees who often incur expenses on behalf of
their organisation, e.g. representatives and travelling technical staff, may
have expense accounts, as will company executives. However, other
employees without expense accounts may need to reclaim money if,
for instance, they visit another organisation and spend their own
money on travelling expenses.

Most organisations set a limit to their expense accounts; no executive
or representative is normally allowed to exceed this unless there is a very
good reason. In many companies, staff need written **prior approval**
before they can undertake a journey or other venture which will cost

the organisation money. This **approval form** is then matched with the expense claim. In other cases, senior staff simply countersign the expense claim to show it is valid. In most cases the employee is expected to attach a receipt for all items recorded on the expense claim.

DID YOU KNOW?

Some organisations issue their executives with credit cards. Then the accounts from the credit card companies must also be checked against the expense claims and expense account limit.

Expense codes

Expenses are usually claimed for the following types of item.

- travel fares, or mileage if the employee's own car is used
- company car expenses, e.g. petrol, car parking, repair bills
- meals whilst away on company business (often called **subsistence**)
- business entertaining
- hotel expenses

Each type of expense will have an expense code, and a code column is included on expense forms. The code is usually entered by the clerk who checks the claim and this enables the organisation to analyse expenses to find out

- how much is being spent on each category of expense
- whether the total expenditure on each category exceeds budget limits
- the total amount of expenses which can be allowed against tax.

The claim must also be carefully checked to see that it contains no items which are not allowed to be claimed by the company.

DID YOU KNOW?

If the Inland Revenue considers that a person is benefiting from part or all of an expense payment (rather than simply being repaid) then he or she will have to pay tax on the additional benefit. A businessman who takes his wife on an expenses-paid trip abroad would probably have to pay tax on the amount allowed for her expenses. This is because her presence is not essential but a **bonus** for them both. In the same way, a representative with a company car who receives an amount for petrol will be taxed on a proportion of this money, as the tax authorities will assume some of the petrol was used for private motoring.

Companies can negotiate **dispensations** with the Inland Revenue for expenses which are essential for their employees. A firm which exports goods and entertains many foreign visitors would be able to negotiate higher business entertainment expenses than a firm which only deals with British companies.

Company allowable expenses

The expenses that are classed as **allowable** differ considerably from one organisation to another. They are likely to include

- all expenses which have been negotiated as a dispensation with the Inland Revenue
- all tax allowable expenses, because the company can reimburse the employee and then claim tax relief on the amount paid.

Tax allowable expenses include

- car repairs and expenses
- hotel expenses
- protective clothing and uniforms
- training fees for a course to improve work-related skills
- essential reference books and *business* stationery
- travel on business trips
- subscriptions to work-related professional bodies.

Non-allowable expenses include

- expenditure on ordinary clothes
- examination or resit fees
- travel between home and business
- fines for breaking the law, e.g. parking fines
- interest on credit cards
- ordinary meals (e.g. at or near the workplace).

DID YOU KNOW?

If you pay your own fees for an NVQ course, are over 18 and not on a YT scheme then you probably qualify for tax relief on your course fees, registration fees and other payments you make related to your award. You are allowed this **at source**, which means you pay less when you register or enrol. For further details, get a copy of the leaflet *Tax Relief for Vocational Training* from your local tax office or talk to your college finance office.

Advances

Some executives or representatives who travel regularly, and are not issued with credit cards, may be given advance payments rather than be expected to pay out large amounts from their own pockets. A record of any advance is made and this is deducted from the expense claim before repayment is made. If the advance is not used in full then the difference must be repaid to the company. If the executive was allowed to keep the difference then this amount would be taxable.

CHECK IT YOURSELF

1 Many organisations have slightly different lists of allowable expenses to the one given above. For instance, you may find that your

organisation is willing to pay your course fees *and* any examination fees – or even pay for your travel to work.

Find out which expenses would be allowed by your organisation and which ones would not.

2   Obtain copies of your organisation's (or college's) expense claim forms and talk through the headings and layout with your supervisor or tutor.
3   Find out if a system of expense codes is used and who would enter these on the expense claim form.
4   Find out if any of your executives have company credit cards or are allowed advances. If so, what type of amount is advanced and to whom?

SPECIAL NOTE

Do be aware that in some cases you may be asking for information which is confidential. Be careful how you ask your questions and be prepared for some refusals. For instance, you may be able to find out how much representatives can claim or be allowed as an advance, but not how much the managing director was advanced on his last trip to New York!

Processing expense claims for payment

On receipt, all expense claims should be checked to ensure

- all receipts are attached
- all relevant columns are completed
- all calculations are correct
- all expenses claimed are allowed by the organisation
- any advance has been recorded and deducted from the total
- all mileage claims are accurate.

The accounts clerk then

- enters the expense codes for each item
- signs the form
- passes it for payment or to the supervisor for authorisation for payment.

Some organisations add the amount to be repaid to the person's next wage or salary. Most repay expenses separately, e.g. once a week. If a cash amount is paid then the amount received must be signed for by the recipient, who usually has to collect it personally. A cheque might be sent instead, either by internal or external mail.

DID YOU KNOW?

Most organisations check the figures put down as a mileage claim against standard mileage charts. These can be found in AA books and other road atlases. Most companies have a standard list, which gives the basic mileage from the company base to commonly visited towns and cities.

1 Make sure you can read a mileage chart! Imagine you work for a company based in London. Look on a standard mileage chart and find out how far you would have to travel to visit the following towns and cities.

- Edinburgh
- Cardiff
- Penzance
- Dover
- Manchester
- Oxford

Check your answers with your supervisor or tutor.

2 Find out the procedure for reimbursing expenses in your organisation.

Types of discrepancy

An expense form may not be passed for payment if it

- contains mistakes in calculations
- has no receipts attached
- is unclear, cannot be read or has essential information missed out
- contains claims for non-allowable expenses or expenses which were not previously agreed by a supervisor or manager
- has mileage claims which exceed the normal journey distance
- is for an excessive amount.

Problem solving

- Mistakes in calculations, wrong claims, missing receipts and unreadable forms are usually dealt with by sending the form back to the claimant. If the mistake is only minor the form may be altered and initialled by the clerk. Rather than make several alterations, however, it is usual to ask the claimant to submit a second form and to destroy the first.
- A claim for an expense which was not previously agreed by a supervisor or manager may be sent to that person for his or her agreement. So will a claim for an excessive amount.
- Staff who regularly complete forms wrongly should be referred to the staff handbook or leaflet showing them how to do this correctly.

If you have any queries at all, you must check with your supervisor to find out what you should do. *Never* pass any claim for payment if you are not certain if it is correct.

VAT and expenses

Virtually every expense claim form contains a separate column for VAT. This is because your organisation can reclaim the money it pays on VAT, if it is itself registered for VAT. There needs to be a system, therefore, whereby the accounts office can quickly and easily total the amounts paid out on VAT.

The VAT column is easy to complete when the VAT amount is listed separately on a receipt. This is known as **plus VAT**. However, in other cases the amount paid is **VAT inclusive**, i.e. not listed separately. If you buy food in McDonalds or petrol in a garage the amount you are charged is inclusive of VAT – you are not told how much the VAT amount is.

In these cases, it may be your job to calculate the VAT inclusive amount.

Working out VAT inclusive amounts

A representative spends £92 on petrol in a week. The VAT rate is 17.5%. The formula to find the VAT included in the £92 is given below.

$$\text{VAT} = \frac{\text{rate of VAT}}{\text{VAT rate} + 100}$$

At the current VAT rate this results in

$$\frac{17.5}{117.5}$$

which cancels down to

$$\frac{7}{47}$$

If you have a calculator then enter $92 \times 7 \div 47$ and round your answer to two decimal places.

Your answer should be £13.70.

This is the amount of VAT paid on the petrol.

The cost of the petrol itself was therefore £92 – 13.70 = £78.30.

You can double check this by using the opposite formula.

$$£92 \times \frac{40}{47}$$

This should give you the same answer (once you round the result again).

The formula can obviously be applied for any rate of VAT, to find out the inclusive amount, although obviously the fraction will change each time.

TEST YOURSELF

What would be the inclusive amount of VAT for each of the following petrol expenses?

a £130   **b** £45
c £60.20   **d** £165.85

Check your answers with your supervisor or tutor.

A final word on confidentiality

Whatever documents you process for payment you must be aware that much of your work will be of a confidential nature. You should *not* discuss

- which organisations are bad payers and how much they owe
- which members of staff can't add up, write legibly, spell properly or work out their own expenses
- the actions (and/or mistakes) of your colleagues
- the amount of money spent on business expenses by senior members of staff.

If you talk about other people's mistakes you can't blame them if they start to discuss yours! And if you start to spread the word that the sales manager spends a fortune whenever he or she goes abroad you could be in serious trouble – and totally misjudging him or her unless you know what is involved in each of the trips.

CHECK YOUR KNOWLEDGE AND UNDERSTANDING

True or false?

1 A delivery note is completed by the supplier.
2 VAT is calculated on an invoice after trade discount has been deducted.
3 All receipts list VAT separately.
4 Only VAT registered suppliers can charge VAT on items they sell.
5 All expenses are allowable against tax.

Fill in the blanks

6 The amount allowed on some invoices for prompt payment is called

_____ _____ .

7 The term _____ _____ means the buyer must pay for delivery.
8 If a company negotiates with the Inland Revenue that no tax will be paid on certain expenses this is known as a _____ .

Work it out

9 You need *two* new computers in your office and have obtained catalogues from several major suppliers. You know the model of computer you wish to buy and have found that this is only advertised by three of the suppliers.

- Computalk, situated locally, is a new company. They want payment in full with order. The price of each computer will be £1450 + VAT. They do not offer a discount but there are no delivery charges. You have heard mixed reports about this company.
- Data Supplies is situated 200 miles away and has been in business for many years. They are quoting £1550 + VAT. They offer 6% trade discount on all orders over £3000. Delivery charges are £20. You

have one month to pay if you buy from them but have no information on their reputation.

● Rainbow Computers is a large company situated 20 miles away. It has been in business for the past three years and has an excellent reputation. Their quote is £1600 + VAT less 5% cash discount for payment within two weeks of order. Delivery charges are £10.

    a Calculate the price you would have to pay if you bought from each supplier.

    b Decide which supplier you would use, taking into account all the information given above, and give reasons for your decision.

    Check your answers with your supervisor or tutor.

10 Overleaf is shown the expense claim form of Ian Bretherton, a new employee who started with your company last month.

    a Check his expense claim carefully. List any errors you find and then calculate the correct amounts. (Assume that his claim that he hasn't received any advances is correct.)

    b Calculate the amounts, excluding VAT, and the VAT columns for all the petrol entries at the current VAT rate. Note that the taxi fare is *not* liable for VAT.

    c Work out the new totals and the final amount due.

    d What documents should Mr Bretherton have attached as evidence of his claims?

BRYANTS & COLE LTD
EXPENSE CLAIM FORM

NAME Ian Bretherton	EMPLOYEE NO 4398	WEEK ENDING 5/3/19-

DATE	EXPENSE CODE	DESCRIPTION	AMOUNT (ex VAT)	VAT	AMOUNT (inc VAT)
1 March	104	Taxi fare - office to Carlton Hotel & return			7.50
	112	Restaurant bill - Five Feathers entertaining Mr Blythe & Mr Hinde of Databank Computers	82.50	14.44	96.94
2 March	101	Petrol - Bristol-Liverpool (185 miles @ 27.6p per mile)			42.56
	115	Hotel accommodation Waterloo Hotel Liverpool	45.00	7.87	52.78
3 March	101	Petrol - Liverpool-Bristol (185 miles @ 27.6p)			42.56
4 March	101	Petrol Bristol-Gloucester & return (72 miles @ 27.6p)			19.87
CLAIMED BY: Ian Bretherton			127.50		244.21

AUTHORISED BY:	LESS ADVANCES PAID OUT:	
	TOTAL AMOUNT DUE	244.21

11 Organise travel and accommodation arrangements

This unit consists of two elements. Element 11.1 involves making travel arrangements by road, rail, sea and air for individuals and groups. Element 11.2 relates to your ability to book accommodation, both for overnight stays and other events.

Element 11.1
Arrange travel for persons

The skills you will need

You will need to prove that you can

- understand instructions for travel requirements
- make sure that the travel arrangements you make conform to specified instructions and organisational procedures
- provide a clear, accurate schedule or itinerary, containing all the arrangements made, for the person making the journey
- make sure that travel documents are complete and accurate
- conform to your organisation's security and confidentiality requirements
- make all travel arrangements within agreed deadlines.

The knowledge and understanding you will need

You will need to know

- the different forms of travel – road, rail, sea and air – and how these compare
- how to make arrangements for individuals and for groups
- how to make travel bookings
- how to prepare itineraries
- how to calculate the cost, route and method of travel
- your organisational rules and procedures on travel
- your organisation's security and confidentiality requirements
- how to understand international time zones.

Organisational procedures for arranging travel

There are very few organisations (if any!) which do not require travel arrangements to be made for staff. Executives, representatives and administrative staff may be involved in making journeys to customers and clients, suppliers and service organisations to attend meetings, conferences and seminars on a variety of topics.

The procedures for planning these trips, making bookings and obtaining tickets and other travel documents will vary, depending on the size of the organisation and the number of times travel arrangements have to be made.

- A small organisation is unlikely to have any specialist staff and will use the services of their local travel agent.
- A larger organisation may have one or two specialist staff who deal with travel arrangements on a centralised basis, but who liaise with the business section at a local travel agents for additional help, advice and for making certain bookings.

In some cases you may want to contact different transport organisations directly (and you will be doing this in the course of working through this unit). However, this is more usual for obtaining information rather than making actual bookings.

DID YOU KNOW?

- Some organisations make so many travel arrangements in the course of a year that they may find it cost-effective to set up their own travel section and employ specialists. However, this is very rare and they are still likely to ask external travel agents to make certain bookings on their behalf.
- The travel agent used is likely to belong to the Association of British Travel Agents – ABTA.

Travel information and planning the trip

The first stage in arranging a trip is planning. If this is done properly, there is less to do later – so never skimp on making sure that you have all the information you need and that you understand exactly what you have to do. Basically you need information on

- how many people are travelling
- the date(s) they are leaving and the date they are returning
- where they are going
- their preferred method of travel
- whether they have any individual requirements, e.g. in relation to disabilities, special dietary needs or language assistance
- whether the cost of the trip is limited in any way.

Therefore all your planning can be categorised under four main headings – **where**, **when**, **who**, **how**.

Remember that the rules for travel within an organisation may limit the type of travel allowed and/or the cost. Check this before you start to plan.

Remember, too, that on many business trips plans have to be altered at the last moment. Another person may need to go as well, another company may be visited in the same trip, dates may have to be flexible, or the return date may need to be left open.

DID YOU KNOW?

It cannot be emphasised enough that you *must* obtain clear information before you start and *understand* what you are doing. You are hardly likely to be popular if you make a booking for three technicians to visit Bavaria instead of Bulgaria because you weren't listening! Misunderstanding travel requests can cost an enormous amount of time and money, *and* make you an extremely unpopular person within your organisation!

CHECK IT YOURSELF

Find out the procedures and rules which apply either in your own organisation or in your college (ask your tutor)!

In particular, check

- who deals with travel arrangements (or whether people can make their own)
- which travel agent is used
- what *internal* documents must be completed for each trip
- whether there are any restrictions on method of travel (e.g. if car, train or plane to a UK main city would all be allowed).

Methods of travel

Essentially, there are four main methods of travel to choose from: road, rail, sea and air. The one you choose will usually depend on

- the distance involved
- the amount of time available
- the reason for the trip
- the budget available.

Many organisations believe that speed is the most important consideration, especially for senior executives. They would therefore usually expect the most rapid method to be used (usually air travel) so that the executive can be there and back as quickly as possible.

However, nowadays there are many trips on which you can mix methods of travel for the best result, and the scope for doing this for continental trips will increase when the Channel Tunnel is fully operational.

Road transport

Road transport includes

- private or company car
- hire car

- taxi
- coach or minibus.

Private or company car

Many people prefer to take their own car with them on fairly short trips, and many business executives who regularly travel on business will have company cars. It is usual for organisations to ensure that these staff are members of a motoring organisation, such as the AA or RAC. In addition to operating a 'get you home' breakdown service, both these organisations can provide information on driving abroad. The AA also operates an information service on route planning, which is useful if your boss is planning to drive on the continent.

DID YOU KNOW?

If your boss is using his or her own car to drive to the airport then there are several organisations which offer secure airport parking at a daily rate. Alternatively, if your boss spends the previous night at an airport hotel, he or she may be able to leave the car there for a specified number of days – though this may be at the owner's risk.

Hiring a car

This is a useful alternative if the traveller

- does not have his or her own car
- is travelling to a country by air and then driving from one place to another (especially if a left-hand drive car is required)
- needs a special car or van for a particular reason (e.g. to transport goods).

A variety of vehicles will be offered to you. Discuss the options carefully – you don't want to book a Fiat Panda or equivalent for the managing director on a sales promotion trip to important customers! Usually price is your best guide if you are not sure of the makes and models.

Be aware that there may be certain restrictions in relation to

- the age of the driver (normally minimum age 21, sometimes 23)
- the number of drivers (you normally pay more if other people want to drive as well)
- where the car can be collected or delivered
- the type of driving licence held; some companies insist upon a 'clean' licence with no endorsements for motoring offences.

Cars can be hired on an unlimited mileage basis or with an additional charge for mileage above a specified limit. Most business people pay by credit card so that there is no problem if some extras are involved. This can be very important abroad – you may think everything has been paid in the UK, only to find that delivery and petrol are charged for upon collection.

In some cases a hire car can be obtained at discount rates if it is linked with air or rail bookings (particularly if your boss is a frequent traveller). Check with your travel agent for details.

DID YOU KNOW?

There is a considerable difference between driving in this country and driving abroad. Most national hire car companies, e.g. Hertz, Avis, Europcar issue help sheets to drivers which gives hints and tips on

- road signs and motoring regulations abroad
- additional documents required – some countries require an International Driving Permit, vehicle registration documents and a Green Card to be available at all times. A Green Card is issued by the driver's insurance company and confirms that the UK insurance cover has been extended to cover European countries
- toll roads, speed limits and 'fast' roads (not usually called motorways) abroad
- obtaining petrol and what to do in case of a breakdown or accident.

As an alternative, ask your travel agent or the AA or RAC for information.

CHECK IT YOURSELF

Find out the names for 'motorways' in Germany, Italy and the United States.

Taxis

Taxis are frequently used by people who do not have their own transport. It may be cheaper to get your boss to the airport by taxi than paying for airport parking for a company car for three days while he or she is away!

It is a good idea to keep a list of local taxi companies which have proved reliable, reasonably priced and have good drivers in well-maintained cars.

Bear in mind too, that many taxi companies also offer a luxury limousine service for special occasions, e.g. for collecting three top executives who are due to arrive from abroad.

Coaches and mini-buses

Coaches are rarely used by business travellers, unless they really detest travelling by train! Your local National Express office can supply details of coaches travelling throughout Britain.

A coach or mini-bus may be hired if you have several people to transport from one place to another. You may be able to hire a mini-bus and provide your own driver – but check if any special driving restrictions are in force.

TEST YOURSELF

Your boss is travelling to Manchester on Tuesday to visit a customer, then flying to Dublin and returning in three days' time. Your company is 85 miles from Manchester. There are *three* options you could recommend.

- He takes his company car to Manchester, reserves a secure parking space (at £2.50 per day) and then drives back.
- He stays overnight at a Manchester airport hotel on Tuesday at the rate of £40 bed and breakfast – he can then leave his car there for nothing.
- He hires a car for Tuesday at the rate of £24.50 and drops this off at the airport. He can then return by taxi (quoted rate £15). This would mean that his car would be available for other users in the company car pool whilst he is away.

1 Which alternative would you choose if you were deciding purely on cost?
2 What are the advantages and disadvantages of each alternative?
3 In what ways would your decision be affected by

   a the time of his flight to Dublin
   b the exact location of the customer in Manchester?

Rail travel

Most business people use the InterCity service to travel from one city centre to another. There is also an InterCity Shuttle service linking several provincial cities with London and an InterCity Voyager service for long-distance travellers from Scotland to the south-west of England.

There is a choice between First and Standard class tickets and, on some trains, the option of Silver Standard for travellers who have paid a full fare open or return ticket. A full fare is payable when a journey is made in the main business travel times. As you probably know from travelling on trains yourself, if you travel late morning or early afternoon the fares are usually lower. However, these times will be unsuitable for people with business appointments during the working day.

It is recommended that you make a seat reservation for your boss if he or she is travelling Standard class. You can decide whether to reserve smoking or non-smoking, or facing the engine or not. Seat reservations are issued automatically to First class and Executive ticket holders. Executive tickets include additional facilities, such as car parking and refreshment vouchers. Special waiting rooms, called Pullman Lounges are available at all main InterCity stations for First class ticket holders with a range of facilities, such as fax, working areas and a teletext service.

Always check to see on which trains a First Class Pullman service is available as this means that your boss can be served at his or her seat and can make a reservation for a full meal if required.

You can purchase a ticket at any British Rail station and from travel agencies which are agents for British Rail. However, some companies have their own Rail Travel Account and can make their own reservations by telephone. In this case they will issue a warrant to their staff. In effect, this is like a ticket which states

- the traveller's name
- the date of departure and return
- the journey details
- the class of travel – First or Standard.

After the traveller hands in the warrant at the station, it is then priced by British Rail and an invoice is sent to the company.

British Rail is in the process of being privatised and split into a number of different operating groups. As a person who books travel it is up to you to keep up to date with changes such as to whom Pullman lounges may be available, and the different types of ticket that may be available in different regions.

This is very much developing yourself and your performance!

DID YOU KNOW?

- If you arrange to meet someone from a train you should always check the name of the station! In many cities in the UK and abroad there are several different stations (think of London), and you could be left standing at the wrong one for a long time if you forget to check this basic piece of information!
- Most trains these days have telephones installed. Make sure the people for whom you make bookings know this – and that they should carry a Phonecard or credit card with them.

CHECK IT YOURSELF

1 Contact the main InterCity service number on 081 200 0200 and ask for a copy of the latest *InterCity Guide*. Read this and check the services now available are the same as detailed in the text above.

2 **a** Find out how your organisation makes rail travel reservations and if warrants are issued.
   b State *two* advantages to the traveller of the warrant system.

3 Go to your nearest main railway station and visit the Travel Centre. Identify the information they provide and booklets they stock. Try to obtain a selection of timetables. If your nearest station is too far away

then your local Rail Appointed Travel Agent should be able to help you.

4 Practise reading rail timetables and comparing fares.

    a Identify the best business train for your boss if he or she wanted to travel on a Wednesday, from your nearest InterCity station to either London or Edinburgh (depending on where you live). Look for the best facilities and check your answer with your supervisor or tutor.

    b Find out the price of a First class *and* a Standard ticket on this train.

DID YOU KNOW?

- 'Le Shuttle' is the name of the train which will be travelling through the Channel Tunnel. Find out details of the Chunnel and its services by ringing 0345 353535 and asking for an information pack.
- French Railways (or SNCF), DER (the German railway service) and other European railways offer a range of services, most connecting with continental ports. There are several high speed routes – and the French TGV trains travel at very high speeds. Look in your Chunnel information pack for details; you will probably find they enclose details of the French railway service with their other booklets.
- Couchettes are available on some continental trains. These are different from sleepers and bed linen is not always provided – in addition, passengers are not segregated by sex.

Sea travel

The only time sea travel is used by business people is when they are travelling to the Continent and (usually) want to take their cars with them. In the case of journeys to France, the Channel Tunnel may make this option unpopular.

The most common method is a **ro–ro ferry** (ro–ro stands for roll-on, roll-off). These ferries take both cars and lorries to Ireland and the Continent. The cost of the ticket depends on

- the number of passengers
- the length of the vehicle
- the facilities required (e.g. sleeping accommodation with or without private facilities).

Alternatives to France are by Hovercraft from Dover to Calais, or by Seacat from Folkestone to Boulogne. Both take vehicles and travel much more quickly than ferries.

Travellers to the Channel Islands can go by ferry or by catamaran (much quicker) from Weymouth.

TEST YOURSELF

Many ferries operate in the UK. Which country would you be going to, and which sea(s) would you be crossing if you travelled from

- Newcastle to Bergen
- Plymouth to Santander
- Holyhead to Dun Loghaire (pronounced Dun Leary)
- Portsmouth to Le Havre?

DID YOU KNOW?

Travellers taking their cars abroad have to check in at the ferryport or hoverport some time before the crossing (this can be up to one hour). It also takes some time to disembark. You must allow for these additional times when planning the journey. Drivers are also asked not to take their vehicles on board with full tanks of petrol.

CHECK IT YOURSELF

1 Check the time it takes to cross the Channel by ferry by visiting your local travel agent and obtaining a brochure which includes this service.
2 Contact Hoverspeed at Dover by ringing 0304 240241 and ask for a brochure on the Hovercraft or Seacat service. Compare the journey times and prices with those of the ferry services.
3 Compare both of these with the information you received on the Channel Tunnel. Which method do you think most business travellers would use, and why?

Air travel

Most business people travel by scheduled air flights, rather than the charter flights you may use to go on holiday. The three normal classes of travel are

- First class – usually very expensive and only used by VIPs
- Business class
- Economy class.

There are several differences between the three, including

- the size, comfort and spacing of the seats
- the service and type of meals offered
- the check-in procedures
- the price!

You might find the different classes called by different names by various airlines. Business class may be club class or mid–class, for instance. If you think of top, middle, and bottom you can't go far wrong!

You can look up flights yourself if you use the *ABC World Airways Guide* or a flight timetable, but most people prefer to contact their travel agent for instant information. However, this method may be unsuitable if you are planning a long journey with several stopovers.

Before you start your planning check several basic facts.

- Does your boss have any likes or dislikes in relation to particular airlines?
- Is he or she a member of a frequent flier programme with a particular airline? These programmes enable people to gain free flights and other facilities and gifts.
- Are there any particular preferences in relation to time of departure or arrival?
- Which is/are your nearest airport(s) and are there direct flights to the intended destination from there – or will you need connecting flights?

If you are looking up the flight details yourself, try to select two or three alternatives before you ring your travel agent.

When you make the booking check that you know exactly

- from which airport and terminal the flight departs and at which one the flight arrives (Remember many cities have more than one airport!)
- how much checking-in time must be allowed
- the time difference between the destination and the UK (*See also page 425.*)
- the flight number.

DID YOU KNOW?

- If your first choice of flight is full, you can usually join a wait list. If this comes up you will be allocated a seat. In the meantime, make a reservation for your second choice and tell the travel agent to cancel this if the first option becomes available.
- You don't have to specify a return date and flight – you can book an open dated return and your boss can make the return booking at the nearest airline office or travel agent when he or she knows the date of return.
- 'Red eye' flights are those which travel overnight from the USA to the UK. They are so-called because people are tired when they land (and may have red eyes!). If your boss is travelling back on the red eye don't expect him or her in the office and eager for work at 9 am that morning! (*See also page 425.*)
- The shuttle is virtually a 'walk-on' airline service between many major UK airports. No reservation is required, though you may feel safer if you have obtained one.

SPECIAL NOTE

A comparison chart for all the main methods of travel is shown opposite.

Travel comparison chart

Method	Advantages	Disadvantages
ROAD **Private car**	Door-to-door Can choose own time to depart/return Relatively cheap method of travelling	Hold-ups through bad weather, road works, traffic congestion etc. Parking may be difficult/ expensive Long distances tiring
Taxi	Ideal for city areas – no parking problems or difficulties finding the address	More expensive than private motoring
TRAIN	Usually quite fast Depart/arrive from one city centre to another Fairly wide network	May be crowded Peak times expensive May have to change trains on some routes May be delays
SEA **Ferry**	Relatively cheap Regular sailing on popular routes Accommodation available	Slow Can be crowded/noisy Boarding/disembarkation can take time Rough seas can make journey unpleasant
Hover-craft	Rapid method of transport Reasonably priced Regular service	May be cancelled in bad weather Limited number of seats and car spaces
Channel Tunnel[1]	Fastest crossing Regular service 365 days a year No booking required Simplified customs procedure	Quite expensive in peak periods Service not yet tried and tested Not scheduled to start full service until 1995 – but may be more delays

continued overleaf

[1]Not really sea – but an alternative to ferry and hovercraft to cross the Channel.

Method	Advantages	Disadvantages
AIR	Very fast Good facilities at most airports Good service en route Minimal check-in times for domestic flights	Expensive Airports may be several miles from city centre May be delays waiting for connections Bad weather can mean delays, rerouteing or cancellations Baggage weight limited

TEST YOURSELF

1 In the airline trade, airlines and airports are known by identification letters. Which cities or airports do you think are represented by the following letters?

LHR　　MAN　　SYD　　DUB　　JFK　　LGW　　ATH

2 *Either* visit your local reference or college library and obtain a copy of the *ABC World Airways Guide* or obtain a copy of an airline timetable from your local travel agent. Ask for one for an international carrier which covers flights to New York.

Look up a flight from your nearest international airport to New York for the last Tuesday of next month, returning one week later. Note down the time of departure and arrival, and the flight number. Make sure you are certain at which New York airport your traveller would arrive! Check your answer with your supervisor or tutor.

CHECK IT YOURSELF

Find out details of the services offered on a major airline to frequent business travellers. A good airline to contact for information is British Midland on 0322 854000 who will send you details of their Diamond Club and Diamond EuroPass.

DID YOU KNOW?

● Your travel agent is connected by computer to all the major airlines and can therefore not only view flights on offer but also make a reservation at the press of a key.

- Pricing air flights can be difficult as there is quite a complicated pricing structure on some flights. Ask your travel agent or the airline to confirm the price to you.

International time zones

When you planned the journey to New York, you may have noticed that the time of arrival in New York was a lot earlier than you thought it would be, and that the return trip took a lot longer than you expected. In fact, on an eight-hour trip to New York, you can expect the time of arrival to be only three hours after the UK departure time, and the return trip to look as though it takes 11 hours!

The reason for this, of course, is that the time in New York is five hours behind UK time. In fact, if you travel by *Concorde* it can almost look as if you arrive before you set off!

Understanding international time zones isn't difficult until you find that sometimes whole days are affected as well! This is particularly true if someone is travelling from Australia or New Zealand to the UK. If you are not careful you will quote the wrong day of arrival – as the trip appears to take about two days!

You need to bear in mind two basic facts when thinking about time zones.

- People travelling **west** (e.g. from the UK to USA) **gain** time and must put their watches back during the flight.

  If you are looking at a ticket for a westbound flight then **add** the time difference to the journey time as it appears on the ticket.

- People travelling **east** (e.g. from the UK to Japan) **lose** time and must put their watches on during the flight.

  If you are looking at a ticket for an eastbound flight then **deduct** the time difference from the journey time as shown on the ticket.

DID YOU KNOW?

People normally cope better when they are travelling west rather than travelling east. Having to live a few hours over again is easier than arriving somewhere when your body clock thinks it is the middle of the night. Hence the 'red eye' – although passengers on this flight arrive in London at perhaps 8 am, to them it may be 3 am or even earlier!

CHECK IT YOURSELF

If you look in your Phone Book, just before the section giving international codes, you will find a map showing international time zones. This can help you work out the difference between any two places. As a second guide, next to each country listed in the phone book, there is also information on the time difference.

Remember that when British Summer Time is in force, the UK is one hour ahead of GMT.

TEST YOURSELF

The following information gives the times of arrival and departure from various places to and from London. Assuming it is winter (GMT) allow for the time difference shown in each case to calculate the actual journey time. All times are given using the 24-hour clock.

1 London – Montego Bay, Jamaica
  Five hours earlier than GMT
  1250 depart – 1800 arrive

2 London – Singapore
  Eight hours later than GMT
  1000 depart – 0700 arrive a day later

3 London – Barbados
  Four hours earlier than GMT
  0900 depart – 1120 arrive

4 London – Bahrain
  Three hours later than GMT
  1800 depart – 0400 arrive a day later

5 London – Sydney
  Ten hours later than GMT
  2100 depart – 0800 arrive two days later

Making bookings for individuals and groups

Apart from the basic information given previously, you may need to consider additional factors, e.g.

- the special needs of certain individuals
- whether discounts can be obtained for group bookings
- whether different or special arrangements have to be made for certain members of the group.

Individual requirements can include special assistance for disabilities, special dietary requirements and even assistance with the language. All travel organisations will do their best to assist with the first two requests *provided you tell them at the time you make the booking.*

Your ability to negotiate group discounts will vary more with business travel than with holiday bookings. In most cases you will simply pay the standard fare multiplied by the number of passengers. However, it is certainly worth asking, as special offers may be in force at the time you book. Bear in mind that if you are hiring a mini-bus or coach for group travel, you should *always* shop around to compare prices, and tell the operators exactly what you are doing!

If different members of the group have different travel plans, then treat them as separate passengers, each with their own requirements. This is safer than trying to work things out for a group and highlighting the exceptions.

DID YOU KNOW?

- In the front of most planes the seats are removable for wheelchairs to be installed.
- People who are poorly sighted or blind can have special assistance at airports.
- Nearly all airlines serve vegetarian options at meal times as standard practice. Other special requests should be made at the time of booking.

Travel documents

Standard documents

Before anyone can travel abroad they need

- a valid passport
- a visa (if certain countries are to be visited)
- travel insurance
- vaccinations (again, only for certain countries).

All passports issued today in the UK have the maroon European format. A frequent business traveller may have more than one passport, especially if he or she needs visas for many countries.

Your travel agent can tell you if a visa is required for a particular country, and obtain this for you. The passport is sent to the Embassy or Consulate of the country concerned and they put the visa stamp in the passport itself. The visa states clearly the date of expiry by which time the visitor must leave the country. In some cases it can take a few weeks to obtain a visa (which is why it can be useful to own two passports).

Travel insurance can be arranged by the travel agent, although some organisations have special or additional cover included on their company insurance policies for business travellers. You should already know that in the EU there is reciprocal health care cover at a basic level for UK citizens, providing they have obtained form E111.

Your local health centre or your GP can give you details of any vaccinations required. Some take several weeks before they are effective, after which time a certificate is issued which gives the date they were carried out and the date a 'booster' is required.

DID YOU KNOW?

Because of the cost of health care in the United States, you may find that the *minimum* cover on some of these policies is about $1 million! This would cover full medical treatment in the case of a serious accident or emergency.

CHECK IT YOURSELF

1 Visit your local post office and obtain a copy of the leaflet *Health advice to travellers* which also includes form E111.
2 At the same time, obtain a passport application form. Note the details required to send for a UK passport and the address of your nearest passport office.
3 *Either* obtain a copy of a holiday brochure and look in the small print under insurance *or* visit an insurance company and ask for a booklet on travel insurance. Find out which accidents and disasters you would be covered against by taking out this insurance.

Other documentation

When the trip is being planned you may have to document your requirements on an internal form, especially if this is being dealt with by a central travel section. Make sure you complete this neatly and fill in all the details accurately.

Whilst you are unlikely to be expected to write out tickets (especially airline tickets), you may be expected to complete rail warrants or write letters of confirmation, e.g. to car hire or coach firms. If you deal with a transport organisation directly, then you may be expected to complete a booking form.

When you receive confirmation back from the operator, check all the details carefully, to make sure no errors have been made. Assemble the documents neatly, together with the schedule and/or itinerary (*see below*) and go through these with the person travelling. Check carefully that nothing is missing and that all requirements have been met.

TEST YOURSELF

Visit a local travel agent and obtain two brochures which contain booking forms. Complete these, making up relevant details. Then check with your supervisor or tutor that you have done this correctly.

Schedules and itineraries

A **schedule** or **travel itinerary** is simply a programme of events for a trip, which lists all travel and accommodation arrangements, in date and time order for easy reference. It may also contain information on business visits to be made and business documents to be taken.

Some executives prefer their itineraries to be typed on A4 paper, others like a summarised version on a small card they can keep in their pocket for easy reference. Here are the basic facts to remember when preparing an itinerary.

- Type all the dates covered by the trip, the destination and the names of those involved clearly at the top.
- List the arrangements in date and time order. *Always* use the 24-hour clock.
- Give full details in relation to travel and accommodation arrangements, e.g.
  - times of departure and arrival
  - flight numbers and terminals
  - check-in time
  - name, address, telephone and fax number of the hotel or car hire firms.
- Start from home (or office) and return to home (or office). Don't complete your itinerary with your traveller stranded 50 miles from home!

A typical itinerary for a business traveller is shown below.

ITINERARY FOR MISS NAOMI LISHMAN
VISIT TO MUNICH

4 – 6 March

Monday 4 March

0600 Company car from home to Manchester airport

0645 Check-in for flight to Munich

0745 Depart Manchester flight BA 398

0945 Arrive Munich – to be met by Herr Schumacher, German rep

Accommodation booked at Hotel Excelsior, Marie Therese Strasse, Munich.
Tel: (010 49) 89 20 38 29
Fax: (010 49) 89 34 28 73.

Wednesday 6 March

1600 Depart Munich office for airport (taxi)

1715 Check-in for flight to Manchester

1815 Depart Munich flight LH 281

2015 Arrive Manchester

To be met by company car for journey home

Your boss, Sandra O'Connell, is travelling to New York next Wednesday from London Heathrow and returns one week later. You have booked her ticket with Virgin airlines. She leaves Heathrow at 1400 hours and arrives at JFK airport at 1540 on VS003. Her return flight is shown as departing at 1815 hours and arriving at 0700 the following day, flight number VS004. A minimum of two hours is required for check-in procedures both ways.

You have arranged for a company car to take her from the office to Heathrow on her outward journey and to collect her and take her home when she returns. Your office is two hours' drive away from Heathrow and Ms O'Connell's home is 90 minutes drive away from Heathrow.

Work out details of the journey times and prepare her itinerary.

Finance abroad

No traveller should leave the UK without sufficient money to pay for the items he or she will require during the trip. The range of options taken to cover this includes the following.

Foreign currency

Some is always required (for taxis, tips, cups of coffee etc.) although it should be kept to a minimum for security. Some countries have restrictions on the amount of local currency you can obtain in the UK or take out of their country. Your travel agent or bank will give your details.

Travellers' cheques

These are available from banks and travel agents in different denominations. The most useful are sterling or dollar cheques which, in some countries, can be used instead of cash in hotels, restaurants and shops – especially in the USA. In other countries it is necessary to cash them in a bank, and the holder must produce his or her passport as proof of identity.

When travellers' cheques are purchased they should be collected by the person who will be using them, as they must be signed in front of the bank or travel agency clerk. A list must be made of all the numbers and kept in a safe place, separate from the cheques.

The cheques are signed once again when they are cashed. If any are lost or stolen the holder must notify the nearest bank office (from an issued list) and can then collect replacements *at no extra charge*.

Credit cards (Mastercard and Visa)

These are acceptable in most countries abroad and can also be used to obtain cash from banks and cash machines. Regular business travellers usually have *both* types of card as one or other will nearly always be acceptable. Each cardholder is given a personal credit limit; having two cards also extends this.

Charge cards (e.g. American Express and Diners Club)

These cards vary in that there is no spending limit *but* the account must be settled in full each month. They are very useful for business travellers who may have to make expensive purchases whilst abroad (e.g. additional airline tickets).

Eurocheques and Eurocard

These are like ordinary cheque books and guarantee cards and can be used to pay for goods abroad or to obtain cash from banks and cash machines. They are acceptable in many places on the Continent and in some other countries outside Europe.

DID YOU KNOW?

Many airlines, petrol companies, hotels and car hire firms issue their own charge cards which usually give discounts to the holder.

CHECK IT YOURSELF

1 Find out what credit and charge cards are used by executives in your organisation and whether these are held individually or are company cards.
2 Find out the difference between an ordinary credit card and a gold card.
3 Contact two or three local banks and travel agents and ask them how much they would charge for supplying you with £500 of sterling travellers' cheques. Compare the rate offered in each case and find out which would be your local best buy.

TEST YOURSELF

1 Look up today's exchange rate in a national newspaper. Then calculate how much you would receive in foreign currency if

● your boss requires £400 in US dollars
● you need to obtain £250 in German marks
● you are asked to get £300 in French francs.

2 Your boss has just returned from Canada with $250. How much would you receive in sterling if you returned this to the bank?

A final word on travel arrangements

You should now have a much better idea of what is involved in making travel arrangements on behalf of your organisation. However, there are a few additional rules which you should always bear in mind and which apply to *all* forms of travel.

- Remember that deadlines are critical when you are making travel arrangements, so treat these jobs as urgent and important! This is particularly the case if you are offered an option and have to confirm it quickly.
- Start a travel file containing timetables, leaflets and other useful information – then you don't have to find out details on the same service more than once. However, be aware that timetables and services change regularly, so keep your information up to date.
- Make friends with the person you deal with at your travel office or travel agency. Don't be afraid to ask questions, to ask for alternatives and to check or clarify details if you are unsure about something.
- Don't discuss details of business trips either with your colleagues at work or outside. You may be breaching security and confidentiality procedures if a particular trip is not common knowledge.

 Note: The 'Check your Knowledge and Understanding' section for this unit is on page 440.

Element 11.2

Book accommodation for a specified purpose

The skills you will need

You will need to prove that you can

- understand instructions for accommodation arrangements
- check that accommodation arrangements meet specified instructions
- provide a clear and accurate confirmation of all arrangements made to the appropriate person
- follow your organisation's requirements for security and confidentiality
- complete the arrangements within agreed deadlines.

The knowledge and understanding you will need

You will need to know

- the different types of accommodation available for residential and non-residential requirements
- how to book accommodation which is required for special events and for overnight stays

- how to make arrangements for individuals and for groups
- the factors to consider when selecting accommodation and associated facilities
- how to book accommodation in the UK and overseas
- your organisation's rules and procedures on accommodation
- the relevance of international time zones to accommodation arrangements.

The types of bookings required

You may be required to make bookings for accommodation which is required on either a residential or non-residential basis. **Residential** bookings are for rooms which are required overnight. **Non-residential** bookings may be required if your organisation needs rooms for a special event, such as a conference or seminar during the day, at the end of which everyone will be returning home. Meals may, or may not, be required.

Organisational procedures for booking accommodation

Within your organisation, accommodation bookings are less likely to be centralised than travel bookings. You may be able to make bookings yourself on behalf of your boss and/or your colleagues as requested. However, you will have to ensure that you do not go against any basic company rules. These may relate to

- the distance which must be travelled before overnight stays are allowed
- the amount of money which can be spent on overnight accommodation
- the amount of money which can be spent on non-residential accommodation for special events
- the rooms and facilities which are available within the company and when these must be used for special events.

You also need to know if there are any special documents or forms you need to complete within your organisation, and who is authorised to sign these.

Planning accommodation requirements

These may range from basic requests for an overnight stay in a UK town or city to accommodation for a three-day conference to include all meals and overnight accommodation for 50 delegates! This element is simply concerned with booking accommodation for such events; other requirements are dealt with in an alternative option – *see Unit 12*.

Remember your travel planning requirements – **where, when, who, how**? The same factors apply to accommodation, although in this case you may have to do some investigation before the 'where' is decided. Check, however, that you know

- when the accommodation is required and for how long
- the expected times of arrival and departure
- who will be using the accommodation and whether they have any special needs (e.g. for mobility, diet or non-smoking rooms)
- how much you are allowed to spend
- the standard of accommodation required (from basic to luxury)
- what type of overnight accommodation is required, e.g. single, twin or double rooms (Note that most hotels today offer private facilities but these can vary between private shower or bath – or both.)
- what additional requirements there are – these may range from special hotel facilities and size of rooms to meals and refreshments or additional visitors on certain days or nights.

Check that you are quite certain that you understand what is required *before* you contact a hotel or a booking agent.

Residential accommodation

You can book overnight accommodation by contacting a hotel directly, by ringing or faxing a booking agency or contacting a major hotel chain. There are several well-known hotel groups which provide business accommodation, including Holiday Inn, Inter-continental, Hilton, Trusthouse Forte, Ramada, Best Western International, Sheraton and Marriott. In each of these cases there are London-based reservation offices to handle bookings worldwide. If you can't find the number, telephone any hotel in the chain and ask them for information.

If you regularly book accommodation both in the UK and abroad, you need some suitable reference books. These include

- *AA or RAC Handbook*
- *Hotels and Restaurants in Great Britain*
- *The Travel Trade Directory*
- *ABC Worldwide Hotel Guide*
- *Michelin Guides* (for European hotels)

Locally you can look in your *Yellow Pages* or telephone your tourist information office for assistance if you are unsure which hotel to contact.

 DID YOU KNOW?

An alternative information source for business travel is New Prestel. *Look back at Unit 5, page 180, where this was covered in more detail.*

Business facilities

Facilities considered invaluable by many business travellers include

- tea or coffee making facilities plus a telephone in the room
- ample car parking space
- 24-hour reception and room service
- early morning breakfast
- laundry and shoe-cleaning services
- fax and other office services
- English speaking staff (if abroad).

The hotel should be centrally positioned if several companies in the area are to be visited. There should also be a good restaurant if business visitors will have to be entertained. Always remember that a business hotel and a family holiday hotel are not the same type of establishment!

DID YOU KNOW?

Most reference books classify hotels by using star categories – the more stars the better the facilities and, usually, the more expensive the accommodation. Below three-star is not usually suitable for business travellers.

Making a reservation

You can reserve a room by telephone or fax. Generally telephone is better as you can check all the details over the phone – though don't try this abroad unless you speak the language well! When you phone, there are some things you need to remember.

- You must specify your accommodation requirements *carefully.*
  - In the UK a double room usually means a double bed – if you want twin beds then book a twin room.
  - Private facilities usually means *either* a private bath or shower is acceptable.
  - Suites can vary but usually include a small lounge, bedroom and bathroom.

- Tell the hotel the expected time of arrival if this is later than 1800 hours. Otherwise the room may be re-let to someone else after this time!
- Make sure the hotel knows if you have any special requirements. For instance, you would have to check there was a lift if one of the party was disabled.
- Find out what time the dining room closes if your visitors want a meal there on arrival.
- Check if there are any discounts in force for group reservations if you are making a booking for several people.
- Check the rate for the room and make sure that you understand whether
  - the rate quoted is for the room or per person
  - breakfast is included.

- Confirm how the bill will be settled. Few hotels will expect to send you an invoice unless they deal with your organisation regularly. Most business travellers today settle by credit card and then reclaim the amount on their expenses (or use a company credit card).
- Ask for directions to find the hotel if it is in a city or town your boss has never visited before.
- Check the car parking facilities (if applicable).
- If you are contacting a hotel abroad directly, remember the time difference before you ring them! They might have a 24-hour reception desk but, as a rule, it is better to phone them when it is daytime for *both* of you!

Always confirm the arrangements in writing, either by letter or by fax. Give your boss a copy to take with him or her in case there are any disputes upon arrival.

DID YOU KNOW?

- If you are discussing credit cards with a hotel abroad it is important that you use the terms **Mastercard** and **Visa.** *Access* and *Barclaycard* mean nothing to someone in another country.
- It is worth noting that British Airways operate a hotel booking service for people travelling with the airline.
- Many hotels chains operate schemes similar to those available to frequent fliers, e.g. Honoured Guest or Gold Pass. If your boss is in one of these programmes try to make bookings at these hotels and quote the membership number when making the reservation.

CHECK IT YOURSELF

1 Visit your local library and obtain a copy of the *Travel Trade Gazette* – note the information given on hotel bookings and agencies.
2 Look through *either* an *AA* or *RAC Handbook or Hotels and Restaurants in Great Britain* and make a note of the contents, how to find different entries and the system used to denote different classes of hotel.
3 Check your local *Yellow Pages* for good business hotels in your own area.

TEST YOURSELF

Your boss, Mr T Brookes, is visiting Bristol on business and will be staying there overnight on Tuesday and Wednesday of next week.

1 Use a reference book to give him a choice of *three* good hotels and list the facilities of each in a memo.
2 Select any *one* hotel on your list and practise booking a single room with private shower for the nights you require over the telephone.

Explain that Mr Brooks may not arrive until about 8 pm and will settle his bill directly by credit card. Ask your supervisor, tutor or colleague to play the part of the receptionist.

3 Assume the hotel agrees the booking. Write either a letter or fax as confirmation and include all the main points of the booking.

DID YOU KNOW?

When you make any travel or hotel bookings you should always

- specify both the day *and* the date (as a double check)
- use the 24-hour clock (to avoid confusion).

Non-residential accommodation

You may work for a fairly large organisation which has several meeting rooms which are regularly booked for different events. If this is the case, keep a list of these rooms, how many people each will hold and who to contact to make a booking. Remember that the better furnished and more spacious rooms will probably be booked up for a few weeks ahead.

If your own organisation doesn't have additional space, or it is all fully booked, then you will have to look outside for accommodation. Most large hotels and several other venues have special meeting rooms and conference facilities which can be hired. You may know of several such complexes in your own area (otherwise look in your local *Yellow Pages* or contact your local town hall or tourist information office for details).

If you regularly need to book accommodation for special events it is worth having a full list of all the alternatives in your own area – together with their rates. You may find that your own organisation has a central list and that some places are recommended and others banned, because they are considered too expensive.

It is less likely that you will be asked to book special accommodation overseas, unless your company has a need to hold a large meeting or conference abroad. In this case you really do need the help of a good travel agent or booking agency. Again, it is a good idea to contact the reservations office of one of the large hotel groups to see if they can help.

Facilities available

The venue you eventually choose must be one which will provide the type, size and number of appropriately furnished rooms for the event. It is therefore essential that you know

- how many people will be attending
- the type of event being held.

This information will help to determine the type of room you need. However, when you discuss your requirements with the reservations clerk you must remember that the layout of the seating will affect the number of people the room can hold. You normally have four choices

- lecture style (in terms of seating choice, this accommodates the most people)
- horseshoe arrangements (for more informal discussions)
- meetings style (with a table in the centre)
- no seating at all (e.g. for a promotional display or exhibition).

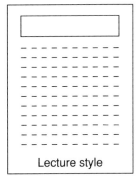

Lecture style

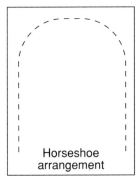

Horseshoe arrangement

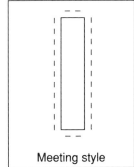

Meeting style

Seating alternatives

If more than one room is required, check the distances between them. If the event lasts more than one day, it is worth finding out if the same room can be used each day, so that people can leave work in there overnight.

Finally, you also need to know the length of time the rooms will be required. Hotel rooms are usually hired out by the half day or full day (not by the hour, which might be the case in-house) and you should check that you have full details of the costs involved.

If the event is important but you are still unsure if the venue will be suitable, and the hotel is fairly local it is a good idea to make a visit to look around and check that the accommodation would be suitable.

If everything seems in order make a *provisional* booking which you will confirm within the next day or two. This prevents anyone following in your footsteps and booking the rooms while you are still reporting back to your boss.

Making a booking

If you are booking a meeting room in your own organisation you simply need to contact the person responsible for recording the bookings. It is a good idea to confirm it in writing, either on Email or by sending a memo. There may be a standard form you have to complete.

For external bookings, once you have comparable information from several sources you should detail this in a memo to the person who made the original request. If you have the option on several rooms for a limited amount of time, so need a decision quickly, make this clear in your memo. If a hotel or other venue is holding the rooms for you for a day or so it is important you confirm to them quickly if you decide you want the booking.

A booking may be made over the telephone but *must* be confirmed in writing. Your letter should give full details of the booking including the dates and any other special requests. Make sure your letter is both accurate and complete, as the hotel will probably use this for reference when setting up the rooms.

DID YOU KNOW?

Some hotels automatically include refreshments in with the price of a room, others do not. You will need to think in terms of

● mid-morning coffee and biscuits
● afternoon tea and biscuits.

You may also be expected to obtain quotations for a buffet lunch or a meal in the evening.

CHECK IT YOURSELF

1 Contact *two* local business hotels and ask them for information on their conference and meetings facilities. Most large hotels produce booklets in which these are advertised. Compare the facilities and the room rates at each one.
2 Find out what other venues there are in your area, by asking your supervisor, tutor or colleagues for information or contacting your local town hall or tourist information office.
3 Find out what meeting rooms are available in your own organisation or college and note the internal system which is used to make bookings.
4 Find out what type of accommodation is regularly used by your organisation or college, and why. Check if there are any rules which determine when rooms must be booked in-house and when external bookings can be made instead.

TEST YOURSELF

Your organisation holds an annual two-day sales conference for its 16 area representatives. Ten staff from head office also attend. The requirements for this event are

● a meeting room for both days large enough to hold everyone comfortably

- a second, smaller room for the second morning when there will be two working groups
- mid-morning and afternoon refreshments on both days
- a buffet lunch on both days and dinner for everyone on the first evening
- accommodation for 20 people – the other six people live near enough to be able to go home at night.

The event will take place on the last Monday and Tuesday of next month.

1 Use the information you obtained from *two* local hotels to make a decision about which venue to use.
2 Make clear notes to prepare for a telephone call. Practise making the enquiry over the telephone with your supervisor, tutor or a colleague playing the role of receptionist.
3 Write a letter of confirmation, detailing all the arrangements. Check your work with your supervisor or tutor.

Some final notes on accommodation

- If you regularly make accommodation arrangements then you may find out a considerable amount of information on people's personal needs. Don't disclose this to other people, either inside or outside your organisation. Equally, don't discuss events which are due to be held, how much is being spent on accommodation, who is going and who is not. The event itself may not be a secret but you will not be popular if all the arrangements you ever make are always common knowledge in your organisation.
- Bear in mind that accommodation, just like travel, always has to be booked and confirmed well before the event. Take deadlines seriously and make a list of what you should do and when. Copy these entries into your diary as a double-check.

 ## CHECK YOUR KNOWLEDGE AND UNDERSTANDING

True or false?

1 Using the 24-hour clock, 2100 hours is 7 pm.
2 On a plane, Club or Business class is more expensive than First class.
3 It is possible for a business person to own more than one passport.
4 The laws and regulations for driving abroad are the same as in the UK.
5 'Le Shuttle' is the name given to the trains which will operate in the Channel Tunnel.

Fill in the blanks

6 The safest way to take money abroad is to buy _____ _____ from a bank.
7 Timetables for all the airlines in the world can be found in the _____ _____ _____ _____ .

8 Instead of a rail ticket, a _____ _____ may be issued to staff who will be travelling by train.

Work it out

9 Your boss will be travelling from Manchester to London by train. He wishes to leave early to arrive in London in time for a meeting which starts at 10 am. He suggests you allow him at least 45 minutes to get from Euston station to the company he is visiting. He wishes to return about 5 pm. He is not bothered about eating on the way home, but would like to have something on the way down. He normally travels First class but realises it will be cheaper if you choose a train with Silver Standard available as he will obviously be paying the full return fare.

Obtain a current timetable for this InterCity service and select a suitable train for both journeys. Detail your findings in a memo and remember to take account of all his requirements.

Check your work with your supervisor or tutor.

10 The directors of your company occasionally go away on weekend residentials to discuss plans for the future of the organisation. You are responsible for reserving accommodation, your colleague is responsible for all their catering requirements.

There are six directors, plus the Managing Director. They will all require rooms for the first Friday and Saturday night of next month, when the next residential is to be held. A meeting room is required for Friday evening from about 7 pm, all day Saturday and Sunday.

They want a good hotel and are prepared to travel up to a distance of 25 miles from your own location.

a Select a suitable hotel which would have these facilities.
b Assuming you have made the booking by telephone, write a letter stating *exactly* what accommodation you require. This letter should also include the seating layout required in the meeting room.

Check your work with your supervisor or tutor.

12 Contribute to the arrangement of events

This unit consists of three elements, all related to assisting in arranging a variety of events, from meetings and workshops to conferences and seminars. Element 12.1 is concerned with providing equipment and materials, Element 12.2 concentrates on the people who are attending and Element 12.3 is involved with providing different types of catering services.

Element 12.1

Assist in arrangements for the provision of supporting facilities and materials at events

The skills you will need

You will need to prove that you can

- provide the quantity, type and quality of supporting materials as directed
- locate equipment and materials to suit the purpose of events within agreed deadlines
- follow instructions for the safeguarding of equipment and materials
- confirm facilities for people with special needs.

The knowledge and understanding you will need

You will need to know

- how to identify the resources required for internal and external events
- how to acquire resources – either from stock or by hiring them
- the security measures to take to safeguard resources
- how to identify and meet special needs requirements
- your organisation's procedures for acquiring resources
- your organisation's security procedures in relation to equipment and materials.

Organising an event

Every organisation holds a number of events each year. These may be purely internal affairs, involving only a few people – or, at the other extreme, many people outside the organisation may receive invitations, the event may be held at an outside venue and generate publicity for the organisation. The type of events with which you may be concerned include

- meetings
- seminars
- conferences
- social gatherings (e.g. the company Christmas party or a retirement buffet lunch)
- workshops
- training courses
- open days
- exhibitions

and many others! Much will depend on the type of organisation which employs you, and the department in which you work. The sales staff, for instance, will be involved with seminars, exhibitions and conferences whereas the staff in personnel will be responsible for workshops and training courses.

It is unlikely that, on your own, you would ever be expected to mastermind the running of an important event. However, you would be expected to *assist* in this process and it is important to those who have the responsibility of organising everything that you

- know what you are doing
- can be relied upon to follow instructions
- clarify any instructions which are unclear or which you don't understand
- realise the importance of deadlines
- report back *immediately* if there is a problem that you can't solve.

The person responsible for co-ordinating the organisation of an important event will be under a lot of pressure to make sure everything runs smoothly. Tempers can become frayed if things go wrong at the last moment. You can help by keeping calm, doing as you are asked and proving that you are a dependable member of the team.

Preparations for an event

The organiser will already have started to plan exactly what is required for a major event in some detail. Even for small, internal events a certain amount of planning is required. Key information will already be known, i.e.

- the type of event
- the number of people involved
- the date(s) on which it will be held
- where it will be held
- the materials and equipment which will be required

● the documents which must be prepared or printed in advance.

The event may be held within the company, at a hotel or other venue – it may even be held in a marquee! The *type* of event will determine the equipment and materials which are required.

CHECK IT YOURSELF

Find out about the type of events which have been held by your organisation (or college) over the past 12 months. Ask your supervisor or tutor for help. In each case try to find out

● the venue which was used
● the number of people who attended
● the additional items which were required
● the type of documentation which was prepared in advance.

Prepared documentation

For most events special documentation is prepared in advance by the organisers. Again this will differ from one event to another but examples include

● **conference**
  – welcome pack for delegates printed folders
  – list of those attending
  – speeches and talks
  – programme of events
  – handouts

● **exhibition**
  – leaflets and brochures
  – handbooks or exhibition guides
  – cards for exhibits/photographs
  – map of exhibition area

● **seminar**
  – handouts
  – worksheets
  – overhead transparencies
  – sales figures/statistics.

Sometimes the printing or reprography will be done in-house. For other occasions an external printer will be required to produce top quality leaflets and brochures. All the documents must be collated properly and the correct quantity available. It is usual to have slightly more than are required on a 'just in case' basis.

It may be your job to photocopy, collate and assemble internally produced documentation. In this case

- make a checklist of *everything* you need
- assemble your items one by one
- check these off when you are certain they are correct
- check there are appropriate arrangements to transport everything to the correct location in time for the event.

Make sure the quality is excellent and everything is ready well before the deadline.

DID YOU KNOW?

- To **table** a paper means what it says – put it on the table before people arrive. If the event is a conference, with only chairs provided, it is quite usual to put some papers on the chairs before the conference begins. This saves the speaker having to hand out papers among a large audience.
- At many events stationery is provided for people to use. People listening to a talk often like to make notes, and hotels which hire meeting rooms will always provide pens and paper – as well as glasses of water or soft drinks on the tables. Make sure you have ordered enough consumable stationery for people to use throughout the event.

Other items and resources

There are many different items which can be required at an event. In some cases, selecting and choosing these can be a key feature in the smooth-running of the event – and may affect how memorable it was for those who attended.

You should be aware that at different events

- the **type** of items required can vary enormously
- the **number** of items you need to organise will also change
- the **quantity** required will depend on the number of people attending
- no organisation could keep the whole range of possible items in stock – it simply wouldn't be worth it!

This does not mean that you will not need to acquire any special items in your own organisation. If events are held regularly, then it would be sensible to purchase the items which are often needed. On other occasions, special items will only be hired for as long as they are needed.

TEST YOURSELF

Below are given *four* different events and then a list of items which would be required. In each case, decide which item is required for which event.

1 Retirement lunch for a director at which his wife will be present. About 25 people are invited to a buffet in an office – temporarily converted for the event – and to see the presentation of a gift on behalf of the organisation.

2 Sales exhibition to be held in a local hotel.
3 Sales conference for 60 sales representatives with talk by the Managing Director followed by presentations on new company products.
4 Garden party and barbecue for all staff, held every summer. Selected invitations to outside contacts.

Items

large screen video
lectern
marquee
promotional balloons with company logo
matting and wooden flooring
china, cutlery and glassware
flip charts
bouquet of flowers
display panels
fridges and freezers
microphone
exhibition stands
pens and keyfobs printed with company name
bunting
writing pads and pens
table linen
video recorder
patio furniture
plants in large tubs
commercial barbecues
overhead projector and screen
engraved cut glass bowl
patio furniture

Items stocked by the organisation

These are likely to include

- all stationery requirements
- basic video equipment
- flip charts
- tape recorder
- trolleys for moving equipment
- basic catering equipment
- tables and chairs.

However, the quantity stocked may be insufficient if large numbers of people have been invited.

Items usually hired

These are likely to include all the other items you dealt with in the exercise above – plus many more! Nowadays you can hire virtually anything, from a hot air balloon to a catwalk, from fish and chip friers to public address systems.

If the event is to be held in a hotel or conference centre then various types of equipment can be provided by the establishment, which will be used to standard requests for videos, projectors, screens etc.

Buying for the event

This is the other alternative. Large items will not usually be purchased, but small promotional gifts will be. In addition you may need to buy items such as lapel badges or pay for the printing of special leaflets or brochures.

CHECK IT YOURSELF

Look through your local *Yellow Pages* to find out about the type of goods which can be hired, and the firms in your area which would supply them. Headings to look under include

- Hire services – functions
- Conference facilities and services
- Promotional items and incentives.

You may find other cross-reference headings listed under these, and is worth looking under all those you can find!

Finally, if you want to think through the range of items required for a major event, you could think about a wedding – and look under Wedding Services in your *Yellow Pages*! Bear in mind that for many company events, specialist people such as photographers and chauffeurs are also hired – just like they are for a wedding.

Organising the hire and purchase of items

When you have decided that you want to hire or purchase an item, make sure you do this professionally.

- Contact at least three suppliers by telephone. State your requirements clearly and obtain different quotations. Discuss these with your supervisor and find out which supplier you should use.
- Confirm your order to the supplier of your choice. You will probably have to send them a company order as this will confirm that the order is official and that they will receive payment.
- If the hire company is not prepared to send your organisation an invoice, but insists on immediate payment when you collect the item, tell your supervisor, who can arrange for you to receive the money from petty cash.
- Note that it is not unreasonable for a hire company to charge a **deposit** which is returnable if the goods are returned undamaged.
- Check their insurance cover (*see below*) for the items you have hired.

- When you collect any equipment, check it works! Do this *immediately*, not on the day of the event when people would panic trying to obtain a replacement.
- Make a clear list of everything you have hired, where from, dates covered and the cost. Use this as your standard check list, and tick off the items as you make the arrangements; a second tick confirms collection and a third that the goods were returned without damage or loss.

Security of resources

It can be more nerve-wracking to hire something than to buy it or get it from stock, simply because you are then responsible for returning it in the same condition in which you hired it! It is sensible *always* to check the hire company's insurance cover and to find out if the equipment or item is covered in case of theft or fire – wherever it will be used. You may find that some policies only cover you if the equipment remains on company premises. If you move it to a hotel in a car, and someone breaks into the vehicle, the equipment may not be covered – so check this carefully. If there is a problem then see your supervisor as your company's insurance policy can usually be extended to cover the item on a temporary basis.

Even if you *are* covered against major disasters, you obviously need to take some sensible precautions yourself.

- Note the serial number of any item of equipment which is being moved to another location.
- If transport has been arranged for these items it is a good idea to go with them yourself and watch them being unloaded at the other end.
- Do not leave valuable items unattended, even for a moment. This includes items such as videos, camcorders and projectors.
- Remember that many cheaper items such as pens, glassware, cutlery, stationery etc. may be very desirable. You would be amazed what can 'walk' when your back is turned!
- When you set up a room with the equipment and then leave it, make sure you lock the door and check that keyholders are restricted.
- Limit the number of people who can use valuable equipment or who can distribute other items. If everyone can 'have a go' then you have no hope of ever finding 'missing' items.
- If your organisation employs security staff it is worthwhile informing them and enlisting their help.

 DID YOU KNOW?

A major hotel in Blackpool ordered 12 new vacuum cleaners. These were delivered, unpacked and left on the corridor of one floor for ten minutes whilst the housekeeper had a word with a guest. When she returned, they had all disappeared!

Special needs requirements

It is quite probable that some of the people who will be attending the event may have special needs. There may visitors who are

- disabled, on crutches or in a wheelchair
- partially or profoundly deaf
- partially sighted or blind.

In addition there may be foreign visitors who have special dietary requirements (*see Element 12.3*) or need an interpreter.

Basic factors to bear in mind include

- **access** – stairs and steps are impossible for many disabled people. There must be a lift in the building or the event must be held on the ground floor. Toilet facilities also need considering – usually there is special provision in most venues for the disabled.
- **space** – wheelchairs take up a considerable amount of room and disabled people don't move quickly. Allow plenty of space for people to move around – and ahead – if they wish.
- **speech** – the partially sighted and blind rely heavily on speech, which should be clear and shouldn't contain constant references to visual items, e.g. '... if you just look at...' Profoundly deaf people would usually have a signer to translate the words into signs. They may have a problem if the speaker uses very technical terms or many slang expressions.
- **printed materials** – you can have printed materials translated into a variety of languages and have handouts prepared in large print for partially sighted people.
- **special assistance** – at any large event a **help desk** is a good idea. If people have a particular special need which you haven't thought about in advance, at least they know where to go for assistance (and you know to make a note of it for next time).

After the event is over

You may think that if you have obtained a variety of items and thought of some good ideas yourself, assembled everything which was needed in the right quantity at the right place and at the right time, and checked everything worked, then you have done your job. Sorry, but this isn't true. There are still several jobs to be done afterwards.

- Retrieve all the equipment which has been used and keep it securely until it has all been returned, either to a safe storeroom or to the hire company. Try to make arrangements to return hired goods as quickly as possible after the event, before they can get damaged.

- Check nothing has been left behind by any visitors.
- Remove all stationery, unused documents etc. Return unused stationery to the store, if special documents will not be needed again then make sure they are thrown away. If any are confidential then put these through a shredder.
- Keep all your receipts and checklists in a file – they will be useful if you are involved in acquiring similar items again
- Make a note of any problems you had whilst they are fresh in your mind. If a particular supplier gave poor service then make a note, and do the same if anybody was particularly helpful.
- If there were any special facilities you forgot to provide then note these down too, for future reference.
- If requested, be prepared to total the amount you spent on different items so that the organisers can match this against the event budget.

 Note: The 'Check your Knowledge and Understanding' section for this unit is on page 463.

Element 12.2

Assist in arrangements for the attendance of persons at events

The skills you will need

You will need to prove that you can

- invite people to attend the event as directed
- provide accurate and complete event directions and supporting documentation to people who attend, in accordance with their role and need
- make appropriate arrangements for transporting people who are attending, within the budgetary allocation
- provide a reception service which gives adequate support and direction for people attending
- route people at events correctly
- keep attendance records in accordance with organisational requirements.

The knowledge and understanding you will need

You will need to know

- how to make transport arrangements
- the procedures for notifying people about events
- registration procedures
- how to identify and meet special needs requirements

- your organisation's procedures for arranging attendance at events
- your organisation's security procedures.

Inviting people to attend events

This can be done in a variety of ways, including

- by telephone
- by memo
- by memo and letter
- by formal, printed invitation
- by advertisement.

Inviting people by telephone is rapid, informal and normally only used when there are a few people involved. A memo is the usual method of notifying people within an organisation that an event will be held. If a few outside people are being asked to the same event, then letters may be sent to them asking them if they would like to attend.

Printed invitations are sent for more formal events involving both internal and external people. Finally, advertisements are used when members of a club or group or the general public are invited. In the first case the advertisement would be placed in specialist magazines or even sent as a direct mail invitation to members. In the second case the event may be publicised in the local paper or on local radio.

TEST YOURSELF

1 Which of the above methods would you use to invite people to each of the following events?

   a An Open Day at a sixth form college.
   b An urgent meeting of five technical staff.
   c A sales meeting which will involve 12 sales representatives and four outside suppliers.
   d An awards ceremony at a university.
   e A conference of computer software designers.
   f The opening ceremony of a new building, to be followed by a formal lunch, with a VIP present.

2 State the main advantages of inviting people to an event by sending a memo, rather than by telephone.

Issuing and recording invitations

Once it has been decided *how* people should be invited, the next decision is *who* to invite. This is usually the responsibility of the event organiser. If any VIPs are involved then they are usually invited *first* – especially if their names will then appear on the main invitations.

Remember that if invitations have to be printed then time must be allowed for this, especially if you are using an outside printing firm.

You are unlikely to be asked to draft an important or formal invitation yourself, but you could be involved in

- telephoning people (to invite them to an informal event)
- writing a straightforward memo
- making a list of everyone who has been invited
- helping to print invitations if they are produced in-house
- sending these out in accordance with your list
- checking off acceptances as they arrive
- chasing up people who have not replied by a specified date.

Informing people by telephone

Make sure you state *clearly* the date, day, venue, time and reason for the event. You should also check with your supervisor if any particular information should *not* be disclosed over the telephone (e.g. the names of the other guests), so that you can deal confidently with any questions you are asked.

Remember to record the responses carefully. If you cannot get through to someone then note down all the attempts you make to contact them, in case your supervisor queries this.

Sending a memo

This sort of memo is usually short and to the point. If a letter of invitation is sent to people outside the company then this is usually done by a senior member of staff and is likely to contain more detailed background information.

M E M O

TO   **All safety representatives**

FROM **Safety Officer**

DATE   **10 September 199–**

SAFETY SEMINAR

A safety seminar will be held in Room 114 on Monday, 21 September, 9 am – 12 noon. The aim of the seminar is to discuss the following items:

1   New protective clothing requirements
2   Accident prevention
3   First aid training
4   Fire fighting courses

Please let me know if you will not be able to attend.

JT

Formal invitations

These are written – and replied to – in the third person. The letters RSVP are usually printed at the bottom – meaning 'please reply'. Usually the name(s) of those being invited is written in by hand.

BARNES ELECTRONICS LTD

The Chairman and Board of Directors have pleasure in inviting *Mr John Davis* .... to the opening ceremony of their new premises by Sir Joshua Legg on Wednesday, 4 May at 11 am. The ceremony will be followed by a buffet lunch.

Chapel Wharf
HIGHTOWN
HG4 9JT   RSVP

HIGHTOWN BANK PLC

Mr John Davis, Manager, has pleasure in accepting the invitation of the Chairman and Board of Directors of Barnes Electronics to the opening ceremony of their new premises on Wednesday, 4 May at 11 am and the buffet lunch which follows.

 DID YOU KNOW?

If you are sending out a large number of invitations and have to match them to written envelopes, there is a danger that you will get bored and put an invitation in the wrong envelope – or even two invitations in one envelope! To prevent this happening, divide your invitations and envelopes into batches of ten. Then separate them into two piles, one for envelopes and the other for invitations. Make sure your recipients match on both sides *before you start*. Don't seal the envelopes until you have worked through the batch and each invitation is safely in its correct envelope.

CHECK IT YOURSELF

Try to find an example of an invitation in your local paper for an event to which the general public are invited. In addition, ask your tutor or supervisor if he or she has any examples of conference or seminar invitations which are restricted to members of a particular organisation or professional body.

The importance of check lists

A check list which shows a list of people who have been invited can be made to serve several other useful purposes, simply by extending the number of columns. In addition to acceptances it can also be used to include

- special requirements (e.g. dietary or mobility)
- transport/parking requirements

and to produce

- confirmation letters, programmes and maps showing the location of the event
- name badges
- registration documents
- other supporting documents, e.g. table plans, place cards.

After the event it can be matched with a visitor's book or attendance register to see if everyone who said they would attend actually did so.

Invitation check list

Name	Address	Invite issued	Replied Y/N	Attending Y/N	Special needs	Transport req'd Y/N

Sending information

If the event is being held at a location which some people may not know, it is usual to include directions (or a **map**) with any letters of confirmation. The letter of confirmation may also include a **programme of events**, which may be typed or printed. (The equivalent at a meeting is called an **agenda**.)

You obviously need to be selective about sending out this material, particularly if there is a mix of internal staff and external visitors. The latter may need a different type of information pack. The information given to any VIPs may also be rather different and the event organiser is likely to handle this him or herself.

 ## DID YOU KNOW?

For some conferences, delegates have to pay to attend. If you are responsible for handling cheques in payment make sure you check these carefully and keep a list of all the money you receive.

Think back to your school speech days! Discuss with your supervisor or tutor the different information about the event which would be given to

● staff at the school
● parents
● pupils
● the visiting speaker
● any local dignitaries (e.g. the Lord Mayor or Lady Mayoress)
● the governors.

Try to identify how this would vary and the consequences of getting it muddled up!

Arranging transport

Most people will probably use their own vehicles to get to the event, but you may be involved in arranging

● taxis
● chauffeur driven cars
● coaches
● a mini-bus.

At some events most people (apart from VIPs) pay for their own transport. In most cases people will be expected to get themselves as close as possible to the venue, e.g. the local railway station. Arrangements may then be made to collect them and transfer them to the actual venue.

A coach or mini-bus is more likely to be hired for a social event where no-one wants to drive.

Chauffeur-driven transport (in more luxurious vehicles) will be provided for VIPs – or they may be collected personally by the event organiser or a senior member of staff.

Remember, when you are organising transport, that you will have a budget to work to. It may seem a good idea to book several limousines to collect 30 guests at the station but your Finance Manager or supervisor is unlikely to share your sentiments!

Reception and registration

At any event there must be some arrangements for greeting people as they arrive – unless it is small, held internally, and everyone knows everyone else.

In a large, external venue, with dozens of strangers attending, everyone arriving will feel rather lost, no matter how confident they look. For that reason there is usually a set registration procedure which everyone follows.

A reception desk is set up in a central point, preferably near to the entrance. It should be staffed by at least two people for a large event, both of whom should be easily identifiable as conference organisers (probably because of special name badges). In some organisations, staff will be expected to be dressed in a special uniform.

On the reception desk there should usually be

- the attendance list
- name badges for visitors (in different colours from those of the organisers), which will also often state the organisation they represent
- a set of specially printed folders, containing all the information and documents visitors require.

Near to the reception desk should be tea and coffee facilities so that people can have refreshments immediately after registration.

If you are involved in registering visitors then

- greet them with a smile
- ask their name
- tick them off your list
- give them a badge and a folder
- give *clear* directions to the room in which the event is being held. Also be prepared to give directions to the cloakroom and the toilets and answer a myriad of questions about the event and the people attending!

DID YOU KNOW?

- Internal signs can save you answering a lot of questions – so can a clear 'you are here' map near the entrance if the building is large.
- If visitors are staying overnight, it is a good idea to ask the hotel reception to let you have a list of names, room numbers and telephone extensions, so that you can pass on messages more easily.

TEST YOURSELF

Four questions which you may be asked on reception are given below. See if you can add *another four* questions of your own – and compare these with those of your colleagues. Then think how you would check that you had this information at the outset.

- Can you tell me what time this is expected to finish?
- Do you know if Mr Brown from Crabtree Engineering is here?
- Is there a telephone near here – and does it take coins?
- Are we in the same room all day?

Attendance records

At some events people are asked to sign in, and complete a visitor's book or attendance record. The procedure carried out will depend on the type of event being held. The reasons for this are

- to match those who *actually* attend against those who *said they would* attend
- to have a list of visitors for the next (similar) event.

People who could not attend at the last minute may be sent an information pack. In other cases the whole list may be used to include on a mailing list for future publicity material.

Security

It is unlikely that you will have gatecrashers or people causing a disturbance at a formal event, unless, perhaps, your VIP is a politician or public figure who has been in the news recently about a contentious issue. If, however, you think there may be any problems it is well worth notifying the security staff either in your own organisation or at the venue where the event is to be held.

CHECK IT YOURSELF

It is important that you attend *at least one* event where guests register as they arrive and/or complete a visitor's book or attendance record.

1 Discuss opportunities for doing this with your supervisor and tutor.
2 Discuss the type of registration procedures used by your organisation or in your college and how these may differ from those you have read about.
3 Find *at least one* example of an event where an attendance record or visitor's book was used – and why.

Note: The 'Check your Knowledge and Understanding' section is on page 463.

Element 12.3

Assist in arrangements for the provision of catering services at events

The skills you will need

You will need to prove that you can

- make arrangements for catering services as directed
- identify and cater for the needs of people attending

- ensure that the costs of catering services are within your budgetary allocation
- make arrangements for catering services within agreed deadlines
- make arrangements for catering services in accordance with organisational requirements
- take precautions to ensure that the provision of catering services provides adequate safeguarding of persons and property at events.

The knowledge and understanding you will need

You will need to know

- the type of catering arrangements which are provided within your organisation
- the external catering services which are used by your organisation
- your organisation's procedures for arranging catering services
- special needs requirements
- relevant legal requirements.

Catering requirements

There are few – if any – events where those attending are not even offered a cup of coffee! In today's fast moving world many business meetings take place over a working lunch – and the Americans are renowned for their working breakfasts!

Seminars and courses will have morning and afternoon breaks for refreshments and there will be a longer break for lunch. Conferences which last several days will obviously include arrangements for evening meals or even a formal dinner.

More social events may include a buffet lunch or a finger buffet – the latter is the more informal of the two. No knives and forks are required and paper plates can be used if you want to avoid washing up!

TEST YOURSELF

Which of the following types of meals or refreshments would you pair with the events which follow?

A   tea and coffee plus biscuits
B   a five-course dinner
C   sandwiches, fruit juice, tea and coffee
D   a finger buffet
E   an informal evening meal
F   a buffet lunch

1   a meeting of the sales staff over a working lunch
2   a leaving party one evening for a member of staff
3   a meeting of all managers at 3 pm one afternoon

4 an evening ceremony for presenting the sales awards for the year, hosted by the chairman

5 lunch for 14 members of staff discussing departmental objectives for the next 12 months

6 lunch for ten customers and their wives, plus the directors of the company

Catering services

The type of catering which can be carried out in-house will obviously depend on the size of organisation you work for. A large organisation, with its own canteen and catering staff, may be able to accommodate all the catering requirements except for evening meals. A small organisation may not even have the facilities for making sandwiches!

Therefore, at one extreme, the only time you may need to use external caterers is in an evening, when the event will probably be held at a nearby hotel. At the other extreme, whenever even snacks are required, you may be asked to call round to the local sandwich bar.

If the event involves only staff and is more social than business (e.g. a leaving party or Christmas celebration) then it may be up to the staff to make their own arrangements (and pay for the event themselves). This can involve booking a table at a local restaurant, outside caterers being hired to provide a buffet or a **Jacob's Join** – where every member of staff agrees to provide one item of food from a pre-prepared list.

Organisational procedures

The events your organisation pays for, the systems to follow to order refreshments and sandwiches, and the amount of freedom you have to choose caterers and hotels yourself will vary, depending upon where you work. However, one factor is always important, and that is the cost. You will never have unlimited funds at your disposal, so all events must have refreshments and catering facilities carefully costed, so that you keep within your budget.

DID YOU KNOW?

Some organisations **contract out** the services of their catering staff when they can. This means that you can arrange an in-house event and, if it is more social than business, you can ask your own catering staff to quote you for supplying the food. But remember, they might not always be the cheapest supplier – it is worth shopping around with outside caterers as well!

CHECK IT YOURSELF

1 Find out about the range of events where food or refreshments are provided in your organisation or college.

2 Obtain examples of the type of catering services provided – and by whom.
3 Find out the average cost allowed for each type of event.
4 Find out about the documents which you would have to complete if you want to request refreshments or food to be provided.

In-house versus external

In-house catering

For routine events, it is a lot easier to use an in-house catering service, even if people do get tired of eating the same type of sandwiches at every lunchtime meeting! Normally the only task for you is to complete a catering or hospitality form which must be counter-signed by your supervisor and then sent to the catering manager. An example of this type of form is shown below.

CATERING SERVICES REQUEST FORM

Requested by .... Dept ....

Date required .... Time required ....

Location of event (state room number) ....

Reason/Function ....

....

Items required	Quantity	Cost★
	TOTAL PRICE £	

Authorised by .... Date ....

Budget to be debited: ....

★ See price list overleaf

If your organisation can also provide buffet meals then it would be sensible to use this service when you can, although you may find the choice rather limited. For that reason, if you have outside visitors attending or many people with special needs who *can't* be catered for in-house, then you may need to make different arrangements.

External caterers

There are basically two options, which are

- hire an outside catering organisation to provide the food for you
- hold the event in a hotel or at a venue where meals are provided.

Outside caterers

Catering organisations can be expected to provide a range of buffet meals. They will also clear away afterwards. Some will provide a cooked meal but may need certain kitchen facilities available, so this can be more problematic. It is worth checking if they also provide cutlery, crockery, glassware and table linen – otherwise you may need to hire this from a different organisation.

Buffet meals are always priced **per head** and start quite cheaply, with basic food such as sausage rolls and sandwiches. If you want a range of cooked meats and poultry which can be carved at the table this will cost you more. Most catering firms will provide you with a series of buffet menus which list the type of food provided in each case and the price.

DID YOU KNOW?

Few people drink alcohol at lunchtime if the event is purely business. You should therefore provide a range of soft drinks and mineral water as well as tea and coffee. The situation is rather different if the event is a celebration or if it is to be held in an evening. In this case both red and white wine may be available. Spirits are seldom offered.

Hotels and other venues

If the event is to be held in a hotel or at a venue where catering services are provided, you need to obtain samples of their menus. These can range from a pub lunch or bar snack to an elaborate dinner! Remember, you should match the type of catering to the type of event – and your budget. You should also note that people usually prefer a lighter meal at lunchtime than they do in an evening.

Be aware that there are usually two types of menus – **table d'hôte** (which is a fixed meal) and **à la carte** (which means people can choose from a varied menu). For a formal dinner you may be shown several ideas for starters, soup, fish course, meat course and desserts – and given the option of

- choosing the same for each person attending (with variations for vegetarians)
- reducing the choice and giving people options to choose from on the night
- reducing the choice and asking people to decide beforehand what they want to eat. In this case you then notify the hotel of their

selections. (This option is really only feasible if the event is for 'in-house' staff only.)

However, you should note that an important factor in any choice of food will be the particular requirements of your guests.

Special requirements

Nowadays everybody has at least one friend who is a vegetarian – if not a vegan. Most major restaurants and hotel groups are used to requests for fish only meals, vegetarian meals and even vegan meals. However you also need to be aware that there may be people who have special dietary requests because of

- their religious or cultural beliefs
- medical problems (e.g. a salt-free diet).

If you are arranging for a buffet to be served you can normally get around most of these problems by making sure that there are plenty of salad and fish dishes (with dressings served separately). If you are trying to arrange a five-course dinner for 30 people you may have more problems.

One way around this is to design a form, which can be included with the invitations, which asks people to specify any dietary requirements they have. Then pass on the problem to the hotel or restaurant you are using. The important thing, so far as you are concerned, is to make sure you check first and then follow up the request to the best of your ability. Consult your supervisor if you encounter real problems catering for a particular guest.

DID YOU KNOW?

If you are entertaining foreign visitors and are unsure about the type of food which would be acceptable then you could contact their country's Embassy or Consulate in London (or even the Foreign Office) for help and advice.

Catering and the law

It is usually inadvisable to offer to do any cooking yourself, even if the event is going to be held in-house, only your colleagues are involved and there appear to be few other alternatives. This is not just because of the work involved but also relates to your responsibility towards food hygiene regulations. You may even be breaking the law if you prepared food for people and *charged* them to attend. (**Note**: This does not include unwrapping sandwiches and party food supplied by Marks and Spencer!)

The reason for this is **safety**. Under the Food Safety Act of 1990 all organisations which offer food for sale have to conform to a whole series of regulations which relate to the preparation, cooking and storage of food. Their kitchens can be inspected at any time by an Environmental Health Officer. This is obviously to prevent food poisoning. You can easily break the law inadvertently – but this wouldn't protect you if someone was seriously ill after the event and you cooked all the food.

CHECK IT YOURSELF

Can you honestly say that, if you were preparing food for an event, you could easily comply with each of the following regulations?

- all cooked and raw meats kept separately to avoid cross-contamination
- separate sinks for equipment
- separate equipment for cooked and raw food
- suitable dress, personal hygiene and training of all food handling staff
- good general hygiene

Talk to your catering supervisor (or refectory supervisor) about these regulations and the differences between preparing food commercially and preparing food at home.

Booking outside caterers

If you decide to use outside caterers – or a hotel – then discuss your needs carefully with them before you make the booking. When you have decided exactly what you want

- confirm the booking over the telephone
- reconfirm it in writing, repeating your exact specifications.

This way you leave little to chance, and have covered yourself if anything goes wrong. Hopefully, if you have done your job well, everything will run smoothly and your guests will be appreciative of the arrangements you made on their behalf.

CHECK YOUR KNOWLEDGE AND UNDERSTANDING

True or false?

1 Name badges are given out at the start of all events.
2 Firms which hire out goods can be found by looking in *Yellow Pages*.
3 Most people attending a conference will require transport to and from their homes.
4 VIPs need special attention from staff.
5 If a hired item is stolen from a company car on a hotel car park, it will automatically be covered by the company's insurance policy.

Fill in the blanks

6 The letters RSVP on an invitation mean _____ _____ .

7 Food hygiene is covered by the _____ _____ Act of 1990.

8 When you hire goods it is usual to be asked to pay a _____ in case of damage.

Work it out

9 Your organisation is running an internal course on a new computer system, due to be introduced in two months' time. Twenty staff will be attending. You are in charge of providing resources for the event and organising refreshments.

No internal facilities are available for providing a mid-day meal or buffet and it has been decided to bring in outside caterers or buy a variety of sandwiches locally.

a Decide on the resources which will probably be required for the event. Bear in mind that there will be a lecture and demonstration in the morning and hands-on practice of the new system in the afternoon.

b Obtain *at least two* quotations from outside caterers and compare the cost of a simple buffet with the cost of buying sandwiches.

State which option you would choose and why.

10 A new member of staff is helping you on reception to greet delegates at your company's annual sales conference. Draw up a check list of points she should bear in mind, and information she should find out beforehand, so that she can meet the needs of those attending without difficulty.

Index